Philip Trower

THE CATHOLIC CHURCH

AND

THE COUNTER-FAITH

*A Study of the Roots of Modern
Secularism, Relativism and
de-Christianisation*

GW00644878

FAMILY PUBLICATIONS • OXFORD

ISBN 1-871217-59-8

by the same author
A Danger to the State (Ignatius Press, 1998)
Turmoil and Truth (Family Publications and Ignatius Press, 2003)

Front Cover: Cologne Cathedral
courtesy of Nicholas Broekman

published by
Family Publications
6a King Street, Oxford OX2 6DF, UK
www.familypublications.co.uk

Printed in England

The Catholic Church
and
The Counter-Faith

"The modern age is often seen as an awakening of reason from its slumbers, humanity's enlightenment after an age of darkness. Yet without the light of Christ, the light of reason is not sufficient to enlighten humanity and the world."

Benedict XVI, Urbi et Orbi message,
25th December 2005

Contents

Contents

PART ONE

WESTERN CIVILISATION
IN THE 20TH AND 21ST CENTURIES:
CORE BELIEFS

Chapter One

PLEASE USE THE FRONT DOOR

For reasons which are understandable if not altogether justifiable, large numbers of us have an aversion to prefaces and introductions. We "want to get down to business," to "get our teeth into the meat of the story or subject." We tend to regard prefaces as superfluous "waffle" in which the author wastes our time either excusing his limitations, arguing with opponents, or explaining things which he should have made clear in the main body of the text. If we read a preface at all, it is usually when we have finished the book, by which time we have often forgotten not a little of what we have been reading, and so much of what the preface was referring to.

This is why I have disguised my preface as an opening chapter. You are much more likely to find you have wasted your time if you don't read it first, since unless you do you will not understand why the book has the shape it does or its principal purpose or purposes. So I hope you will forgive this small initial deception. It will be the only deliberate one.

My first and immediate aim, then, is to complete the investigation into the historical roots of the current crisis in the Catholic Church which I began in *Turmoil and Truth* (Ignatius Press and Family Publications, 2003). However, this sequel has a larger and more long-range objective. There would, I believe, have been room for a book of this kind even without the changes and disturbances that marked the last four decades of the 20th century.

Let me explain. Until a short time ago, Western Christians took it for granted that they were living in what was still basically a Christian culture. Christian beliefs and principles were the norm from which all other beliefs or forms of unbelief, however widespread, were deviations. Then suddenly they have found themselves part of a culture in which they are not only a minority, but which is increasingly at variance with most of its own previous beliefs and practices. As a result they are often at a loss to know how far they can go along with the new ways of thinking and acting. Where do they have to draw the line? Can any of the pre-existing lines be redrawn? And if so, where should they run?

Their situation is not, in fact, unlike that of the Christian converts from paganism of the 1st century AD, except that for the early pagan converts it was the same situation but the other way around. The first converts from paganism had grown up taking as their norm the ideas and practices of the Graeco-Roman world into which they had been born.

After their conversion, however, they found themselves members of a minority which looked at the way in which the majority lived through very different eyes. Majority opinion could no longer be regarded as part of the natural order of things, and to begin with many must have found it as difficult to determine what was acceptable and unacceptable in the age-old pagan way of life as Christians today find it to thread their way through the dramatic changes of the last fifty years. How far could they go along with established custom? Did it all have to be rejected? And if not, which areas of what had previously been their daily living and thinking could continue as before?[1]

As we see from the *Acts of the Apostles*, this last question, once asked, rapidly introduced a process of discernment which not only embraced practical matters (like whether one could eat meat that had been sacrificed to idols), but also subjected the speculations of philosophers to scrutiny.

The early Church Fathers took the lead. But contributing in their smaller way would have been countless other Christians, lay and clerical, whose words were never written down or whose writings have perished.

The first and longer part of this book is intended to make a contribution to a similar process of discernment with regard to what we call "modern thought" – the mental substratum of modern Western societies, and the source of many of our semi-conscious assumptions. As I attempted to show in *Turmoil and Truth*, such a process has been going on in the Church for around 200 years; and there can be few of the new theories and ideas that have surfaced during that time on which she has not given guidance or instruction. The number of documents is enormous. Greater still is the secular literature on the subject. We even have Dictionaries of Modern Thought. But as far as I know, there has been no examination of its principal components and their implications for Catholic belief from a Catholic point of view – at least not for non-academic English readers.

The main components I have chosen are: the doctrines of the 18th

---

1. Down to the end of the persecutions, Christians were often divided as to whether, in spite of the persecutions, the Roman state was an instrument of divine providence or, because of the persecutions, a work of the devil (Fliche et Martin, *Histoire de l'Eglise*, vols. I & II).

century Enlightenment; the theory of evolution and its derivatives; the schools of post-Cartesian[2] philosophy which have had most influence on Catholic thinking; the human sciences; and the more radical theories of 20th century liberal Protestant theology. The findings of the exact sciences are the only major component I have omitted because in so far as they are exact, they no longer provide any serious obstacle to the Catholic and Christian world-view. Of these components, the doctrines of the Enlightenment are, for the purposes of this undertaking, by far the most important.

"Modern thought" could be defined as the sum total of what modern men know, or think they know, with the doctrines of the Enlightenment as their soul or informing principle. It is these doctrines which now give modern thought and Western culture their coherence, shape and sense of purpose.

Nothing like them, no such universally accepted thought-system seems to have existed in the ancient world. Even after Rome had unified the Mediterranean basin politically, its intellectual and cultural life remained far more of a spiritual free-for-all where no one world-view had it all its own way. It does not much matter in what order you read the other chapters or groups of chapters in this book, provided you begin with the first five on the Enlightenment.[3]

---

2. "Cartesian" refers to René Descartes (1596-1650). In the history of philosophy he is considered the father of modern Western philosophy.

3. "Post-modernism" and "New Age" religions are often written about as if they had supplanted the self-confident progressivist outlook hitherto characteristic of Western civilisation. My reading of the evidence is different. To me, post-modernism looks more like a temporary failure of nerve on the part of the more sensitive members of our cultural élites. There is no sign of any widespread failure of nerve in the literature coming from Western government departments, the majority of our universities, or the United Nations. "New Age" religions are another matter. They can best be seen as palliatives to ease the pain left by the decline of Christianity, a malaise which the bouncy optimism of the Enlightenment project is incapable of soothing or curing. The Enlightenment has great things to say about humanity as a whole and the more or less remote future, but little to console the individual who happens to be unsatisfied or unhappy in the present. So New Age religions are likely to be with us for a considerable time. Nevertheless I would see them as essentially a surface phenomenon, like the mystery cults which flourished with the growth of the Roman Empire and the decline of local religious loyalties. They can be compared to lichen on trees, duckweed on ponds, or icing on cakes, which do not affect the tree, the pond, or the cake themselves, just as the mystery cults did not affect the structure or policies of the Roman state or the main outlines of Graeco-Roman culture.

This then is the main purpose of the first two and longer parts of the book: to throw the light of revelation on the mind of the Western world as it moved from the second into the third millennium, and from Christianity into an apparently all-embracing secularism.

The last and shortest part of the book is more directly related to recent events in the Catholic Church. It is designed to show how difficult the process of discernment I have been talking about can be in practice. To illustrate the point, three chapters are devoted to the later thought of Fr Karl Rahner, the Church's chief theological heavy-weight during the 30 years from around 1960 to 1990 (six years after his death). Theologians are the principal channel through which doctrinal developments or deviations enter the mainstream of Catholic thinking. They also create the intellectual style in which, at a particular epoch, divine revelation is transmitted via the clergy to the Catholic people. In both these respects, Fr Rahner, above all other theologians of the period, deserves studying.

The two remaining chapters describe the history of the movement for liturgical reform, the direction given to it by the Second Vatican Council, and the ways in which the Council's decree on the subject have been interpreted and implemented, since the liturgy is the expression of the Church's life most directly affecting the beliefs and spiritual life of the clergy and faithful as a body. The liturgy is the means through which the Church collectively responds to the offer of divine revelation and divine self-giving. It is like the young woman's "I do" to the young man's "Do you love me?"

But for the present, Rahnerian theology and the liturgy lie many chapters ahead. We are still in the front hall of the building, as it were, and from there we pass into the main saloon where the doctrines of the Enlightenment, prefaced by a brief survey of the way they have developed since they were first preached nearly three hundred years ago, are spread out on tables for our examination.

We are all familiar with them even if we don't always assemble them together in our minds as a creed. They can be classified as: belief in perpetual progress; in the power of unaided human reason to resolve all human problems, to ensure that the rights and dignity of all are respected, and to lead humanity to a final state of spiritual and material happiness and perfection; in liberty, equality and fraternity as the indispensable ingredients of that happiness; in democracy and the pursuit of human rights as the infallible means of securing them. Evil, when it is given consideration, is chiefly thought to be due to ignorance and can therefore effectively be overcome by the right kind of education.

We are now so familiar with this catalogue of principles for right living and thinking that we are unaware of their having anything novel or surprising about them. We tend to regard them as self-evident truths without history or mystery behind them, like two and two equalling four, or, if we are believers, in their being as unarguably true and obligatory as the Ten Commandments.

But are they true, either in whole or in part? And if they are, in what sense or respect? And where did they come from?

Please pass into the next room and discover the answer to these questions for yourselves.

Chapter Two

WHAT WAS THE ENLIGHTENMENT?

There are two facts about the Enlightenment which it is essential to grasp if we are to understand its true historical significance. The first is that, regardless of how it began, it became far more than just another movement in the history of ideas, like the Romantic movement. What happened in the drawing rooms, libraries and coffee houses of 18th century Europe resembled in at least one crucial respect what happened in the deserts of Arabia in the 7th century AD. A new world religion was born.

Clearly there were and are great differences. Islam had one, and only one, founder. The Enlightenment, on the other hand, as a coherent body of dynamic ideas, was the work of a succession of men of letters, and its first converts were nobles and sophisticated city-dwellers. Islam's converts were in the main desert tribesmen.

Nevertheless, the title "religion" can, I believe, be justified in so far as the teachings we shall shortly be examining in greater detail provide their own particular explanation of the meaning and purpose of life and our final destiny as a race; they present those teachings as the sole path to salvation as well as universally valid for all peoples; and they are spread by a high proportion of their adherents with missionary zeal.

That we are truly dealing with a religion was recognised by Pope Paul in his closing speech at the Second Vatican Council. "At the Council," he said, "the religion of God made man" had encountered "the religion of man aspiring to be God." He did not of course mean that there had been official representatives of secular humanist societies debating with the bishops in the Council Hall. He was referring to the fact that much of the Council's work was directed towards showing how far the doctrines of the Enlightenment are compatible with Catholic belief. There was an implicit recognition on the part of the Council that the cult of "man aspiring to be God," as Pope Paul put it, is now the Church's main intellectual and spiritual rival, beside which Islam pales into insignificance.

Liberalism,[4] secularism or secular-humanism, socialism, communism are

---

4. Throughout this and the following chapters, the word "liberal" is used in a philosophical sense, the significance of which will become clearer shortly.

merely the new faith's main denominations (freemasonry being a survival of the original 18th century form). Their adherents may differ about how the final goal is to be reached (is the principal instrument of salvation to be politics, revolution, social engineering, improved education, extra productivity, mind manipulation, or genetic tinkering?) and about which of the ingredients of happiness matter most (liberty, equality, fraternity, human rights, an abundant cash flow or sexual licence?) But they are at one as regards the new message of salvation itself: paradise in this world, brought about mainly or entirely by human effort.

Although this new "faith" was not initially regarded as incompatible with belief in God, and in the eyes of multitudes of Westerners is still seen in that light, for a core of committed believers, man rapidly replaced God, if not as an object of worship, then at least as worthy of a quasi-religious veneration. There may no longer be a God whom one can offend by sin, but there exists Humanity against which it is possible to commit crimes.

For the first hundred years or so, this unbelief was of a straightforward rationalistic kind, the atheism of sceptical 18th century French abbés – as it remains for a large part of the unbelieving West. Religion is just superstitious nonsense fit only for servants and peasants and promoted by priests for their personal advantage; the sooner it is done away with, the better. But after passing through the sombre tunnel of German romanticism and philosophy, of which Marxism and Nazism have been the principal political offshoots, a more "mystical" atheism emerged, owing its origin mainly to the German philosopher Feuerbach (1804–1872). It is this which Pope Paul VI seems to have been referring to when he spoke of "the religion of man aspiring to be God."

According to Feuerbach, man invented the idea of God before he was old enough to realise that what he imagined to be the attributes of a Supreme Being – omnipotence, omniscience, absolute goodness – were really, in latent form, his own attributes. Man will therefore never fully flourish until God, or the notion of God, has been wiped from men's minds. God, or the idea of God, is man's natural enemy. Human progress therefore demands war to the death against Him or It. Feuerbach was the father of what can be called Promethean atheism.[5]

We are now so used to atheism as a socially acceptable profession of belief, that it is difficult to realise what a unique phenomenon modern atheism is.

---

5. Prometheus: ancient Greek hero who stole fire from the gods to benefit men in the gods' despite.

There have no doubt been atheists since the beginning of history – whether parish-pump atheists or sophisticated intellectuals like some of the ancient Greek philosophers, or, in China, 12th century Sung mandarins. But never before have there been committed groups of atheists believing that they have the one true solution for all the sorrows and problems of mankind, and bent on converting the great mass of humanity to their viewpoint by reason, by persuasion, or if necessary, by force. Our atheist brethren will no doubt cry out against this description. But if they look at the historical facts, how can they refute it? There can be no question that the vast majority of atheists genuinely want to benefit their fellow men. What they can't or won't admit to is that they are apostles of a missionary world-view bearing most of the marks of a religious "faith." Atheism, as we have noted already, is not a necessary component of that faith. But after three centuries, sad to say, it has become the culturally strongest component.[6]

The second of the two facts which I said it is necessary to grasp if we are to understand the full historical significance of the Enlightenment, is that this new "world religion" is in its deepest roots and in many of its practical objectives a Christian heresy.

Taken individually, its teachings either have their origins in Christianity, like the raising up of the poor and lowly, or, like the brotherhood of men, have always had a prominent place in the Christian scheme of things. Collectively, they are the product of 2000 years of a Christian way of looking at the world. It is impossible to imagine them occurring in the form they do in any civilisation or culture so far known to history other than a Judaeo-Christian one. Nor have they in fact done so. They can be accurately described as "secularised Christianity," or a falling away from Christianity while at the same time carrying bagfuls of the total Christian patrimony along with them. This is especially true in the political and social fields where the emphasis on constitutional government or the rights of man and his dignity represent a recovery of topics and themes well known

---

6. Perhaps one of the most penetrating observations about modern atheism can be found in Pope John Paul II's *Sign of Contradiction*, a series of sermons preached during a Lenten retreat to the papal household when he was still Archbishop of Cracow. When, the Pope remarks, the Devil told Adam and Eve that if they ate the forbidden fruit they would become like God, our first parents did not really believe him, nor when the temptation has been repeated down the ages have any of their descendants. The proposition too obviously violates common sense. Only in the last 200 years has Satan found men really prepared to take him at his word.

to the Middle Ages, but swamped by the late Renaissance cult of fame, glory and princely absolutism – a development which helps to explain the Catholic Hilaire Belloc's otherwise surprising enthusiasm for many aspects of the French revolution.[7]

This is what makes the whole Enlightenment "package" so singularly difficult for the Church to handle. It is not something totally alien as paganism was. We have all been influenced by it to some degree, while many Christians seem to believe that, except for disagreements about God and Christ and perhaps the sixth and ninth commandments, they and their secularist or secular humanist counterparts are on the same wavelength in regard to more or less everything else. About not a few things, they may well be. Unfortunately, only too many tend to be children of the Enlightenment first and Christians by way of addition. They fail to see that, when wrenched from their Christian context and raised to the status of absolutes, the notions to which the children of the Enlightenment give priority, such as liberty and equality, no matter how good in themselves, can receive a quite different significance and even become appallingly destructive – like crates in a ship's hold that have broken loose in a storm and go crashing against each other until they are smashed to pieces. Outside the context of a world designed by a Creator for a purpose, it is impossible to make a harmonious whole of them.[8]

Some remarks by Pope John Paul II on one of his last visits to Poland show the extent to which the doctrines of the Enlightenment are, from a Catholic and Christian standpoint, a confusing blend of benign and toxic elements. "In the name of respect for human dignity, in the name of liberty, equality and fraternity," he exclaimed in one of his speeches, "I cry out, 'Do not be afraid! Open the doors to Christ.' " However, in another address he was moved to talk of the need to defend human freedom "in a social context permeated by ideas of democracy inspired by liberal ideology"

---

7. Benjamin Franklin, for example, tells us that his contributions to the United States' constitution were influenced by his conversations with the Paris Benedictines. We can also trace a connection, via Descartes, between 18th century rationalism and medieval scholasticism.

8. In spite of often noble intentions, vastly more people have been killed in the wars and revolutions of the last two hundred years which sought to establish one or other of the principles of the Enlightenment as a panacea for all human ills, than in all the religious wars and crusades since the time of Constantine (e.g. the death toll for communism has been estimated at between 50 and 100 million persons), if only because in the past populations were so much smaller.

and of a "spiritual disorientation" caused by "various liberal and secular tendencies."

This is why Chesterton and Bernanos could speak of the modern world being full of Christian virtues (or ideas) gone mad, and why the Church's attempts to recapture these Christian runaways and relocate them in their proper context is proving so taxing.

It also explains Pope Paul's warning to well-intentioned humanists. Paul VI was the most sympathetic and sensitive pope so far to the good present in Enlightenment principles. But, he told his hearers, they would only continue to live while attached to the parent bush (Christianity). Detached from it, they would eventually die.

One could perhaps sum up the Catholic and Christian position thus. Viewed from the perspective of the sum total of human goods, the Enlightenment creed is defective in two ways as a guide to human living and human endeavour: it is defective because of what it excludes; and it is defective in giving first place to secondary goods.

A third characteristic of the Enlightenment is more generally recognised. All religions have their more fervent and less fervent members. But apart from that, the ideas we are considering have, right from the start, been embodied in two contrasting forms: a strongly dogmatic European form, with republican France for its showcase, and a milder and looser Anglo-Saxon or Anglo/North-American form, with the United States as its most dazzling shop window. While atheism and its promotion have always been high on the agenda of the dogmatic form, the Anglo-Saxon form has never been regarded as irreconcilable with belief in God or Christianity. There have always, of course, been plenty of adherents of the European form in Anglo-Saxon countries, and followers of the Anglo-Saxon form in Europe.[9] Nevertheless, the distinction remains valid and is of the first importance for understanding the history of the last two centuries and the entanglements in which it has involved men.

With regard to toleration, on which the Enlightenment has always laid so much stress and which we all value when it is to our advantage, two things can be said. No society has ever tolerated everything; what distinguishes societies and civilisations from one another is what they do and don't tolerate.

---

9. John Stuart Mill is an example of an Englishman committed to the European form (see his letters to Auguste Comte on the difficulties of preaching Comte's positivism in England), while Chateaubriand and still more de Tocqueville are representatives of Anglo-Saxon liberalism in France.

Secondly, it is a universal weakness for people who are, or see themselves as, the guardians of some body of belief or opinion, to regard the ideas they are upholding as their personal property, to interpret any attack on or criticism of those ideas as an attack on themselves, and to react accordingly. Pope Urban VIII's relationship with Galileo is an obvious example. But the weakness is not confined to Christians or religious people. To illustrate the point, here is an admission by a distinguished palaeontologist:

"Steve Gould my friend and co-developer of the notion of punctuated equilibria [and I] ... have been accused on many occasions [of saltationism – a heresy in strict Darwinian eyes]." "I am, I almost hate to admit," the speaker goes on, "basically rather conservative and driven, at least in part, by a desire to be taken seriously. That has always meant staying within the fold of orthodoxy – all the while, of course, still looking for a better fit between the material world and our descriptions of it." (Niles Eldridge, *The Pattern of Evolution*, New York, Freeman and Co., 1999.)

Finally, there is the widely assumed connection between the Enlightenment or its associated atheism and the development of modern science and technology. But this popular idea is a case of *post hoc, propter hoc* ("what happened first must necessarily be the cause of what happened second"). The foundations of Western science were laid by men who were nearly all Christians of some kind. If, from the 18th century on, more and more scientists have become atheists, we can see this as an effect rather than a cause of scientific advance. The more successful and powerful we become, the harder it is to keep a sense of proportion about ourselves.

It is equally illusory, I believe, to think that, without the Enlightenment, we in the West would not enjoy the social and political advantages that we now do. Indeed we might well have reached them by a less tortuous and painful route.

With these generalisations in mind, we can now look briefly at the way that the ideas we are considering have developed and interacted over the last 300 years. I shall not be dealing with personalities, nor shall I be trying to assess how much good or harm each denomination has done in its efforts to realise its goals. My purpose in this chapter is simply to show how they came into existence.

It is a familiar story, but I hope to throw a light on it that brings out features which you had not perhaps noticed before.

Chapter Three

THE DENOMINATIONS

When we look for a place to begin, we find ourselves early in the second half of the 17th century. The Peace of Westphalia (1648) has brought the religious wars to an end and we are aware of being in a new spiritual climate. It was like the stillness after a storm. There was time to reflect, and a certain weariness about religious issues. Had it all been worthwhile? Couldn't men live in peace even if they differ about religion? Surely they could agree about the existence of God and the laws of nature, since these are truths open to reason, and leave it at that? Through improved communications the mood spread across Europe to Russia in the east and across the Atlantic to the New World in the west.

I am talking, of course, about the thinking, reading and writing classes. The great bulk of men and women were unaware of and as yet untouched by the change. Today, of course, we all think and read. But for men and women of the type I am speaking of, thinking, reading and writing were their life's blood.

In Catholic Europe, Jesuit education had long made the entrance to this aristocracy of intellect much easier for bright boys from poor families. Pierre Bayle (1647–1706) is an example. A Protestant pastor's son, he studied philosophy under the Jesuits of Toulouse for a while. Then, through his literary journal, *Nouvelles de la république des lettres* and his *Dictionnaire historique et critique*, he helped to turn what had been a mood into a movement, and give it international cohesion. He was not alone. The proliferation of periodicals of this kind had in miniature an effect not unlike that of the Internet today.

As a result, the sense of lassitude rapidly dissolved and was replaced by growing confidence. The achievements in mathematics, astronomy, chemistry and physics of men like Descartes, Leibniz, Kepler, Galileo, Boyle and Newton, had at last begun to reverse the backward-looking mentality of the Renaissance. They had finally taught European man to see himself as superior to the Greeks and Romans rather than as their perpetual pupil, and therefore to direct his thoughts towards a future full of new possibilities instead of towards a past which might be rivalled but never surpassed. The idea of building a perfect world, which St Thomas More and the Italian

Dominican Campanella had played with a century and more earlier, flickered on the horizon and seemed increasingly to be a possibility.[10]

By now we have reached the turn of the century. So far the flow of ideas had been changing men's way of thinking by a sort of osmosis, with England and Holland providing most of the input. It had given them new viewpoints, new expectations, new enthusiasms (Progress is inevitable; Nature is the best teacher; Reason must have the last word; God has set the machine going, but it's up to men to do the rest). However, there was no directing or driving force behind them until the rise of freemasonry in England, and the advent of the French *philosophes* in France.[11]

I shall not try to assess the role of freemasonry in the promotion of Enlightenment ideals over the next three centuries, mainly because of the difficulty of reaching an accurate judgement without an enormous amount of detailed research. There is a mass of literature from the Masonic and non-Masonic sides, but as far as I can see, no historian of distinction on the non-Masonic side has been prepared to write a full-scale account of masonry, whether in its deistic or atheistic form, as a cultural, social and political force in Western society. It simply has to be assumed as a presence in the background – one factor among others. This is not a very satisfactory state of affairs; it is rather as though the history of England since the Reformation were to be written without mentioning the Anglican Church. But that's how it is.

For the *philosophes*, masonic or otherwise, the ideas that had been taking shape were not to be left to make their way as best they could. They were to be actively promoted, which was achieved largely through the plays, tales and poems of Voltaire, and through Diderot's encyclopedia. Soon there would scarcely be a gentleman's library between St Petersburg and Lisbon whose shelves these works would not be adorning. They became for the European gentry and upper middle classes what volumes of the Church Fathers were for the monks in their still unsacked monasteries and priories.

---

10. We could of course have begun with the Renaissance humanists. Among some of St Thomas More's predecessors and contemporaries, we find an intention similar to that of the leading figures of the Enlightenment: the launching of a purely humanistic culture divorced from any supernatural dimension. But they were not numerous enough at that time to turn it into a self-sustaining movement.

11. Clement XII in 1738 was the first Pope to forbid Catholics to be freemasons, and similar prohibitions have been issued by subsequent popes. The reason is freemasonry's repudiation of the Judaeo-Christian revelation, and its claim to be a higher religion capable of subsuming all other religions under its wings.

Simultaneously, in the Catholic Church, or in religion as such, the *philosophes* found an adversary to be overcome, something which is always helpful to the advancement of causes.

This first phase in the development and spread of Enlightenment doctrines in their dogmatic French form was optimistic and relatively a-political. There was admiration for the English constitution and later for the American colonies in their war of independence. There was also, not without reason, criticism of the existing French social set-up. But the *philosophes* who, for the most part, were brilliant writers and publicists rather than philosophers, were not averse to absolute monarchs, provided they had the right ideas and carried out reforms of which the *philosophes* approved. Confidence was momentarily shaken by the Lisbon earthquake of 1755 – how can a beneficent Nature let her children down so badly? – but was soon recovered and lasted to the eve of the Revolution.[12]

The next stage, which overlaps the first, begins with the arrival in Paris of the young Jean-Jacques Rousseau. Just how momentous and extraordinary his influence was to be, just how bizarre the disparity between the kind of person he was and the society he mesmerised into drawing up its own death warrant, is, through familiarity, no longer easy to appreciate. It is as though a 1960s hippy had wandered into a meeting of the Royal Society or the American Academy of Sciences, and been unanimously elected president. I shall have more to say about him shortly. The only point I want to make here is that it is Rousseau who first politicised the Enlightenment doctrines and injected into them a messianic religious dynamism. From the publication of *Le Contrat Social*, justly described as the Revolution's bible, politics rather than education came to be seen as the main highway to the earthly paradise.

As for the Revolution itself and the Napoleonic period, we can see their role as largely experimental and missionary. Paris under the Revolution becomes a kind of laboratory for testing what happens when Rousseau's ideas are put into practice, while the revolutionary and Napoleonic armies, with the zeal of early Christians, carried the notions of liberty, equality, fraternity and democracy, hitherto heard of only, for the most part, by

---

12. For an account of the Enlightenment down to the end of the 18th century, Carl Bekker's *The Heavenly City of the French Philosophers* (1935), and Paul Hazard's *The European Mind 1618–1716* (English edition 1953), and *European Thought in the 18th Century* by Hollis and Carter (1953) are still among the most rewarding and penetrating studies.

educated ears, far and wide across Europe to men and women of every social stratum. Is it altogether unfair to compare it to an Islamic *jihad*?

Outside the dogmatic and missionary French sphere of influence, the milder, looser Anglo-Saxon or Anglo-American Enlightenment, strengthened by the success of the American war of independence, had also been consolidating itself and extending its membership, and when the world began to take stock of things again after 1815, the followers of both forms started calling themselves "liberals," a decision which has not made life easier for teachers, school children and historians.

Liberalism of this period reigned with only minor challenges until 1914, and for the first half of the 19th century was the religion (in the sense of path to salvation) of both the financial and economic overdogs and the urban and industrial underdogs, until after the middle of the century the disenchanted underdogs and their champions started to look elsewhere. It was also *par excellence* the religion as well as the political creed of a large part of the new European middle classes and the now greatly enlarged European intelligentsia. As a cultural force it competed with the clergy for spiritual leadership. The accent was on individual liberty, safeguarded and made practicable by representative institutions and republican government. In the name of liberty and democracy, things good and bad were swept away, and others good and bad introduced to replace them. Inevitably interests and aspirations sometimes clashed. "Free trade," a panacea for some, was anathema for others. Likewise free love. There was much championing of the rights of minorities and subject groups of which the abolition of slavery was an obvious high point. In foreign affairs, energy was directed towards undermining long-established empires by encouraging national liberation movements. However, before the end of the century, not all liberal regimes were averse to collaborating in the acquisition of colonial possessions overseas.

In France, the epicentre of dogmatic liberalism, the government of Louis Philippe was an attempt to hold off more radical interpretations of the democratic idea, which might have endangered individual liberty, with an English compromise. Similar compromises were tried in Spain and Italy that lasted longer. But in France the compromise rapidly failed and dogmatic liberalism finally came into its own with the arrival of the French Third Republic.

From this point on we can justify using the word "secularism" for this characteristically French brand of liberalism, since the first item on its agenda for the next forty years was its war on Catholicism and its attempt to make atheism, in law if not in fact, a state religion. The second article was republicanism. The French attempt was the model for similar experiments throughout the Latin American world, with Turkey and Mexico becoming the first fully secularist states in the early 1920s. In France, however, the march towards a fully secular state was held back by the still large numbers of practising Catholics and the need for national unity during the First World War.

In the First World War and the subsequent economic crises of the 1920s and '30s, classical 19th century liberalism, in both its mild and dogmatic forms, after triumphing for over a century, met its *Götterdämmerung*, and, with the success of the Russian Revolution, its cultural influence and intellectual prestige passed to collectivist theories of government and social life and collectivist political parties originating during and immediately after the French Revolution. For the best part of two centuries they were to be the religion for a large part of the rapidly growing European industrial working class, and, in their more moderate forms, won them great benefits. Before 1918, the more extreme forms lived a largely underground life, erupting from time to time in revolutionary outbursts here and there across Europe.

Within this collectivist egalitarian denomination, Marx occupies a position similar to that of Rousseau in the democratic liberal tradition. He was founder and prophet of its most powerful current, he was the author of its scriptures, he gave it its unparalleled missionary dynamism, and he provided it with an incomparably challenging war cry: "Workers of the world unite; you have nothing to lose but your chains." Next to this, the call for "liberty, equality and fraternity" sounds almost pallidly abstract.[13]

So after 1922, when Marxism became the state religion of the Soviet Union, we find ourselves with three major denominations rather than two jockeying for first place, and at the same time provoking resistance movements on the part of bodies of belief or opinion, mainly local nationalist movements, that dislike or disagree with them.

From the 1930s on, the reaction of many Western liberals of both kinds, the European and the Anglo-American, to their newly empowered rival is not unlike that of moths to a flame or rabbits to a cobra. Some are attracted, others repelled. But the common roots and underlying unity of purpose linking all three denominations produced that curious phenomenon, "No

---

13. It is an historical irony, surely, that what seems to have done most to lift the chains from Western workers is technology and a sophisticated system of borrowing and lending money (capitalism).

enemy to the left," and that equally curious aberration, people who call themselves "liberals" admiring or making excuses for perhaps the longest lasting and socially and psychologically devastating tyranny known to history.

Within the Western liberal intelligentsia, the intellectual prestige of Marxism remained high from the 1930s up to the collapse of the Soviet Union in 1989, while from 1918 to 1960, old-fashioned 19th century liberalism as a socio-cultural or spiritual force had been in a state of near eclipse. However, with the revival of Western economies after 1960, what seemed like a second great liberal age began. But of which kind?

At first it appears to be an amalgam of several kinds. In spite of Marxist meddling from without, the student revolts of the 1960s and the beginnings of the sexual revolution leave the impression that the ghost of Bakunin, father of anarchism, had temporarily taken charge. However, when things settled down and the next half-generation decided that money-making was more enjoyable than lounging about, smoking drugs, and cocking snooks at authority, it seemed more as if a revived Anglo-Saxon or Anglo-American liberalism, with its practical common sense and emphasis on free enterprise, was going to be the directing or guiding force of the coming age. And to some extent it has been, at least in the United States. But in Europe it is otherwise. Dogmatic liberalism or secularism, with its antipathy to religious belief and determination to impose its own code of what it considers right and wrong, regardless of its once stridently proclaimed devotion to freedom of speech and expression, seems to be rapidly supplanting the Anglo-American kind.

After this rapid survey of the way the main denominations stemming from the central core of "enlightened" belief have taken shape, we can now turn to looking at each of its doctrines individually.

Chapter Four

PERPETUAL PROGRESS

When the message that things were not only getting better and better, but were going to go on getting better until they became perfect, was first preached, its recipients – luckily for the preachers – were in a mood to listen.[14]

They had not only been enjoying a longish period of domestic peace. For the upper classes and upper middle classes there had been a general increase in wealth and comfort, a situation which tends to encourage people to believe that their personal good fortune means that everything is getting better for everybody.

To begin with, as we have seen, progress was attributed to human intelligence. Men were backward because they were ignorant: proper education would set everything right. But soon progress came to be seen as a tendency operating throughout nature independently of man. The most usual way was to think of it as a physical force like one of the elements. Then Hegel introduced the idea that the forward march of things follows the pattern of an argument between philosophers, Darwin made it dependent on the fight for survival between contending species, and Marx on the clash of classes.

How did these ideas slip so easily into the European consciousness without anyone noting their novelty? No one had ever doubted that things had got better at different times and places. But after a spell they had usually got worse again. What reason was there for believing that now, even if there should be occasional relapses, they were destined to go on getting better until they became perfect?

There were, in fact, no reasons. But there was a strong cultural climate

---

14. Although belief in perpetual progress initially seemed a harmless enough idea, it was loaded with social and political dynamite from the start. Clever, prosperous and healthy people can amuse themselves with the idea of an earthly paradise in the distant future. Life is already a reasonable facsimile of heaven for them. Not so for the poor. If heaven on earth is to replace heaven after death, they are going to want heaven on earth instantly, now. Perhaps the greatest harm the Enlightenment has done is holding out so many cruelly unrealisable promises at the same time as it offers others which are in fact realisable.

inclining people to think this way. The idea came from the Jewish–Christian belief that history has a beginning, a middle and an end – a direction and purpose. Although the idea is now widely taken for granted, it had nowhere established itself outside of the Judaeo–Christian world.

All other great civilisations known to us, when immune from Jewish or Christian influence, have taken the view that time and history, like the planets, follow a cyclical course. Whatever has happened once will, after the passage of enough time, happen again, and these recurring cycles will repeat themselves *ad infinitum*. (Scientific belief in the theory of an oscillating universe seems to be a partial return to this ancient idea.) History is essentially futile, while matter is often seen as evil or an illusion. Wisdom consists in escaping from the wheel of time or the burden of matter by contemplation, leading to the individual's spiritual absorption into the "One."[15]

The fact that many Westerners have continued to believe in history's having a beginning, end, direction and purpose so long after they have rejected the grounds for such a belief is a tribute to the power of mental habit, but nothing else. Obviously there are vast differences between Neolithic times and now, but there is nothing in philosophy, science or history to assure us that the gains in natural knowledge and artistic and technical achievements must go on forever, or that they are destined for a triumphal climax in this world. The Enlightenment simply took over Christianity's linear view of history, removed God, and placed the "kingdom of heaven" inside, instead of outside, time. It is in this sense that we can call the religion of perpetual progress a Christian heresy.

It is also a simplification of human history which wins assent only by ignoring its mysterious and intractable factors.

When we talk of things getting better, are we simply thinking about faster cars, improved central heating, more powerful space rockets? Surely not. Who would want to be that crass? Isn't it the whole collection of ideas, activities and achievements which go to make up what we call "civilisation" and "culture"? But they vary in value and do not all progress in the same way or according to the same laws.

Perhaps the best way of understanding the problem is to see civilisation

---

15. The uniqueness of the Judaeo-Christian world-view and its importance for the development of modern science is compellingly presented by the historian of science, Stanley Jaki, building on the work of the early 20th century French physicist Pierre Duhem. See *The Road of Science and the Ways to God* and *The Saviour of Science* (Edinburgh, Scottish Academic Press, 1978 and 1990).

as having a "soul" and a "body." Religion, philosophy, manners and morals make up the "soul." The body comprises the things like literature, art, architecture, science and technology which we can lump together under the term "culture." Soul and body interact. They form one whole. But unless we distinguish between them in the way I have suggested, the ambiguities implicit in the notion of progress remain irresolvable.

The West, even when pursuing spiritual goals like the reign of justice and peace, attaches most importance to the "body." Justice and peace will be achieved by technical means – better political structures, social engineering or psychological manipulation.

For the Church, the "soul" has priority. The measure of a civilisation is not, in the first place, cultural or technical achievements, however good and pleasing to God they may be in themselves. Civilisation's highest achievement is the transformation of the human heart under the influence of grace. A loving, united family, no matter what its material circumstances or level of culture, is "more fully human" and therefore civilised (at any rate supernaturally) than one whose members, even though they have polished manners, are cold and selfish. Nor is justice dependent on advances in knowledge. A primitive society could be more just and peaceful than a highly developed industrial one.

It is the same when we turn from the state of men's hearts to the contents of their heads. If we compare a culturally backward community where there is knowledge of God and respect for his laws with a learned society steeped in unbelief and moral relativism, the total of intellectual darkness is, from the Church's point of view, greater in the latter.

Civilisation in this deeper sense is a matter of the slow building-up of mental and moral habits, rather than of sensational leaps forward in the technological and cultural spheres, and its continuation depends on millions of unknown people maintaining what has already been achieved.[16]

No doubt, had there been no Fall, "soul" and "body" would have progressed hand in hand. As it is, however, too much or too rapid growth in the "body" can impede the growth of the "soul" or send it into decline. As we get richer or more powerful we do not necessarily get better. It is as simple as that. Progress in virtue is not a linear ascent, as increase in knowledge and know-how tends to be, but it advances and

---

16. Enlightened thinking about progress is often contradictory. If the past was as bad as it is often claimed to have been and everything has to be rebuilt from the ground up, then there has never been any progress.

retreats in individuals and civilisations beneath or within the other kinds of historical change.

Many other components of civilisation seem to follow this fluctuating, rather than steadily ascending, course. As a work of art, Chartres cathedral is neither an advance on the Parthenon nor a regression from it. They are simply different, like the daffodil and the rose. Moreover, while architectural and artistic techniques can improve, with technical improvement there is often a loss of artistic power.

The same applies to civilisations as a whole. The best periods usually come fairly early on and are marked by a certain simplicity. As they ripen and grow in wealth and technical mastery, a coarsening sets in. We see it when we compare fifth century Athens with the Hellenistic age, or fifteenth century Florence with the Florence of the Medici Grand Dukes in the following century. Moreover, as distinct things with their own charms and qualities, civilisations grow, flower, and fade, now in one place now in another, and, once destroyed or dissolved in a different culture, they are gone for good.

The idea of a super-culture at the end of time somehow combining all the virtues and beauties of past cultures may be a nice idea, but it overlooks these patterns of growth and decay. The nineteenth century tried it in architecture and interior decoration, and the result was, for the most part, a collection of pastiches. That you cannot blend cultures without killing them is something conservationists recognise. They are challenging the notion, dear to Teilhard de Chardin, that what is complex and high-powered is in some absolute sense necessarily better or more beautiful.

The scientific and technical advances of the last three centuries do not readily fit into a textbook pattern of progress either. Up to the late Middle Ages, the world's main civilisations had developed to a great extent independently, with all but one, the European civilisation, reaching much the same technological and scientific level, then stopping short in a state of arrested development or collapse. Suddenly from that one has burst a firework display of discoveries which have enriched whole populations in ways that make Roman emperors look like paupers.

The single world civilisation that appears to be coming about as a result will undoubtedly be "higher" in the sense of more powerful. The "body" will be physically stronger, with possibilities for immense good and immense evil that everyone can see. But the "soul"...? One can easily conceive of a great civilisation of rich, healthy clever people who had supposedly "solved" all their social problems and yet were thoroughly wicked. Already, much that our contemporaries see as progress actually represents regress, and certainly should be seen as such from the Christian perspective.

Here, science-fiction writers often show more wisdom than many theologians and university professors. In their "worlds of the future" or in outer space, the struggle between good and evil goes on undiminished, super-technology notwithstanding.

The main problem for the Church is that in giving her newly developed teaching about the role of civilisation and progress, she has to do it with her rival breathing down her neck and large numbers of her children lending both ears to the rival's message. The more she insists that there is not going to be a heaven on earth this side of the Last Day, the more she exposes herself to the charge of not being wholehearted in her commitment to human welfare, while the more she speaks about "transforming" the world, or building a better one, the more her children are likely to conclude, and indeed do conclude, that she secretly does believe in an earthly utopia and that turning the world into a universal Hilton hotel is what the Church primarily exists for. Many of the Western faithful of all kinds and degrees are now children of the Enlightenment first and Catholics second. They think in the categories of the Enlightenment, make its priorities their own, and see progress, rather than the struggle between good and evil and the salvation of souls, as the central theme of human history.[17]

Whether or not the Church wins the immediate battle of words with her new religious rival, the realities of history and human nature make it clear that she rather than that rival is the truest friend of human welfare, in spite of not being able to promise a heaven on earth. By telling her children they must do good at all times, whether civilisation is advancing or retreating, she cannot fail in the long run to produce the most persevering benefactors of the human race. The best proof can be found in St Benedict, with his rule and his religious order sowing the seeds of a new civilisation while his own was falling apart around him,

---

17. According to *The Catechism of the Catholic Church* (CCC), "God created the world for the sake of communion with his divine life, a communion brought about by the 'convocation' of men in Christ, and this 'convocation' is the Church. The Church is the goal of all things" (art. 760).

and there seemed every reason to despair of civilisation's future. What comparable motive for courage and perseverance can atheism offer in the face of history's inevitable setbacks and tragedies?[18]

---

18. "The orthodox Christian is committed to believing in the ultimate victory of good over evil, but not necessarily in the triumph of the Church ... in this world...Where in the Gospels is He (Christ) recorded as assuring his followers of a triumphal march through history?" Nor did He claim "that if his followers encountered difficulties and opposition they should set to work revising his teaching and adapting it to the spirit of the age. He looked for persevering loyalty." (*Memoirs of a Philosopher*, Frederick Copleston SJ, London, Sheed & Ward, 1993, pp. 205–6.) With regard to civilisation and culture, the ancient Greeks perhaps had an inkling of this truth in the myth of Sisyphus. Every time the ex-King of Corinth got the stone which he had to push up a hill almost to the top, it slipped aside and rolled down to the bottom. The history of civilisation and culture is a bit like that. They are part of God's plan. They are the stone we have to roll up the hill. But in this world we are never going to get it to the top either. After the Last Day, when we have done what we can, God will carry it to the top for us.

Chapter Five

THE PRINCIPLES OF 1789

It has been well said that in the religion of the Enlightenment, liberty, equality and fraternity take the place that faith, hope and charity occupy in Christianity. Without them there is no "salvation." We will start by putting liberty under the microscope, not only because it comes first in the triad, but because in the West it has always had pride of place. The French revolutionaries planted "trees of liberty." We do not hear of anyone yet having planted trees in honour of equality or fraternity.

Liberty and liberties

Liberty is a mystery of our innermost being, which we understandably value as one of our most precious possessions. Coupled with the faculty of thought, it is what makes us human. The two things are inseparable. A will without a mind to direct it would be like a rag flapping in the wind – in this case the winds of impulse; and a mind without the power to decide what to think about would not be a mind but a machine moved by forces springing from something other than itself – the biochemical rhythms of the brain. The master would be the slave of the servant. Still more do we value being able to give outward expression to this inner liberty and rationality.

So liberty has two meanings: the power of choice (which is only truly choice when it is rational); and the absence of restrictions, internal and external, which prevent us from carrying out our choices.

Western man is almost exclusively concerned with the absence of external restrictions. About the power of choice he mostly says contradictory things. While loudly asserting his right to choose as he pleases, he will only too often be subscribing to deterministic and behaviourist explanations of human conduct which make a nonsense of liberty. He wishes to be free to do what he wants; but unfree, it seems, when the question of moral responsibility arises.

The Church, in contrast, resolutely upholds the power of free choice and the importance of its not being impeded by illegitimate restrictions. But she puts the accent on *right* choice, and gives first place to removing the *internal* restrictions on its exercise – disordered impulses, passions and habits of sin.[19]

However, the best way to understand how widely these two views of liberty are separated, I think, is to glance at the history of the Western cult of liberty.

Leaving aside Luther's call for each man to be allowed to interpret the Bible in his own way, we can take as its starting point the struggle of the 17th century English land-owning class with the monarchy. Its origins, in other words, were aristocratic. The aristocrat, *qua* aristocrat (that is before he is touched by grace), wants to do as he pleases with his property and dependants and not be interfered with in the enjoyment of his amusements and pleasures. Liberty therefore means being a miniature absolute monarch within the boundary of his estates.

The cry for liberty was next taken up by the merchant classes. For the merchant and industrialist as such, liberty means above all freedom to make money in the most profitable way. Then liberty became the rallying cry for writers and artists, with unrestricted self-expression more and more regarded as the necessary condition for great art and literature.

Adam Smith is a symbol of the mercantile concept of liberty; Lord Byron simultaneously of the aristocratic and artistic ideals. Later, literary and philosophic liberals would, inconsistently, forbid the liberal merchant to make money as he pleases, while insisting on their own right to express anywhere and at any time whatever opinions they pleased. (The demand for liberty was rarely first on the agenda of workers' movements. Decent pay and living conditions, and security of some kind, were felt as more urgent.)

Finally, as I mentioned in the last chapter, with some of liberty's devotees in Germany, the cult of liberty turned into a Promethean revolt against the idea of limitations of any kind, including those of nature itself, or the condition of being a creature. The cry for liberty became a cry for god-like autonomy and power, which in the more frenzied writings of Nietzsche reaches a high point of strident defiance.

Although all these calls for liberty, with the exception of the last, often contained reasonable and just demands, among others that were not, a single idea can be seen gradually taking shape and finally prevailing: Liberty is a beatific state to be enjoyed for its own sake, an idea which Rousseau helped to make look respectable by providing it with philosophical foundations.

---

19. See Leo XIII's encyclical *Libertas Praestantissimum*, 1888.

The young Rousseau was a natural vagrant. Bliss for him was wandering at will about Europe without settled occupation. (We can see today's world-wandering students as the young Rousseau multiplied by the million.) Life in society must therefore be shown as a fall from this primitive state of innocence. The playboy millionaire, with all the time and money he wants to satisfy his whims and fancies, consequently becomes the truly fortunate man. (Anarchism is an attempt to extend this individualistic view of liberty to society as a whole.)

The result was a head-on clash with the principle of equality, since equality can only be established by limiting the free play of liberty. (Turning partial goods into absolutes inevitably breeds conflicts of this kind.) This is why, right from the start, Western liberalism has always spoken with two voices, subsequently embodied in opposing political systems: "Do as you please" and "Do as I tell you"; or why, though strongly individualistic to begin with, so much of Western liberalism has turned out collectivist and authoritarian. But both kinds of "liberals," libertarian and authoritarian, remain in principle hostile to law and authority, even if law and authority have to be tolerated and even intensified until the application of correct social and political procedures have made everyone virtuous.

For the Church, in contrast, liberty is not a beatific state to be enjoyed for its own sake. The power of choice, and the freedom to carry out our choices, exist so that we can serve God as men, not as machines. Restraints on freedom, internal or external, are bad in so far as they prevent us from doing what God has willed for us as our calling. Freedom is a means and not an end, a precondition for carrying out a work – which, I quickly add, does not exclude relaxation and recreation. We need liberty for the same reason that a lumberjack needs to throw off his jacket before swinging his axe.

We all know this from personal experience. One of the mysteries of liberty is that, as soon as we use our power of choice, our liberty *seems* diminished. If I want to be a good pianist, I must stick to my instrument, even though at the same time I may feel the urge to do other things. If I am invited to visit India, I cannot simultaneously go to Spain. Yet everyone knows that the *impression* of having lost some of one's liberty is false; that I wouldn't increase my freedom by abandoning the keyboard or having second thoughts about my air ticket; that in making a choice and sticking to it, far from having lost my liberty, only then have I found its meaning and am able to feel truly free. In contrast it is when we are unable to make up our minds that we feel least free. We say we are "prisoners of indecision," just as the playboy millionaire is frequently the prisoner of boredom. The unemployed have liberty; the misery of unemployment is lacking the means to make use of it.

When liberty is looked at in this way – as the necessary condition for carrying out a work – law and authority appear as the allies and friends of liberty rather than its enemies. Neither liberty, law, nor authority exists for its own sake. All three together are there for the sake of a higher good, the service of truth and right.[20] But in order to do right, which we know through having discovered the truth, we need the internal authority of self-discipline, in itself an act of free choice. Self-discipline enables us to listen to the voice of reason rather than to less desirable voices. Meanwhile, a just external authority and a system of laws prevents others from interfering with our liberty to carry out our right decisions, or keep us from interfering with theirs. They surround us with the necessary "room for action."

They also help to support us in our right decisions. If we are endangering ourselves by abusing our liberty, it is a blessing to have it curtailed. As ingredients of happiness, the friendship of God and a good conscience, at least for believers in God, are infinitely above physical liberty.

To have a truly balanced understanding of what is at stake, it is perhaps better to think of liberty in the plural rather than the singular. Liberty prospers when men aim for a limited number of recognised "liberties." In this situation, fewer laws from on high are needed. Authority can be devolved. When liberty *in the abstract* becomes the cry, authority eventually has to bear down harder and multiply laws to counteract the abstraction's disintegrating social consequences.

Yet liberty, law and authority are linked at a still deeper level. Creatures, just because they are creatures, can only fulfil themselves and be happy by following the laws of their being, which the laws of the state should ideally reflect. Going against the laws of their being may be an exercise of free will, but it is not an exercise in self-fulfilment. It is an act of self-frustration. It demonstrates the existence of freedom only in the way that illness demonstrates the existence of health. For instance, if we eat to excess, we shall be *confined* to bed.

These "laws of our being" are not a strait jacket surrounding us from

---

20. See John Paul II's encyclical *Veritatis Splendor*. Its necessary connection with truth is the main emphasis of the Pope's teaching on liberty. Liberty divorced or detached from truth ceases to be liberty.

without. They are the cause and source of our freedom. Like our bone structure, they uphold it from within. They are what makes any activity, free or otherwise, possible.

From all this it will be seen that, by her teaching on the nature of the human soul and its likeness to God, the Church is today philosophically the principal and often the only champion of the very possibility of free choice and action. Meanwhile, the doctrinal confusion in the Church, the departures from the priesthood, the disintegration of religious orders and the frequent paralysis of authority when dissenting theologians cry "liberty in danger," show how deeply the anarchic Western non-Christian concept of liberty has entered into Catholic minds.

Equality and equalities

Equality and fraternity are easier to understand than liberty, because, unlike liberty, they are not a mystery of our inner being. They have to do with our relations with other people.

When we look at men in general what we see is not equality so much as equalities. We are obviously equal in having a common nature and certain common physical and spiritual powers and needs. Then, with the awakening of the moral conscience, we realise that we have certain common rights and obligations, a state of affairs marking us off from our furred, feathered and fishy friends and foes.

These are the equalities we know by observation and reflection. Knowledge of our other essential equalities we owe to God. All of us, from the most physically or mentally perfect to the most deformed, He has told us, are made in His image. All of us He loves with an immeasurable love. All of us He wishes to save. He gave His Son to die for the sins of each and all. In that Son's Body, the Church, baptism gives all a fundamental equality, regardless of office. Thus far, there is neither "Jew nor Gentile, slave nor free, male nor female." These, one would have thought were equalities enough to satisfy any reasonable being. After that come the inequalities.

Even the most dedicated egalitarian realises that we are unequal in intelligence, artistic gifts, strength of will, psychological and emotional balance, powers of leadership, and physical strength – how could he not, seeing that his whole life is dedicated to frustrating the natural consequences of these inequalities. He will also probably acknowledge, at least in secret, that we are unequal in virtue, since in caring about equality more than his neighbours, he must at least on this point see himself as better.

In the next world inequalities loom even larger. In heaven there are higher and lower orders of angels, greater and lesser rewards, the last shall be first, and although God loves us all beyond anything we can imagine, He loves some more than others. Equality is not something, one could say, in which God seems all that interested. Fairness, harmony, mutual service, yes; but not, it would seem, equality as such.

When we turn to the modern world, we find it as much at loggerheads with itself about equality as it is about liberty. Its Christian ancestry has left it with a passionate attachment to the notion of equality, yet its favourite philosophical and scientific fancies leave room for only the barest minimum of it. If we are not descended from a single human pair created by God, there could well be races mentally as well as physically "superior" or "inferior," depending on one's standards of judgement.

Probably the chief contribution to intellectual confusion has been identifying equality with sameness, and sameness with justice. If people are in some deep sense equal, it is felt, they ought not to be different. At least they ought not have differing amounts of the goods of this world and the next.

This view of equality seems to have persuaded many Catholics that inequality is something intrinsically displeasing to God, and, as Christians, they are bound to root it out wherever they find it, whether it is a matter of pushing women towards the priesthood, or the laity in large numbers into the sanctuary. It also seems to have infected them with a deep-seated prejudice against the very notion of hierarchy (higher and lower functions and degrees of authority).

Certainly, as designed by God, hierarchy in human affairs is not meant to be like an Indian caste system – something fixed forever by birth. Its purpose is the harmonious functioning of a varied whole, whether Church, society, or universe, for the glory of God and the benefit of all, with love, mutual service and mutual respect as the hallmarks. The Christian notion of hierarchy also sees the basic equalities as more fundamental than the inequalities. The ideal Christian delights in being little, whether he is at the top, middle or bottom of the pile. Nevertheless, hierarchy is so much a part of the way God has designed the worlds visible and invisible, including the Church, that its place in the divine scheme can hardly be ignored without serious damage to happiness as well as faith and common sense.

Fraternity, Natural and Supernatural

Fraternity or brotherhood is the nearest that any of the "principles of

1789" gets to being an absolute good, even if most recent attempts to establish universal brotherhood make one think of the disillusioned French revolutionary who went around saying mockingly "Be my brother or I'll kill you," until he was arrested and guillotined. Unless we act in a sufficiently brotherly way in this life we are likely to lose our entrance ticket to the eternal brotherhood in the next.

There are two questions to be considered. Are men brothers in fact? And if so, how can they be brought to behave in a more brotherly fashion?

The Church, following divine revelation, says that they are indeed brothers: descended from a single human pair, they are members of the same family. On top of this they have the capacity for a higher kind of brotherhood: brotherhood in Christ. Christ is the link between these two kinds of brotherhood, natural and supernatural. In taking on human nature, Vatican II tells us, Christ "in a certain sense" united himself with every man. Because of this, all men are brothers *of* Christ and as such are damaged reflections of Him. When we see Christ in the poor, for instance, we do not first ask whether they are Christians or Hindus. But men only become brothers *in* Christ when, on entering the Church, they become members of His Mystical Body.

Yet brothers though they may be in these two ways, men cannot be brought to act in a brotherly fashion by natural means alone. They have a natural tendency to love their kith and kin, and in normal circumstances will entertain a certain fellow-feeling for their kind outside the family; but neither instinct will be strong enough by itself to resist strong impulses and passions of an opposing kind. For that they need grace.

Initially, the thinking of the fathers of the Enlightenment and the Revolution about brotherhood had some points in common with the Church's own. They believed in a real brotherhood of men based on our common human nature, and, if they were deists, on the fatherhood of God as well. But grounds for this belief were, in different ways, rapidly undermined first by Rousseau, then by Darwin.

Rousseau atomised humanity. We think of brothers as belonging to a family; but for Rousseau, men and women come into the world as isolated individuals. The family counts for nothing. In keeping with these principles he placed his four illegitimate children in an orphanage as soon as they were born. The only relationship that mattered for Rousseau was a legal one (the "social contract"). Men agree to give up some of their liberty for the advantage of communal living. Darwin further undermined human brotherhood by abolishing our first parents and making the behaviour of

Cain towards Abel the model for human advancement.

Nevertheless, making men behave like brothers continues to be proclaimed as a duty and a possibility. This, it is thought, can be done by ordering them to think of each other as brothers, and training them in the right rules of conduct. In addition there is now the tool of psychological conditioning. Modern doctrines of human brotherhood are really forms of Pelagianism, and they seem to have turned most Western or Westernised Catholics into Pelagians or semi-Pelagians too without their knowing it.[21]

For these de-supernaturalised Christians, natural brotherhood is ranked above brotherhood in Christ, while getting people to be sociable and friendly is equated with making them holy. Reliance is placed on natural means, like group dynamics and similar psychological techniques, rather than supernatural means such as teaching people their faith, or encouraging them to pray, fast and confess their sins. Man, it is thought, can perfect himself by his own efforts alone. Believers and unbelievers are equally capable of "transforming the world."

Left to themselves, as we can see from the history of the last two hundred years, the principles of 1789 are like wild bulls on the rampage. Only the Church can tame them. But can she recapture them, we may wonder, before they smash up the Western "china shop"?

---

21. Pelagius (c.360 – c.420), denied the reality of original sin and the need for grace to achieve perfection and salvation. He was the only Briton to propound a major heresy. In the last 30 years, complaints about a new wave of Pelagianism in the Church have been frequent.

Chapter Six

SALVATION BY POLITICS

It is now more or less a commonplace that the French Revolution was two revolutions in one. A revolt started by the aristocracy against the monarchy's attempts to reform the *ancien régime* became a revolution by a section of the educated middle classes, who in the name of the rights of man and democracy, wrested power from the king and aristocracy, to be followed by a social revolution in which an urban proletariat tried to wrest power from the educated middle classes. The first succeeded. The triumph of the second was delayed for over a hundred years, and when it finally took place, under the banner of socialism, in a country at the opposite end of Europe, it turned out to be not the triumph of the proletariat, but of professional revolutionaries and an intelligentsia ruling for the supposed benefit of the proletariat, with a rigour far surpassing that of any of its previous masters.

Are democracy and socialism, then, opposed political theories or part and parcel of the same thing? The answer is a bit of both. The goals are the same – human happiness through the reign of liberty, equality and fraternity. The differences are about priorities. Should liberty and the rights and interests of the individual come first, or equality and the rights of the collectivity? Let us take a closer look.

Democracy – What Is It?

When we ask ourselves what people today mean by democracy, we find two conflicting conceptions tumbling about in Western minds. I will call them *common-sense democracy*, which is not democracy in the literal sense, and *theoretical democracy*, which is not in the literal sense practicable.

For most people, *common-sense* democracy means political systems like those of the United States, the United Kingdom and France. There must be separation of powers; rulers are elected for limited periods to make them attentive to the wishes of the ruled; all adults have the right to vote; public office is open to anyone who cares to compete for it; decisions are by majority vote; no one can be arrested without a warrant or left in prison without trial, and the law is the same for all. We speak of it as "representative government." Some of the features listed are found in different types of government. I have mentioned them because they are in most people's minds when thinking about what they believe to be the special virtues of democracy.

The underlying ideas are that government should to some degree be for the benefit of all and that a people or society is something organic: a union of families and individuals who, while having many things in common, including a common history and culture, also fall naturally into like-minded groups with different views and interests.

Common-sense democrats, one could say, do not believe in government by the people, but in the greatest degree of consent, consultation and representation of the people consistent with stable and effective rulership. If we look at them without preconceptions, we see that common-sense democracies are more like the mixed systems favoured by St Thomas, combining monarchical, aristocratic and popular features.

This is especially true of the United States and the present French Republic. Political systems are not always what they seem. The United States and France, for all that they are called democracies, are really elected monarchies limited by powerful representative institutions. England is a republic with a powerless hereditary president. Soviet Russia, though atheist, resembled a theocracy; the same men decided what was to be believed as well as how the country was to be run.

The French revolutionary tradition has propagated some of the principles of common-sense democracy, but it did not originate them. What it did originate, basing itself on Rousseau, was *theoretical democracy*.

The basic principles of *theoretical democracy* are that there exists such a thing as "the people," an aggregate of equal units all having the same needs, thoughts and will; that together they are the source of truth, right and the power to command obedience; that the people should rule, either directly by intervening day to day in the details of government, with no decision being taken without their knowledge and consent, or in the sense that the rulers are merely their mouthpieces. For a man to have to submit to an authority other than his own is an affront to his dignity and a limitation of his humanity.

There is a close connection between Rousseau's idea of democracy and Luther's concept of the Church as a people acting together directly under the inspiration of the Holy Spirit. Rousseau's difficulty was that, in leaving out the Holy Spirit, he could not explain why the people should always be of one mind and will. Hence his second most famous idea.

By what right can the collective mind and will compel the individuals, absolutely free by birth, who make up the people, obey its authority and laws? Because of the *social contract*. Having freely (in the person of his remote ancestors?) entered into the contract, the free individual remains his own master because the collective mind and will are now *his* mind and will. Can he withdraw from the contract? No. It is for keeps. Those who disagree with the collective mind and will are no longer part of the people. They have become severed limbs, enemies of the people. The people is ... the majority? Those with the right ideas? Here theoretical democracy becomes evasive.

The theory of the social contract is an attempt to explain the origin of society and political authority without God; to show why men and women who are assumed to be subject to no one but themselves should accept laws manifestly coming from outside them, and not always to their liking. It is assumed that social living is artificial, not natural.

Owing to the influence of Hobbes, Locke, and Rousseau in Western education, many common-sense Western democrats, when they talk about democracy, unfortunately often have a number of these ideas in mind too. This intermingling of two discordant conceptions of democracy (common-sense and theoretical) based on fundamentally different principles, explains most of the confusion surrounding the subject and not a few of the world's present political difficulties.

Everyone knows that government by "the people" is impossible. Even with the most representative of institutions, the real ruling is done by a relatively small number of men and women. They also know that fifty-one per cent approval of a policy or measure does not make it right. And in what sense is an activity like the formation of public opinion, whether by the media or the intelligentsia, a democratic undertaking? Is it not rather an aristocratic one? If a writer or thinker first forms public opinion on a topic and the people then vote accordingly, whose will has prevailed? The people's or the writer's? Voltaire was in no doubt. "Opinion governs the world and philosophers govern opinion" – though the kind of philosophers he had in mind should more properly be called publicists.

Indeed leadership of any kind is hard to reconcile with the notion of government by the people or popular sovereignty. Most nations and cultures have been hammered or moulded into shape by remarkable men who, whether good or bad, tend to appear unexpectedly on the stage of history like rabbits out of a conjuror's hat.[22]

---

22. A similar process of moulding is presently being conducted by the European Commission in Brussels. If European union succeeds, even after a referendum, the moulding will have been essential to the final outcome.

In spite of this, *theoretical democracy* is widely seen as the ideal. This is why we have so many well-intentioned liberals seeking to realise the principles of theoretical democracy within the framework of our common sense democracies until they crack at the seams. Such liberals feel guiltily that the will of the majority ought somehow to make wrong things right, even if it doesn't; that the people ought to rule, even if they can't; and that liberty and equality ought to be maximised even if the attempt is going to burst the seams of democracy. The breakdown of parliamentary democracies in Europe in the 1920s and 1930s was partly attributable to this cause.

Where does the Church stand?

"By her mission and nature, the Church is not bound to any one culture, or to any political, economic or social system."[23] She blesses any legitimate social or political institutions in so far as they embody the principles of her social teaching (which we will come to shortly). With regard to democracy, one could say that she supports the common-sense kind against the theoretical kind. In today's world, common-sense democracies seem to provide the best framework for achieving that balance between individual and community rights which the Church's social teaching calls for.

The aspect of common-sense democracies which the Church does not endorse is their attitude to "popular sovereignty." Common-sense democracies have now taken over from theoretical democracy the notion that sovereignty (the right to command obedience) comes from "the people" or the majority vote, not from God. In so far as they accept this principle, first passed into law by the French constituent assembly in June 1789, modern states have moved from a Christian foundation to an atheist-humanist foundation. We can therefore see the French Revolution as incorporating three not two revolutions: a political revolution, a social revolution, and a metaphysical revolution, as the transference of power from God to Demos has been called.[24]

The fact that many Catholics now think that democracy (however understood) is the only legitimate form of government, that majority opinion ought not to be opposed (except when it is an opinion with which they disagree), and that the Church should be restructured "democratically," is another example of how much more their minds are formed by the teaching of the Enlightenment and the Revolution than by the teaching of the Church.

---

23. *Gaudium et Spes*, 42.

24. I am indebted for this tripartite distinction to Geneviève Esquier of the French Catholic weekly *L'Homme Nouveau*.

Socialism and the Social Teaching

Until Rousseau came along, no one except the odd philosopher had thought it necessary to presuppose an aboriginal social contract in order to explain why people lived together in families, tribes and nations. They took it for granted that human life had been social from the start. So the rise of socialism can be seen as first of all a reaction to the libertarian individualism of Rousseau and the economic individualism of Adam Smith (the good society results from each man pursuing personal self-interest.) It was also, of course, a reaction to the horrors of early industrialism. Individually, the poor were weak; but united they could be strong.

Anyone who has ever thought about the subject is familiar with the three basic socialist principles: co-operation rather than competition at work; as equal, or a nearer-to-equal distribution of the products of work; and communal ownership. The emphasis is on interdependence. Equality and brotherhood take precedence over liberty.

Before the French Revolution, the men and women who had put these basic principles into practice in the most thoroughgoing fashion had been Europe's monks and nuns. We also find movements like the Diggers of the English Civil War (1640s–1650s) attempting to realise them in non-religious context. Then, after the revolutionary and Napoleonic armies had driven most monks and nuns from their homes in the name of liberty, equality and fraternity, some of the first attempts to apply the basic principles in a secular setting were made by the early socialist Robert Owen, who founded a number of co-operatively organised communities in Great Britain and the United States in the 1820s and '30s. The word "socialism" came into use around 1835. Owen's communities eventually failed. But the 19th and 20th centuries have seen the foundation of countless similar co-operative and communal enterprises with a strongly utopian or religious bent.

Socialism's partly religious origins have influenced all subsequent forms of socialism, the irreligious included. They also explain its attractions for certain Catholics. If monks and nuns can live by what looks like a blueprint for the kingdom of heaven as well as a quick fix for horrendous social conditions (if you forget about original sin), why shouldn't everyone else be made to?

So socialism begins as a theory of ownership and human relations, and only becomes a theory of government when the attempt is made to apply the basic principles to whole societies and nations.

Fourier and Saint-Simon (a descendant of the malicious duke and diarist at the court of Louis XIV) were among the first thinkers to draw up plans for a "rationally" organised industrial society. Their primary interest was efficiency and productivity. Saint-Simon's system foreshadowed the corporate socialism of Mussolini and early fascism. It emphasised class co-operation under the leadership of captains of industry and scientists.

Mainstream socialists, in contrast, remained attached to the principles of theoretical democracy: the powerful were not to be trusted; power should be with the people; the people or workers must be the directing force. There was also an important terminological change: communal ownership came to be identified with state ownership. The state must own the means of production and exchange. All of them? The different schools of socialism can be distinguished by the degree of state ownership and control they advocated.

If history followed logic, the next step would have been something like the modern welfare state. But this was beyond the reach of 19th century socialist parties. So the welfare state only arrived about thirty years after the setting up of the first fully socialist state, by revolution in 1917, had given the governments of Europe a fright of such almighty proportions that they are only now recovering from it. The Russian revolutionaries called their system communism, but it makes more sense to call it despotic socialism.

Despotic socialism, which justifies its claim to be democratic by an appeal to Rousseauistic theory coupled with linguistic sleight of hand (the party incarnates the popular will) is, in essence, the imposition on a whole people of a way of life that can only be effectively lived by freely consenting small groups with a strong religious motivation. Lacking that motivation and consent, the rulers are confronted with the same difficulty as Calvin at Geneva, and the French revolutionaries in Paris. Can people be brought to live at a high level of virtue solely by government authority and police surveillance?

Marxism is simply the most wide-ranging and devastating attempt to answer the question in the affirmative. It is surely delightfully ironic that it should have collapsed in Europe in the 200th anniversary year (1989) of the outbreak of the French Revolution, and that its aged and exhausted rulers should have been referred to by the Western media as "conservatives."

Nevertheless, despotic socialism remains a standing temptation not only for rulers faced with serious economic difficulties, but also for generous-hearted young people suddenly confronted with extreme poverty on a massive scale for the first time.

How far can socialist aims and ideals of a non-Marxist stamp be partly

49

incorporated into common-sense democratic systems without denaturing them or ruining them economically? This is the question the majority of the world's nations, new and old, are now facing.

To understand what the Church has to say on the subject, we have to distinguish between socialism as a philosophy of human relations and ownership of property, and socialism as a theory of government. The Church has a social philosophy and social principles but no specific social and economic plan, just as she has principles of just government without being committed to any one political system.

The first of those principles is what she now calls the *principle of solidarity*. The principle of solidarity does not exclude reasonable competition or the notion of social order or hierarchy, but it puts the accent on co-operation. It says that, whatever the economic or social set-up, men should live together as brothers, not fight or try to over-reach each other. Neither cut-throat free enterprise nor class struggle can be the mechanism of social progress; only ethics can. Without ethics there can only be social regress.

The principle of solidarity is an extension of Leo XIII's principle "Capital needs labour, labour needs capital" to every sphere of life. To summarise what she has in mind, the Church has recently been using the word "socialisation." No society ought to be socialist. But the institutions of every society should reflect the fact of its being a "commonwealth" or "common weal." There seems to be a certain affinity here with the thinking of "Christian socialists" like the 19th century Anglican, Frederick Maurice.

Secondly, the Church recognises only two absolutely necessary and unchanging social units or unities: *the family* ruled by parents, and *the social whole* (tribe, community, nation or state) ruled by a legitimately established government. Between these two there can be any number of other public or independent bodies and associations running social and economic life, side by side or in ascending order according to the *principle of subsidiarity* (a higher body ought not to do what can be done just as well by a lower body).

The fact that the family is the smallest social unit does not, however, mean it is the least important. On the contrary, all other associations exist for the benefit of families and individuals. The family is the place where the future citizens receive their deepest formation, in personal virtue and social living. Societies, like those in the West, that undermine family life are simply piling up bombs in their basements.

The elements in socialism which first attracted the Church's condemnations were the revolutionary methods of gaining power advocated by the most influential 19th century socialists: their plans for total state control, and their denial of the right to private property. "Property is theft," said the French socialist Proudhon.[25]

The Church allows the overthrow of tyrannical rulers by force only in extreme circumstances. To paraphrase Pius XI, the "cure must not be worse than the disease." As for total state control, the Church will not allow that God has given any man or group of men the right or power to establish the universal reign of justice. That will come later and be His doing. What He has decreed in the meanwhile seems to be that mixture of sufficient authority and liberty enabling men to seek and serve Him freely in peace and tranquillity.

For the same reason, she has always defended the right to private property. Many have seen this as a championing of the well-off. But there are millions of small property owners throughout the world who, by Western standards, are poor. In championing men's right to private property, the Church is championing their liberty and independence. The expression "wage-slave," for the property-less worker, still has meaning.

However she does not regard private property as an unqualified right. A man may not for instance, just for the hell of it, burn his Rembrandts, or tear up a pile of bank notes. Property is to be seen first of all as a *stewardship*. It should also be distributed as equitably as possible. Great concentrations of wealth can be infringements of other men's right to property. The just wage and the just price should also limit the free pursuit of wealth. Economic life should not be left entirely to the operation of blind forces or conflicting egoisms.

To get these points across, the Church has recently been speaking about private property having a "social dimension" (it must be used in ways that benefit our neighbour or at least don't harm him) and emphasising the biblical doctrine of the *universal destination of earthly goods*.

The universal destination of earthly goods does not mean that everything belongs equally in equal amounts to everybody. It means the world was made for the benefit and enjoyment of all, and that everyone has a right to an equitable share.

To sum up, if we look at the social and political changes, revolutions included, of the last two hundred years, carried on in the name of liberty, equality, fraternity and democracy, what we see running like a crystal stream through the thickets of horrors and follies is a confused quest for a system of laws and institutions which will protect the rights and interests of the weaker

---

25. *What is Property?*, 1840.

or less gifted members of society without stifling the energies and enterprise of the strong or talented, which are also necessary to the common good. This is the Christian thread at the heart of modern political history. Governments and social and economic institutions are meant by God to be for the advantage of all, not just a few. But how is the goal to be realised? Should it be by limiting or increasing the powers of the state? This is where madness begins.

The main madnesses are thinking that government is basically an evil which can one day be done away with; that its chief business should be promoting liberty and equality rather than the common good; that there is a single political formula for all situations; that politics can do the work of ethics and religion; and that at the end of the road lies a socio-political paradise.

These madnesses underlie the attempts to harness the Church to the promotion of different forms of political or social "emancipation," of which South American liberation theology was until recently the most notable. Liberation theology can be seen as the last and most radical version of the early 20th century Protestant social gospel. The main thrust of Christian practice should be raising the poor everywhere at least to a minimally reasonable level of prosperity. Poverty in the sense of destitution can and should be abolished.

Before the Industrial Revolution, such an idea would have seemed inconceivable to most people. Distributing what wealth there was more widely had had its advocates, but not abolishing poverty *as such*. The mass of mankind had always been poor, and with the scarcity of resources at the time, it was difficult to see how it could ever be otherwise. However, as the Industrial Revolution gathered strength, there was a change of mentality. What had once seemed inconceivable, now seemed possible. By the 1960s, the idea that through "development" the poor countries of the world could eventually be raised to the level of the rich West was almost a commonplace among people concerned with these matters. Development meant turning ancient agricultural countries and civilisations into efficient industrial ones through loans, gifts and technological advice from the West. "Development," said Pope Paul, "is the new name for peace," introducing, thereby, an additional idea – that war is principally due to want.[26]

These are not notions that can be dismissed lightly, or even dismissed at all. The idea that everyone is meant to share in the good things of life, provided they have not in some way disqualified themselves through their

---

26. In so far as the idea of abolishing poverty includes the idea of "abolishing" the poor, it is an idea, I suggest, which Christians need to look at carefully.

own free will, is, as we have seen, a thoroughly Christian one. The Church's problem has been this: she is not in the business of producing utopias, but she *is* in the business of making men righteous and binding up the wounds of the afflicted. How was she to get her children to see the difference? The rise of liberation theology was the most notable example of her lack of success in the 1980s.

As a specific teaching, liberation theology began in the 1960s when certain heterodox Latin American theologians with strong social views became disenchanted with Pope Paul VI's belief that poverty could be overcome by "development." Development was too slow a process. They wanted wholesale relief for the poor *now*. So they inevitably turned to revolution. But their radicalised social gospel is not just "Catholicised" Marxism of the Soviet brand. From Marx, certainly, they took over the idea of class conflict as the mechanism of social progress. But the rest of their system, as will become clear in a later chapter, is the Lutheran biblical critic Rudolf Bultmann's religious modernism in a political mode.[27]

The Church, in liberation theology, exists to establish "the kingdom" – a kingdom of equality and peace.[28] But the Church, according to the liberationists, is not herself the kingdom, not even, as Vatican II says, "the seed of the kingdom." She exists to serve the kingdom, to help bring it about. This at least is true of the "institutional Church," the Church's leaders with their rules, regulations and "structures" like dioceses and parishes. However, over and against the institutional Church stands the "people's church," the "popular church." In the popular church, the people are organised in small communities[29] under lay leaders, who in turn take their cue from "pastoral workers" (clerical or lay), for whose instruction and guidance, we are told, liberation theology was developed (not in the first place for academics or the people themselves). From the pastoral workers, the members of the small communities learn to interpret the Bible in the light of their experiences and life situations through which they discover

---

27. The principal liberation theologians were Gustavo Gutierrez, Leonardo Boff, Jon Sobrino, Juan Luis Segundo.
28. Is "the kingdom" to be in this world or the next? Or does the first glide into the second without a break? These questions are left hanging in the air.
29. Small or basic communities, *communautés de base*. It is necessary to distinguish between the heterodox and politicised basic communities of liberation theology, and the many small communities now scattered all over the world, who meet for religious instruction or prayer under lay leadership because of a shortage of priests. These the Church encourages.

the Bible's principal message: man's right and duty to agitate for his total liberation from every form of oppression, starting with the unjust social and political structures of his own time and place. Eventually this will lead to the liberation of the entire universe from suffering and limitation. The two things are part of a single cosmic process.

That the world is full of injustices of every kind, no one will deny, nor men's right to correct them by legitimate means in so far as they can, without committing further or worse injustices. But that anyone can read the Bible and think that this is its main or only message is incomprehensible. What mainly strikes one is how closely the liberation theologians' message resembles that of the Jewish zealots of New Testament times, whose influence was one of the reasons so many of Christ's hearers failed to understand Him.[30]

As for the stages through which the revolution must pass, or the way society will be organised once all oppressive structures have been laid low, liberation theology is, unlike Marxism, deliberately silent. Truth, for liberation theology, is discovered in and through action. Set the revolution going and the necessary next steps will automatically reveal themselves.[31] Likewise with the organisation of "the kingdom" when it arrives. One has to admit that this is an ingenious way of avoiding a lot of very tiresome questions.

Liberation theology was at the height of its influence between the second meeting of the Latin American bishops' conference at Medellin in 1968 and the third meeting at Puebla in 1979, at which John Paul II started the process of defusing it. In the mid-1980s, the Congregation for the Doctrine of the Faith in Rome issued two documents, the first detailing its errors, the second setting out the Christian notions of freedom and liberation.[32] Since then liberation theology has suffered two blows: the collapse of communism in eastern Europe, which has temporarily discredited rapid revolutionary

---

30. Christ "did not wish to be a political Messiah who would dominate by force... His kingdom does not make its way by blows." (*Dignitatis Humanae*, 11).

31. This idea comes from the "critical," anti-dogmatic Marxism of the Frankfurt Institute for Social Research founded in 1923 in partial opposition to what its members regarded as crude and unsophisticated Soviet Marxism. Frankfurt Marxism was Marxism for sophisticated Western intellectuals who did not like being dictated to. They "unearthed" and gave pride of place to the writings of the supposedly more "libertarian" and less dogmatic young Marx. The best known member of the Frankfurt school was Herbert Marcuse, who became an American citizen in the 1930s, and the hero of American student radicals in the 1960s.

32. *Instruction on Certain Aspects of the Theology of Liberation*, August 1984, and *Instruction on Christian Freedom and Liberation*, March 1986.

solutions; and the departure of large numbers of the South American poor into the Protestant sects. They wanted to hear about a better life in the next world rather than an improbable paradise in this one.[33]

This does not mean, however, that liberation theology's underlying principles are no longer operative. They are apparent in radical feminism, which is already proving even more troublesome, and they have also played a part in the middle-class North American and European religious revolt, which is hardly surprising seeing that, in spite of the Latin American liberation theologians' claims to the contrary, their theology is just a by-product of European political modernism.[34]

The main difference between the two groups is that the European and North American middle classes, having just about all the political, economic, and social advantages they could want, agitate against ecclesiastical rather than social and political "structures." With Fr Hans Küng as their Bolivar, they look kindly on political liberationism abroad, and at home favour priestless parishes or small groups under lay leadership, either because this helps to blur the distinction between clergy and laity, or because they accustom the faithful to women in apparently "priestly" roles. Dutch Catholics immediately after the Council were the first to pioneer this view of the Church, which has appropriately been called "Dutch elm disease." The "We are Church" ("Wir sind Kirche") movement of the mid-1990s in Germany and Austria is another example of the same mindset, which, as we shall see later, has its roots in Bultmann's ideas about Christian origins.

---

33. Was this flight a sign of the times? If so, there has been considerable reluctance to read it.
34. The Tübingen Catholic theologian, Johann Baptist Metz, a pupil of Karl Rahner, and member of Concilium's editorial board, was among the leaders of the movement which rejected Pope Paul's reliance on development as the proper method of social progress and turned to revolution instead.

Chapter Seven

HUMAN RIGHTS AND HUMAN WRONGS

"I believe in human rights." We could call this the last article of "enlightened" Western man's creed. But what are rights, and where do they come from? Rights, which include our legitimate liberties, can be defined as a legal entitlement to the things we need to fulfil our destinies. We need life, food, work, truth, love, a family, reasonable security, all sorts of things. But the right to them is not something we give ourselves. Like law, rights are a gift from the Author of existence. Without Him there are no rights; there is only the superiority of force or cunning. If God does not exist, said Dostoevsky, anything is possible. In different words Nietzsche said the same thing. It was the foundation stone of his philosophy of the superman.

A look at the Ten Commandments (the oldest declaration of human rights and duties) gives us an additional insight. From the point of view of Western man, the Ten Commandments put things back to front. The Decalogue is a list of our neighbour's rights in regard to us, not our rights in regard to him. The command not to kill is a declaration of his right to life; not to steal, of his right to property; not to commit adultery, of married people's right not to have their spouses filched from them. In other words, for every right there is a corresponding duty and we are meant to think about our duties towards our neighbour before we start thinking about his duties towards us. The first three commandments, of course, are about God's rights over us. We have none over Him.

Groups as well as individuals also have rights, as does the community as a whole, or the government acting on behalf of the community or on behalf of God, because, human life being social, there is a common good to be pursued as well as a multitude of individual goods.

Harmonising this multiplicity of interlocking goods and claims has always been one of the chief tasks and difficulties of government. Where individuals, groups and the community as a whole all have their rights, there is justice. Justice is not equality or sameness but right order; everyone doing what they ought to be doing and receiving what they should receive. But anything approaching this state is only possible when men are just, which means willing to give God, as well as our neighbour, His due. Because justice now mostly means justice between men without reference to God, the older word "righteousness" better describes what the Bible has in mind when it speaks of "justice." True justice involves three parties, not two.

This is where the Church comes in. It is not the Church's business, as we have already seen, to provide a detailed blueprint for social and political life. Her role is to make men just, in the above sense, by feeding them with religious and moral truth and the means of grace. Good laws and institutions can help to keep men just or righteous. But they cannot *make* them so.

Added to all this, the Church has recently been insisting that the search for rights and justice will be futile without mercy and charity, another lesson the 20th century should have taught us by now.

We tend to think of mercy as opposed to justice, a concession to sentiment. But we come nearer the truth if we see it as justice looking down on men and things from a higher plane, and therefore able to take in motivations and mitigating circumstances often invisible to human justice. "Father, forgive them for they know not what they do" was the voice of Justice viewing injustice from this loftier position. A passion for justice without mercy eventually corrupts the heart as surely as a passion for money does. "Justice without mercy becomes cold and cutting."[35]

Such, more or less, is the Church's view of justice and men's rights, of which the modern quest for justice and human rights is a well-meant but disordered offshoot. Once again, history helps to explain what went wrong as the movement, step by step, cut itself loose from its Christian moorings.

Anglo-Saxon in origin, it began, like the quest for liberty, with an aristocratic and gentry demand for the limitation of royal or central government authority (subsequently enshrined in the English Bill of Rights, the American Declaration of Independence and the US Bill of Rights, and the French Revolutionary Declaration of the Rights of Man). From the start, therefore, there was a tendency to absolutise the individual's rights without a corresponding emphasis on duties, an imbalance which did serious damage to the common good.

Some early drafts of the French Declaration had sought to introduce a list of duties.[36] But the attempt was defeated. Had the duties been listed or given equal emphasis in these declarations, and had the European middle classes, who were the immediate beneficiaries, paid more attention to them, the next century might not have seen the demand for rights become, to the extent it did, a conflicting working-class demand for the limitation of the power of employers in favour of employees with a corresponding agitation

---

35. John Paul II, message for World Day of Peace, 1 January 1998.
36. W. Doyle, *Oxford History of the French Revolution*, 1989.

for an increase of central government authority.

Meanwhile, God's rights were being increasingly ignored, and the belief was gaining ground that relations between men can be made just and a state of absolute justice reached without making men themselves just. "Social and political structures" can do the work of religion and ethics.

Certainly when rights are genuine and sought within the context of the common good, the Church unhesitatingly supports their pursuit. Bad laws and institutions should, within the limits of what is possible, unquestionably be corrected. But if you give people in general the impression that all they have to think about is their rights, they will not only start imagining they have rights to things they have no right to, but you are training them for social war rather than social living.

However, what has given the Church the most trouble since the 1960s is one particular right rather than the pursuit of rights in general. I refer to the right to freedom of speech, of opinion and of expression, particularly of religious belief and opinion.

In the liberal camp there is general agreement that this right, like other rights, comes from man, not God; but about the extent of any limitations there is disagreement. For libertarian liberalism, only one thing is certain. Restrictions should be as few as possible. Words that could result in damage to person or property should in most cases be discouraged. But the possibility that they might cause moral or spiritual damage is dismissed as of no consequence.

Authoritarian or dogmatic liberalism, on the other hand, while agreeing with its libertarian counterpart that the question of moral or spiritual damage is irrelevant, has always been more restrictive. Wherever it gets into the saddle, it has never been reluctant to limit free speech about the things that concern it. What, for Christians, are blasphemous films may be tolerated. But insulting references to people's race or sex should be punished by law, and political opinions considered to be smacking of "fascism" curtailed – fascism too often being understood as anyone or anything opposed to liberal opinions. Dogmatic liberalism is not permissive or unprincipled. It simply has different principles or priorities.[37]

---

37. The case of the French sociologist Roger Garaudy, a convert to Islam, is a good recent example. In February 1998 he was fined £12,000 for infringing a law making it illegal to question anything defined by the French state as a "crime against humanity." (*Daily Telegraph*, London, 28/2/98) He had claimed that the holocaust, while an "atrocity," was morally no worse than the bombing of Hiroshima and Dresden. However, neither French nor European law regards these latter events as crimes. So it is legitimate to approve of them, as it is of abortion.

The views of only too many Western Catholics are now an uneasy synthesis of the libertarian and strict liberal views. What authoritarian liberalism condemns (racism, sexism, fascism) will be condemned, and what libertarian liberalism clamours for (abortion, divorce, pornography) will, in the name of pluralism, be considered to some degree allowable, with theologians, in the name of academic freedom, claiming an unlimited right to teach what they please, even if it conflicts with the aims of the university or college employing them. In doing so, they are in fact invoking a spurious individual right to destroy other people's right to freedom of association.

For the Church, what God has given us in the first place is not a right to think and say whatever we please, but a duty to seek and speak the truth. Man is by nature a being made to look for truth, above all the Truth which is God. This, not an illusory human autonomy, is the basis for the right to religious freedom.

The right to religious freedom, therefore, is not a right to think or say what could be wrong or erroneous. Because God wants men to come to him freely, it is simply a right (for groups as well as individuals) not to be impeded by the state from expressing our sincerely held religious beliefs and opinions, even when erroneous, unless they genuinely do serious harm to our neighbour, public morality, public order or the common good. Such is the main thrust of the Second Vatican Council's Declaration on religious liberty, *Dignitatis Humanae*.

Hitherto the Church had taught that other religions could be tolerated for the sake of the common good, but had no right as such to existence. She was thinking of those religions as systems of belief impregnated to a greater or lesser degree with error, which cannot be the subject of rights. *Dignitatis Humanae* moved the focus of attention from the systems to their members considered as men and women in some way in search of God and trying to please Him.

In giving this teaching, the Declaration states, it is developing the teaching of recent popes on the inviolable rights of the human person and the constitutional order of society (Leo XIII, Pius XI, Pius XII and John XXIII are cited in the footnotes), while leaving intact the traditional teaching on the moral duties of individuals and societies to the one true religion. If they see it is true, they must embrace and uphold it.[38]

---

38. "They could not be saved who, knowing that the Catholic Church was founded as necessary by God through Christ, would refuse either to enter it or to remain in it." *Lumen Gentium*, 14 and *Ad Gentes*, 7.

But what do the terms "harming our neighbour," "public morality," "public order," and "the common good," the sole limitations on the right, mean? How far do the rights of the state in limiting public expression of religious belief extend?

For the Church, "public order" and "public morality" mean more than keeping crime to a minimum and preventing riots in the streets ("public peace"). Public order means that the state has a duty to see that a country's public life and laws are in accord with the natural law. (The state cannot prevent all vice, but it should try to limit it and certainly not encourage it.) God has given social as well as personal life a shape with the natural law for its outlines. It should also favour belief rather than irreligion. Since we are social beings, the best state of affairs, consequently, even if it is no longer the normal state of affairs, is when a people together with its rulers publicly acknowledge God's existence and sovereignty. Things are then better for everybody, even unbelievers. This was clearly the view of the majority of the American founding fathers: "In God we trust."

Dignitatis Humanae does not see the morally and religiously neutral state as the ideal either, even if a superficial reading can give that impression. It also allows state recognition of the majority religion, provided that minority religions, with the already mentioned provisos, can practice their beliefs freely. As for states which use force "to wipe out religion throughout the world or in a particular region" they are violating the rights of men and of God.[39]

Where *Dignitatis Humanae* chiefly differs from earlier teaching about the obligations of the state is in not claiming that governments have in all

---

39. Contrary to what many Catholics now seem to think, *Dignitatis Humanae* does not regard religion and irreligion as on the same level. "The civil authority ... must recognise and look with favour on the religious life of its citizens ... it must help to create conditions favourable to the fostering of religious life ... It has the right to protect itself against possible abuses committed in the name of religious freedom" (art. 6). "It is a serious transgression of God's will and men's rights when force is applied to wipe out or repress religion either throughout the world or in a single region" (art. 7). However, the American Fr John Courtney Murray, one of the principal advocates for a shift or development in the Church's teaching about religious freedom, and an important contributor to the text of *Dignitatis Humanae*, found questionable "the prominence given (in the final text) to man's moral obligation to search for the truth, as somehow the ultimate foundation of the right to religious freedom." The fact that "the notion appears four times" he finds excessive and a misunderstanding by the Council Fathers of the "twentieth century state of the question." However, the main point, surely, is not the number of time the notion appears, but whether it is true for the 20th, 21st, and any other century.

circumstances a duty to recognise the Catholic Church's claims.

Here, it seems to me, we see the Church recognising the implications not only of a changed historical situation, but of the fact that faith is a gift.

For many centuries her teachings in this field had been directed mainly at Christian rulers and societies. It was assumed that they knew or had the power to know who and what she is. But since the 1920s she has been increasingly drawn into relations with non-Christian rulers and states who do not (as yet) have the gift of faith. The Church bears manifest signs of its divine origin. But to give full assent to her claims, a special grace is needed which may not have been granted. Non-Catholic and non-Christian rulers, can, however, have access to the truths of natural religion (existence of God and natural law) through the exercise of their reason. This far, then, they do have moral and religious obligations.

So with regard to religion, "the common good" has two elements. Everyone should be able to seek and serve God freely; but not in a way that threatens public peace, offends against the natural law (public order and morality), or jeopardises the genuine rights and stability of other religious bodies.[40]

Confusion about the teaching of *Dignitatis Humanae* is due to the suddenness with which it swung the focus of attention from the requirements of the common good to the good of the individual, and to its having failed to show satisfactorily how its developments related to the traditional teaching.[41] The beginnings of the attempt to bridge the gap at the level of official documents can be found in the *Catechism of the Catholic Church* (see the references to *Dignitatis Humanae* in the index).

---

40. The common good: "The sum total of those conditions of social life which enable men to obtain a fuller measure of perfection with greater ease. It consists chiefly in safe-guarding the rights and duties of the human person" who "has a moral obligation to seek the truth, especially religious truth" (D.H., art. 6).

41. "Substantial identity of doctrine was indeed affirmed but not demonstrated." These words, which could well have been said of *Dignitatis Humanae*, were actually written about the Council of Chalcedon, 451 AD, in relation to some of the formulas of the preceding Council of Ephesus, 431 AD (Tixeront, *History of Dogmas*, Maryland, Christian Classics, 1984). According to Bishop de Schmedt of Bruges, the relator who introduced and defended the draft of D.H. at Vatican II, the demonstration of the identity of its teaching with the traditional teaching would have to be done by theologians after the Council. Unfortunately, only too many of its interpreters have confused "public order" with "public peace." In other words they only allow the state the right to intervene in matters religious where they seem likely to provoke public disturbances, not where they involve an infringement of the natural law.

How, in the light of the Church's present teaching are we to understand the restrictions imposed in the past on minority religions in Catholic states? By the requirements of the different elements of the common good in particular circumstances. We don't have to maintain that statesmen and churchmen in every age applied those requirements in the best possible way. But we need to remember that most of the minority religions that the Church had to deal with entered history as revolutionary movements committed to her overthrow, not to mention that of the political and social *status quo*.

This raises a question of a more general kind. Is not any society, whether secular or religious, going to try and protect itself against attempts that threaten to destroy what it holds most precious? Whether we like it or not, the Church's attitude in the past was not unlike that of the Allies after World War II in putting the Nazi leaders to death. And what are liberals most concerned about today? The religious liberties of the fundamentalist sects? Or the need to control them?[42]

We also, I think, need to ask whether any government or state can ever be religiously or philosophically totally neutral – as Fr Courtney Murray seems to have believed.[43] Can a people or state hold together in the long run without some kind of consensus about life's meaning or what should and should not be done? And if that consensus is not Christian and Catholic, what is it going to be? The history of the twentieth century suggests that the theoretically neutral liberal state is either an illusion or a transitional stage on the way to something very different. "Political correctness" is already giving us a foretaste of what that different something will be. In "political correctness" we see "liberal fundamentalism" levering its own Decalogue into place. Genuinely libertarian liberalism will soon be a thing of the distant past.

This should be no cause for surprise. Over two hundred years ago, Jeremy Bentham, English liberalism's earliest "moral theologian," a man full of well-intentioned plans for making men happy according to his own view of what was best for them, had called talk about rights "nonsense on stilts." And so, without a transcendent Giver of rights, it is.

---

42. Outside the Anglo-Saxon political sphere, so-called "liberal" states had never had any qualms about restricting religious freedom; for example, the French third republic, Switzerland, Mexico, Ataturk's Turkey, or contemporary Russia.

43. For a criticism of Murray on this point, see David L. Schindler, *Communio*, Winter 1997, pp. 748–9. Underlying Schindler's criticisms of Murray is his different view of the relations between nature and grace.

PART TWO

SECONDARY INFLUENCES

Chapter Eight

THE SHIFT TO THE HUMAN SUBJECT IN PHILOSOPHY

Why Philosophy?

It would be difficult to deny that the attempt to put "modern philosophy" at the service of the Church has not so far produced the fruits that were expected from it, while at the same time it is responsible for many of the Church's present problems.

But why should the Church have anything to do with philosophy? Does it really have any need for it?

If asked to give a really truthful reply, the reaction of many Catholics, I suspect, would be not unlike that of the 7th century Arab invader of Egypt, who, when asked why he had burned the great library at Alexandria, replied that if the books in it contradicted the word of God they were wrong, while if they agreed with it, they were superfluous.

But that has never been the attitude of the Church, even if St Paul was at pains to explain that he was preaching something much more than a philosophy. Whether using or refuting philosophical ideas, the Church has always taken philosophical ideas seriously, because she quickly saw that unless men's fundamental "philosophical" notions were right it would be harder for them to accept and understand revealed truth.

Formal philosophy simply does in a detailed and systematic way what all men do from time to time in a loose untidy way – use their natural powers of thought to make sense of themselves and the world around them. What kind of thing is this? What is it made of? Who made it? What is it for? How did things come into existence in the first place? Is everything changing all the time, or is there something that remains stable underneath the change? Out of questions like these arose the different branches of formal philosophy, because although common sense hits the mark much of the time, it is not an infallible guide all the time; things are not always the way they appear to be on the surface.

The main branches of formal philosophy are or were: natural philosophy, now called "science," which deals with the physical and biological worlds; epistemology, the study of how we know; logic, about reasoning correctly;

moral philosophy, concerned with the goodness or badness of human acts; metaphysics, which penetrates through the world registered by the senses to its immaterial or abstract "substructure" – we could call it the science of primary causes, first principles and essences; and natural theology – the search for the supreme cause and final purpose of things. When not impeded by prejudice, the mind moves naturally from speculating about created things to searching for their uncreated cause.

In spite of philosophy's reputation as something recondite, the rough and ready kind of philosophical thinking that precedes formal philosophy is in fact as much a normal human activity as breathing and eating; and, contrary to the bulk of current opinion, metaphysics is the most normal of all. Man is a naturally metaphysical creature. If you doubt it, try carrying on a conversation on any reasonably serious subject without using abstractions like "something" or "nothing," "cause" and "effect," "quantity" and "quality," or "matter" and "form." We talk about being "substantially" in agreement, or things being "essentially" the same, though we cannot touch or weigh what in this case we mean by a "substance," any more than we can an "essence."[44]

Where then do these notions come from?

A fashionable view among some thinkers and theologians, as we saw earlier, is that they have been culturally imposed on us. We in the West have been indoctrinated with Greek or Hellenistic thought patterns. But if so, how are we to explain the fact that numbers of peoples who know nothing about the ancient Greeks have words for equivalent concepts, or if not, easily assimilate them; or that people who refuse to allow words like "substance" and "essence" any philosophical value cling to them for everyday use.

The alternative explanation is that these basic building blocks of thought are generated (one could almost say instantaneously and automatically) as soon as the human mind comes into contact with reality. The intellect, so to speak, "reads them between the lines" of the data provided by the senses. Greek philosophers used expressions like matter and form, substance and accident, essence and existence, not because they had a special 4th century

---

44. "All men and women are in some sense philosophers and have their own philosophical conceptions with which they direct their lives." John Paul II, encyclical *Fides et Ratio*, 30. The word "substance" in philosophy does not mean what it means in ordinary speech. It does not mean a kind of matter, like treacle or hair cream. It first meant the unchanging "core" of a thing, and then its total being, that which transcends while embracing the parts.

BC way of looking at things, but because, as Gilson has pointed out, coming first in the long line of formal philosophers, they were the first to see these elemental truths.[45]

Other philosophers have denied the reality of change, or held that matter is evil or an illusion. From this we can see how important it is for the Church that men's fundamental notions should be right. Disbelief in the reality of change would make repentance or the Real Presence impossible, while the notion that matter is evil or an illusion conflicts with her teaching about the goodness of creation and the reality of Christ's human nature.

Christian Philosophy

But where was the Church to find a valid system of philosophical notions through which to explain her teaching, apart from those already provided by common sense?

The answer was nowhere. When she came into the world, no such system existed. The available systems – Pythagorean, Platonic, Aristotelian, Stoic, Epicurean, Neoplatonic – although they contained varying amounts of truth, were not individually wholly satisfactory. It took time to discover this. But eventually she learned that to have a philosophical explanation of reality completely to her liking, she must forge it for herself by taking whatever was good in existing philosophies, correcting it where it was necessary with the help of revelation, and carrying on from there.

In this way there came into existence that body of philosophical truth known as the *philosophia perennis* (the good-for-all-time philosophy), or Christian philosophy, of which the medieval philosopher-theologians called the scholastics were the principal builders, with St Thomas Aquinas as chief luminary.

The *philosophia perennis* does not claim to provide a finished picture of reality in all its details. Its claims are twofold: that from the philosophical standpoint, it has got the main lines of the picture right; and that it provides

---

45. Pope Paul called this universal capacity for metaphysical thought "the natural metaphysics of mankind" (*Mysterium Fidei* (1965), 24). He was answering Catholics who had been trying to get the Church to drop her teaching about transubstantiation – her way of explaining what happens to the bread and wine in the Mass – on the grounds that modern philosophy has rejected the notion of metaphysical substance and therefore modern men can no longer understand what the Church is talking about. The Pope replied that the concept of substance is not peculiar to any particular school of philosophy; it belongs to the natural pattern of human thinking everywhere.

a body of permanently valid principles and concepts which no philosophical explanation of this or that aspect of reality, or reality in its totality, can ignore with impunity. It could never, for instance, make room for the Zen Buddhist denial of the principle of contradiction (contradictory assertions cannot be true of the same thing at the same time). But it can absorb philosophical explanations of hitherto unexamined, or incompletely examined parts of reality, provided they are not in contradiction with its basic principles. All that matters is whether any novelties can be shown to be true.

The scholastics' analytical approach and systematic method, coupled with the value they attached to reason, and their conviction that the universe is ultimately intelligible throughout, because it is the work of an intelligent and purposeful Maker (it contains mysteries but not absurdities) created a climate of opinion which had much to do with the rise of modern science.[46]

The main weakness of the *philosophia perennis*, as St Thomas and the medieval scholastics left it, lay in being encumbered with ancient Greek notions about physics, which its guardians were reluctant to shed when these notions were challenged by the new mechanistic physics originating in the late medieval schools of Paris and the astronomy of Copernicus and Galileo.[47]

It was assumed by friend and foe alike that there was a necessary connection between the strictly philosophical components of the *philosophia perennis*, which were of enduring value, and these disproved scientific hypotheses. So, as the exact and applied sciences went from triumph to triumph, scholasticism became discredited through guilt by association, not only in the eyes of the Church's opponents, but eventually in those of some of her own children. Meanwhile, Luther, with his subjective emotional approach to religion (not "Is it true?" but "What does it mean for me?") had set most of the Protestant world against the *philosophia perennis*. His passionate, self-filled, self-willed spirit could not fail to find its ordered objectivity repugnant.

Finally, in the 17th century, the *philosophia perennis* was to suffer from misguided attempts to reconcile it with the beginnings of what is now called "modern philosophy."

---

46. The case was first made early in the 20th century by the French physicist Pierre Duhem, and has since been even more convincingly presented in the English-speaking world by the historian of science Fr Stanley Jaki.
47. In the same way that science today would seem to be encumbering itself with irrelevant philosophical notions.

Modern philosophy

René Descartes (1596–1650), one of the world's most powerful intellects and a mathematician of the first order, is usually considered the father of modern philosophy. However, he launched into European thinking two ideas that the world would probably have been happier without.

The first was his method of systematic doubt. Everything should be called into question, nothing accepted as true until its truth has been established with unshakeable certainty.[48] This led him to the conviction that the only thing we can know with absolute certainty is the fact that we think. What seems to be the outside world may look real, but we could be dreaming, having an hallucination, or be the victim of diabolical deceit. However, I unquestionably know that my thoughts are real and so that I who think them am real too. *Cogito ergo sum* – I think, therefore I am. All subsequent certainties depend on this one. Our thoughts, not things, must therefore be the starting point of all future philosophy. The outside world exists, but we do not know it by direct contact. Its existence has to be proved by logical deduction from what we know about our thoughts.

By breaking the connection between the human mind and the outside world, which it is the mind's purpose to penetrate and understand, Descartes plunged the greater part of modern philosophy into an epistemological[49] quagmire from which it has ever since been struggling to emerge, thereby becoming the progenitor of modern idealism or subjectivism. If the first and only thing we indisputably know is our thoughts, how can we establish the existence of anything else? In spite of heroic efforts to show it can be done, no one has so far succeeded to everyone's satisfaction, and many consider it impossible.

The opposite of modern idealism is realism. For the realist, the first thing we know, the starting point of knowledge, is not thought but things. *Res sunt*: "things exist." We know by direct intuition, that is, without consciously thinking about it, that the things we touch and see are outside our minds. Only after first knowing things do we realise that we have thought about

---

48. Descartes was looking for a way round the elegant scepticism of his predecessor, the French essayist Montaigne (1533–1592) in his *Essais* and *Apologie de Raymond Sebond*. Montaigne took the not very original position that philosophers all disagree and there is no way of establishing which of them is right.

49. Epistemology: the branch of philosophy which studies the relationship between reality and the ideas and pictures of it we have in our minds, or the way we know whatever it is that we know.

them.[50]

The standpoint of the Church, the world at large, and of most philosophy before Descartes, is realist. The clash between these two starting points, realist and idealist, the one objective in its approach, the other subjective, explains much that is taking place today, including, I suggest, some of our children's behaviour and not a little of what we may hear from politicians.

Descartes' method of systematic doubt also introduced the "critical spirit" into Western life. No one doubts the importance of a good critical sense (not taking everything at face value). But the critical *spirit* is something rather different. It can often be the enemy rather than the friend of a good critical sense. It starts with the assumption that, up until now, error is what has chiefly prevailed in the world. Whatever is or has been commonly thought or done is almost certain to be wrong – an idea that was axiomatic with the thinkers of the Enlightenment, and now seems to have become axiomatic for large numbers of Christians.

If the method of systematic doubt was the first of Descartes' less desirable legacies, the second was his idea that all thinking and proof must follow a mathematical pattern – which gave birth to modern rationalism. By rationalism I do not mean the grand metaphysical systems of Descartes' immediate successors like Spinoza, Leibniz and Malebranche (a Catholic priest), which are now as dead as dodos. I am thinking of the vulgar rationalism of the 18th century "age of reason," which to some extent is still with us: only simple clear ideas can be true, and conversely, whatever exists must be capable of being expressed in simple clear ideas.

The objection to rationalism is not that it values reason, or even overvalues it, but that it limits our powers of knowing *unreasonably*. It restricts them to one particular form of knowing, making certainty depend on the kind of proof that, as in mathematics, forces us to assent. But many, if not most, of the really worthwhile things in life are not known in that way, nor is certainty about them so reached. Married couples are a case in point. A man can know his wife loves him. He can know it with certainty. But if he wanted mathematical certainty, he would have to do without sleep; he would have to watch her day and night, which would defeat its purpose. Under those circumstances she would cease to love him. That way lies madness.

---

50. I would go further and suggest that the real starting point of knowledge is when a baby first recognises that outside objects – its mother in the first place – are not part of itself.

The other main objection to rationalism is the impoverished world-view it generates. Where a rationalistic outlook reigns, the most striking features of God's creation, its majesty, mystery, poetry, and "magic" drain away like the light from a landscape when the sun sinks below the horizon.

Eventually, this kind of rationalism provoked the backlash we know as the romantic movement, with its cult of the individual and his feelings, which found philosophical expression in German idealism. By an irony of history, Descartes was unintentionally the originator of both movements.[51]

Kant's Copernican Revolution

After Descartes had philosophically shut men up inside their minds, the English philosopher John Locke (1632–1704) redecorated the prison's interior, the Scot David Hume (1711–1776) locked the door and the Prussian Immanuel Kant (1724–1804) threw away the key.

For John Locke (1632–1704), the basic stuff of the mind was not pure thought or innate ideas, but sense impressions. He was the father of English empirical philosophy, and less directly of what we can call "vulgar empiricism" (only what we can touch and see exists or can be the object of genuine knowledge.) A blend of vulgar rationalism and vulgar empiricism is

---

51. A third undesirable Cartesian legacy should also perhaps be mentioned: his solution to what is now called the mind/body problem. In the *philosophia perennis*, a human being is a single entity or substance made up of matter and form, the soul being the form of the body. Descartes tended to identify soul with mind and made mind and body two separate "substances." He and his followers then had to go through fantastic contortions to explain how they interacted. His radical separation of soul and body also made it easier for 20th century thinkers like the English philosopher Gilbert Ryle to caricature the Christian concept of the soul as "the ghost in the machine." It explains too why contemporary theologians like to talk about "the whole man" instead of about our bodies and souls. The intention is to correct the idea that the Church subscribes to "Cartesian dualism." However, the Church does subscribe to the separate survival of the soul after death. Attempting to correct Descartes' errors does not justify avoiding the word *soul* or *spirit* as has happened in English translations of the Bible and liturgy. The most glaring example is in the English Jerusalem Bible, where Christ's words "What does it profit a man if he gains the whole world and loses his soul?" are changed to "loses his life," which renders the passage meaningless, as well as being a mistranslation. The Greek word *psyche* does not mean life. It might well be worth gaining the whole world if we were only going to lose our lives. We all do that anyway. A learned Dominican, one is told, has written a treatise maintaining that at death, instead of going straight to heaven, the soul is put into some kind of cold storage until the general resurrection. To appear in heaven without a body, it seems, would be indecent.

generally the philosophy of today's run-of-the-mill scientist and Westernised man in the street.

In making sense experience the starting point of knowledge, Locke was returning to the standpoint of St Thomas and the scholastics. But how do ideas originate? Here, being locked inside the Cartesian mental prison, Locke took a different path. They arise, he concluded, from the same group of sense impressions repeatedly appearing together in association on the inner movie-screen of consciousness. Seeing them always together, we form the idea of an object (rock, cat, or tree), of laws (solid objects always falling downwards), or of cause and effect (stick striking body followed by loud cries). Locke did not doubt that our ideas tell us something true about the outside world, but he seems not to have seen all the implications of his way of explaining their origin. The more astute David Hume did.

Hume argued that if a group or sequence of sense impressions appears in association fifty times running, there is no reason to think those same sense impressions will appear in association the fifty-first time. Our belief in the existence of things with fixed natures, or an enduring substance or essence has no rational foundation. Nor has our belief in cause and effect. All we can be sure of is the presence in our minds of a stream of not necessarily related sense experiences.

Hume, of course, did not really doubt the existence of objects, or laws of cause and effect. No man is an empiricist or an idealist when he eats his dinner or cashes money at a bank. Hume wanted to finish off metaphysics, because metaphysics, as we have seen, is the ladder by which the mind ascends from created things to their uncreated Cause. Having achieved his purpose – having, as he thought, made philosophy commit suicide – he took to writing history. With Hume, one could say, sin enters into modern philosophy.

Hume also fathered the notion that judgements of value – recognising that an action or thing is noble or ignoble, beautiful or ugly, right or wrong – are nothing but expressions of personal likes and dislikes. They tell us nothing objectively true about the object or action judged. Today this is called "separating *fact* from *value*." This idea, given currency in the 20th century by the English philosopher A J Ayer, is also encapsulated in the idea "you can't get an *ought* from an *is*."

The short answer to this unsubstantiated assertion is "Why not?"

Let us suppose that Hume or Ayer saw a giraffe with three legs. Would their reaction have been:"this proves our theory that the collection of sense impressions to which we attach the name "giraffe" has nothing fixed about it. At any moment it could include "giraffes" with two legs, six legs, or no head. Is not their reaction more likely to have been: "What's wrong with that giraffe? It *ought* to have four legs. How did it lose one?" Every creature has its own special form. If we find it deviating from that form, we say it is "deformed."

It is the same when we turn from objects to actions. Physical actions, like physical things, are recognised by all sane people as having a right and wrong "form." They ought or ought not to have taken place in the way they did. So this time let us suppose that one of our two philosophers has been clobbered over the head by a mugger. Can we imagine him, as he sinks to the ground, murmuring: "It's all right. It's only a fact not a value"; or "It's only an *is*. You can't get an *ought* (or *ought not*) out of it."

What, of course, Hume chiefly wanted to show us was that there is no absolutely unchallengeable basis for moral judgements. From this it follows that whatever can be done may be done, an idea widespread today in the fields of science and medicine as well as in morals.[52]

Such, more or less, was the state of affairs when Kant discovered Hume, and, as he described it, "awoke from his dogmatic slumbers."

Convinced like Locke and Descartes that philosophy must begin inside the mind, and deeply impressed by Hume's arguments about the origin of ideas, Kant was nevertheless unwilling to follow Hume into scepticism. He was a philosopher to the core; he was not prepared to help philosophy cut its own throat. He saw moreover that Hume's account of the origin of ideas threatened science as much as philosophy. If belief in cause and effect or the reality of objects was an unjustifiable assumption, what happened, for example, to the Newtonian law of gravity? If Hume were right, how could one be sure that a day wouldn't come when apples would appear to fall upwards from trees rather than downwards? Kant was an admirer of Newton as well, believing that he was something of a scientist himself.

His attempt to answer Hume resulted in his philosophical "Copernican revolution." Copernicus had shown that the earth goes round the sun, not the sun round the earth. Kant would show that the human mind determines the way reality looks, rather than reflecting the way reality is. However, since the "structure" of the human mind is basically the same in everyone, dealing in the same way with the incoming sense data, apples will always look like

---

52. It is ironic that Descartes' enterprise, which started as an attempt to refute the scepticism of Montaigne, should have ended in the much deeper scepticism of Hume.

apples and continue to fall downwards rather than upwards, even though there may be no such things as "apples" and "upwards" and "downwards" in the mysterious "noumenal" world of "things in themselves."[53]

Thus did Kant think he had salvaged science from Hume's scepticism and breathed back life into the corpses of philosophy and morals. Whether he actually succeeded is another matter. What he unquestionably did was to turn philosophy's gaze more decisively than ever away from things to thought, making human thought the arbiter of what is or ought to be.

Hegel's Evolutionary Pantheism

From the tide of philosophical subjectivism let loose by Kant, Hegel, his most influential successor, stands somewhat apart.

Everything, for Hegel (as we saw on an earlier page) – cats, dogs, babies, mountains, governments, armies, ideas, appetites, feelings, doctors, carrots, poetry, *haute cuisine*, you, me – is a thought, or part of a thought, of the Absolute Mind or *Geist*, as it argues itself into self-knowledge zig-zag fashion through our minds and the events of history. A first thought gives rise to a second and contradictory thought, leading to their fusion in a third

---

53. It is true that our knowledge is conditioned by the limitations of our minds. As St Thomas says: "receptum recipitur in modo recipientis – a thing is received in a manner suited to the recipient." God and the angels see more deeply into things than we can. But that is not what Kant is saying. For Kant, all knowledge is basically knowledge about the workings of our minds. Only the flood of incoming sense data has some kind of connection with reality outside us. After that the mind takes over, processing the sense data in three stages. First it gives the sense data the "forms" of sense and time. Then it "categorises" them, that is to say, shapes them into things of different classes and kinds in their various relationships to one another. The result is "categorial knowledge." This is the field where science operates. Finally, to give coherence to this vast mass of processed sense data, to simplify it and make it more manageable, the mind conceives ideas like the notions of God, the world and the soul. This, the now exploded world of metaphysics, is the "transcendental" level of knowledge. In everyday speech "transcendental" means having to do with a world outside and above us. In Kant it means precisely the opposite. It refers to the part of the intellect furthest removed from external reality. Transcendental ideas do not have objective validity. They are mental conveniences – like name tags for docketing large bundles of papers so that they are easier to handle. The rejection of revealed truth in favour of "experience," would seem to have its roots in Kant's separation of phenomenal from noumenal reality and "categorial" from "transcendental" knowledge. It also explains the terrific business German philosophy makes about reconciling subject and object.

thought, which in its turn generates a contradictory opposite followed by another fusion and so on. Such is Hegel's famous dialectic (thesis, antithesis, synthesis).

Karl Marx "stood this on its head" – mind is a product of matter, not matter of mind – making this inverted version the basis of his dialectical materialism. For Marx, clashing classes were the motor of history, for Hegel clashing ideas. Hegel summarised his version of the process as "being is becoming," which is like saying "standing up is the same as lying down."[54]

Before It started to think, the Absolute appears to have lived in a dreamlike subliminal state, having initially brought Itself into existence – "posited Itself" – out of nothing. In his later years, Hegel came to regard the Prussian state as the most advanced expression of the Absolute's attempt to understand and express Itself.

However, as the Absolute Mind grows in self-awareness, the objects of Its self-consciousness (the material and biological contents of the universe) become in some way detached from It, as if enjoying an independent existence of their own. They confront the Thinker as something other than Itself. The result is a feeling on the part of the Absolute of partial estrangement or "alienation" from Itself, which is repugnant to its desire to be a unified whole. Time and history represent the effort of the Absolute, not only to discover who It is, but to reunite Its objectified self-knowledge with Its subjective self.[55]

Hegel could be said to have initiated the obsession with change which is such a feature of contemporary thinking. It is true that the notion of biological evolution was already in the air. The growth of historical knowledge and an increasing familiarity with other civilisations had likewise helped to prepare the way; if customs vary, people began to think, perhaps everything else is a matter of taste and opinion. But Hegel's evolutionary pantheism gave to change its dominant philosophical position as the all-

---

54. In a fit of exasperation, the German physicist Ehrenfest described the Hegelian dialectic as "a succession of leaps from one lie to another by way of intermediate falsehoods" (Jaki, *The Road of Science and the Ways of God*, p. 198).

55. Hegel's objective or absolute idealism bears a certain resemblance to Neoplatonic world-views current in the first three centuries AD which influenced some of the Church Fathers. They saw the universe as a flowing forth or emanation of "the many" from the cosmic One followed by a return ending in general reunion. However they differed from modern pantheisms in not being evolutionary. The notion of progress was absent. The further things got from the source, the less real and good they became.

important feature of reality.[56]

Kant and Hegel continued to dominate European philosophy throughout the 19th century, and are still powerful forces today. But at this point we must pause to look at the effects of the philosophical currents we have been following on theological thinking.

The Religious Reaction

To begin with, as Descartes' ideas became part of the spirit of the age, there was a general surrender to his rationalism. Whether writing or teaching, theologians tended to handle Christian doctrine as though it were a kind of religious mathematics whose propositions must of their nature compel assent or only be denied by people guilty of stupidity or bad faith. Protestants were affected as much as Catholics. Alien though the idea was to the spirit of their founder, Lutheran theologians, under the influence of philosophers like the Lutheran Christian Wolff (1679–1754), began to systematise their theology into what has come to be called Lutheran scholasticism.

Consequently, when, with the romantic movement, the reaction began, it took the form of a deep and irrational prejudice not only against abstract ideas, but against any kind of clear systematic thought in connection with religion. System and abstractions, it was felt, of their nature deform or falsify religion. System and clarity were for science; religious knowledge should be indefinite and misty. Under the influence of this idea, a supposed opposition between the Greek and Hebrew minds was discovered.[57] The sin of the Greek mind, described as "essentialism," was, so it came to be maintained, its inability to think except in "static essences." The virtue of the Hebrew mind was its love of what is concrete, dynamic and historical. Abstract was set against concrete, static against dynamic, as though these complementary aspects of reality could only be enemies, incapable of

---

56. 19th and 20th century papal documents mostly have Hegel's absolute idealism or its derivatives in mind when they censure "immanentism." In Catholic teaching, God is both transcendent and immanent; transcendent in that the Creation is not part of Him, immanent in the sense that He is present everywhere by His power. The censured meanings are that God is developing with and through the universe which is part of Him, (Hegelian immanentism), or that he only speaks to men or can be found by men in the depths of their hearts (Kantian immanentism or agnosticism). Atheist immanentism holds that the universe contains within itself everything necessary for its existence and expansion; it is self-moving and self-explanatory.

57. The idea is found in writers as diverse as Matthew Arnold and Lucien Laberthonnière.

living in peace together in the same world.[58]

This is the remote origin of the neo-modernist war cry "the faith is not a set of abstract propositions to be believed." Even if today that cry has been transmuted into a shout of protest at having to believe everything the Church teaches, we are also hearing the last echoes of the romantic movement's objection to Descartes' attempt to reduce all thinking and knowledge to a mathematical pattern.

The reaction to rationalism among theologians began, as we have seen, in Lutheran Germany. Almost to a man, its leading religious thinkers made personal religious experience the sole valid field of philosophical and religious inquiry. With Schleiermacher it had been a "feeling of absolute dependence." With Otto it was a "sense of the holy," with Lotz an "awareness of value" and so on. These spiritual or psychological phenomena, they believed, were the only escape roots by which the imprisoned Cartesian ego could find its way to God.

In the circumstances of the time, this philosophical and theological "retreat into the interior" or "shift to the human subject" as it is now called, had the appeal of clever tactics. Unbelief was conducting its war of nerves on religion, using science as its battering ram. What science could not explain today, it was boasted or insinuated, science would be able to explain tomorrow, eventually providing a natural explanation for the universe itself. But, so our frightened champions of the subjective philosophical approach persuaded themselves, science could not follow man into the sanctum of his heart and attribute everything that went on there to material and mechanical causes. Alas, they had not foreseen the coming of clinical psychology with its invasion of the sanctum through the basement, where it would attribute everything it found there to unsatisfactory relations with Mum and Dad and nastier things still.

With Catholics, the influence of Cartesian rationalism lasted longer, the Catholic Church having always given reason an ampler role in religion than had been customary among Protestants.[59]

---

58. Abstract ideas, or the aspects of reality outside our minds to which they correspond, do not exist independently of concrete things, as Plato thought. But they are as much a part of reality as are the architect's plan for a house or the physical laws which keep it from falling down.

59. The French literary critic, Charles du Bos, recounts how when he became a Catholic around 1930 some of his fellow Catholics looked on him with suspicion because he insisted that the mysteries of the faith cannot be reached by reason alone. These Catholics were unwittingly contradicting Vatican I's declaration (aimed principally at Günther) that there are revealed mysteries inaccessible to human reason alone. Cartesian rationalism is a kind of caricature of the scholasticism from which it partly derives.

When it eventually came, the Catholic reaction took two forms. First, in response to Pope Leo XIII's encyclical on Christian philosophy, *Aeterni Patris*, as we likewise saw earlier, the search began for a Thomism, purified of Cartesian and post-Cartesian distortions. This led to the formation of at least three distinct Thomist schools: the quasi-official neo-Thomism of Fr Garrigou-Lagrange and Jacques Maritain, who presented their updated Thomism in a more or less timeless form; the "historical" Thomism of Etienne Gilson and the scholars of the French Dominican house of higher studies at Le Saulchoir in Belgium, who in interpreting the medieval scholastics wished greater weight to be given to the historical conditions which had influenced them (the Maritainian neo-scholastics, they said, were too dependent on the 16th century commentators on St Thomas, John of St Thomas and Cajetan – their Thomism was not fully faithful to the Master's thought); and finally, the "transcendental" or "Louvain" Thomism originating with Cardinal Mercier but more fully developed by the Jesuit Fr Joseph Maréchal.[60]

Transcendental Thomists wanted to shift St Thomas's realism onto a subjective Cartesio-Kantian foundation. The basic Cartesio-Kantian premise, they argue, has to be accepted. About this Descartes and Kant were right. There can be no going back on it. The mind at first knows only its own thought. But that does not mean it is forever enclosed within the walls of its personal experience. A proper analysis of the act of thought shows that the inner "dynamism" or "intentionality" of the human mind of its very nature presupposes a world outside itself about which genuine knowledge is possible. For this reason, transcendental Thomists call their method "critical realism."[61]

---

60. Within these three schools, as one would expect, there were differences of opinion on particular points. For instance, among the neo-scholastics of the first kind there were disagreements in the 1930s about whether the rights of the individual or the requirements of the common good should have priority. Meanwhile, "Louvain" Thomism had produced a vigorous offshoot, favoured by Karol Wojtyła, the future Pope John Paul II, at the Catholic university of Lublin in Poland where he taught philosophy for a time.

61. This is not unlike Blondel's belief that, on analysis, human action necessarily presupposes the search for an end outside this world. In this respect Blondel's "method of immanence" and transcendental Thomism clearly belong to the same philosophical trend, the first analysing the "dynamism" of the will, the second that of the intellect. The principal transcendental Thomists since Maréchal have been the Germans Rahner and Johannes Lotz, the Austrian Emerich Coreth, and the Canadian Bernard Lonergan.

All this may seem rather abstruse for a book of this sort. But the "subjectivising" of St Thomas's epistemology was an important factor in the philosophical and theological in-fighting of the second half of the 20ᵗʰ century, with most Thomists maintaining that the results of the "subjectivising" are not really Thomism.[62]

Other Catholic thinkers, reacting against rationalist influence, began, like their Lutheran counterparts, pressing for a philosophical and theological "shift to the human subject" that would involve a much wider opening of the doors to German idealism, with the pressure increasing as the new theology took shape during the 1940s and '50s.

In principle, a philosophical and theological taking into account of subjective experience is perfectly reasonable. Our moods and states of mind are as much a part of reality as the Milky Way and plant life. They too can be used to point the way to God and help us to understand his intentions for us. St Augustine, St Bonaventure, and Newman all used this more personal or psychological approach. The crucial questions were whether the "shift" was to be partial or total, whether elements of the subjective German approach were to be used to complement or supplant the *philosophia perennis*; and of which of the by now numerous kinds of philosophical subjectivism the Church should make use?

Since the early 1900s, two major new arrivals had appeared in the field of German philosophy, and it is at these that we must now look.

---

62. See "Transcendental Thomism, A Critical Study," in *One Hundred Years of Thomism* by Robert J. Henle SJ, Houston, Texas, Centre for Thomistic Studies, 1981. Early in the 20ᵗʰ century the American philosopher Josiah Royce had already foreseen "that a resurgent Thomism might give way to the Kantian legions and their demand that the epistemological issue be settled first, (that is before any other philosophical question could be debated) a fear later shared by Etienne Gilson." (See Jude P. Dougherty, Dean of Philosophy C. U. A., Washington, *FCS Quarterly*, Winter 1998.) In fact Gilson maintained in two books that once you adopt the Cartesian premise, there is no way of solving what came to be called *le problème du pont*, how to bridge the gap between the imprisoned Cartesian ego and the outside world. See, *Réalisme méthodique*, and *Réalisme thomiste et critique de la connaissance*, Paris, Vrin, 1936 and 1939 (English trans. *Methodical Realism*, Christendom College, Va., 1990, and *Thomist Realism and the Critique of Knowledge*, Ignatius Press, 1986).

Chapter Nine

EXISTENTIALISM: HEIDEGGER AND SARTRE

After the end of the first modernist outbreak, Bergson's *Creative Evolution* had continued to exercise an influence in France, and James's *Pragmatism* in the United States, while during the 1920s and 1930s English philosophers were increasingly pre-occupied with the intricacies of *linguistic philosophy*. But by the 1960s, all three schools of thought had been outstripped by a formidable German newcomer, a newcomer, not only powerful in academic circles, but with a world-wide popular following.

The arrival of a fashionable new philosophy is like a tropical deluge. For a short time it washes everything else aside, while anyone without a roof of solid religious beliefs over their heads, or the umbrella of a rival philosophy, gets soaked. Then the rain stops and people say to each other "it's over." But they are mistaken, or at least partly. Its terminology and attitudes having become part of the common vocabulary and stock of ideas, and there follows a long period during which it continues to exercise an influence in a subliminal way, in spite of subsequent downpours of quite different ideas. So it has been with *existentialism*.[63] There has been nothing like it since Rousseau took educated Europe by storm in the late 18th century.

The first raindrops began to fall with the liberation of Paris in 1944 and the discovery of the new philosophy by the more literary members of the allied armies. Through the 1950s, as growing numbers of the Western intelligentsia fell under its spell, the shower turned into a steady downpour. By the end of the 1950s the downpour had become a deluge mounting to torrential proportions in the late 1960s and early '70s, the era of student revolt. After that its force began to slacken and, by the mid-eighties, it was

---

63. Since writing this chapter, I have come to look at existentialism in a less unflattering light. In existentialism we hear the voice of twentieth-century man desperately crying for help and gasping for air as he feels himself being suffocated by enlightenment rationalism and scientism. As an alternative to asphyxiation, existentialism may not have been the best remedy, but it did help a lot of people find their way back from infidelity to belief in God of some kind. However, I have decided to leave the chapter as it is because the "case for the prosecution" is so much less often heard than the "case for the defence."

being looked back on as something belonging to the past. Yet at every social level throughout the Western world, it continues to influence secular and Christian thinking, speech and attitudes profoundly. To appreciate this it will only be necessary to recognise how many of the characteristically existentialist words which I have italicised in this chapter, are now part of everyday speech. However, before coming to existentialism itself, we must first glance at the three thinkers who provided a large part of the building material.

The Forerunners
Søren Kierkegaard (1813–1855)

Kierkegaard, the movement's true forefather, who first used the word *existential* in its modern philosophic sense, was a gifted but idiosyncratic and eccentric Danish Lutheran, whose view of life and human nature was based on the experience of his conversion (he had lost his beliefs at university and recovered them when about twenty-five), which in turn was influenced by his neurotic reactions to certain episodes connected with his father and his fiancée. His father had once cursed God and the son thought he shared his guilt.

For Kierkegaard, faith or belief is a basically mindless act – a leap in the dark. A man *commits* himself to Christ without having any reason for doing so, having been urged to make the leap by what he has gone through emotionally beforehand. The emptiness and *absurdity* of life without God and the consciousness of his own nothingness have led him from anxiety and dread through anguish to despair. The pain of the despair drives him to jump outside himself, and in so doing he *encounters* God. (It is true that God often uses unhappiness to make us think about him. But thinking, under the attraction of grace, should lead to knowledge, confidence and love, not to jumping off a cliff.)

Even after his conversion, the Kierkegaardian Christian continues to live in a state of partial dread and anguish because he is daily faced with the necessity of making decisions while having no way of knowing what God requires of him. He has total freedom and total responsibility for his acts, but no guide as to what will be right or wrong in different situations or what the consequences of his acts will be.

Like many of the thinkers we have just been considering, Kierkegaard had a passionate dislike of metaphysics and objectivity, his works being full of diatribes against both. (An understandable antipathy to Hegel's highly abstract and artificial system was partly responsible.) And he had a similar dislike of doctrine and universally applicable moral principles in religion. The way things look to the individual, the way he feels about or experiences them, is the criterion of truth, which is different for each of us. As for moral choice, every decision should be governed by the situation in which it is made. We must take our courage in both hands, Kierkegaard says, not knowing whether the outcome will be salvation or damnation.[64]

Kierkegaard's psychological and rhetorical brilliance, the fact that his arguments provide useful ammunition against the cruder forms of rationalism, determinism and materialism, that he was trying to make his contemporaries realise that belief in Christ and following Christ should be a matter of deep conviction rather than social conformity, unfortunately led many of the 20th century's most influential Christian thinkers, anxious to stir up Christians as they saw unbelief spreading, into under-rating his limitations as a thinker. He was a kind of hot-gospeller for intellectuals, delivering his message in print instead of from a platform. However he remained largely unknown outside Denmark until long after his death. It was only when a German edition of his writings appeared just before and during World War I that his influence began to be widely felt.[65] Since then it has been incalculable. His writings have transformed Christian thinking everywhere.

Friedrich Nietzsche (1844–1900)

Nietzsche's contribution was not as great, but was still significant. The son of a Lutheran pastor, and a classical scholar so outstanding that he was offered the chair of philology at Basle before he had completed his doctorate, he is best thought of as a deranged visionary and soothsayer rather than a philosopher in the academic sense. His main life's work, conducted through a series of passionately written attacks on the men, beliefs and culture of his

---

64. A view of things which has had profound repercussions in moral theology. "Situation ethics," "proportionalism," "consequentialism," all boil down to the same thing: the moral law can never be precisely the same for everybody in all circumstances. For some existentialists, one's *Sitz im Leben* or life situation is seen as inseparable from one's self. "I am myself and my circumstances," as the Spanish existentialist José Ortega y Gasset put it.
65. The translation, published by the firm Eugen Diederich (1911–1917), could be seen as a landmark in European intellectual history comparable to Lessing's publication of the Wolfenbuttel Fragments which had set radical biblical scholarship on course 150 years earlier.

times, could be summed up as the demeaning of everything Christianity had built up over 1900 years, and the exalting of all the disordered passions it had tried to tame.

The idea at the heart of his message was that "God is dead," by which he meant that not only is there no such being as God, but that the majority of influential people in the Western world now know it. However, they are hiding the fact because they fear the consequences; this must no longer be allowed. No matter how painful it may be, they must be made to face the fact that they have no one to rely on but themselves. Since man is totally free, no laws bind him. Since there is no such thing as absolute truth, everything is allowable. Man must dare and achieve, making his own morality and "truth." But most men are mediocrities. So the future must be in the hands of the strong, the self-disciplined and cunning.

The only things preventing the triumph of Nietzsche's supermen are the values of a decaying Christianity. Christianity is based on sublimated class resentment. Exalting virtues like humility is the poor and the weak's way of getting back at the capable and the strong. There must therefore be a "transvaluation of values." Christian meekness must be condemned, manly pride applauded, weakness regarded as despicable, strength glorified. His ideal society was aristocratic in the worst possible sense, with one law for the ruling class, another for the ruled. The suffering of slaves is of no consequence. Eugenics should be seen as a typically Nietzschean enterprise.[66]

Some of his criticisms of 19th century Christianity may partly have hit the mark. But the measure of a philosopher is not what he sees wrong, but how he plans to put things right.

Nietzsche's atheism, it will be seen, has a passionate and dramatic quality quite different from the rather smug self-satisfied atheism of the French Enlightenment. He hated with the vehemence of a Karl Marx and far surpassed him in implacable invective. He detested Kierkegaard. During his last twelve years he was insane. However he was not a German nationalist nor was he anti-Semitic, in spite of the disastrous effect of his teachings on the Nazis. Perhaps the most surprising thing about him is the reputation he

---

66. "Values clarification" in education would seem to have roots in Neitzsche's "transvaluation of values." It can have a legitimate use; we "clarify our values" when we go on retreat: are we putting first things first, we ask ourselves, and how far does our life conform to them? But equally it can be and is employed as a technique for persuading people to question the "values" they have hitherto adhered to when these are not approved by the teacher.

continues to enjoy in the halls of philosophy. It is as though Genghis Khan were honoured with a statue in the hall of the UN General Assembly.

Edmund Husserl (1859–1938)

During the last decades of the 19th century, German idealism underwent a subtle change. Hitherto the object of inquiry had tended to be some particular aspect or faculty of the human soul – reason, conscience, will, feelings of some kind, or in the case of Fichte, of the underlying self or *ego*. But towards the end of the period the inner man began to be regarded as an undifferentiated sea of mental and psychic phenomena, all of more or less equal standing and value, into which the philosopher could dip his net in order to extract for examination whatever happened to attract his interest. This sea of phenomena eventually came to be called the "contents of consciousness."

Mapping the movements of the human spirit, its desires, reactions and emotions in every conceivable set of circumstances, had, in an unsystematic way, been one of the achievements of the great 18th and 19th century novelists. There can be no mood, emotion, or state of mind and heart left unanalysed or described by them. But no one had yet thought of using this material to construct a philosophy of man – both of what he is and what he ought to be – based on his subjective responses to life as it unfolds from birth to death.

The thinker who did most to set the ball rolling in this direction was Edmund Husserl, the father of phenomenology. As a philosopher, however, Husserl, who taught philosophy at Göttingen from 1900 to 1916, and thereafter at Freiburg, was more important for his method than his conclusions.

The phenomenological method consists in isolating or "bracketing" a particular emotional or spiritual experience – guilt, shame, anxiety, friendship, fidelity – and studying it with complete detachment. All earlier preconceptions about its origin, nature, or relation to the rest of the contents of consciousness must first be set aside. The practitioner then moves slowly round the experience, looking at it from every angle, and in so far as is possible, empathises with it, in the hope that it will at last reveal its true significance as a component of the "human subject" and where it comes in the hierarchy of importance.

What is the relationship of the contents of consciousness to the outside world? Do they give us objective knowledge about it?

In the earlier part of his career, Husserl appeared to be moving from an idealist to a more realist stance. He had studied in Vienna under the Catholic philosopher Brentano and Catholics interested in these matters began to prick up their ears. Around the beginning of World War I, numbers of his pupils having become Catholics, it was thought that he might too. But these hopes were dashed. He did not enter the Church and any movement in a realist direction went into reverse towards the end of his life. He had perhaps been an idealist all along.

The Founders
Martin Heidegger (1889–1976)

In spite of his rejection of the name "existentialist," Martin Heidegger was the founding father of existentialism. Drawing on the ideas of Kierkegaard, Nietzsche and Husserl, it was he who, in the 1920s and '30s welded it into a distinctly recognisable new philosophical theory.

A lapsed Catholic and ex-seminarian, Heidegger held chairs of philosophy first at Marburg (1923–29), then Freiburg (1929–45), being forced to retire in the latter year because of his connections with the Nazis. He believed, and publicly claimed, that from the time of Plato all philosophers had approached reality in the wrong way. Now, for the first time he was going to put philosophy on the right track. But, like other tenacious if misguided thinkers, he found his ambitions greater than his capacities. He was never able to finish his major work, *Sein und Zeit* (*Being and Time*, 1927), which was to establish his claims.

In Heidegger's existentialism the mind is not just dethroned, it is all but abolished. To use it for thinking in the normal way by distinguishing object from object (cat from mouse or mouse's tail from mouse's body) or objects outside us from objects in our minds (object from subject) is treated as a kind of sin. It is regarded as falsifying reality, which is envisaged as a kind of liquid continuum like treacle or soup.

To know reality or Being (reality in its most generalised form), there must be a total surrender of self to *experience*, a plunging of oneself into the treacle or soup (the self being part of the soup, though possibly the soup, or the experience of being in the soup, is just an extension of the self – which of these alternatives is not altogether clear). This self-surrender to *experience* is called *openness* or *openness to Being*.

What Heidegger seems in fact to be trying to do is re-establish contact with external reality – from which he has cut himself off through adopting the idealist starting point – but by-passing reflective thought. By a passive experiencing of *Being* or *openness to Being*, he seems to believe that not only will reality and the mind be brought into touch again, but reality will reveal itself to the philosopher in its true colours.

But what, it may be asked, is the use of this kind of knowledge, except perhaps to the individual who receives it, if the attempt to express it in intelligible statements or propositions radically falsifies it?

Needless to say, having in theory dethroned the mind, in practice Heidegger proceeds to use it in the normal way, employing abstractions and propositions like other men, in order to explain, via Husserl's phenomenological method, what kind of being he thinks man essentially is.

The answer seems to be a disembodied "stream of consciousness" in search of solidity but never finding it. Men and women are not beings with a substantial reality from conception onwards. They are non-beings who materialise in a void as the recipients of *experience*. Man's existence, as the famous existentialist axiom has it, precedes his essence. His accumulating *experiences* determine what he will one day be. But in fact existentialist man never has an essence, since what he essentially *is* only comes about at the moment of death when the accumulating units of experience can be added up – presumably by his friends after the funeral – and then he no longer in any sense *is*. When existentialists speak of man's *nothingness*, they do not mean his nothingness before God as Christians do; they mean it more or less literally. Although men are distinct from things, and can never be completely absorbed by them, without things to experience they would cease to be.

Given, then, that each of us lives inside the bubble of his personal life, there is no way of showing that, as descriptions of reality, one person's experiences are any better than anyone else's. That is why you can "do your thing" while I "do mine" without harm to oneself or society.[67]

However, there are certain fundamental experiences common to all men.

Heideggerian man finds himself *thrown into the world* without knowing

---

67. Even travel agents have been touched by existentialist notions and terminology. Instead of inviting us, as they formerly did, to visit Africa or have an African holiday, they now urge us to have "an African experience." This is because, in an existentialist world, you do not go to foreign countries or meet concrete people, animals and things, you undergo a stream of subjective impressions. In the early '90s, a pub overlooking the Thames carried a notice reading, not "Try our sandwiches," but "Try our sandwich experience." The big question was, did the experience involve a real sandwich?

who he is, why he is there, or where he has come from; actually, where he finds himself is not so much in the world as imprisoned in a subjective field of vision called his *horizon*.[68] His basic states are *care* (he is condemned to preoccupation with apparently pointless tasks), and *anxiety* (*angst* or *dread*). Like Kierkegaard, he constantly has to make decisions, but, while he is responsible for the remotest consequences of his smallest acts, every situation is different and there are no rules to guide him. So he moves through life, haunted by the flight of time, burdened by a sense of *guilt*, while trying to reach *self-understanding* through the experience of *his life situations*, and *to realise his possibilities*. Another condition of his existence *is projecting himself into the future*. Since his situation is always changing, this involves moving from *horizon* to *horizon*, altering his understanding of the meaning of existence as he does so, until he reaches death, the *final horizon*, and the last of his *possibilities*, which puts an end to him.

Existentialist literature is full of rather pretentious talk about death – as though it were a recent discovery. Existentialist man is not a little angry and sorry for himself that he cannot have unbelief, happiness and immortality all together. There are even Catholic theologians who now speak of death as though it were a gloomy indignity.

The words italicised in the above paragraph are known as *existentials*. The *existentials* are the supposedly most elemental human experiences. Together they define what a man is. They are the fundamental constituents of "being human," or of human nature, in so far as Heidegger would allow such a term. What he has actually done is metaphysicalise and universalise the feelings and outlook of an unhappy guilt-ridden atheist. It is therefore not surprising to find him concluding that life is *meaningless* and *absurd*.

The once fashionable word "happening" in connection with the theatre and arts expresses this viewpoint. A "happening" is an event or object deliberately intended to startle by its meaninglessness.

Another *existential* is the experience or state of *fallenness*, the existentialist equivalent of original sin. On finding himself thrown into the world, or in the state of "being there" (*Dasein*), he is continually in danger of falling into *inauthentic* living. Inauthentic living means submerging oneself in wordly things and preoccupations and adopting the standards and values of the crowd in order to avoid asking the really important questions in life; one

---

68. One would have thought most people's primal experience would be of "lying in the arms of their mother," not being "thrown into the world."

makes oneself part of the crowd (*Das Man*, the collective man, as Heidegger calls it). The chief characteristics of Das Man are idle or shallow talk and idle curiosity. Das Man is always looking for something new to occupy him so that he does not have to face his real situation. All this is the basis for a strong and not unjustified critique of modern Western societies and their overpowering preoccupation with technology and busyness.

However, underlying Das Man's inauthenticity or shallow preoccupation with externals, even if he is unaware of it, is a deep dread or anxiety (*angst*), and herein lies his path to salvation. *Angst*, when strong enough, can catapult a man into *authentic* living. *Authentic* living means facing the realities of our situation, our nothingness and the inevitability of death, and starting to ask the really important questions. What does it mean to exist as a man? What indeed *is* existence?

But Heidegger does not really answer these questions. All he tells us is that to live authentically, we must "think of Being." In turning away from things and opening ourselves to Being we shall find light and joy. In fact, in his later philosophy, under the influence of the German poet Rilke, Heidegger often seems to be promoting a kind of atheistic mysticism. Instead of thinking in the ordinary sense, the philosopher, through his passive *openness* to or contemplation of Being, seeks some kind of communion with it.[69]

This highly unsatisfactory conclusion no doubt explains why so many existentialists decided that, since life remained absurd whether you thought about Being or not, it was up to the individual to give life whatever "meaning" he or she liked.

Jean-Paul Sartre (1905–1980)

Sartre, a propagandist of the first order, is better known as a writer and playwright than as a philosopher, and it was chiefly through his novels and plays that existentialist ideas eventually reached the general public.

After starting life as a philosophy teacher, with a short spell in Berlin (1933–34), he had already written a novel, a volume of short stories, and two phenomenological studies by his mid-thirties. Then came World War II. He was called up in 1939, a year later taken prisoner, and, after yet

---

69. Perhaps we can see in Heidegger's identification of modern industrial society with inauthentic living and his rejection of Das Man in favour of the contemplation of Being, a relic of his time as a Jesuit novice. Being has become an atheistic substitute for God. It is the same with the turn from inauthentic to authentic living. St Ignatius' *Spiritual Exercises* had a similar purpose. Only the final goal is different.

another year, released. Returning to Paris, he joined the resistance, but at the same time was able to complete his major philosophical work *Being and Nothingness* (*L'être et le néant*, 1943).[70] He emerged from the war an active communist sympathiser, if not a party member, and remained a propagandist for left-wing causes to the end of his life, in spite of quarrels with Stalinists over Stalinism at different times. 20,000 people attended his funeral.

As a philosopher, Sartre's vision of things is basically the same as Heidegger's, but being a child of the French Revolution, he gives more of his attention to man's will and freedom than to his supposedly fundamental experiences.

For Sartre, the mere passive reception of experience is not enough to confer existence. A man only truly exists by continual acts of will.

The human will is pictured as a kind of eddy in the liquid continuum of reality. Man is the hole made by the whirlpool of his free will in the treacle or soup. If he stops exercising his will, the hole closes and his existence is swallowed by the treacle. Any restriction on his free will is therefore an attack on his existence. This is why the characters in Sartre's novels and plays, if not Sartre himself, find other people and objects "nauseating." The "other" can resist their wishes and thereby threaten their existence.

It is also one of the reasons why people now *become* persons instead of *being* persons. You become a person in so far as you are able to act consciously, make decisions, and realise your possibilities. If through sickness or poverty you are incapable of doing any of these things, you cease to be a person, which, though Sartre does not say so, means that in principle you can be dealt with accordingly. Abstruse philosophical notions have a surprising way of producing far-reaching public consequences.[71]

However, at this point in the unfolding of Sartre's existentialism there is a change of key from minor to major, or tragic to heroic. Taking over from Kierkegaard and Heidegger the distinction between authentic and inauthentic living, Sartre gave authentic living a different style and goal. The despairing Sartrian existentialist, instead of leaping into the arms of God like Kierkegaard, or losing himself in "thinking about Being" like Heidegger,

---

70. Contact between French intellectuals and their German counterparts serving in the German army during the occupation of Paris seems to have been, if not much advertised, an accepted part of the war time scene. (See obituary of Ernst Junger, *The Daily Telegraph*, London, 18th February 1998.)

71. Translated into Christian terms, this is sometimes seen as meaning that people are not Christians as a result of their baptism and beliefs. They are in a state of perpetually "becoming" without ever fully being Christians, and having to prove it to themselves and others by conspicuous good works.

commits himself to the service of man, after the example of the heroes in the novels of Albert Camus. In so doing, he *transcends himself* and *encounters the other*. He opens himself to, communicates or enters into a meaningful relationship with the other. He is conscious of a new sense of *responsibility*. He becomes "a man for others," putting himself at their disposal. In this way he breaks out of the lonely world of his personal experience.

In fact of course, if life is really a string of unintelligible happenings, there is no reason why one kind of commitment should be superior to another. Gardening, stamp collecting or overthrowing the state should all be equally authentic occupations. In practice, however, it was soon agreed, that the only cause worth committing oneself to was "transforming the world" in alliance with some party of the radical left. French existentialists now had a blueprint for *realising their possibilities* and *making their future*.

The history of human thought is full of strange alliances, but none has been so strange as this which, with Sartre and other politically left-wing existentialists like Merleau-Ponty as the marriage brokers, has brought perhaps the most individualistic philosophy ever invented (if we overlook Ayn Rand's Objectivism) into the service of political collectivism.

How did they come to this decision?

In the encyclical *Humani Generis* (1950), Pius XII explains it as follows. "They (the existentialists) attribute to our appetitive nature a kind of intuitive faculty, so that a man who cannot make up his mind what is the true answer to some intellectual problem need only have recourse to his will; the will (without reference to the mind) makes a free choice between two intellectual alternatives. A strange confusion," the Pope continues, "between thought and volition."[72]

Meanwhile, those who live in an "inauthentic" way, the collective Das Man, receive an even more severe drubbing from Sartre than they do from Heidegger. They are like the reprobate in Calvinism destined for damnation, or the bourgeois in Marxism, only fit for the firing squad. However, as death wipes out "authentic" and "inauthentic" alike, Das Man, in drifting through life, as he is supposed to do, without committing himself to anything in particular (except, possibly, supporting his family, bringing up his children in the love and service of God and quietly fulfilling the duties of his state) has perhaps chosen the wiser course.

But how were the newly committed faithful to be prevented from relapsing into the nihilism towards which any form of atheist existentialism

72. *Humani Generis*, 33.

necessarily points people?

The situation was saved by the philosopher Ernst Bloch who, while fishing in the contents of consciousness, had discovered the phenomenon of human hope. Clearly this was a constituent of human existence as fundamental as anxiety or guilt, and from it he constructed his philosophy of hope, later given a Christian turn by the German Lutheran theologian Jürgen Moltmann. But Bloch's existentialist hope is not Christian hope – trust in God's providence and his promises of eternal happiness. It is hope in man. It represents frightened existentialist man whistling in the dark when he fears that the forces he now possesses are going to be too much for him to control, and he will blow up the world before he can build the only paradise there is going to be.

Throughout the 1960s and '70s, the two existentialisms I have been describing, nihilistic and social-activist, ran side by side. But in the end the nihilistic message won most supporters. If people wanted to be social activists, they looked to Marx or Marcuse. Existentialism thereby became the door through which large numbers of Westerners entered what is now called "the post-modern age"; in other words, ceased pinning their hopes on perpetual progress and adopted "doing their own thing" as their philosophy of life.[73]

Weighing the results

Although its two most powerful exponents were atheists, existentialism does not, of course, have to be atheistic. Kierkegaard, its progenitor, as we have seen, was a Christian, so is the French Protestant philosopher Paul Ricoeur; and the German philosopher Karl Jaspers (1883–1969) initiated an influential school of theistic existentialism.[74]

The appeal of existentialism for Christians lay, in the first place, in its

---

73. That the notion of "doing your own thing" triumphed over that of "being a man for others" is surely demonstrated by the speed with which marriage and family life began to break down just when the existentialist downpour was at its heaviest. In an age when "commitment" or "being committed" has never been so much talked about, fewer and fewer people want to commit themselves permanently to anything.

74. Christian existentialism: defined by Anglican Canon David Edwards of Westminster as "a style of theology inspired by Søren Kierkegaard, which tests every doctrine by its derivation from human experience and by its power to illuminate human existence. It rejects metaphysical speculation about eternal essences even when this is hallowed by dogma, and it attempts to demythologise the Bible" (*Fontana Dictionary of Modern Thought*, 1981). Demythologizing the Bible, however, while characteristic of Bultmann's existentialism, is not necessary to Christian existentialism as such. Kierkegaard would hardly have tolerated it.

teaching about authentic and inauthentic living; about the importance of not just drifting through life, and of putting oneself at the service or *disposal* of others. If it could be shown philosophically that a man only concerned with his private interests, or a man who buries himself in distractions or business in order to avoid having to ask questions about the real meaning of life, was only half a man – that to be fully a man one has at some point to make some decisive choices, get outside oneself, be a *man for others*, and more important still, like Kierkegaard, seek an *encounter* with something outside and above this world – then the Christian view of man was well on the road to being proved right philosophically. In these respects existentialism can be seen as a philosophy of spiritual conversion. However, separating the benign from the toxic elements has proved more difficult than expected.

Its chief defect as a philosophy, I believe, is the ambiguity surrounding its use of the word "experience."

The majority of people when they talk about "experience" mean something that has happened to them or something they have lived through, in other words their contact with something going on *outside* them (objective experience). When they want to refer to what goes on *inside* them, they mainly talk about having a "feeling" or "impression" (subjective experience). Because existentialism uses the same word for contact with objective realities and subjective feelings, feelings are raised to the same level and given the same value as real knowledge. Granted that all forms of modern idealism have had difficulty in drawing the line between waking and dreaming or seeing and imagining, it could hardly have been otherwise.

Its second major defect, I suggest, lies in the way it pits "experience" against reflective thought, as though they were rival ways of knowing, with experience as the superior contestant – rather than seeing them as complementary stages of the same process. In existentialism, this already long-established anti-intellectual current reaches its apogee.[75]

Experience, however, whether external or internal, is only the starting point of knowledge. It is true that knowledge received at second hand often needs to be complemented by experience. Practice deepens our understanding of theory. But experience *by itself* tells us very little, apart

---

75. The summer issue of *Communio* for 1996 was largely devoted to "Christian experience" and the problems surrounding the notion. "The complexity attendant upon a careful definition of the two concepts – experience and theology – increases prodigiously whenever we try to make a single coherent statement about both," admitted the author of the opening article.

from the fact of its being pleasant or unpleasant. Many people have the same experiences over and over again, and, because they do not reflect on them, repeatedly make the same mistakes. To acquire knowledge, seeing, touching, hearing, smelling, tasting are not enough. We must think about what we have seen and touched. Thinking, however, necessarily presupposes at least a modicum of abstract ideas and propositions.

To illustrate the point, let us take the example of a man from a remote part of the world who has never come across electricity before. In his bedroom he sees a loose electric wire. On touching it he receives a shock and is convinced that he has been bitten by some kind of snake, until the owner of the house explains to him what electricity is. We should not think much of his intelligence if he replied: "I refuse to believe it. Your abstract knowledge does not correspond with my experience."

As we all know, the way things are does not always correspond with the way they appear or how we experience them. The old lady on the airplane who gives the nice young man in the next seat some of her money to invest has "experienced" his charm. But some reflective thought involving abstractions and propositions, like "he could be a crook," would have been more useful. If we stayed permanently at the level of experience, we should still be believing that the sun goes round the earth.

I say all this because persuading the faithful that personal experience is a superior form of knowledge to the teaching of the Church and should be the ultimate authority in determining what is to be believed or done has been modernism's most effective weapon in its war against the Church's magisterium.

To show how it is used, let us take another example. Jim and Jane get married. The Church, following divine revelation, tells them they are now one flesh till "death do them part," and so they feel it to be for a time. But then things go wrong and their experience sends a different message. They now feel like two separate warring pieces of flesh, so they listen to Fr X who tells them that, because of this, they are no longer married. Having absorbed the idea that truth must always conform to personal "experience," they are soon concluding that because the "experience" of receiving holy communion resembles the experience of eating and drinking bread and wine, then that is what they are in fact consuming. This would explain why repeated polls show that in countries like the United States, something like 75 percent of Catholics no longer believe in the Real Presence.

The same approach applied to religious teaching in schools has had similar results. Since the late 1960s the majority of young Western

Catholics have lapsed once they leave school, if not sooner, largely because, instead of being given Catholic doctrine, they have been taught (if it can be called teaching) to analyse their feelings about or reactions to God, their parents, the "experience of being a Catholic," or life in general. Their teachers are often happy with this method since, having lost the faith themselves, they are naturally reluctant to teach as true what they no longer believe to be so.

In reality, very few of the things God has revealed are directly accessible to experience. If they were, it would hardly have been necessary to reveal them.[76] The same is true of many scientific propositions; they are likewise inaccessible to direct experience. Indeed they frequently appear to flout it.

What modernists are in fact doing, when they pit experience against doctrine, is exploiting the fact that experiential knowledge is always more vivid than theoretical knowledge or knowledge at second hand, and because more "vivid" is felt to be more "real" or "true." Seeing someone crushed to death by a lorry immediately in front of us makes far more of an impression than the deaths of hundreds killed in an earthquake 2000 miles away. It takes a mental effort to make ourselves appreciate that each of those far-off deaths is of equal importance. Raw experience says the opposite; the death I have just witnessed matters more. It is the difference between what Newman in *The Grammar of Assent* calls notional and real assent. What we have never experienced can seem unreal, even though we know it is true or has happened.[77]

This largely psychological problem does of course mean that, for pastoral purposes, it is important that the "experience" of Christian parish and family life should not be a counter-witness to the supernatural truths

---

76. This is the meaning of Tertullian's *Credo quia absurdum* ("I believe just because it is absurd"). Not "absurd" in the modern sense; but not directly accessible to reason or the senses.

77. This is why, for Christians, meditation is so important. We need to bring the truths revealed by God down from the notional to the real level, whether it is a question of supernatural mysteries beyond the reach of imagination or the contents of the Gospels, which we can imagine. This, Newman maintains, is always more effectively achieved, at least in the case of preaching, when the faith is presented in concrete imagery rather than abstract terminology. What is given to the mind in abstract terms, tends to remain "notional." Concrete imagery makes the truths of the faith real in a way that has an impact on personal living. This is probably true in general. The only thing the great cardinal seems to have forgotten is the number of people swept off their feet by abstractions like liberty, equality and fraternity.

those institutions embody and should teach. To this extent, the way people "experience things" does matter. Grace can and does triumph over the most adverse circumstances. But parish and family life should not be an obstacle to ease of belief. They should not provide genuinely disagreeable experiences.

However, if we want to measure the true value of "experience" as a source of religious knowledge, we need only look at the non-Christian religions past and present. With the exception of Judaism and Islam and some later cults, which are based on real or supposed revelations, all have, or have had, their origins solely in what must have been "experiences" of some kind. Why then have they differed so widely?

Existentialism also seems to be responsible for the now widespread use of the term "faith experience" among Catholics.

This can have a variety of meanings. It may mean the speaker thinks that faith is something which hits you over the head like a blow from a sledge hammer without any way of accounting for it. One minute you don't believe, the next you do, and that's all there is to it. Or it may refer to the speaker's own experiences in prayer. On the other hand, it may describe what he thinks happened on the first Easter Sunday: when the disciples saw Our Lord, they were having "faith experiences." If they had not already believed He was still alive, they would not have seen him.

During the synod of bishops in Rome on catechetics in 1977, it was seriously suggested that the faithful should somehow be polled and their personal spiritual experiences collected to form the basis for a special "catechism of experience." There would then have been two competing catechisms, one based on experience, one based on doctrine. The demand did not make the running, and the Church eventually dealt with the question more than a decade later by including numerous quotations from the writings of the saints, mystics and other holy people in the *Catechism of the Catholic Church*.

The writings of the saints are of course a source of genuine religious knowledge. They provide most of the material for what is called mystical theology. But though their writings may deepen our understanding of what God has revealed, they never contradict it.

To sum up, existentialism is in fact far from being the philosophy of concrete existence or reality it claims to be. The *philosophia perennis* and St Thomas have a much better title to that honour since they tell us how things exist in themselves. Existentialism only tells us how they appear to exist or what we feel about them, or, in the case of our minds, wills and emotions, not what they objectively are, but how we experience their operations. The right and proper name for existentialism would have been "experientialism."[78]

---

78. The problems surrounding this subject also result from regarding *abstract* and *concrete* as belonging to separate realms. But if the abstract did not inform the concrete, the concrete would be a shapeless mass of sub-atomic next-to-nothingness.

Chapter Ten

PERSONALISM: BUBER, MARCEL, SCHELER

As a recognisable philosophical current, "personalism" dates from the early 20th century and was, like Bergson's "creative evolution," part of the general reaction against the crude materialism of much mid- to late 19th century philosophy – the kind that Belloc aptly called philosophy's "vulgar dwarf" who throughout history has repeatedly kept forcing his way into philosophical high society only to be as repeatedly pushed out. The result of the reaction was a growing number of "philosophies of the spirit" of which personalism has been the most enduring. People do not have to be certain about God's existence in order to discern that there is more to us than flesh, blood, bones, and a nervous system.[79]

In this chapter I will look at the personalism of Martin Buber, Gabriel Marcel and Max Scheler, leaving to the next chapter the personalism of Jacques Maritain and Emmanuel Mounier.

The personalism of Buber, Marcel and Scheler, which we could call "spiritual personalism," has its roots in Kierkegaard. Like existentialism, of which it is a near relation, it tries to establish the kind of beings we are by analysing our spiritual states and emotions. However there is a significant difference. The leading personalists, unlike the leading existentialists, have all been theists or Christians. Roughly one could say that where the heterodox reformers favoured existentialism, the orthodox inclined to personalism.

The personalism of Maritain and Mounier is of a different brand. I earlier called it "socio-political personalism."

Martin Buber (1878–1965)

If one were asked to decide which two words did most to influence or even change religious discourse in the second half of the 20th century, it would be difficult, I think, not to choose "dialogue" and "community."

---

79. The concept of "person" came from Christian Trinitarian theology of the 4th century. Before that it barely existed in ancient philosophy. The first thinker to use the term "personalism" (around 1903) seems to have been Charles Renouvier, a pupil of Auguste Comte turned ethical theist.

Before the 1950s "dialogue" and "community" were words with relatively limited and humdrum meanings. Then suddenly one not only heard them used much more frequently and in a wider variety of contexts, but they appeared to have become invested with an almost mystical significance, as though referring to realities of a metaphysical or supernatural kind. Indeed, one began to meet Christians who left one with the impression that, for them, the whole content of their faith could be summed up in these two words – a state of affairs, I think you will agree, which still persists.

That is why I am going to look at the ideas of the man largely responsible for this change in a bit more detail than I have done in the case of other thinkers. My hope is that by the end of the journey you will understand more clearly in what sense the Catholic Church has given its assent to the meanings attached to these two words and in what respects it holds back from them. It will also, I think, throw more than a little light for you on why the liturgy of the mass is now so often understood and practiced in the way it is.

Born in Vienna of Jewish parents, and educated there and in Berlin, Martin Buber taught history and the philosophy of religion at the university of Frankfurt from 1922–33. Then in 1936 he fled to Palestine where he became professor of social history at the Hebrew university in Jerusalem until 1951. In the post-war period he worked to bring about better relations between Jews and Arabs and Jews and Germans. Indeed, in every respect, he seems to have been a man not only of high intelligence but also of outstanding nobility of character.

However, rather than being a philosopher in the strict sense (someone who grapples with technical philosophical questions), he is better thought of as a sage preaching a spiritual "way" based on a mystical theistic humanitarianism, strongly influenced by Judaism and Christianity, which he called "the life of dialogue."

His family being typical members of what is called "the Jewish Enlightenment," his intellectual formation was at first like that of other young men of his kind and generation; well-mannered atheism or agnosticism with a thorough-going rationalism as its guiding principle. In spite of this, in early manhood he took a different course.

Three things helped to change his mental outlook: hasidism, oriental and Christian mysticism, and the writings of Kierkegaard which he came across in that order, although on a more superficial level he remained a typical European intellectual, mentally sophisticated and interested in everything going on in the worlds of science and thought.

Hasidism, a revivalist movement which swept through European Jewry in the 18th and 19th centuries, had the most lasting effect. Its followers, the hasidim, emphasised love, joy, religious fervour and delight in God's creation in contrast to the strict observance of the Law insisted on by orthodox rabbis. At their religious services they danced with the Torah and prayed with wild gestures.

Buber first came across hasidism when, as a boy, his father took him to visit an hasidic community near his grandfather's house in Galicia (southern Poland). There, for the first time, he saw or thought he saw what he was never to forget – a genuine "community." This vision of the "community" as something living and breathing in contrast to the seemingly lifeless artificiality of normal social forms, was to become the lodestar of all his future thinking.

The effect of the experience was not instantaneous. But in 1904, when he was 26, he underwent something like a conversion if not to hasidism as its followers understood it, at least to certain of their ideas, many of which had been taken from that centuries-old mystical under-current in medieval Jewish thought, the Kabbalah, which in its turn had been strongly influenced by 2nd and 3rd century gnosticism.

These semi-gnostic ideas had to do with helping to release the divine sparks of God's exiled *shekinah* or goodness and glory, which supposedly became separated from his *en-sof*, or transcendent essence, and imprisoned in creation during the process of its making. Each spark was held to be surrounded by a hard shell of darkness (*quelipot*), which, though a kind of evil, was not regarded as an active or personal force but represented whatever is not fully under God's dominion or can be considered resistant to his will. The reunion of these divine sparks with God himself, and the restoration of the original harmony which existed before creation took place brings about the redemption of the world. In so far as the divine sparks are present in man, each of us can help to release them by perfecting his or her own life and helping others to perfect theirs.

So much for hasidism.

The study of oriental and Christian mysticism also helped to wean Buber from the rationalism and unbelief of his upbringing. But by about 1920 these influences had begun to decline. The mystic's search for personal union with God, he decided, was too self-centred and withdrew men too much from daily life.

Then towards the end of World War I, he came across Kierkegaard. The discovery helped him to fuse his ideas into the system or teaching which was to make him famous. Although he later adapted and added to that teaching, he never changed its fundamentals. It first saw daylight in his book *I and Thou* (1922).

This little volume of 120 short pages has had as great an impact on Western thinking as all Kierkegaard's books together. In form and style, it resembles a collection of sayings by a Chinese or Indian wise man (the *Tao* of Lao-tzu for instance) rather than a work of philosophy. The language is semi-poetic, thoughts are expressed in short loosely-connected paragraphs or aphorisms, and from time to time conversations take place between unknown speakers. As for the message, even if at first reading it seems a bit enigmatic, it is relatively simple, revolving round a few recurring themes which we can now look at with, I hope, a better chance of understanding how he arrived at them.

The Life of Dialogue

In Buber's "life of dialogue," the supreme reality is the human person in relation with other beings. We are always in a state of relationship to someone or something other than ourselves and cannot exist except in such a state. Relationships rather than individuals could be called the stuff of reality. However they are subject to important qualitative differences.

All relationships, whether between men and God, men and men, or men and animals, plants and inanimate things, are of one of two kinds: either I–Thou relationships, or I–It relationships. A *Thou* is a person; an *It* is a thing.

I–It relationships are those in which we look at or treat other beings as in some sense things, whether they are things or not, and it is assumed that this necessarily happens whenever we look at or think about them objectively or with any kind of detachment. In doing so, it is asserted, we are turning them into objects for use. Buber characterises more or less all I–It relationships as selfish. Detached observation and objective thought therefore involve from the outset something which appears to be at best regrettable, at worst to be deplored. Objective thought about God is especially regrettable because "it turns God into an object" – an objection which hardly seems reasonable seeing that we cannot think about anything without at least making it an object of thought.

In I–Thou relationships, on the other hand, we meet the Other not as a thing but as a person. Instead of trying to understand the other objectively and reach factual conclusions about him, her or it, the I makes itself "present" to the Thou or Other. This means more than being physically present. It means more than trying to give the Thou one's full attention without prejudices or preconceptions. It involves a kind of spiritual intercommunion not unlike that described by poets and nature mystics, when they feel momentarily united to whatever they are contemplating as if it had suddenly become part of themselves. However for Buber this kind of interpersonal communion ought to be the norm, achieved by a conscious mental act. By contrast, I–It thinking places the other in a kind of outer darkness resembling the *quelipot* of *hasidism*, which is the very opposite of "being present."

I–Thou and I–It relationships are also seen as constituting two different spiritual worlds or fields of reality, in one of which we are always immersed. Not a minute of our lives falls outside one or the other. For the ordinary purposes of life, it is true, I–It thinking and I–It relationships are unavoidable, even necessary, but only I–Thou relationships are fully real. They bring into existence the world of "spirit," spirit being what has most reality. The more, therefore, that men can generate I–Thou relationships, the more the element of "spirit" or reality grows. I–It relationships, on the other hand, take place in a quasi-unreal world inimical to spirit, and the more they prevail the more spirit and reality are diminished.[80]

However I-Thou relationships are not just a matter of interpersonal communion. After making themselves present to each other, the I and Thou enter into "dialogue." In dialogue, each party affirms the other's "truth" or right to be the way he or she is, while presenting himself or herself without pretences or concealment. To try to influence the other, or change his or her point of view would turn the I–Thou relationship into an I–It relationship.[81]

Situations and events should be approached in a similar way. We must see each situation and event as something unique and let its uniqueness tell us how to deal with it. Trying to apply ready-made rules will prevent us from seeing it as it is.

All I have said so far had to do with relations between individuals. But we are members of society as well and most group relationships are of an I–It quality. Nevertheless, by fostering a spirit of dialogue, the spiritless conglomerations of individuals that most modern societies are can be turned

---

80. By "spirit" Buber seems to mean something resembling what Christians mean by "grace" and "charity."

81. That the liturgical bulletin of the archdiocese of Paris should be called *Présence et dialogue* is a good indication of the extent of Buber's influence.

into living communities.

Since communities are the place where men are most completely themselves and reality is most fully achieved, building communities of I–Thou related persons is the real object of Buber's "way." If the members are of one mind as well as one in heart, that is good but not, it seems, essential.

In so far as communities are of one mind, the pattern for their relationships with groups thinking differently should be that of I–Thou relationships between individuals: mutual forbearance and the affirmation of each other's right to be the way they are.

Finally, at the highest level, Buber's teaching envisages a world network of I–Thou related communities, and this is what "the life of dialogue" summons its followers to promote. "The solidarity of all separate groups in the flaming battle for the becoming of one humanity is, in the present hour, the highest duty of each."[82]

As you will have seen, all this amounts to much more than a philosophy of world-wide social harmony. One could call it hasidism stripped of its overtly gnostic elements, but retaining its central gnostic idea – that of redeeming creation by releasing the exiled sparks of goodness in men and the world from the evil or darkness those sparks are embedded in. But evil for Buber was no more a personal or positive force than it had been for the hasidists. He appears to identify it with our elemental instincts and passions in their untamed state. These, along with all life's forces, good and "evil," will, through "the way of dialogue" and community building, one day be drawn into harmony with each other and the supreme Thou, thus bringing about the redemption of the entire universe.

Buber also seems to have believed that God had to create the universe in order to have a Thou for his I to enter into dialogue with.

Such then is Buber's spiritual way or "life of dialogue." I will consider its pros and cons as far as the Catholic Church is concerned after looking more briefly at the personalism of Gabriel Marcel.

Gabriel Marcel (1889–1973)

Gabriel Marcel was even less typically a philosopher of the 19th and 20th century type than Buber.

---

82. Speech, 27th Sept. 1953, after receiving the peace prize of the German book trade. Seeing what his people had just gone through, Buber's viewpoint is understandable. But for Christians, humanity does not have to become one. In Adam, it already is one. The battle, flaming or otherwise, is about how much it sides with good or evil.

The child of an agnostic father and a Protestant mother, for whom religion was largely a matter of ethical behaviour, he left the Sorbonne without completing his doctorate and thenceforward made his way as a critic, editor and essayist. He also wrote plays and music, using his plays as vehicles for his philosophical ideas, but without achieving box-office successes like Sartre. Philosophically, he started like so many other young men of the time as an idealist, but was converted to an "existentialist" approach by his experiences as a Red Cross worker in World War I. This meant rejecting systematic philosophy. A philosopher, he came to believe, must participate in ordinary life, rather than observing it with detachment from a university chair, if he is to have anything useful to say philosophically.

Increasingly interested in "the religious dimension of experience," in 1929 he became a Catholic, and by the 1940s was an influential figure in Catholic intellectual circles in Paris. His rejection of the pessimistic existentialism of Sartre and Camus, and adherence to Kierkegaard and Buber, marks his passage from existentialism to personalism. Although his method and many of his ideas closely resemble Buber's, he always insisted that he had arrived at them independently. His conclusions are also more modest, less wide-ranging. He had no ambitious panaceas for world harmony like Buber.[83]

Two ideas in particular show the drift of his thought. He draws a distinction first between *problems* and *mysteries*, and secondly between *having* and *being*.

"Problems" are matters we approach from outside and solve by intelligence. "Mysteries" are things we experience – like love, freedom, friendship, evil, existence itself – which you have to be involved in to understand. Thinking about them has its value, but a purely objective approach and clear-cut answers are impossible. In mysteries, subject and object are so intertwined that they cannot be separated.

The distinction between "having" and "being," specifically mentioned in *Gaudium et Spes*, emphasises the simple truth that the kind of people we are is more important than the things we possess. *Having* (it is claimed)

---

83. There is no reason to doubt Marcel's having reached his conclusions independently. The resemblances simply show that the thinking of men subject to the same influences and preoccupied with the same questions is likely to converge. Uncharacteristically for a French intellectual of his stamp, on the other hand, in the 1930s he became involved with the moral re-armament movement, an attachment which seems to have survived World War II. In 1958 he edited a volume of "testimonies" in support of the movement, called *Fresh Hope for the World*.

establishes an egocentric relationship with people and things; it gives us power over objects, whether they are possessions or ideas. We cannot escape from having; but *being* (i.e. the kind of person we are) is more important since it transforms our relationships. When people value being more than having, the dichotomy between the self and its opposite or object melts into mutual interchange or interpersonal communion.

Other simple truths prominent in Marcel's philosophy could be summarised as follows:

People are more important than anything else; each is unique and precious. We should never allow their professional function − as garage mechanics, bankers, opera singers, waiters or waitresses − to dull our awareness that they are first and foremost human beings. They should always be treated as persons, not things. On the other hand, in spite of our uniqueness, we are social beings. But society should be more than an agglomeration of individuals.

Like other thinkers influenced by modern subjectivism, Marcel tends to see man as starting as a prisoner inside himself, though a prisoner of his selfishness rather than his thoughts. The way of escape is being involved with others. This is part of the essence of being human. If a man is faithful to the true dynamism of his being, it will carry him outside himself to "the other," beyond the other into the community, and through the community to the discovery of God. He summarised this progression in the formula: "person − *engagement* (commitment) − community − reality." Community appears as the highest reality. Self-centredness is the supreme sin because it inhibits the birth of genuine community where alone men become fully men and reality fully exists. He called this teaching a "metaphysics of hope." The metaphysics of hope was his answer to the existentialism of absurdity and despair.

Pros and Cons

The attractions of Buber's and Marcel's personalism are undeniable, and their appeal to the reform-minded is easy to understand. Modern man may be uncertain whether he has a soul; he may even hotly deny he has one. However he is unlikely to deny he is a "person" (meaning by that, something more than an animal, machine or thing), and should be treated accordingly. But an analysis of the notion of personhood leads ineluctably to admitting the existence of a non-material, non-biological component. The argument for the existence of the soul is already half won.

Emphasising our "personhood" would also, it was thought, help remove misunderstanding about the Church's teaching on the body-soul relationship, mentioned earlier (see note 51, p.73). For the Church, the body is a constituent part of the human being or person (in contrast to the angelic person). Although the soul is the more important part, since the way the soul acts decides where soul and body together will end up, nevertheless a soul without a body (for example, a soul in heaven before the general resurrection) is an incomplete human being. Surprisingly, many Catholics do not seem to have appreciated this particular feature of their faith to the extent one would have expected. Indeed, not a few appear to have thought that it would be nicer to be forever in heaven without one's body, thereby giving atheist humanism yet another weapon to clout the Church over the head with. The Church, it could say, and did say, was anti-body, and so anti-human. It was to correct this misapprehension that the idea of speaking about the salvation of "the whole man" rather than the salvation of "souls" came into fashion, although "saving your soul" is a biblical expression.[84]

The insistence on the human person as this world's highest good ("man," the Second Vatican Council would say, "is the only creature in the universe God has willed for its own sake") had other advantages. It was an approach intelligible to rulers and employers no longer moved by the fear of God or a hereafter, and suitable for combating the dehumanising factors of contemporary life: the primacy of economics and production over religion, morality, culture and the good of families; an exclusively technological, bureaucratic or business outlook; the 20th century's slave camps and torture chambers.

The attractions of "dialogue" as a method of spreading the faith have already been noticed. The explosive state of the world commended it as now the safest and seemingly most Christian way of resolving social and international conflicts.

Finally, the communitarian aspects of personalism appeared to provide the principles for a Christian "third way" between the extremes of Marxist

---

84. Mt 16:26; Jas 1:21; and 1 Pt 1:9. St Athanasius speaks of "the salvation of the whole man" in his letter to Epictetus of Corinth. However the hullabaloo modernism makes about "the whole man," as we already know, has a different motivation. See *Turmoil and Truth*, Ch. 14, footnote 8. Since it makes no distinction between matter and spirit and sees the eternal salvation of the "whole man" as more or less a certainty, it necessarily follows that improving earthly living conditions ("salvation of the body") is the only thing that really matters.

collectivism and liberal individualism.

These were the main "pros" of personalism.

At the head of the list of "cons" we must put the misunderstandings to which Buber's distinction between I–Thou and I–It relationships are subject. It is true that we often do make use of each other, or sometimes unconsciously treat others as though they were things. In this sense I–It relationships are unquestionably bad. But it is also quite possible to think objectively about other people, their virtues, faults, qualities or even peculiarities, without in the least regarding them as things, still less as things to be made use of. Close personal and emotional involvement between people, on the other hand, can include serious wrong-doing or blind them to things about each other which it might be better for one or other of them to know. What couple having an illicit love affair would not insist that their relationship was of the spirit-generating I–Thou variety?

This identification of interpersonal involvement with moral righteousness, and of objectivity with sin (or at least to some degree), seems to have been at least partly responsible for that notable decline in common sense about human nature and human relationships characteristic of so many of today's caring compassionate Christians, the like of whom have not, I think, been seen since Rousseau's men and women of feeling flooded over Europe in the late 18th century, baring their souls and sensibilities to the public gaze.

The notion of "dialogue" is also open to misunderstanding. Buber's notion is not identical with the Church's. For the Church, dialogue or talking things over in an atmosphere of charity and good will, is an apostolic method. The primary purpose is to reach agreement about an objective truth. For Buber its main purpose was to promote mutual respect followed by enhanced fellow-feeling, or the universal tolerance of all views not physically or in some other immediately observable way damaging to man. As such, it can, for Christians, provide an excuse for avoiding difficult topics and relegating unpopular truths to the realms of the irrelevant or undiscoverable.

Thirdly, we meet again the idea that people are not fully human to start with, but become so, this time through having a Thou to enter into relationship with. Thus while theoretically the human person is the focus of attention in Buber's philsophy, in practice relationships between people seem more important. Robinson Crusoe on his island was barely human until Man Friday turned up, and when he did, the really precious thing was the encounter itself, they themselves being significant only as the poles between which it took place and that made it possible. Encounters and relationships are treated as goods and ends in themselves and given the kind of substantiality usually associated with concrete things.[85]

This objection applies even more at the community level. Since the community is a network of personal relationships, generating "spirit" on a greater scale, the community, or "building community," is seen as having a quasi-sacramental sanctifying power, and easily becomes an object of worship. In the community the troubled are reconciled with themselves and psychologically tranquilised, while the divided learn to live together, forgetting their disagreements. Only when taking part in community activities is a person fully a person. What the community believes easily becomes a secondary consideration.[86]

In fact, as we all know, there are relationships and encounters in life which should be avoided and communities from which one ought to separate oneself (like Abraham from Ur, Lot from Sodom, Elijah from the priests of Baal, and 20th century Christians from certain political parties). In loving others, that is willing and working for their good, we often have to say "no" to them; to be shut not open, at least to some of their wishes and desires. And while it is true that we are always in relationship with the Supreme Thou, without whose presence we could not exist, God is an I who needs no Thou in order to be; and however delightful and necessary human companionship is, it is not the source of our being, and occasionally has to be dispensed with. We sometimes need to be less with others in order to be more ourselves, ourselves as God wants us to be. We should also perhaps add that the selfish are just as much human beings as the unselfish. They are then *damaged* human beings, not *semi*-human beings.

As a spiritual way or religion in its own right, Buber's personalism, if its limitations are not clearly recognised, can become a rival to Christ's way. Christians who adopt its terminology and ideas are easily led into adopting it in its totality. One does not need special powers of penetration to see that many Catholics today are far more interested in preaching Buber's doctrine of world redemption through dialogue, community building and

---

85. The *philosophia perennis* is often accused of "reifying" concepts, that is treating abstractions as though they were things, but there seems to be no philosophy that does not do it to some degree.

86. To detail the effects of all this on Western Catholic liturgical practice since the early 1970s would be superfluous. In only too many parishes, generating a feeling of community has supplanted the worship of God. The worship of God is being made to serve a purely pastoral purpose.

promoting social harmony, than in redemption and salvation in Jesus Christ. Buber had the noblest intentions, and social harmony is a great natural good, but it is not the same as redemption and salvation in Jesus Christ, and when advanced as a substitute for the Gospel amounts to something like a betrayal of it.

Marcel's personalism, more modest in its aims, is nowhere in direct conflict with Catholic belief. Its chief weaknesses are its anti-intellectualism, the weight given to personal involvement as a factor in arriving at truth, and its failure to provide a logical way of moving from the particular to the general. How can we make any true statements about mankind as a whole, if we are restricted to the level of personal experiences and life situations?

Max Scheler

None of the major conciliar reformers seems to have had any special interest in Scheler. But his personalism was an important influence on Pope John Paul II, and if only for that reason needs to have something said about it. John Paul II's personalism incorporated elements from all the major personalists: Buber, Scheler, Marcel and Emmanuel Mounier. But only Scheler was the subject of one of his two doctoral dissertations.

Son of a downtrodden Lutheran estate agent with an intellectually ambitious wife, Max Scheler (1874–1928) twice entered and twice left the Catholic Church.

His first seemingly superficial conversion at the age of 14 did not last long. There followed a morally chaotic period as a student and young university teacher which led to his losing his post at Munich and forfeiting the possibility of a professorship anywhere in the Kaiser's Germany. In abilities, character, and lifestyle he was more like a gifted novelist or café intellectual than an academic. But perhaps just because of this he was an exceptionally successful and captivating teacher.

Moving to Göttingen to be near Husserl, his unofficial lectures, applying Husserl's phenomenological method to the analysis of feelings like love, hate, shame and resentment, were soon attracting more listeners than his master. By making Husserl's phenomenology more intelligible and attractive, Scheler helped to put phenomenology on the map.

In 1912 he married a Catholic and three years later underwent a second more serious conversion. (There had already been, from the Church's point of view, an irregular first marriage followed by divorce.) Under Scheler's influence, several members of Husserl's circle, Jewish, Gentile and unbelieving, became Catholics too. They included Edith Stein, who later, as Sister Teresa Benedicta of the Cross, became a Carmelite nun, died in Auschwitz, and was canonised in 1998.

During World War I, he lectured widely in Germany and abroad on behalf of the Central Powers. Defeat, however, worked unexpectedly to his advantage. The Weimar Republic, of which he theoretically disapproved, was indifferent to moral delinquency in its university professors and in 1919 he received a professorship at the newly founded university of Cologne. Shortly thereafter he divorced his second wife and married a third time, leaving the Church again, this time for good. He died in 1928, just after taking up a new professorship at Freiburg.

In Scheler's personalism (at any rate during his second Catholic period) man is first of all a person because he is capable of seeking and responding to God (he has a "permanent possibility of responding to religious experience"), and knows himself as a being answerable for his acts – he knows himself as a responsible adult "subject," not an object. It is by reflecting on his acts that he can best discover the kind of person he is, distinguishing between those which he does in common with animals and those which are peculiar to him.

Personhood is therefore something that grows and shrinks. It increases the closer one draws to God and the more responsibly one acts, diminishing in so far as one goes into reverse. In other words, one can be a human being without being fully a person. For Christians, fullness of personhood would be sanctity.

Man is also a being who responds to "values." This is the most distinctive feature of Scheler's personalism. The capacity to recognise and respond to an ascending scale of "values," and their opposites or "disvalues," is the second thing that sets man above all the other beings we directly know. He can see things and actions as pleasant or unpleasant, useful or useless, noble or common, beautiful or ugly, holy or unholy (religious values). In addition there are moral values (and disvalues), determining the goodness or badness of human acts. Moral values can co-exist with any of the other five categories. They span and connect them like the arches of a bridge.

The philosophy of values is known as *axiology*. Modern value philosophy is responsible for our now talking about religious, Gospel, family or political "values" rather than goods, truths, principles or teachings. Many consider this a dangerous concession to subjectivism, since, owing to Hume (as we have seen), only too many modern philosophers regard judgements of value as mere matters of taste and opinion. Things are good or true, depending on the *value* men attach to them.[87]

However, on this point Scheler was in disagreement with the mainstream of German idealism. He regarded "values" as existing independently of our minds (even if, in the way he writes about them, they sometimes seem to float about in a void like Platonic ideas, having only a passing relationship to particular things).

How do we apprehend or recognise values, particularly moral values? Here, although still writing as a Catholic, he began to part company with the Church. For the Church, judgements of right and wrong are acts of reason. Scheler, on the other hand, believed they are given through feeling and the experience of acting in "our lived situation." Once again we find feeling and willing coming before thought. We know whether an act is good or bad in the doing of it. Logically, although Scheler did not say so, we should actually have to commit murder to know it was wrong. Secondly, Scheler says, values can only function "uncoercively." They should therefore be allowed to draw or repel us by feelings of love and hate. They ought never to be imposed by force. Nor can they take the form of a universal command. Since each man is in a different situation and a bundle of different experiences, there can be no universally applicable moral principles. Christ was a model, not a commanding authority. His commands were expressions of his "intentional" feelings at particular moments in regard to particular situations. The only common factor in ethics is whether the "whole man" is oriented towards the Supreme Person or not. In these respects Scheler has contributed to the idea of the fundamental option and the spread of situation ethics.

Scheler's ethical theories, which made their first full dress appearance in his book *Formalism and the Ethics of Substantive Values* (Part I, 1913; Part II, 1916), were intended as a *via media* between the subjective ethics of Kant (an inner sense of obligation tells us what is right), and what he regarded as the too "legalistic" ethics of the Catholic Church (there are certain things which have to be done in all circumstances without exception, and even if we ourselves cannot always see why, Catholics can be sure of these things because the Church tells them so.)

Scheler was also fascinated by sociology. This led him to speak of values becoming personified or incarnated in certain ideal types, who then become models for particular societies. This led him to what are now some very unfashionable conclusions. World War I was, he believed, above all a conflict

87. The notion of value can be seen as the subjective equivalent of the concept of the good. It looks at the good as it appears to us rather than as it is in itself.

between rival "value systems." The Central Powers represented the virtues of hierarchically ordered and integrated traditional societies, where primacy was given to co-operation and duty; the Allies stood for the bourgeois ideals of the Anglo-Saxon world directed towards individual satisfaction and profit.

Personalism and John Paul II

John Paul II's discovery of Scheler came about accidentally – as these things often do.

Could Scheler's philosophy of values be made the basis for a Catholic system of ethics? Such was the theme taken by the future pontiff as the subject of his second doctoral thesis. His answer was "No." A valid ethical system could not be built solely on feelings and personal experiences. But having been thus introduced to Scheler, he found other things in Scheler's personalism which pleased him: the phenomenological method; man as a responsible "sovereign person" open to values outside himself; Scheler's insistence on making "the whole man" – body and soul, mind, will and emotions – his starting point.

The Church's devotional life has always allowed plenty of outlets for the affections and emotions. But theology, at least in recent times, had tended to regard emotions and feelings with something like mistrust – almost as if it would have been better had God made us without them.

For John Paul II, on the other hand, man is supremely a being who *feels*, as well as thinks and wills. As a definition of man, "rational animal" may do for a start. But a lot more needs to be said. Jesus, the perfect man, felt every worthy emotion, even anger. An unfeeling man would be a defective man.

In all this the Pope, like the philosopher Dietrich von Hildebrand, another phenomenologist, saw the possibility of what never before seems to have been attempted: developing a philosophy and theology of that mysterious entity the human heart, seen not only as the "seat of the affections," but as man's deepest centre where all the faculties of body and soul interlock and receive their special colour and tone; where, if "the heart" is well disposed, they are warmed and made radiant; if ill disposed, chilled and congealed. Holy Scripture, in speaking of this deepest centre, uses the word "heart" far more often than "soul" or "spirit," and even refers to God's "Heart." John Paul II has spoken of God as "the Great Heart." [88]

---

88. Von Hildebrand's *The Sacred Heart*, (Baltimore, and Dublin, Helicon, 1965), is subtitled "an analysis of human and divine affectivity."

However, it would be misleading to suggest that John Paul's personalism is only concerned with our affections and emotions. It is no accident that the title of the English translation of his main philosophical work should be *The Acting Person*.[89] His main philosophical interest was ethics: right action, the role of the will and its freedom. Few Popes can have praised freedom so much. But as Western societies have increasingly used the call for freedom to relativise morality, he more and more insisted, particularly in the encyclical *Veritatis Splendor*, that freedom ceases to be true freedom when it is not linked to knowledge of the truth.[90]

The shift to the human subject in Catholic philosophy and theology has unquestionably been one of the most risky operations ever allowed by the Church, which is perhaps one of the reasons why, in God's providence, John Paul II became Pope. He alone of the then eligible figures would seem to have had the qualifications to guide the Church through the maze of German subjectivism, without a total surrender to it. But in the twenty-two years between the beginning of the post-conciliar rebellion and his election to the papacy in 1978, the philosophical damage already done was beyond the power of any one man to rectify. The *philosophia perennis* became the subject of an international campaign of vilification and mockery. Even where not totally rejected and abandoned, it was pushed on to the sidelines. Subjectivism and relativism permeated the teaching of theology, and in the general confusion philosophy itself became discredited.

---

89. The title immediately brings Blondel to mind, and correctly. In his *The Mind of John Paul* (p. 148), George Huntston Williams, for many years Professor of Divinity at Harvard, and personally acquainted with the Pope, speaks of the influence of Blondel's *L'Action* on his thinking. And in the age-old debate between Thomists and Scotists (followers of the medieval scholastic Duns Scotus, beloved by the English Jesuit poet Gerard Manley Hopkins) about whether the human intellect or will plays the more crucial role in our journey towards beatitude and its enjoyment throughout eternity, the Pope definitely sides with the Scotists, crowning his preference by beatifying Scotus in 1992.

90. Before embarking on his doctoral thesis about Scheler, Pope John Paul had studied Thomism under Garrigou-Lagrange in Rome, and his philosophy is often presented as a blend of Thomism and personalism. This is true in so far as his epistemology is realist – we have real knowledge of a real outside world. But Huntston Williams gives the impression that he found the analytical scholastic method less to his taste than the more suggestive phenomenological approach.

Chapter Eleven

PERSONALISM: MARITAIN AND MOUNIER

I
Jacques Maritain (1882–1973)

Owing little if anything to German philosophy, Maritain's personalism had its roots in St Thomas, the Enlightenment and French humanism, and its goals were as much practical as speculative.

The son of an unbelieving Republican father and a Protestant mother, as a young man he had been attracted to socialism. Then came his conversion to Catholicism (1902) and discovery of St Thomas. It was as a metaphysician and Thomist that Maritain made his reputation between then and 1927. During that time he adopted the more or less conservative political views of the group of Dominicans with whom he first came into contact, and for a time was associated with *L'action française*. But on its condemnation by Rome, he rethought his political position. He reverted to being a social and political liberal and as such he remained. However the temper and tone of his liberalism fluctuated.

During the economic crisis of the 1930s he was further "to the left" (i.e. critical of free enterprise or liberal capitalism) than during the 1940s when he was teaching in America. Closer contact with the United States gave him a greater appreciation of the virtues of American-style democracy. This was followed by a flirtation with the American political radicalism of the American populist agitator Saul Alinsky. In extreme old age after the death of his wife, he retired to the house of a religious order.

He was not invited to take part in Vatican II – only to read a message at the concluding ceremonies. Nevertheless the bulk of what he had written about the human person and human society had already been taken into the mainstream of the Church's social teaching, had strongly influenced the development of that teaching by the Council, and was amply used by the three "conciliar popes," John XXIII, Paul VI and John Paul II. Since the essentials are in what I have written in chapters 6 and 7 about the Church's social teaching, there is no need to go over them again, and I will confine myself to the problems arising from his famous book *Integral Humanism* (1936), in which he started to give his personalist principles an historical and evolutionary development.[91]

That there were problems, he himself became uneasily aware as soon as the Council was over.

"Thanks especially to Emmanuel Mounier," he wrote in *Le Paysan de la Garonne* (Paris, Desclée de Brouwer, 1966, pp. 81–82) "the expression 'personalist and communitarian' has become something of a catchphrase for French Catholic thought. I am not without some responsibility for this myself... It is from me, I think, that Mounier got it ... but when I see the way it is now being used, I am not very proud of it. For it is clear that, after paying lip-service to the 'personalist,' it is really the 'communitarian' which those who use it cherish."[92]

He also complained of the large numbers of clergy and laity for whom "the only thing that matters is the temporal vocation of the human race, with its march, embattled but victorious, to justice, peace and happiness" (*The Peasant of the Garonne*, p. 56). "Hardly is the word 'world' pronounced when a gleam of ecstasy lights up the face of one and all."

Today it is difficult to read these words without being taken aback, seeing that in not a few people's opinion, *Integral Humanism*, or elements of it, were responsible for the very situation he was lamenting.

In spite of his great contributions to Catholic social and political thought, Maritain was always less sure-footed in this field than as a metaphysician. His goodness of heart, weak historical sense and seemingly poor understanding of what most ordinary people are like, often led him to identify what he would have liked something to be with what it could be or ought to be. And he was at his least sure-footed when he wrote *Integral Humanism*. The Spanish Civil War was just about to erupt; Hitler was already in power in Germany; France was embroiled in the struggles between the Popular Front and the political right; and these ephemeral secular conflicts all left their mark on the book. However, the source of the problems, according to the late Cardinal Siri of Genoa, lay deeper.

Cardinal Siri of Genoa called *Integral Humanism* "a philosophy-theology of human history," and it is here, he says, that we find the key to all Maritain's thought about society, politics and the meaning of history, that key being the radical separation he makes between our earthly and heavenly callings or between secular and salvation history. Both are willed by God. But they

---

91. The book was initially a series of six lectures given at the University of Santander in Spain in the summer of 1934.

92. Eng. trans. *The Peasant of the Garonne*, London, Geoffrey Chapman, 1968, p. 51.

move along separate tracks one above the other, towards distinct goals, like trucks on a two-tier Californian super-highway.

The cardinal illustrates his point with two quotations. "The secular order has in the course of the modern age built up for itself an autonomous relation with regard to the spiritual or consecrational order which in fact excludes the notion of instrumentality. In other words, it has come of age. This is ... an historical gain, which a new Christendom must know how to preserve" (I.H., p. 170).

The second quotation is the book's enigmatic last sentence. "Thus human history grows, for it isn't a process of repetition, but of expansion and progress ... drawing near at the same time to its double consummation – in the absolute below, where man is god without God, and in the absolute above where he is god in God."

The Church has always distinguished between the natural and supernatural orders, just as the scholastics distinguished between men's natural or supernatural vocations or "ends." But for the scholastic, the two ends were intertwined. No scholastic before Maritain, I think, had ever forced them so far asunder. Furthermore, for the scholastics, man's natural end was something realised in the here and now. They did not think of history as having a natural end.

Maritain's reason for separating the two orders as radically as he did was partly tactical. As already mentioned, he wanted Catholic laymen to be free to collaborate with all "men of good will" in what he called the "common task," with minimal interference from the clergy. To this extent, the idea will be enshrined in the conciliar teaching as "the autonomy of secular realities" (see *Turmoil and Truth*, Chapter 14). Maritain's "common task" was the socio-political counterpart of the new theologians' "human endeavour," and it meant more than winning decent pay and conditions for the "fourth estate" as he called the working classes. The common task meant "a substantial transmutation where the fourth estate will come ... to ownership, to real freedom, and a real participation in political and economic enterprise" (I.H., p. 268).

At this point we meet an idea which takes us deeper into Maritain's mind. Every man is an individual; but only a man who is his own master is fully a person. A gardener, for instance, working for the personal advantage of another rather than himself or the community, is fully an individual but only partly a person. This is why any kind of social or industrial "paternalism" (i.e. philanthropic employers looking after their employees' welfare, rather than the workers seeing to it for themselves) is reprehensible.

The common task, therefore, has as its second and higher goal the bringing of men to full "personhood" by freeing them from everything that limits their "personal expansion and autonomy." "The natural end of the history of the world is the mastery of nature by man, and the conquest of human autonomy," or setting "the human person and the different human groups (races, classes and nations) free from servitude or subjection to other men" (*The Peasant of the Garonne*, pp. 40–41). To achieve this end is man's "historic vocation."

It is also the direction in which history as a whole is moving. In spite of serious setbacks, "history" is on the side of the common task. When the task is complete, secular history will have come to its term. This does not mean, Maritain is quick to assure us, that it is bound to reach it; he is not preaching a doctrine of inevitable progress like the 18th century French encyclopedist Condorcet. But if the process is frustrated "the end is premature and the book stops in the middle" (I.H., p. 238). We have the impression that, as far as this world is concerned, God's plan will have failed.

Although the spirit of the Gospels has played its part, the primary agents of this necessarily forward movement of history are the natural appetite for human liberty in the human will and the ideal of liberty in the human mind. The *appetite* drives men towards their goal from within, after the fashion of Bergson's *élan vital*, while the *ideal*, glittering mirage-like in the future, pulls them forward like a magnet. The combined actions, one propulsive, the other attractive, are responsible for the "ascending forces of history."

The ascending forces are all movements, political or otherwise, working towards the goal of total emancipation. Collaboration with Marxists was therefore sometimes possible for tactical reasons. Even if Marxists horribly distorted the movement of history, they were not resisting its general thrust, unlike fascists, who, being opposed to the movement of history, could never be allies. Social and political movements "of the left" incarnated the inner drive of history. In them, Maritain saw coming to birth a "third age" of the world. Although earthly history is "impure and dark," he tells us, nevertheless it is "the history of an unhappy humanity on the march towards a most mysterious deliverance" (I.H., p. 243).

However the most important questions are left dangling in the air. Is this deliverance natural or supernatural? If natural, it presumably takes place in time. Are we therefore to assume that once men are free and autonomous they will all behave like angels? And what about all the people who have died without becoming free and autonomous? Are they incomplete persons in heaven? We are simply told that "the history of time enigmatically prepares its final consummation in the Kingdom of God" (I.H., p. 103) and that once "the ideal towards which the human person aspires" has been realised and history has "achieved its end," Humanity will have "passed beyond history."

It is not without significance, I think, that in the little book published in New York in 1942, from which I have taken this last quotation, *Les droits de l'homme et la loi naturelle* (*The Rights of Man*, London, Geoffrey Bles, 1944, see pp. 20 & 22) he points out the similarities between his thinking on these topics and that of "the great paleontologist Teilhard de Chardin." Indeed *Integral Humanism*'s "evolutionism" could be called the political counterpart of Fr Teilhard's cultural and cosmic evolutionism. Later, when people began to understand better what "the great paleontologist" was actually saying, Maritain was to take a decidedly different view of him.

However, the problems really begin when Maritain tries to explain how the "common task" is to be realised in practice.

Having made the "freedom, expansion and autonomy" of the individual or human person the fundamental principle of socio-political life, the "pluralist" society or state (the one with a wide variety of views about fundamental questions) has to be the ideal. That all Western societies are now pluralist is not just a fact, it is an "historic gain." "We must give up seeking in a common profession of faith the source and principle of unity in the social body" (I.H., p. 168).

Maritain had inherited from his socialist past and French republican forebears a deep-rooted aversion to the idea of the "confessional state" (a state where the rulers and laws express the beliefs and principles of one religion because it is the religion of the great majority of the people, and minority "faiths" have to keep a low profile). Necessary perhaps in their time, they should now be relegated to the scrap heap. The Church should have no direct influence on attempts to realise humanity's natural or temporal end.

On the other hand, as a Catholic philosopher, Maritain knows that truth and right are still higher goods, and that for men, being social by nature, there is a common good as well as a good of the individual. How in such a radically pluralist state are these higher goods to get a foot in the door? How are the citizens to be kept together as a people without some kind of agreement on basic questions?

It was to answer these questions that Maritain invented his "integral humanist" state or new non-denominational "Christendom" – surely one of the most curious exercises in political philosophy ever undertaken by a self-proclaimed democrat.[93]

His integral humanist state will, he tells us, be politically democratic (it will presumably have universal suffrage and representative institutions of some kind) and Christian in inspiration. However, the real power lies with those he calls the *cives praeclari* (the enlightened ones). The *cives praeclari*, who may be of any religion or none, are not state officials elected by the people, or part of the political system. They are self-appointed groups of intellectuals and members of the "proletarian elite" who guide public opinion towards the fulfilment of the common task from out of sight, like members of communist party cells or Masonic lodges. Maritain himself says they will fulfil the same function as kings in the past; elsewhere he compares them to medieval religious orders (I.H., pp. 162 & 165).

The "Christian inspiration" will come from the Catholic *cives praeclari*, of whom, it is assumed, there will be a few in each group. They will not try to impose their religious beliefs on the other members of the group. But their practical ideas about what needs to be done will in the end be adopted because of the intrinsic reasonableness and rightness of what they propose. Thus, says Maritain, the Christian viewpoint "will have prevailed ... but in a secular and pluralist way" (I.H., p. 168).[94]

But why should unbelievers and non-Christians unfailingly accept what is reasonable and right? Isn't this Pelagianism: believing that men can unfailingly see and do what is right by their natural powers alone? No, says Maritain, because the *cives praeclari* – "even when ... ignorant of or alien to the profession of Christianity" – are already in a state of grace (I.H., p. 162). Willing, as they do, the right social and political ends, they are "set in a state of moral rectitude"; they are by definition virtuous men and as such must be under the influence of grace (I.H., pp. 162–3). More than that, in embracing Maritain's socio-political ideals, they have unconsciously embraced Christianity itself. "Comprehended in the fullness and perfection of the truths which it (the common task) implies, it takes

---

93. Maritain was a natural intellectual aristocrat and couldn't help knowing it, just as he knew that democracy in the literal sense is a fiction and that there are limits to the liberties which even the most perfect "pluralist" state can allow. His reluctance to face these realities – dictated by his longing for a world free of injustices – largely, I think, explain the contortions and contradictions which characterise his book.

94. It is curious that at the very time Maritain was introducing his Spanish audience to these ideas, an unknown Spanish priest was training young laymen in a task that had at least resemblances to that of Maritain's *cives praeclari*. However, the founder of Opus Dei's aims were much less ambitious and more unequivocally Catholic.

in all of Christianity; yes, the whole of Christian ethics and dogmatics," even if it does not demand "in its beginning a profession of the whole of Christianity from each man" (I.H., p. 200). Therefore, Maritain argues, "a city animated by such elements will in reality be, to an extent, under the reign of Christ" (I.H., p. 163).

The moral stature of the *cives praeclari* will at the same time make them acceptable to the masses, even if the masses are not capable of appreciating the wisdom of their leaders' policies. Why the masses should be ready to follow good rather than bad leaders is not explained. In fact, Maritain's attitude towards the masses is equivocal. Sometimes he speaks of them as though they were to be passive instruments of the *cives praeclari*, or even obstacles to their aims (I.H., p. 169). At others the masses themselves seem to be the principal driving-force behind history. We hear of their "historic mission." We are told that the "destiny of humanity depends largely on their attitude and action" (I.H., p. 230). Are the masses too all in a state of grace? It often seems so. "The guiding star ... of this new humanism, the idea at its heart ... will not be that of God's *holy empire* (sic) over all things, but rather that of the *holy freedom* (sic) of the creature whom grace unites to God" (I.H., p. 156).[95]

What about the citizens who reject his grace? That, however, is an incidental point. Whether or not the masses are all in a state of grace, the *cives praeclari* and the masses together will prepare the ground for the new Christendom with "a vast and multiform work ... of propaganda and organisation" (I.H., p. 267). "A spiritual warfare" and "a social and temporal strife" will have "to be waged by all those who share the same human ideal" (I.H., p. 230).

But will working at the common task be enough by itself to hold the citizens of the "new Christendom" together? Here Maritain contradicts himself. First, he tells us that "we must renounce the search for a common profession of faith." A "simple unity of friendship" and the pursuit of religiously and morally neutral goals will be sufficient (I.H., p. 167). The citizens will be united by a "minimal" kind of unity "on the plane of the temporal." On the next page, however, he tells us that the "simple unity of friendship does

---

95. Maritain's exaltation of the individual's holy freedom provoked a famous controversy between a group of his followers and the French Canadian Thomist Charles de Koninck, who maintained that it would render social life all but impossible. See *De la primauté du bien commun contre les personalistes*, Québec, 1943. Maritain replied in 1947 with *La personne et le bien commun*.

not suffice to give form to a social body." Nor do common practical aims. Without a "a definitely ethical and religious specification" (I.H., p. 166) the city "cannot be veritably human" (I.H., p. 168). So the citizens are to have a common religion, the new Christendom is to be a one-religion state after all, even if Maritain calls it a spiritual ideal and it is centred on man rather than God. Its chief articles of belief are "the dignity of human personality and its spiritual vocation, and of the fraternal love which is its due."

In other words, having carefully excluded the Church from any direct influence over temporal affairs, Maritain has in fact brought religion and politics together again by the back door. The *civis praeclarus* is a kind of bishop of the religion of human dignity, liberty and brotherliness, guiding both spiritual and temporal affairs.

Disconcerting too in a different way at this period of his life is the manner in which left-wing clichés dominated his political thinking, and revolutionary rhetoric, at times, his writing. All modern states are categorised as communist, fascist, or bourgeois liberal. The only worthwhile people seem to be intellectuals, workers and peasants (I.H., p. 267). Liberal bourgeois states are treated as incapable of reform. Trying to tinker with them is "opportunism" or "empiricism"; they must be "liquidated" (I.H., p. 256). "Modern civilisation is a worn-out vesture" (I.H., p. 201). The future "can only be born of an essential rupture" with the past (I.H., p. 259).[96]

Does the state have an obligation to uphold natural morality? Only in so far as the people adhere to it. "The body politic does not know another truth than that which the people know." The state being pluralist, this means that "civil legislation should adapt to the variety of moral creeds of the

---

96. The rupture and "the inauguration of a new Christian order," Maritain says, "demand '*means*' which are proportionate to that end." Did that include the use of force? Up to a point. The question is discussed on pp. 240–250. By instinct and conviction Maritain was, of course, for peaceful means, which he sets out at length. But he was in a dilemma. The left was attacking him for having, in an earlier book, preached political "disengagement." He replied by citing the Church's teaching about the conditions for a just war and just insurrection. "I hold that the Christian should not refuse such a use of *just* force, when it is absolutely necessary" (I.H., p. 246). But he was also provoked into statements like: "Force and the use of force implies also violence and terror and the use of all the means of destruction. These things also can be just in certain defined conditions" (I.H., p. 241): and "fear of soiling ourselves in entering into the context of history is a pharisaical one... to stain our fingers is not to stain our hearts." (I.H., p. 243) Statements of this kind will later be grist for the mill of South American liberation theologians, who will see themselves as partly indebted to *Integral Humanism* for some of their key concepts.

diverse spiritual lineages which essentially bear on the common good of the social body." (*Man and the State*, pp. 166–9, cited in "Maritain, Personhood and the State" by Prof. Charles E. Rice, *The Wanderer*, 9 Sept. 1982.) But suppose the people have conflicting ways of life? Or immoral ones?

There is a curious similarity between the views expressed in *Integral Humanism* and those of certain French traditionalists. With both there is an underlying assumption that you can get a society made up largely of non-Christians to live like Christians. The difference is about the means. Where the traditionalists think you can do it by recapturing control of the state, Maritain imagined you could do it by stealth.

One regrets having to criticise this great Catholic philosopher, who was in so many ways a good and loveable man. *Integral Humanism* was not his final word about man and society. But it was his most widely read "word," and the span of its influence stretched from the orthodoxy of Pope Paul to the heterodoxies of Gustavo Gutierrez. It was to be the principal source of today's Catholic political utopianism.[97]

In the *Peasant of the Garonne* he uttered a final cry of anguish at the way some of his ideas had been used, accusing Catholics after the Council of kneeling to the world. But one cannot help feeling that he had given it some fairly profound bows himself.

II

Emmanuel Mounier (1904–1950)

Emmanuel Mounier, better than any other figure of his time, I think, exemplifies the dilemma of generous-minded young French Catholics who, wanting to "do something" about atrocious social conditions, found themselves trapped between the three political ugly sisters: communism, fascism and anti-religious liberalism.[98]

A gifted, initially pious and introverted young Sorbonne graduate from Grenoble, Emmanuel Mounier, first appeared on the French Catholic scene

---

97. For Gutierrez on *Integral Humanism*, see Siri, *op. cit.*, p. 96.

98. For this sketch of Mounier and his personalism, I have relied on John Hellman's fair-minded and detailed study, *Emmanuel Mounier and the New Catholic Left, 1930–50*, University of Toronto Press, 1981. Also available in English are Mounier's own *Personalism* (London, 1952) and *Be not Afraid: Studies in Personalist Sociology* (New York, 1954).

around 1927 when he began attending the famous weekly gatherings of Catholic intellectuals at Maritain's house in Meudon on the outskirts of Paris, and rapidly made a name for himself as editor of the monthly *Esprit*, which he founded with the help and support of Maritain and Gabriel Marcel in 1932. For the rest of the thirties, Maritain and Mounier were linked in a curious master-disciple relationship in which the master often seemed to be running to catch up with the disciple.

Mounier had received a narrow philosophical formation and had limited powers of philosophical thought. (Maritain once complained that his articles were "a host of contradictory affirmations.") But he had determination, a strong attachment to certain key ideas, and gifts as a publicist. Added to this, he voiced what many of his generation were confusedly thinking – which for Maritain often proved an irresistible attraction. Consequently while Maritain frequently rebuked Mounier for excesses and imprudences, not a few of these excesses found their way into Maritain's own writings of this period, though usually in more guarded language.

Integral Humanism represents the highpoint of Mounier's influence on Maritain. After Maritain's departure for the United States in 1939, it declined. This was largely because of their opposing views about the merits and demerits of democracy and fascism. Maritain never wavered in his opposition to fascism. In spite of *Integral Humanism*'s many amorous sidelong glances towards the extreme left, he always remained strongly attached to the democratic idea (government in some way by as well as for the people.)

Mounier's position was more equivocal. Although he has often been presented as a typical Catholic "of the left," and during the last five years of his life threw his weight behind Christian–Marxist dialogue, he had previously spoken favourably of certain fascist movements (Hitler was the betrayer of *true* fascism), and with the outbreak of war gave qualified support to Vichy. He believed unashamedly in the role of élites. But he was plucky and in a certain sense unworldly. When the Vichy authorities imprisoned him for nine months he went on hunger strike in protest. In spite of this, he continued to regard them as the legitimate government and greeted the liberation of France by the allies with mixed feelings.

The jump onto the Marxist bandwagon as soon as the Fourth Republic was in place, however, was not the cynical opportunism it seems at first sight. Given Mounier's beliefs, there was logic in it.

Mounier saw himself as a religious reformer who, on his own admission, knew little about and cared little for politics, yet nevertheless was simple enough to believe that he could use the great political movements of the day to clear the ground for a spiritual revolution which would bring about the universal reign of brotherliness and unselfishness through a reversal or "transvaluation" of reigning "values."

The great barrier to that revolution, in his view, was the selfish individualism of "bourgeois civilisation" with its rotten parliamentary institutions and capitalist economics. Seeing it purely as an instrument of that selfishness, Mounier had nothing but hard words for parliamentary democracy. Democracy meant the French Third Republic. Whatever the faults of fascism and communism (and Mounier was one of the first to denounce Stalin's brutalities and Hitler's persecution of the Jews) they at least recognised that social life should be co-operative or corporate. If therefore one or other of them could be used to sweep away bourgeois civilisation, so much the better. Mounier and his groups of *Esprit* readers, whom, by the mid-1930s, he had welded into something resembling a movement – they met for talks and discussions – could then infiltrate and spiritualise whatever political systems resulted.[99]

Today, only Mounier's advocacy of Christian–Marxist dialogue is remembered, partly because his contacts with fascism proved inconvenient to his left-wing admirers, partly because after World War II Mounier largely rewrote the history of his movement. Like other reformers, he was not averse where necessary to sacrificing historical particularities to the interests of his vision.

But how Catholic was that vision? This is the other area of ambiguity. Underlying his Catholicism was a private "religion of the spirit," which is what he was chiefly interested in propagating and which was to work his spiritual revolution. It had three components.

The first was a variant of Maritain's personalism with elements from Scheler, Marcel and Buber. Most of this, with which we are already familiar, was consistent with Catholicism. The human person is the highest created good, but it only discovers itself in a community inspired by brotherly love. However, Mounier put much less emphasis on the individual's freedom and autonomy than Maritain. Brotherly love and social living came first. Personalism was the instrument destined to regenerate Europe by bringing bourgeois civilisation to

99. Initially, Maritain seems to have seen Mounier's *Esprit* groups as a foreshadowing of his *cives praeclari*. "Even now," he was writing in 1936, "under the most unpromising conditions, and with the awkwardness of first attempts, the first steps have been taken" (I.H., p. 266). Towards the end of his life, Mounier founded a small community dedicated to living a common life according to personalist principles.

its knees. Through personalism, people would at last learn to prefer people to things and the good of the community to their own private good. These aspects of Mounier's personalism were to leave their mark on the social encyclicals of John XXIII, Paul VI and the Christian humanism of John Paul II.[100]

The second component was an evolutionary world-view coupled with an emphasis on the primacy of spirit over matter, which he had initially acquired from his philosophy teacher at Grenoble, Jacques Chevalier, a disciple of Bergson. Chevalier also implanted in him a typically Bergsonian aversion to abstract or systematic thought.

In Mounier's thinking, anyone who believed in "spirit" was a potential ally for his religious revolution. He saw Christianity, in Hellmann's words, as first and foremost, "a superior way of life for all people even if they did not share its supernatural beliefs." No specific doctrines were denied, but, in order of importance, belief in "spirit" and brotherly love tended to come before belief in the Creator God or the Blessed Trinity, and "the central acts of Christian drama" – sin, redemption, and resurrection – which were to be "set aside" (Hellman, p. 255).

Later, Mounier came under the influence of Teilhard de Chardin. The December 1937 issue of *Esprit* "heralded Teilhard's work as of ... exceptional importance." The editor found "reassuring" Teilhard's idea that conflicting political movements, democratic, fascist and communist will ultimately "converge," being all part of a single evolutionary forward march (Hellman, p. 128).

Finally there was Nietzsche, whom Mounier discovered during the Second World War. Nietzsche was a more potent influence on him than Marx ever was. Indeed at one point he confessed to knowing little about Marx, though hoped to read more of him. In Nietzsche, Mounier found support for certain already existing sympathies and antipathies which came more from his temperament than his intelligence. By nature rather timid and indecisive and despising himself for being so, he was attracted by compensating qualities and people, such as daring, energy, force, strength of will, action, manly vigour, heroic figures, even violence. Believing, as he did, in élites as the only really effective agents of historical change, he had a corresponding contempt for what he judged weakness, mediocrity, self-seeking and compromise.

---

100. *The New Catholic Encyclopedia* sums up this aspect of Mounier's personalism as: "belief in the person as a spiritual being, maintaining his existence by adhering to a hierarchy of values freely adopted and assimilated...The person freely involves himself in the world while maintaining a spiritual detachment from, and transcendence over, the material aspects of civilisation. Personalism (so qualified) means 'engagement in action' in contemporary civilisation" (art. "Mounier, Emmanuel").

Reading Nietzsche not only brought these sympathies and antipathies to white heat, they provided him with a formidable arsenal of invective for attacking bourgeois civilisation (Nietzsche's *bête noire* too), and for everything he disliked in the Catholic Church.

Mounier's hostility to the greater part of existing Catholic life and practice did not begin with his discovery of Nietzsche, and that there were things to criticise has already been made plain. What is not so easy to explain is why his hostility should have been so all-embracing and uncompromising from early on. He does not seem to have had harsh parents or an unhappy childhood. Perhaps we can attribute it initially to his having listened to conversations between Jacques Chevalier and his disgruntled modernist friends. However, reading Nietzsche made his animosity near paranoic. He ended by becoming incapable of seeing almost anything good in Catholicism past and present. Why hadn't the Church managed to abolish poverty, persuade people to value things of the spirit above material goods, and make all men love each other? By the late 1940s he was wondering whether Christianity had not been a blight rather than a blessing for the human race. Perhaps there never had been any genuine Christianity. Perhaps it was only now beginning. "Who are the first Christians?" he asked, and answered "Perhaps ourselves," meaning himself and his *Esprit* readers (Hellman, p. 199).

Such was the explosive mixture of things acceptable and unacceptable which this (oratorically) ferocious prophet and apostle of brotherly love spread abroad through *Esprit* immediately before and after World War II. *Esprit* did not have a vast circulation. But Maritain's support and the distinguished writers he and Marcel persuaded to contribute to it, gave it prestige. The early readership included many names eventually to become famous: the future cardinals Journet, de Lubac, Congar and Daniélou, Fr Marie-Dominique Chenu, non-Catholic Christians like Berdyaev, and unbelievers like the philosopher Merleau-Ponty. Outside France its main impact was in Québec, Belgium and Poland.[101]

---

101. Hellman notes Mounier's influence on the *Znak* group in Poland, on the avant-garde review *Cross Currents* in the U.S., and the Canadian magazine *Cité Libre*, one of whose founders was the future Canadian Prime Minister, Pierre Trudeau. *Znak* published articles by the future John Paul II. The other two periodicals were designed as American and Canadian versions of *Esprit* (*Emmanuel Mounier and the New Catholic Left,* p. 328). According to Fr Chenu, *Esprit* was learned and rather difficult to read, nevertheless he considered its influence decisive. Its positions, he says, were "vulgarised" in reviews like *Sept* and *Temps Présent* and "a host of books" (Hellman, p. 292). Seeing that the critics of "bourgeois Catholicism" tended to associate it with an attachment to the Church's devotional life and practices, these "vulgarisations" must have contributed considerably to the violent post-conciliar assault on those practices.

Chapter Twelve

THE EVOLUTIONARY IDEA

The evolutionary idea is so much a part of Western thinking that there can be no one with a Western education unaffected by it. But with ideas that are built into our minds from earliest childhood, we are often unaware of what *precisely* we are harbouring. This chapter is therefore devoted not to determining whether "evolution," in the usually understood sense, took place, but to unpacking the "idea" to see what it actually contains, and to what, without their often realising it, it is committing Christians when they start trying to "baptise" it.

Even highly qualified people often launch into the topic as though unaware that the word "evolution" now has four quite distinct meanings. These are supported by evidence, or open to objections of varying weight and value, so it is not surprising that the subject is such a thorny one. We are all familiar with those different meanings in a rough and ready way, but they tend to exist in our minds in one single undigested lump.

However, since a situation has come about where to offer even a mild criticism of evolutionary theory exposes one to the danger of being written off as a crank, I first want to ensure that, if I do make some critical comments, I am seen to be in good company. Here then are four quotes from men of impeccable scientific credentials:

"No amount of argument or clever epigramme can disguise the inherent improbability of orthodox evolutionary theory; but most biologists feel it is better to think in terms of improbable events than not to think at all" (Zoologist James Grey of Cambridge, 1954).

"To say that the development and survival of the fittest is entirely a consequence of chance mutations seems to me a hypothesis based on no evidence and irreconcilable with the facts. Classical evolutionary theories are a gross over-simplification of an immensely complex and intricate mass of facts, and it amazes me that they are swallowed so uncritically and readily for such a long time by so many scientists without a murmur of protest" (Nobel prize-winner Sir Ernest Chain, co-discoverer of penicillin, 1970).

"The view that evolution can ultimately be understood in terms of genetics and molecular biology is clearly in error" (Steven M. Stanley of Johns Hopkins University, 1974).

"Evolution [has become] in a sense a scientific religion; almost all scientists have accepted it and many are prepared to 'bend' their observations to fit with it. [. . .] I have always been slightly suspicious of the theory of evolution because of its ability to account for any property of living beings. I have therefore tried to see whether biological discoveries over the last thirty years or so fit in with Darwin's theory. I do not think that they do. To my mind, the theory does not stand up at all" (H S Lipson, CBE, Professor of Physics, University of Manchester Institute of Science and Technology, in the May 1980 issue of *Physics Bulletin*).

One could make a long list of such statements, but we do not have unlimited space.[102]

A second introductory point: evolution is about change. So before embarking on the subject we ought at least to be clear in our minds about the difference between the two main *kinds* of change.

These are *accidental* and *substantial* change. Accidental changes are the ones that modify the appearance or "surface" of a thing without making it a different thing. Substantial change (in so far as it is possible) turns one kind of thing into an altogether new thing. It has received a different nature or form. It has been *transformed*. Alternatively, it is broken down into its physical components and ceases to exist as that particular thing – as happens to our bodies at death.[103]

This immediately helps us to see the difference between evolution and the apparently similar but actually different form of change we call "development." The two words used to be used interchangeably for any movement from one state of affairs to another. But since Darwin it has become necessary to distinguish between them.

---

102. The above and similar quotations in this chapter are taken from Fr. Stanley Jaki's *The Purpose of It All*. Other statements critical of the theory by qualified authorities can be found in *Darwin On Trial* (Inter-Varsity Press, 1991) by Phillip Johnson of Berkeley University, California, *Darwin's Black Box* (1996) by Michael Behe, and *The Design Inference* (1998) by William A. Dembski. The most recent book to summarise the inadequacies of Darwinism from the philosophical and scientific perspectives can be found in *Uncommon Dissent: Intellectuals Who Find Darwinism Unconvincing*, edited by William A. Dembski, ISI Books, 2004.

103. Fairy stories are full of substantial changes – princes changing into frogs, etc. – but in real life, outside what Catholics believe happens in the Mass, there seems to be much less substantial change than we imagine. With good reason we call the change from caterpillar to butterfly, or sinner to saint, a transformation; but it is still the same being in a different physical or spiritual state. Perhaps the history of civilisations and governments provides us with the best examples of substantial change or "transformism."

Evolution is basically about substantial change, one class of things becoming another class of things. *Development,* in contrast, is not about things becoming different things, but about things becoming more fully themselves. It is about the *unfolding* of a thing's hidden powers and possibilities, even though the thing itself remains what it was. It could be called the highest kind of accidental change.

We are now perhaps better prepared to pursue our original purpose.

Descent from a single life form

The first meaning of the word "evolution" is the one we know best. According to this theory, the different kinds of animals and plants were not created different from the start, but came into existence through descent from a single primitive life form and through a process of change and transformation lasting millions of years. Higher forms, including men, "grew" or were drawn out of break-away groups of lower forms. The French word *transformisme,* initially used sometimes as an alternative for "evolution" to describe this real or supposed process, gives the best idea of what is supposed to have happened.[104]

Evolution in this first most basic sense is not an established fact but a scientific hypothesis suggested by the work of 18th and early 19th century naturalists like Buffon, Linnaeus and Cuvier who were interested not so much in how the different kinds of animals and plants came to be the way they are, but in classifying them into groups and sub-groups (orders, families, genera, species, etc.) based on their anatomical similarities and the position of fossils in the rock strata. If living forms could be grouped in families like this, might they not all descend from a single common ancestral type rather than a group of separate and distinct archetypes? Darwin did not invent this idea. Lamarck seems to have been the first to formulate it systematically. But Darwin collected the greatest body of information about animal and plant life in apparent support of it.

In saying this I am not denying that Darwin's formidable powers of observation, patience, attention to detail and tenacity of purpose place him among naturalists of the highest rank. Unfortunately, the nature of his studies, and still more what seemed to him their implications, carried him into the

---

104. For example, *La crise du transformisme,* by F. Le Dantec (Paris, F. Alcan, 1910). Dantec, an avowed materialist, was a professor of physiology at the Sorbonne. As early as 1910 the theory was seen as being in a state of crisis.

world of philosophy and metaphysics which he was not equally equipped to deal with. In developing a cosmology and anthropology which ignore questions of an order higher than the geological and biological – questions like the origins and role of goodness, beauty, love and intelligence – he ended, even if unintentionally, like Marx and Freud, in turning the public mind of the Western world upside down, and not, by and large, to its benefit.[105]

In spite of this, evolution in this first sense is not incompatible with belief in God. God *could* have brought animals and plants into existence in this way. The important question is: did He in fact do so? Is the evidence advanced in favour of the theory adequate? As we have just seen, not all scientists think that it is – at least not on the evidence we have seen so far.

Right from the start, the major headache for evolutionists, non-Christian and Christian, has been the lack of what are called "intermediate forms." If evolution happened as supposed, the rocks should surely be filled with the fossils of creatures in a state of semi-transformation between one species and the next. Not just the odd difficult-to-classify case, which with a stretch of the imagination might be an intermediate form, but literally *thousands* of indisputable intermediate forms. But they simply are not there.

As anyone who has gone into the subject knows, species appear in the fossil-bearing rock strata "very suddenly, show little or no change during their existence in the record, then abruptly go out of the record." So says the curator of the Field Museum in Chicago, David Raup, writing in 1979. Long before that, Darwin's friend and ally Thomas Huxley had noted that the idea of gradual change was incompatible with the fossil record. How too do we explain things like fossils of trees which run up through several rock strata (polystrata) that were supposedly laid down at intervals over millions of years? Or the innumerable mammoths found in the Siberian permafrost with fresh grass in their stomachs? (Without a sudden, catastrophic drop in temperature, the grass would have been found digested.) There are abundant examples of geological phenomena such as these which suggest that the challenge to gradual and lengthy geological change, one of the foundations of evolutionary theory, is still very much alive.

These and similar problems may not be conclusive arguments against an evolutionary origin of species, but they are not easily dismissable. In the

---

105. The story that the beauty of the peacock's tail made him feel sick may not be authentic, but it makes the above point. There is good reason why the existence of beauty in the animal and plant worlds should turn the stomach of any committed Darwinian. If form and system imply a supreme Mind, beauty implies a supreme Artist.

present state of knowledge, what the rocks, fossils and animals have to tell us about the remote past remains deeply mysterious. It is like an inscription in a language which no one yet knows fully how to decipher.

The Church's most authoritative statement about evolution so far is to be found in Pius XII's encyclical *Humani Generis* (1950). Catholics, he said, may believe God could have created the animals and plants by some kind of evolutionary process, and even that He might have used the body of some kind of higher ape for the body of the first man. But the result was something utterly new and different. The body was united to an immortal human soul created directly by God, and was transformed in the process. With regard to evolution in general, the Pope warned, Catholics must remember that they are dealing with what is still only an hypothesis. Although the first chapters of *Genesis* are not history or a scientific description in the modern sense, they are not to be treated as a jumble of Jewish folklore without doctrine or truth of any kind. In some way, still to be determined, they do "come under the heading of history."[106]

Choice by Chance

The second idea that people have in mind when they talk about evolution is the theory of "natural selection" or "the survival of the fittest." This is an hypothesis about how the transformation of one species into another actually works, and in its initial form this was indeed Darwin's creation, even if he drew heavily on the geological uniformitarianism of his friend Sir Charles Lyell.[107] To mark the

---

106. Denzinger, 3898. Subsequently, in his less authoritative *Message to the Pontifical Academy of Sciences* (22 October 1996), John Paul II spoke of evolution as a theory rather than a hypothesis, thereby attributing to it a greater degree of probability. This was the point given most attention by the media. More important, but largely unmentioned, was the Pope's insistence that each human soul is directly created by God. It is not a product of evolution or nature.

107. *Uniformitarianism*: the theory that the earth's surface has been shaped slowly over immense periods of time by the same forces acting today in the same way as in the past. Lyell's uniformitarianism, based on the theories of the Scottish geologist James Hutton, displaced the previously reigning "catastrophism," systematised by the French anatomist Cuvier – the theory that the earth's major physical features were the result of periodic world-wide geological cataclysms rather than small local earthquakes, volcanic eruptions, and floods. Cuvier's theory fell into disrepute with many scientists of the post-Enlightenment period, partly, even I think one can fairly say *largely*, because it lent credibility to the biblical account of the Deluge, a narrative which is not of course limited to the Bible, but which is found in varying forms in the traditions of many cultures around the world.

difference between these first two meanings of the word "evolution," we can therefore justifiably call the second "Darwinism."

"Natural selection" was not in fact an altogether new idea either. The fact that weak or unhealthy members of a species tend to get killed off is a matter of observation which had hitherto been interpreted as one of nature's ways of keeping a particular species healthy. The novelty of Darwin's theory was in turning the idea around and claiming that it could be the starting point for producing a fresh species. If nature kills off weak and ill-adapted members of a species, she must favour strong or better adapted ones. To this idea he then joined two other well-known facts, long exploited by gardeners and breeders of domestic animals. Not only do all members of a species vary slightly; by mating the ones varying in the same way you can emphasise a particular tendency until you get, not a new species, but a recognisably different sub-type. Variant forms, whether produced by men or nature, are the development of the hidden possibilities latent in a type or species. It is rather like a theme and variations in music. With regard to species as a whole, variation is always a matter of accidental change.

But might not nature do blindly, Darwin asked himself, what the selective breeder does knowingly, and even go much further? Bit by bit, generation after generation, might not an accumulation of small variations favourable to particular animals in their struggle for survival terminate in a new organ or body structure, eventually resulting in a new kind of creature, in the sense of its being unable to interbreed with the 'parent' form from which it arose? In other words, might not a long chain of accidental changes somehow lead to a substantial change, not in individual members of a species, but in a section of the species itself? A "species" is of course an abstraction, so what is envisaged is a *metaphysical* change.

What Darwin was proposing was not, of course, "natural selection," since selection means choice, and only minds can choose. This is why his theory soon provided as many headaches for its inventor as had the theory of evolution.

Darwin, as we have seen, thought in terms of small variations and an environment that changes extremely slowly. An accumulation of small variations sufficient to produce a new organ or body structure must therefore take millions of years. But what value is a developing organ until it is fit for use?

The going gets harder still when we try to imagine the evolution of complex organs like the eye or the digestive system. We have to imagine a cluster of changes, each useless in itself, but all converging over millions of years towards a common end without knowing it. Today, critics of Darwinism describe such a hypothesis as violating the "principle of irreducible complexity." They are saying, in effect, that while it is possible to make additions to an already existing system (like, for example, the internal combustion engine) which were not foreseen from the start, it is impossible for the *basic* requirements which enable the system to function as the particular system *it is* to be a random collection of parts assembled without plan or purpose.[108]

Darwin himself admitted that "in not a single case" could he prove that natural selection had "changed one species into another,"[109] while Huxley confessed that the idea of gradual change was incompatible with the fossil record and wondered why, in the case of gradual change, variations should occur at all.

By the 1920s, Darwinians were finding it increasingly difficult to paper over the cracks. Renamed "neo-Darwinism," the theory had already had to be modified to take account of discoveries in genetics, as it would later have to assimilate the findings of molecular or micro-biologists. Meanwhile a partial return to some of Cuvier's ideas was taking place. It could be called "neo-catastrophism." An increasing body of geologists and palaeontologists was re-exploring the evidence and deciding that the shaping of the earth's surface, far from having always been slow and uniform, was due in great part to periodic upheavals on a world scale, and that the various species we know today did not emerge slowly over the millions of years hypothesised by Darwin, but rapidly in "jumps" of thousands, even possibly mere hundreds of years. This aspect of neo-Darwinism, popularised by Stephen J. Gould, is described as "punctuated equilibrium." When one of these catastrophies strikes, according to David Jablowski of Chicago University, "it is not

---

108. In the words of the philosopher and logician Professor Peter Geach, "there can be no origin of species, as opposed to an Empedoclean chaos of varied monstrosities, unless creatures reproduce pretty much after their kind; the elaborate and ostensibly teleological mechanism of this reproduction logically cannot be explained as a product of evolution by natural selection from among chance variations, for unless the mechanism is presupposed there cannot be any evolution." (From "An Irrelevance of Omnipotence," *Philosophy* 48 (1973) p. 330, quoted Brian Davies, *An Introduction to the Philosophy of Religion*, OUP, 1993, pp. 112–113.) See also Neil Broom, *How Blind is the Watchmaker?*, chapter 10 (Inter-Varsity Press, 2001).

109. Nor, so far, has it been possible to produce a genuinely new species by selective interbreeding, even using the famously fast-breeding fruit fly. On the other hand, were a genuinely new creature to be produced by genetic engineering, it would of course be proof of intelligent intervention, not of evolution by natural selection.

necessarily the most fit that survive; often it's the most fortunate."

Small changes or "tweaks" in the genetic code, it is argued, possibly brought about by sudden ecological change, can effect large changes in the appearance of an organism. Obviously this is an attempt to get around the problem of the absence of intermediate forms. But how big a change? If the tweak produces what is still a variation, no matter how large, in an already existing species, then the need for intermediate forms in the rock strata remains with the addition of a new problem: the genetic code has to "know" how to give the kind of tweak *exactly* suited to the particular ecological disaster that precipitates it. If, on the other hand, a sufficiently strong tweak *can* produce a totally new species, then the whole Darwinian theory of transformism by natural selection is in ruins. For according to this version, the origin of species would lie *not* in a long process of supposed trial and error, but in sudden changes in the genetic code which occur for reasons and in ways that no one as yet knows. This can only mean that we are back where the whole debate began, on the mechanism which drives the evolutionary process from a single primitive life form.[110]

Yet another challenge to mainstream Darwinism (old and new) has come from the proponents of the "anthropic principle," which means that, when looked at as a whole, the universe seems to have been "fine-tuned" specially to produce an environment capable of supporting human life. At innumerable points in the course of the universe's development, if things had gone only a little bit differently, human life would have been impossible. How could this possibly have happened by accident?

To parry this apparently lethal thrust, champions of a self-generating universe, like the indefatigable Richard Dawkins and Daniel Dennett, have suggested that the existing universe is only one of an ever-multiplying number of alternative ones. Since the process is never-ending as well as self-generating, they claim that it is statistically bound one day to throw up a universe capable of supporting human life, without the help of any intelligent agent. If by nothing else, one cannot help but be impressed by their ingenuity and pertinacity.[111]

---

110. It is worth noting that in our own day we can witness sudden ecological change producing the death of species and not their dramatic change into new ones.

111. In the 4th century BC, the Greek philosopher Epicurus also postulated the existence of an infinite number of universes. However in his case they seem to have come into existence and then disintegrated one after the other. (Cf. St Augustine, *The City of God*, Bk XI, chapter 5.)

But through all these adaptations, what in the eyes of Darwinists of every stamp is the essential feature of the theory has been preserved. Darwin made it possible for men who do not want to believe in God, to believe the impossible without seeming mad; namely, that things can make themselves.

So while the arguments for and against evolution in the first sense (transformism) have to do with evidence, those for and against it in the second sense (natural selection) are largely about logic, or trying to circumvent it.

It will also be seen that the debate over the origin of things is not a straightforward one between evolutionists and creationists; there are two intertwined debates. The first is between believers and unbelievers about whether you can have a "creation" without a Creator and "law" without a Lawgiver. The second is between believers about whether God brought things into existence rapidly, and as far as living things are concerned, from directly created species; or over aeons from a single initial life form ("creationists" versus "theistic evolutionists"). In point of fact, even if the "creationists" regard the Christian evolutionists as a Trojan horse in the City of God, both are "creationists" in the sense that they see God as the supreme and final cause of everything. What divides them is the methods God used and the nature of the difficulties to be overcome. While the creationists have to reconcile their position with the anatomical and geological data (why, for instance, was nature apparently "red in tooth and claw" before the fall of man?), the hardest question for the "extended creationists" or theistic evolutionists is how, if God did not directly intervene in the evolutionary process, he used secondary causes to bring about foreseen results. Natural selection, as we have seen, is incapable of accommodating the notion of foresight, although it is implicit in the very nature of biological forms.[112]

---

112. I am, of course, simplifying a highly complex situation. Within and between these two groups there are many shades of opinion. Taking them together, they range from biblical fundamentalists at one extreme to Teilhardian pantheists at the other. In between we find, for instance, scientifically qualified anti-evolutionists, who, following the example of St Augustine, would not interpret the six days of creation literally, and base their objections entirely on scientifically observed and established facts. On the other hand, being a Christian evolutionist does not necessarily mean dismissing the first chapters of *Genesis* as irrelevant Jewish folklore; God is recognised as having had a purpose in allowing them to be composed as they were. I am talking in both cases about Christians who are seriously interested in the subject. As for the majority of today's Christians, I think their attitude could be summarised as: "No matter how you understand it, evolution is a fact. As for the way God fits into it all, heaven knows. Let the theologians worry about that."

Before leaving Darwinism, something should also be said about its social consequences.

Christians were not alone in foreseeing the brutalising effects that the theory was bound to have once whole populations learned to think that ruthless competition was the mechanism of progress. Marx, the Nazis, and unprincipled factory owners all appealed to it to justify their theories or practice, while unbelievers like Bernard Shaw, the philosopher-novelist Samuel Butler, and the socialist thinker Prince Kropotkin cried out in protest. Even Huxley, Darwin's ally, was aware of its implications. "The moral progress of society," he wrote, "depends not on imitating the cosmic process (i.e. the evolutionary struggle for survival) but on combatting it."[113] But why should there be such a thing as moral progress in an amoral purposeless universe, and how are we to explain a blind cosmic process suddenly reversing itself to bring that progress about?

It is curious how few, if any, dedicated Darwinists are willing to face the inconsistency of their position in this regard. They are often pacifists and by and large anti-war, while refusing to recognise that their world view justifies, indeed demands, not only war but genocide. They believe in equality. But if we are descended from a multitude of competing hominids (polygenism) rather than a single human pair directly created by God (monogenism) there could well be superior and inferior races. Once again it is a case of residual Christian attitudes surviving in largely anti-Christian surroundings.

The root of the problem seems to lie in a scientific mindset which, over the last two centuries, has concentrated more and more on the first two of Aristotle's four causes of things, to the neglect of the third and fourth. The tendency makes its first noticeable appearance with Francis Bacon's *Novum Organum* (1620), and in the 18th century receives a powerful thrust forward from Diderot's *Encyclopédie* with its emphasis on the pursuit of purely "useful knowledge."

By "causes," Aristotle meant the answers to the four most fundamental questions we ask when confronted with anything new. What is it made of (material cause)? How is it made and how does it work (instrumental cause)? What makes it and maintains it as the kind of thing it is (formal cause)? For what purpose was it made (final cause)? Whether the seemingly exclusive preoccupation of the majority of today's scientists with the material and instrumental causes, and their indifference to the formal and final causes, is a

---

113. T. H. Huxley, *Evolution and Ethics and Other Essays*, New York, 1914, p. 37, quoted Jaki *op. cit.*

consequence or contributory cause of modern atheism is hard to say. What is unquestionable is the impoverished one-dimensional understanding of the cosmos it has generated.

No Christian should doubt that investigating the secrets of nature is good in itself. But where scientific inquiry is pursued without a modicum of interest or philosophical grounding in the formal and final causes, we also observe a tendency for it to become spiritually and even physically lethal. The original author of the Faust legend seems to have foreseen it a good half century before it began.[114]

Ongoing Evolution

We now come to evolution's third meaning. Most people take it for granted that the process is still going on. For this, however, it is difficult to see evidence of any kind. If evolution were continuing, we ought to see countless creatures with physical features in every stage of semi-development. But they are not only absent from the fossil record; they are absent, when they ought to be present, here and now before our eyes. It is no good saying, as people do, "Ah, but evolution works very slowly. That's why you can't see it happening." No matter how slowly it works, the logic of the theory demands a multitude of forms in every conceivable state of semi-development at every moment of biological history.

The only reason people believe in continuing evolution, I think, is that once you have committed yourself to the existence of such a process, it is difficult to explain why it should stop. The biologist Julian Huxley and his friend Fr Teilhard de Chardin tried to get round the difficulty by maintaining that the "evolutionary drive" now expresses itself through human progress. It is no longer bothered with animals and plants. But this is just a supposition to get around an inconvenient fact.

Evolution as Demiurge

The fourth and final idea that people seem to have in mind when they talk about evolution is that something called Evolution with a big "E" is responsible for the whole history of the universe. Under the impulse of this mysterious force everything is continually changing into something different and better, in spite of hiccups like the First and Second World Wars.

---

114. See John Morton, *Man, Science and God*, Collins, 1972, especially p. 16.

At this point we have moved from science to philosophy, even if it does not sound much as if it deserves the name "philosophy." It is really just the Enlightenment's doctrine of perpetual progress biologised and cosmologised.

But what do the apparently unchanging physical and chemical laws which governed the formation of the galaxies, the planets and the Earth have in common with the random process called "natural selection"? Do atoms and molecules vary like animals and plants so that some are "selected" by favourable circumstances for further development and others rejected? Do stars struggle with each other for survival? If not, why include their formation under the concept of evolution? Giving a single name to activities in different fields operating according to different laws should bring a blush to the cheek of any genuine scientist or philosopher.

Evolutionists of this stamp also tend to leave out of their account the evidence for things having in many places moved from a better to a less good state – deserts, for instance, where there were once savannahs and forests. The Earth and the universe often show more signs of running down than being built up. They could be compared to a car, which will one day wear out, but meanwhile has enough energy and staying power to carry its passengers to their destination – a view which seems to chime with the second law of thermo-dynamics and the notion of entropy, not to mention Christian eschatology.

When unbelieving scientists and philosophers talk about evolution as a kind of demiurge responsible for the origin and history of the universe, they are simply bringing in a substitute for God through the back door after kicking Him out of the front door. This is because the universe so obviously has intelligence, design, purpose and foresight written all over it, that it is impossible to talk about any part of it for long without falling into the language of intelligence, design, purpose and foresight.[115] It is equally

---

115. The hidden "vitalism," the assumed, if not admitted, presence within the evolutionary process of a life-promoting drive or "striving to become," which is accepted by people who deny the existence of design and purpose, is elegantly explored by the philosopher E. Tomlin. At the everyday level it is most readily detectable in nature programmes on television where animals or plants are praised or blamed for having adapted well or badly to new challenges, as though each species had a collective mind and knew what it was doing. The problem had, of course, been confronted by the French philosopher Bergson over a hundred years ago. Realising that it is impossible in the long run to discuss the cosmos and its history intelligibly without recognising and trying to explain the apparent directive purpose behind or within the process, he posited his pantheistic *élan vital* or evolving God to explain it.

impossible to think about the thing as a whole without looking for a single ultimate cause, the way Einstein was always looking for a single formula that would explain all physical phenomena. To be forever seeking all-embracing causes is the natural bent of the truly scientific mind. But must not the supreme cause of the universe be something other than the universe itself?

Talking about Evolution with a big "E" enables people to enjoy the luxury of a supreme cause which is halfway between a Something and a Someone, and both "in" the universe while not quite identical with it. It allows them, when convenient, to talk about it as if it had a mind, and when inconvenient, as if it didn't. What matters is that it should not have a *plan*, so that men are left free to run the world as they please.

One sees how wise Pius XII was to warn Catholic scholars to exercise "the greatest caution" when studying the scientific hypothesis and trying to reconcile any authentic findings with the data of revelation; and he could have said the same about the philosophical theory.

It has been one of the Church's misfortunes that the man who made the most ambitious attempt at a reconciliation, Fr Teilhard de Chardin, should have been totally impervious to these warnings.

Chapter Thirteen

TEILHARDISM

It may now be difficult for readers who were not yet adults during the years of Teilhardo-mania, running from about 1958 to 1982 or thereabouts, to understand why I have devoted a whole chapter to the ideas of this eminent theological eccentric. Surely they may well say to themselves, no reasonable person could possibly take such outlandish stuff seriously. So why bother with it any more? Surely his flights of fancy, even if they once captured the imaginations of certain people for a time, cannot have had any serious or lasting effect on ordinary Catholics.

Unfortunately one has to say they have – both on the ordinary and the extraordinary. Many distinguished people, for reasons I will explain shortly, have thought and still think Father Teilhard de Chardin was a world genius, while his mystical evolutionism has profoundly modified the way countless western or westernised Catholics interpret the fundamentals and priorities of their faith.[116]

However, perhaps the best way to present and explain Fr Teilhard's

---

116. Cuenot's *Teilhard de Chardin* (London, Burns & Oates, 1965) was the first major study by an admirer, and the Carmelite Fr. Philippe de la Trinité's *Rome et Teilhard de Chardin* (Paris, Fayard, 1964) the most widely read early critique. The best still available guides to Teilhard's thought I have come across in English are *Teilhardism and the New Religion* (TAN Books, 1988), a detailed analysis of his world-view based on his published writings, by the American mathematician Wolfgang Smith, and *Teilhardism and the Faith*, the masterly little summary and critique of his leading ideas by G. H. Duggan, S.M. Born in Vienna, Smith, after a distinguished research career in aerodynamics, and teaching posts at MIT and UCS, became professor of mathematics at Oregon State University. Fr Duggan was for many years professor of theology at the Marist seminary in New Zealand. Quotations from Teilhard marked (W. S.) and (D.) in the text are drawn from these first two writers. Both give the appropriate references to Teilhard's works. Quotations marked (M.) are taken from Maritain's *The Peasant of the Garonne*, (London,, Chapman, 1968). Quotations marked (T.P.) are taken from *The Teilhard Papers*, I, II & III, published in the American monthly *Triumph*, between November 1971 and January 1972. These contain passages from the letters and the greater part of the text of three essays in which Teilhard expresses his views with less than usual circumspection. Included is the section of *The Human Sense* which, when initially published in 1971, the *Fondation Teilhard de Chardin* omitted.

radical reinterpretation of Catholic and Christian belief is to start with the peculiarities of the man.

The Man

In the first place, like Loisy, Tyrrell, and Brémond, he always had in him a strongly adolescent streak, though of a different kind. If in them we can see symptoms of the *enfant terrible*, Fr Teilhard de Chardin makes one think more of the self-contained adolescent obsessed by a single all-absorbing idea or hobby, the "odd-ball" loner whose deepest thoughts even his parents can never quite plumb.[117]

Born in 1881, Fr Teilhard entered the Society of Jesus in 1899, studied in Jersey and England when the Jesuits were expelled from France in 1902, with a three-year interlude teaching in Cairo, and was ordained in England in 1911. While in England he was involved in the discovery of the fraudulent Piltdown man, though as the faker's dupe, it seems, rather than a conscious collaborator. From 1912 to 1914, he studied palaeontology in Paris. During the First World War, he declined to act as a chaplain, enrolling instead as a stretcher-bearer and receiving the *légion d'honneur* for bravery. After the armistice he was appointed a professor of geology at the Institut Catholique in Paris. He was thus too young to play a part in the first modernist crisis, and throughout his life remained unknown to the general public. But from 1922 – when an essay calling original sin into question accidentally reached Rome – he was a person about whom the highest authorities in the Church were increasingly worried. Had they got a new Galileo or a major heretic on their hands? Opinions were divided. Although forbidden to teach or publish, he wrote prolifically, and these unpublished productions were read by those who mattered.

Since his superiors were anxious to keep him out of sight as much as possible, from 1926 to 1946 he mostly lived abroad, in China and elsewhere, travelling and taking part in anthropological and palaeontological expeditions. In China he participated in the discovery of the Peking man, whose authenticity has also been challenged. The fragments were lost

---

117. The most embarrassing example of this adolescent streak – embarrassing in a supposedly major Catholic thinker – is his "stage-struck" attitude to science. Identifying spiritual progress with scientific progress, he treats scientific research as the highest activity of the human spirit. Science "will absorb the spirit of war and shine with the light of religion." (W. S. p. 163)

during the Japanese occupation; only plaster casts survive. However his collaboration in the discovery led to his being looked on as a palaeontologist of note, and when he returned to Europe in 1946 he was welcomed by a large part of the Parisian intelligentsia like a king returning from exile. What his admirers hoped for, what his vindication, if ever it came, would represent, was the death and burial of Adam and Eve, the Fall, Original Sin and eternal punishment – the "cruel doctrines" as they were coming to be called – along with the baptism of evolution in one or all of the four meanings discussed in the previous chapter. Pressure mounted for him to be allowed to publish his principal works, *The Phenomenon of Man* and *The Divine Milieu*. But the authorities in Rome stood firm. Since he continued to advance his ideas in spite of prohibitions, in 1951 his superiors sent him to the United States, where he died five years later.

After his death an international committee of friends and admirers, *La Fondation et Association Teilhard de Chardin*, started to publish his manuscripts. Books by and about Teilhard, backed by a massive international publicity campaign, poured from the presses. It is true that there were dissenters from the chorus of adulation: Gabriel Marcel and Daniélou both had serious doubts. So did von Balthasar. Gilson called Teilhardism a "theology-fiction" which, if it meant anything, meant "that Christianity ... must disappear." Maritain (after the Council) described it as "a gnostic theogony in the style of Hegel." Von Hildebrand spoke of its author's "crass naturalism," and Cardinal Journet included among the beliefs to which adherence to Teilhardism necessitated saying goodbye:"creation, spirit, evil ... Original Sin, the Cross, the Resurrection, the Second Coming and the Last Judgement" (*Nova et Vetera*, Oct–Nov, 1962). But the critics were in a minority. For the most part the Catholic reading public was taken by storm. *The Divine Milieu* and *The Hymn to the Universe* became spiritual reading for many of the clergy, bishops included, and by the time the Council opened, second- and third-hand Teilhardism was reaching the pews.

On 30th June 1962, the Holy Office in Rome issued a warning against "the ambiguities" and "even serious errors" which, it said, "abounded" in Teilhard's writings. Bishops and others in authority were exhorted "to protect the minds" of those in their charge against these dangers. But the warnings mostly went unheeded. It was generally assumed that Teilhard had reconciled Darwin with Christianity, and everyone breathed a sigh of relief. What the majority did not realise was the extent to which Teilhard had immolated Christianity on the altar of Darwin. This was partly because Teilhard had tailored *The Phenomenon of Man* and *The Divine Milieu*, his two most widely read books, to get them past the ecclesiastical censors; partly because his editors did not immediately publish the essays and letters in which his views appear at their starkest; partly because of his peculiarities as a writer and thinker.[118]

The Thinker

Despite his own and other people's claims to the contrary, Fr Teilhard was only in a minimal sense a scientist; his achievements in this field were, to say the least, modest. Nor was he a philosopher or theologian, though ranging widely through all three fields. He was a visionary. He was not searching for truth. He had already found it. Science, philosophy and theology were called in to make the truth of what he had "seen" credible to other people. But they were not the path to it.

This "truth" which he had seen began to take possession of his mind, it appears, while he was still a boy. Although very intelligent, top of his form in all subjects, says the abbé Brémond, who taught him for a time at his Jesuit school in the Auvergne, it was impossible to arouse the slightest gleam in his eyes, for he was living in another world "utterly absorbed in one overpowering passion." The passion was, at that time, for stones and geology. But around 1914 he discovered "evolution," and from then on evolution – in the sense that nothing is complete, everything is in a state of becoming, God included, God and the universe making up a single evolving whole – became the master idea not only dominating his thought, but receiving something akin to worship and adoration. "Man is nothing else than evolution become conscious of itself...The consciousness of each of us is evolution looking at itself and reflecting..." Man "is at one with and responsible to an evolutionary All." It "can give or refuse itself" (Duggan 28–29). Such is his vision. In *Le Christique* (written a month before his death), he expressed his amazement at the "superiority of what I see, in relation to what I have been taught"

Secondly, he was a missionary. "What increasingly dominates my interests,"

---

118. "Evidently I must find a certain orthodox way of putting things if I am to get across my experience without distorting or weakening it." (D. p. 12, quoting *The Making of a Mind*, Collins 1965, p. 244.) Even critics like Maritain and Gilson were taken in for a time. Maritain, in the main text of *The Peasant of the Garonne*, and Gilson, in an article *Le cas Teilhard de Chardin*, bent over backwards to give Fr Teilhard wherever possible the benefit of the doubt. Later, after reading critiques by Claude Tresmontant and Cardinal Journet, Maritain added an appendix to his book admitting that he had underestimated the extent of Teilhard's departure from the faith. Gilson's final estimate is mentioned below.

he wrote to his cousin Léontine Zanta in 1936, "is the effort to establish within myself and diffuse around me, a new religion (call it a better Christianity, if you like), where the personal God ceases to be the great neolithic proprietor of the past to become the Soul of the World which the stage we have reached religiously and culturally calls for" (*Letters to Léontine Zanta*, Paris 1965, pp. 127–8; in J.M., p. 118, footnote).

Many years later he would astound Etienne Gilson, when they met at a conference in New York, by speaking casually of the "religionless Christianity we've all been waiting to hear about." Gilson was equally non-plussed an hour or so later to see him attentively reading his breviary. "When you can't wait to hear about religionless Christianity," Gilson commented, "why in the blue blazes would you be a Jesuit? And if you already are one, why waste time reading your breviary?" He also noted the curious way Fr Teilhard "snapped to attention" every time the word "evolution" was mentioned during the conference, the way "a priest in choir doffs his biretta at the name of Jesus" (*Letters of Etienne Gilson to Henri de Lubac*, No. 5, Ignatius, 1988).

Initially, Fr Teilhard had had considerable qualms about the project he had embarked on. "Sometimes," he had written in 1922, "I am a bit frightened to think of the transposition to which I have to subject the vulgar notions of creation, inspiration, miracle, original sin, resurrection, and so forth, in order to be able to accept them" (Duggan, p. 18, from *Lettres*, Grasset, Paris, p. 32). But his fears soon seem to have evaporated.

A final peculiarity is his indifference to logic and consistency, and his self-admitted preference for intuition and "sensing." "I do not know of another thinker," wrote von Hildebrand, "who so artfully jumps from one position to a contradictory one, without being disturbed by the jump or even noticing it."[119] It is also frequently difficult to know when he is using figures of speech and when what he is saying is meant to be taken literally. He continually claimed to be writing as a scientist, and therefore about experimentally verifiable material, yet the bulk of his writings are a mixture of philosophical and theological speculation, in which metaphysical and supernatural realities are treated as though they operated according to the laws of physics and chemistry. His one undoubted talent was for conjuring glittering cosmological mirages out of high-flown spiritual rhetoric.

All this made it relatively easy for his admirers, when faced with some

---

119. See "Teilhard de Chardin: a False Prophet" in *Trojan Horse in the City of God*, Franciscan Herald Press, 1967, p. 229. This section also appeared in the English-language edition of *L'Osservatore Romano* for 2 August, 1973.

particularly astounding assertion, to claim that, in the light of alternative passages, it did not really mean what it seemed to mean. However, there was soon enough hitherto unpublished material along with critical studies to show that the more "astounding" assertions represented the deepest level of his thinking, and that when brought together reveal a distinctive system or world-view.[120]

Basically, that world-view is a conflation of Darwin and Bergson with Christ playing the role of Bergson's *élan vital*.

Teilhard's Universe

That everything was moving forward and upward from a state of dispersal and randomness and converging towards a state of organisation and unity was in many ways more important and fascinating to Fr Teilhard than the nature of that final state or the Being responsible for bringing it about. "If I were to lose in succession my faith in Christ, my faith in a personal God, and my faith in spirit," he wrote in 1934 in China, "it seems to me that I should continue to have faith in the world (its value, its infallibility, and its goodness) this is ... definitely the first and the only thing in which I believe" (W.S., p. 129, citing *Christianity and Evolution*, p. 99).

However, it was not quite the world or the universe as most of his fellow Christians have thought of it. Christians have always seen the universe as a harmony of particular things or groups and kinds of things. Within this harmony, each particular thing or group has its own value and place reflecting in some way the goodness and wisdom of the Creator, and all together by their existence and activity sing a hymn of praise to Him.

For Teilhard, no particular thing or group of things has value in itself. Everything is a mere step or stage on the way to something better and more complex, and, once its evolutionary usefulness has passed, can be cast aside without regrets. By temperament Teilhard, like Hegel, was a monist – a thinker for whom vast wholes or totalities are the all-important thing.

What is the universe made of?

Early in life, Teilhard cast aside the distinction between matter and spirit. Matter and spirit are the "outward" and "inward" faces of a single cosmic stuff (*Weltstoff*). In every grain or atom of matter there is already a tiny

---

120. While some of his admirers have tried to maintain that he did not have a system, Cuenot maintains that he did.

germ of spirit, spirit being identified by Teilhard with consciousness. The seeds of spirit or consciousness grow and develop as matter organises itself or is organised into ever more complex units or wholes, according to a supposed law of "complexity-consciousness." This at least seems to have been Teilhard's final position, though he sometimes speaks as though there were originally nothing but matter.[121]

In spite of Teilhard's adulation of matter – "my divine matter" (Duggan 46, from *The Heart of the Matter*) – the emergence of spirit or self-consciousness, out of matter is evolution's basic purpose, a process he calls "personalisation." "All that exists is matter becoming spirit" (W.S., p. 34). The vegetable and animal life enveloping the planet, which he calls the "biosphere" and pictures as a kind of skin, is merely the preparatory phase for personalisation.

However, the appearance of man, or of individual men, is not evolution's final goal. According to a second Teilhardian law, in addition to being a process of "complexification," evolution is even more a process of "unification." Its ultimate aim is to weld all the individual human consciousnesses into a single super-consciousness or super-mind, which he calls the "noosphere," dedicated to the exploitation of the earth's resources through scientific research and technology. When the noosphere is fully formed, humanity will have passed into the "ultra-human." (The ultra-human is Teilhard's substitute for the supernatural.) It is on this final stage – the coming into being of the noosphere – that humanity has now entered.

Actually, if we like to think of the universe as a gradual unfolding of latent potentialities, it is clearly a process of diversification rather than unification. First there was a single life form, then a multitude of different ones. But that is by the way.

Is the noosphere just a world state dominated by scientists (the noosphere's higher brain cells), or are we to envisage a super-person? Many texts seem to favour the second alternative. What, he asks, is "the growing compulsion to think and act collectively which so disquiets us," but "the first portents of the super-organism which," he adds (perhaps sensing the aversion such an idea might evoke in his readers) "is preparing ... not to mechanise and submerge us, but to raise us ... to a higher awareness of our personality" (W.S., p. 178). (This attempt to give the noosphere a more

---

121. The idea, known as *panpsychism*, that there is a fragment of "soul" in everything, already had quite a history. Teilhard gave it a different twist but he was not its originator.

pleasing appearance, however, should be compared with Teilhard's views on its right to use force and compulsion cited later.) Elsewhere he says of it "of all living things we know, none is more really, more intensely living than the noosphere" (W.S., p. 87).

Elsewhere he describes the "noosphere" as a "sentient protoplasmic layer ... an ultimate envelope, taking on its own individuality and gradually detaching itself like a luminous aura." It "is not only conscious but thinking" and "from the time I first became aware of it," he found concentrated in it "the essence or rather the very soul of the Earth" (W.S., p. 89).

Teilhard's God

But where did it all come from and how did it all begin? According to St Thomas, there is a close connection between the way one understands God, and the way one understands creation (ST 1a 32,1 ad 3), and of no one is this more true than of Fr Teilhard, who early came to the conclusion that "since God cannot be conceived except as monopolising in Himself the totality of being, then either the world is a mere appearance – or else it is in itself a part, an aspect, or a phase of God" (W.S., p. 111; S.C., p. 80). He chose the second alternative, calling his system a "superior form of pantheism" and adding that the ecclesiastical authorities were quite right in suspecting as much (Duggan, p. 42).[122]

How then are the two parts of the whole, God and the World, related? His answer resembles the attempts of the Neoplatonists of the 3rd century AD to explain the relationship between the "One" and the "many."

Before the cosmos began, matter, even if of the most tenuous kind, existed together with God in a state of unorganised simplicity. Teilhard calls it "pure multiplicity," "a sort of positive nothingness," or the "scattered shadow of God's unity," which from all eternity God saw beneath His feet," and which "cried out to exist," a cry which eventually God was "not able to resist." This is why Teilhard keeps insisting that "to create is to unite" rather than, as Christianity teaches, to make something out of nothing. What cries out for existence must already have some kind of existence. And if we have any lingering doubts, we have only to ponder texts like "God

---

122. In *Le Milieu Divin*, on the other hand, he goes to some lengths to deny the charge of pantheism. However, anyone still believing that *The Divine Milieu* is anything more than window-dressing or that Fr Teilhard's cosmic vagaries have anything really Christian and Catholic about them should read *The Human Sense*, where his contempt for the Church and the faith are expressed at their crudest.

only completes Himself in uniting Himself" and "what gives Christianity its vitality is not the sense of creation's contingency but the sense of the mutual completion of God and the World" (M., p. 264).

This would seem to be the basis for Teilhard's objection to the distinction between the natural and supernatural orders and explains his famous outburst to von Hildebrand about St Augustine: "Don't mention that unfortunate man. He spoiled everything by introducing the supernatural" (W.S., p. 201).

How then does God satisfy the cry of "pure multiplicity" for fuller existence and His own need for completion? One's immediate impression is of a swimmer diving into a swimming pool. God has "to immerse Himself in the multiple in order to incorporate it into Himself," organising and unifying it from within (M., p. 265). But not after the fashion of an all-powerful intelligent creator. In taking the plunge He is transformed into a blind Bergsonian life-force, groping its way forward by trial and error. We are even told that God "corpuscilises" Himself, as though the divine substance became atomised and mixed with the "multiple" like sugar in salt (D., p. 37). This is why matter, as it develops towards spirit, can be called "divine." It is God's outer crust or the overcoat He is gradually weaving for Himself.

Bizarre as all this may sound, it follows logically from Teilhard's wholesale acceptance of the theory of natural selection. If we are to have God *and* natural selection, God has to create without a plan. We have to rule out "the intervention of an extra-cosmic intelligence" (W.S., p. 21). "God cannot create except evolutively" (W.S., p. 14, quoting C.E., p. 179), and evolution proceeds "only through strokes of chance." In plunging into "the multiple," God becomes subject to the general law of evolutionary development. "Groping is *directed chance*. It means pervading everything so as to try everything, and trying everything so as to find everything" (W.S., pp. 11–14).

This brings us to the origin of "evil." Early in *The Phenomenon of Man*, Teilhard tells us that his book is "nothing but the story of the struggle in the universe between the unified *multiple* and the unorganised *multitude*" (W.S., p. 86). The multiple or many, even if it originally cried out to "exist," has a built-in resistance to the efforts of the One to organise and lift it to a higher state of existence. Evil, we therefore learn, is not due to malice, angelic or human. It is an inevitable side-effect of the evolutionary process. "In our modern perspective of a Universe in a process of cosmogenesis," the problem of evil "*no longer exists*" (sic). Since the Multiple is "essentially subject to the play of probabilities of chance in its arrangements," it is "absolutely unable to progress towards unity without engendering Evil here or there – by statistical necessity" (M., p. 265). So sin in our earliest ancestors (multiple not single) could scarcely have been blameworthy. Even at our present stage of "hominisation" it must be largely a matter of ignorance, incompetence and miscalculation. Evil is even said to be a "sign and effect of Progress" (M., p. 123). If there is such a thing as sin, it is refusal to co-operate with evolution, or opposition to the direction in which the process can be seen to be moving.

At this juncture, however, Fr Teilhard introduced a conflicting idea. It is as though he felt that, reduced to a mere life force, the One would not be strong enough by itself to overcome the intractability of the multiple. He had also committed himself to believing that, not only was evolution a process of unification, everything in it was converging through space and time towards a single point of arrival like the apex of a cone far ahead in the future, an assumption which required a different explanation. So he divides God in two, leaving one half still immersed in its struggle with the "multiple," and placing the other half at the end of the evolutionary process from which it pulls the multiple forwards and upwards by attraction. This he called the "Omega point." The climax of the evolutionary process will be the meeting and unification of the noosphere with the Omega point, at which moment the noosphere passes into the ultra-human. "I see in the World a mysterious product of completion and fulfilment for the Absolute Being Himself." God "in some way 'transforms himself' as he incorporates us" (W.S., p. 104).

Teilhard's Christ

This was the cosmology to which, in Fr Teilhard's mind, the Catholic faith had to be adapted if it was to have any chance of survival.

It was his curious belief that he could demonstrate "scientifically" that the universe was not only a process of "complexification" and "convergence" giving birth to ever higher states of consciousness, all converging on a supreme consciousness or Person, but that this Person must be Christ. Such was the basis of his apologetic towards unbelieving scientists. It is the Eternal Word who, as the "Cosmic Christ," plunged into the Multiple to become the motor of evolution, and simultaneously stands at the end of the process as the Omega Point ("Christ Omega"). So far, scientists have been less responsive to the idea than theologians.

In support of his thesis, Fr Teilhard invoked the Christian doctrines of the Church as the Mystical Body of Christ, and the *pleroma* or final "reconciliation of all things in Christ" after the last day. But he gives them a meaning radically different from the Church's. Teilhard identifies the Mystical Body, not with believers in Christ who adhere to Christ's teaching, but with his noosphere or collective consciousness of the human race's higher elements as it passes into the ultra-human at the end of history. Meanwhile, his *pleroma* or reconciliation of all things in Christ is, in Christian disguise, a Neoplatonic bringing together of the Multiple with the One, or the two aspects of an eternally existing divine/sub-divine cosmic whole.

We can say, indeed, without exaggeration that Fr Teilhard was not interested in Christianity. He retained from his pious childhood a devotion to the idea or "person" of Christ. He was also as a Jesuit committed to preaching Christ. But the teaching of Christ meant nothing to him. The one indisputable truth was Western evolutionary humanism, whose message he even suggests in one place is the voice of evolution itself pointing out the way ahead. The only thing evolutionary humanism lacked was a place for a God of some kind which it was Christianity's privilege to supply. Apart from that Christianity must be totally refashioned. We must "without delay ... modify the position occupied by the central core of Christianity... The 'God of the Above' has to be replaced by a Christianity re-incarnated in the spiritual energies of matter" (W.S., pp. 23–24).

Once this is achieved, "Creation, Fall, Incarnation, Redemption – these great universal events cease to appear to us as accidents dated and distributed over the course of time (an infantile perspective, which is a perpetual scandal to our experience and reason): all four become co-extensive with the duration and totality of the World" (T.P., I, p. 13). Redemption is not the God-Man making satisfaction for sin; redemption means the evolving cosmic Christ gradually overcoming the statistical errors of evolution as he struggles to carry it towards the "ultra human." "It is Christ in very truth who saves – but should we not immediately add that at the same time it is Christ who is saved by evolution?" (W.S., p. 118)

But if from the start, as he says, Christ "was present in all things as a soul that is painfully gathering its embryonic elements," why did he have to appear in the flesh? (W.S., p. 124). In order, it seems, that he could emerge from the cosmic process and take his place outside or at the "end" of it as "Christ Omega," drawing "all things to himself." With the Ascension, He was "raised to the position of Prime Mover of the evolutive movement of complexity consciousness" (W.S., p. 96). However it remains difficult to understand how, if Christ is evolution's Prime Mover, he can also be spoken of as "the end product of evolution, even the natural evolution of all beings" (D., p. 63, citing *Hymn to the Universe*).[123]

As for the Church, his views about it are best seen in his letter of 4th October 1950 to an ex-Dominican who had lost his faith, explaining why he should remain in the Church instead of leaving it.

"Christianity," he tells his correspondent, is "a broad mystical current" with "the astonishing reality of the 'Risen Christ' as its object," which has "extraordinary powers of adaptation and vitality." Nevertheless, among the various channels which have carried the current down the ages, only "the Roman stem" or "phylum," as he calls the Catholic Church, has the biological strength and flexibility (in spite of the contemporary signs of sclerosis) to "carry through and underpin the transformation I look forward to." The right thing therefore is to remain in the Church and "work for a transformation from *within*" (D., p. 66).[124]

It is also noteworthy that although Fr Teilhard had by now become a New Age cult figure, he was far from being a "friend of the earth" or, on other matters, what is now regarded as "politically correct." Many of the private letters reveal a Nietzschean ruthlessness and quasi-Faustian idolisation of applied science belying the gentle smiling face of the photographs.

"In exploding the atom bomb," he says in *The Future of Mankind*, "we took the first bite at the fruit of the great discovery, and this was enough for a taste to enter our mouths that can never be washed away." And was it not further cause for rejoicing that "the greatest of man's scientific triumphs happens also to be the one in which the largest number of brains were

---

123. On this point Teilhard makes conflicting statements. Most of the time he speaks as though Christ only started to exist when evolution began: the universe is in a process of giving birth to Christ (*Christo-genesis*). Elsewhere he talks as if Christ already existed, fulfilling the role we imagined had been assigned to God the Father or the One. "The Redeemer could penetrate the stuff of the cosmos, could pour himself into the life-blood of the universe, only by first dissolving himself in matter, later to be reborn from it." (W.S. 121). However, it would be vain to look in Teilhard for any coherence on this topic, much less a coherent doctrine of the Trinity.

124. Teilhard was both agitated and indignant when he discovered that the recipient of the letter had been showing it around, and his admirers later went to considerable lengths to keep its contents from being known. It seems first to have appeared in print in *Le Concile et Teilhard*, by Maxime Gorce (Neuchâtel, Switzerland, in 1963) then in France in an article by Henri Rambaud in 1965, which was translated into English and published the following year in the English periodical *Approaches* and then in *The Wanderer*.

enabled to join together in a single organism" (W.S., p. 192). But the release of nuclear energy was a mere prelude to the glories lying ahead. These included:"the vitalisation of matter by the creation of super-molecules"; the "remodelling of the human organism by means of hormones"; the "control of heredity and sex by the manipulation of genes and chromosomes"; the "readjustment and internal liberation of our souls by direct action upon the springs gradually brought to light by psychoanalysis" (W.S., p. 194).

A few years earlier he had called the Italian war against Abyssinia a "war of construction." The earth, he wrote to a friend, had a right "to organise itself by reducing, even by FORCE (sic), the refractory and backward elements... In the last analysis, I am with Mussolini" (letter to Maurice Brillant). In the same vein, in *Sauvons l'humanité* (1937), he finds that "fascism opens its arms to the future," it is a "blueprint for the world of tomorrow," and even "a necessary phase during which men have to learn their business as men." French resistance to Germany was "defence of egoism and the status quo" (T.P., I).

After World War II, he switched his support to Marxism. Fascism had proved an evolutionary "groping" in the wrong direction. Marxism and Christianity, he now discovered, were "fundamentally inspired with an equal faith in Man." Was it not therefore "incontestable that they will eventually come together on the same summit?" "In the nature of things everything that is faith must rise, and everything that rises must converge ... we can do no other than plunge resolutely forward, even though something in us perish, into the melting pot of socialisation" or "the stream of the whole in order to become part of it" (W.S., pp. 186–9).

His views about race were of the same stamp. Not all men are equally "hominised," i.e. human. The Chinese, for example, were "arrested primitives .. whose anthropological substance is inferior to ours." Should the "human stratum" turn out not to be homogeneous, it "would be necessary to find for the Chinese, as for the Negroes, their special function which may not (by biological impossibility) be that of the whites" (T.P., III).

The Ethiopians he considered "the survival of a splendid human type – but how ill-fitted, it would seem to follow our forward march..." (January 1929). Then, fearing he had shocked his correspondent, he added "J. will say that I am cruel and not sufficiently Catholic," but "progress implies an unquenchable force that insists on the destruction of everything that has outlived its time." He had earlier anticipated with equanimity the possible liquidation of the Mois of Thailand, "who are so picturesque but belong to a bygone age," along with the surrounding "deer, elephants and peacocks."

"Temperamentally," he added, "I am not disposed to think this way; it is through reflection and deliberation that I passionately welcome the life that is coming without allowing myself to regret anything of the past" (May 1926, T.P., III).

The history of the Western world since the Renaissance is full of intellectuals who liked playing with fire without realising that it burns. Max Stirner, a hen-pecked teacher in a Berlin girls' school, authored the most violent of 19th century anarchist tracts. So we do not have to conclude that, had he had the power to, Fr Teilhard would necessarily have put any of the above ideas into practice. We can say with Nobel-prize-winning Sir Peter Medawar that "before deceiving others, he has taken great pains to deceive himself" (W.S., p. 110). It is also unlikely that his more esoteric ideas were ever widely understood, and by the 1980s he had ceased to be a best-seller. For all that, as I have already said, his influence on the faithful at large was to be profound.

What did they think he was saying? We can begin with the three truths in the overall message. There has probably never been a guru, no matter how deluded, whose entire message has been false, and the fact that these particular truths were not ones the faithful had hitherto been taught to give much attention to goes some way perhaps to explaining their apparently intoxicating effect on them. The first was that the universe is something great and glorious, something that it is a religious duty to admire and appreciate. The second was that the development of nature's resources was, from the beginning, part of God's overall plan. The third was that Christ is to be worshipped not only as God but as Lord of the universe and its history, for whom it has all been created.

As for their interpretation of the rest of the package, it could be summed up as follows. Evolution explains everything. In general, everything is getting better and better and contemporary Western culture expresses the direction in which the forces of evolution are currently moving. The Church should therefore adapt herself to it as much as possible. Her principal task should be co-operating with the forces of progress in building a better or perfect world, which is the same as building the kingdom of God. Many if not most of the Church's doctrines and practices belong to outmoded phases of the evolutionary process and should consequently be abandoned or re-interpreted. On most issues, Western liberalism is right and the Church wrong. Sin is not nearly as serious either in itself or its consequences as we previously thought. "Saving the world" – collective action in favour of material improvements – is as important as or more important than saving souls.

Fr Teilhard's writings created what can be more powerful than a creed. They created an ethos and a mindset. It was to become the mindset of countless Catholics in the post-conciliar period. How could the Council's interpretation not have run into difficulties?

Chapter Fourteen

MOSTLY ABOUT FREUD

We have to include the principal "human" or "behavioural sciences"–psychology, sociology and anthropology – in our survey of "modern thought" if only because they and the Church are concerned with the same subject: men and women as spiritual beings, with the Church taking the higher faculties of the soul (the area of rational free action) as its principal field, while the human sciences study mainly impulsive, conditioned or unconsciously motivated thoughts and behaviour. It would be more accurate to call them the "semi-human sciences." They are genuine branches of knowledge, but they deal with what is least rational in us.

About the value of the human sciences' factual content (when it really *is* factual) no one is in doubt. They have accumulated a mass of useful data about human behaviour and motivation. Nor did the Church wait for the Second Vatican Council to recognise their right to a place in the scientific pantheon. The late Polish Cardinal Wyszynski (d. 1981) was a graduate in the social sciences of the University of Lublin and later a sociology professor. As for the Council, its decree on the training of priests says that the teachings of modern sociology, as well as those of psychology and pedagogy, should be used by those responsible for priestly vocations and by priests themselves in their pastoral work.[125] What the Council fathers assuredly did not expect was that their modest injunction would be interpreted as a command to deluge the faithful with psychological and sociological theories of greatly varying worth.

There is a number of reasons why the human sciences raise problems for the Church. The first is that there are areas where the fields of competence of the priest and human scientist, although distinct, overlap. The same human actions, individual or collective, can include an element of compulsion or conditioning and an element of moral fault.

---

125. See *Optatam Totius*, on the training of priests, arts. 11 & 20. "The Church does not scorn serious study of psychological and sociological elements of the religious phenomena, but firmly rejects the interpretation of religiosity as a projection of the human psyche or the result of sociological conditioning" (John Paul II, General Audience, 14th October, 1999).

Then there is the fact that, while most human scientists insist that scientific inquiry ought to be "value free" – that is to say unaffected by metaphysical or moral presuppositions – there are few who do not at some point stray into the fields of philosophy and ethics. This is in fact true of scientists in general, but it applies above all to human scientists. It could hardly be otherwise.[126] How can you study human beings or human behaviour without forming ideas about what they essentially *are* (a metaphysical judgement) and still more how they *ought* to act (a moral one)? We find many human scientists not only ready to do this, but mostly eager to do so. Unfortunately, however, the "values" of the most significant figures in these fields have seldom coincided entirely with those of the Church.

That brings us to the prevailing ethos of the human sciences. Reflecting the mindset of the leading figures in the field, it tends to be determinist or reductionist, or both. It is hardly necessary to define determinism: all human actions are externally conditioned. Reductionism means believing that there is nothing more to human beings than what one's particular science has to say about them. It is difficult, I think, even for those who are not reductionists or determinists, not to be affected by this ethos.

Finally there is the tendency of the public, from which Catholics are not immune, to regard anything calling itself a science as an *exact* science, which of their nature the human sciences are incapable of being, and therefore to see them as the highest authority on everything human.

In fact, what the Church knows about human beings is far greater and always will be than anything the human sciences can tell us, and that is because she knows from revelation and reason what men fundamentally are, and, from her long experience of shepherding them through history and its trials, how to give them the most important kind of "psychological" health and guide them to their final end. Being a Catholic does not of itself make

---

126. If we look at the question closely, we find all scientific thinking and writing falling into one of three kinds. We can call them descriptive (about things that exist and the way they act or develop); explanatory (about why they are the way they are and act as they do); and finally prescriptive (about the use they can be put to or the way they should be made to act). While it may be possible and even desirable to keep the first two activities "value free," (description and explanation or scientific inquiry in the strict sense), it is impossible when it comes to deciding what is to be done with the knowledge acquired. Only a minority of scientists believe that just because a thing can be done it is always right to do it. Many of the physicists who contributed to splitting the atom were deeply troubled by the production of the atom bomb. Others today have reservations about genetic engineering.

a man a good psychologist or sociologist. But it is arguable that the greatest advances in the human sciences will come only when their practitioners take the Church's knowledge of man as their guiding light.

I will begin with psychology.[127]

From Aristotle to Freud

Psychology, the science of the soul, is not a new science. At least from the time of the Greeks, thinkers and writers have discussed the nature of the soul and its faculties and tried to account for the different types of human temperament and behaviour.

Aristotle's *De Anima* is the first and most enduringly impressive work on the subject. Like St Thomas and the medieval scholastics, he focused mainly on what is common to all men – the virtues and vices, passions and appetites, the way they interact and their effects on the personality as a whole – rather than trying to explain individual peculiarities. The latter task was first tackled systematically by his disciple and the editor of his manuscripts, Theophrastus. Theophrastus' *Characters* was translated into French in the 17th century by La Bruyère who added a collection of "character" portraits of his own. The great playwrights, poets and novelists have also provided a mass of insights into human behaviour and differences of temperament.[128]

Such more or less was psychology down to the late 19th century. It was called "rational psychology" because it dealt with men in a normal state of

---

127. History is usually classified as one of the human sciences. However, it has always been widely recognised that the understanding and writing of history is as much an art as it is a science. Collecting and verifying the facts, the strictly scientific part, is only laying the foundations. For the way historical studies affected the understanding of doctrine and theology in the period after 1920, see Appendix I.

128. Theophrastus and La Bruyère used the word "character" where we should probably use the word "temperament," meaning the qualities and peculiarities we are in some sense endowed with from the start. By "character" we tend to mean what we make of ourselves by our free choices, with or without the help of others. Hence "character building" and "character formation." A weakness of much modern psychology is the lack of any theoretical basis for this important distinction; We build our character with and through our temperament, but sometimes this has to include going against it. The word "personality" seems to embrace temperament and character together. For centuries, the most popular explanation for the differences of temperament was, of course, the theory of the four humours. They were attributed to the prevalence of one of four bodily fluids: blood, phlegm, yellow bile, black bile, the resulting temperaments being named "sanguine," "phlegmatic," "choleric," and "melancholic."

mind. Obviously insanity was recognised, but it was little understood.

Modern psychology was born when, towards the end of the 19ᵗʰ century, the focus of interest shifted from the mentally sound to the mentally and emotionally sick, giving rise to new theories about the nature of the soul and its activities.

However, in order to avoid misunderstanding, before looking at these theories, I want to draw a distinction between the ideas of the famous figures who first propounded them, and the practice of the millions of psychiatrists and psychologists at work around the world today.

Today's psychiatrist has basically two remedies open to him: drugs, increasingly used for serious cases, or talking to his patients and getting them to talk to him. In regard to the latter, the successes, which should not be discounted, would seem to depend in the main on the experience, intelligence and natural wisdom of the individual therapist more than on theory; the wise pick only what they find useful from the different psychological orthodoxies. So criticism of aspects of modern psychological theory should not be seen as criticism of psychiatric medicine in general.[129]

The main point about modern psychological theory is that it is no longer about the soul. The difference between spirit and matter is either not understood or not recognised. "Psyche" has come to mean whatever goes on inside us above the biological level, and "psychology" its explanation in terms of quasi-physical dynamisms. For the modern psychologist, psyche is the equivalent of the phenomenologist philosopher's "contents of consciousness."

In so far, therefore, as modern psychologists do not believe in the soul, or the factors that contribute to spiritual (in contrast to psychological) health and sickness – virtue and vice, sin and temptation, conscience and guilt (genuine, not neurotic guilt), they do not know what the thing they are dealing with essentially *is*. They are like doctors trying to treat people's bodies while ignoring the fact that they have heads.

The main lines of most present-day public thinking on the subject have come to us from the Russian physiologist Ivan Pavlov (1849–1936), and the Austrian and Swiss psychologists Sigmund Freud (1856–1939) and Carl Jung (1875–1961).

---

129. Even the "orthodox" are sometimes compelled to make theory bow to common sense. A strict Freudian I know was once describing a patient she had been analysing and having little success with. "In the end," she concluded, "I decided the woman was just thoroughly selfish."

Pavlov's contribution to modern psychological theory was fairly straightforward. Whether he intended it or not, his "behaviourism," based on his studies of "conditioned reflexes" (his salivating dog must be as famous as Hamlet or Hitler) gave renewed vigour to the notion, already familiar for over a century, that man is just a body and the body a machine. La Mettrie had propagated the idea in his *L'homme machine*, (1747), and the American educationist John Dewey (d. 1952) popularised it with his explanation of mind as "an adaptive function" of the body. Pavlov can be considered the father of modern experimental psychology, which subjects normal as well as abnormal people to tests to see how they will react, with the possibility of finding ways to get them to act differently.

Freud's theories were more subtle, but ultimately no less materialistic. The role of the unconscious as a major determinant of human behaviour was the first of his ideas to revolutionise Western thinking. It was not the discovery of totally unknown territory, but an attempt at organised exploration and deeper penetration through the interpretation of dreams and the association of words and ideas.

The Hidden Depths

Although it was not at once appreciated, this new or increased knowledge of the psyche's hidden depths provided striking confirmation of what the Church has always taught about the effects of original sin: how deeply rooted self-love and disordered desire and passions are, how much of them there is that escapes easy control by the reason, how prone we are to concealing our real motives from ourselves. Modern psychology has stripped the facile optimism of Pelagius and Rousseau of any trace of plausibility once and for all. It has also made everyone more aware of the factors that diminish blameworthiness. We can more easily understand why we are ordered so sternly not to judge, and can say with Christ of our opponents, "Father, forgive them, for they know not what they do," even when they appear to be fully conscious of it. All this can be of help to confessors.

As a therapeutic technique, exploring the unconscious proved beneficial in so far as it uncovered the causes of certain kinds of obsessional behaviour, hitherto incurable: the suppression of long-buried memories of painful past experiences. Bringing them to the surface, it was found, could of itself bring relief or a return to sanity. It was like lancing a boil or purging the stomach. Such is the fundamental idea underlying psycho-analysis, and even much of everyday psychological practice. At a superficial level it has affinities with relieving one's mind by telling one's troubles to a friend. Psychoanalysis no longer enjoys the prestige it once had. But the idea that dredging the unconscious for the causes of particular troubles and bringing them to the surface is good therapy remains influential.

The difficulty has always lain in knowing whether the memories are genuine or due to auto-suggestion or to a desire to please or impress the therapist, and whether exposing them to the air could not in many cases be like pulling the scab off a wound. Then there is the problem of the advice the therapist gives his patient about how to handle himself and his life once he is cured or as part of the cure. Many psychologists would say this is not the therapist's business. But, given the nature of the relationship between therapist and patient, it hardly seems possible for a therapist not to convey to his patients some idea of what he personally believes to be a rational or right way of thinking and living, and for it to have no influence on them. This is where, from a Christian standpoint, a therapist's character, beliefs and principles must be of vital importance.

The fathers of the modern movement had initially, of course, been concerned with serious mental disturbance (madness or psychosis). Freud had moved into psychology after witnessing the cures or partial cures of mentally deranged patients by means of hypnosis worked by Breuer in Vienna and Charcot in Paris, under whom he studied for a time. But eventually he found hypnosis unsatisfactory and developed psycho-analysis as a substitute.

However, once it was discovered that nervous disorders likewise often had psychological rather than physiological roots, they spent more and more of their time treating neurotics. (Although serious neurotics are often victims of strange compulsions, they are emotionally disturbed, but not mad.) Then during the 1920s and '30s, growing numbers of practitioners moved from treating the seriously neurotic to the mildly neurotic (people suffering from unreasonable fears and anxieties), and from there to normal people suffering under the strains and stresses of life (the background to many of today's counselling services).

In the process a distinction was introduced between the unconscious and the subconscious. Not everything below the level of consciousness was to be seen as lying at the same psychic depth. The contents of the unconscious were held to be beyond the knowledge of its possessor. Without a psychologist, it could not be recovered. With the subconscious it was otherwise. The subconscious is to be seen as the region immediately below consciousness where we are continually absorbing impressions, forming ideas, reaching conclusions and even making decisions without adverting to the fact either fully or at all. But the contents are not so deeply buried that they cannot be fairly easily brought to the surface by the owner himself, with or without outside help. It is the region, in biblical terminology, of the heart's "secret thoughts," the place where we can bury unpleasant memories, without this necessarily having seriously disturbing results; or hide "secret designs" of the kind that cause Holy Scripture to speak of the heart's "deviousness."

The subconscious is important for the subject of this chapter because it is the area where psychological counselling and religious guidance or spiritual direction mainly overlap. A man who talks all the time about himself may be partly or largely the victim of a compulsion. It is his way of overcoming a sense of insecurity. Or it may be a moral fault: he is thoroughly self-centred. When St Teresa of Avila said that one of her hardest tasks was getting her nuns to own up to their faults, she was saying neither that they were deliberately lying, nor that they were incapable of discovering those faults with a little effort and good will.[130]

The extension of the psychologist's field of operations that I have just mentioned, had a number of consequences that, for good or ill, were to be important for both Western society and the Church. It helped to spread the theories of the new psychology to a much wider public than would have been the case had psychologists confined themselves to treating the insane. It turned psychologists into universal authorities on how to be happy – or less unhappy. And more important still, it began to obscure public understanding of the difference between psychological illness and health on the one hand, and moral or spiritual illness and health, which in the case of Catholics meant the difference between psychological counselling and spiritual direction.

A little anecdote will illustrate all three points. A priest I know was summoned to the bed of a construction worker fatally injured in a fall from a building. On reaching the hospital he found the family gathered round the dying man's bed. When the priest had given the last rites, he turned

---

130. Alfred Adler tells a story perfectly illustrating the point. A small boy was making his parents' life intolerable. They brought the child to see him. A principle of his therapy was destroying what he called "false good faith," so at the end of the first session he said: "Now there's something I want you to say to yourself every morning when you wake up." The boy's eyes opened wide with curiosity. "I want you to say to yourself," Adler went on, "I must remember to make my parents as miserable as I can today." This time the boy looked at him with amazement. The cure had begun.

towards the wife intending to give her some words of consolation and encouragement. Instead she asked to see a hospital "counsellor."

The reaction of many Church authorities when priests and religious started having crises of faith after the Council tells a similar story. Instead of sending for wise and experienced spiritual directors to get them back on track, they called in psychologists, as though loss or disturbance of faith were a psychological disease. And in a well-known seminary, there was for a long time a course on psychology, but none on the Trinity. This, however, illustrates the prestige of psychology rather than confusion about its proper role.

The reverse side of this coin is the idea, prevalent in the public at large, that men and women who are psychologically well balanced – that is to say, sound in mind, in control of their emotions, and tolerably content with life – have nothing more to worry about. Among Christians it has, I suggest, been one of causes of the decline of the "sense of sin," and in the Catholic Church of empty confessionals.

However, the chief negative consequence of the new psychology's exploration of the unconscious has been the idea that the bulk of people's faults and misdeeds can be attributed to causes over which they have little or no control. People have been seduced into being "non-judgemental," not only about their fellow men, which can be a good thing, but about themselves and the objective rightness and wrongness of actions which of their nature demand an adverse judgement. Even criminals these days, we are told, have learned to blame their crimes on their parents. One result has been a tendency among the clergy to see hearing confessions as an occasion for giving psychological counselling. Of course, people are affected by their upbringings, and a minority are seriously damaged psychologically. Our sympathy for them, however, should not obscure the fact that most men have the ability, with God's help, to rise above bad experiences, and even if those experiences have left a mark, to learn to live with them. Only in extreme cases is the spiritual so completely subordinated to the psychological that a person can no longer be held responsible for their actions.

In the Church, one of the chief sufferers from the increased reluctance to admit responsibility for one's actions, either because of psychological damage in childhood or supposed immaturity, has been the marriage bond.

At a time when men are widely proclaimed as having at last "come of age," more and more annulments are being given by Catholic diocesan marriage tribunals on the grounds that the couples applying for them, even when considered old enough to vote, receive university degrees, fill responsible well-paid jobs handling other people's money, and generate children, were too immature at the time of their weddings to understand the meaning and obligations of what they were doing. Most marriages throughout history have been between couples in their teens. Are we to consider them all invalid? Rome keeps protesting; but little attention is paid.

The Rebels in the Basement

Freud's other contribution to the transformation of Western thinking is, of course, the dominant role he gave to sexual instinct.

His picture of the human psyche is like a house on three floors. In the basement is the libido (a kind of nursery of unruly drives and passions, mostly sexual, clamouring to get out); above comes the ego or central self (source of rational decisions); and over that again lies the domain of the superego – a kind of psychic "top floor" from which the injunctions received in childhood from parents, teachers and other authoritative voices continue to be transmitted, often against the householder's will. (It is like having a stereo which you can't switch off ceaselessly playing in the attic.) The ego appears as a kind of psychic Cinderella between two ugly sisters issuing contradictory instructions. This in its way is not a bad description of how, in our fallen state, we sometimes feel about ourselves.

However, the Freudian ego is not to be identified with the Christian soul, the thing that keeps the human whole together, any more than the superego is to be equated with the voice of right reason or conscience.[131] For Freud, the libido is the substantive part of the human psyche. The ego is merely a psychic superstructure which the libido creates and subjects itself to in order to survive. The libido somehow knows that it would destroy itself or be destroyed by rival egos if it gave free reign to its impulses (murdered

----

131. For Christians, what psychiatrists would designate as the superego would include conscience without being limited to it. Not everything that "authority figures" tell children they should or should not do is a matter of right and wrong. Part of growing up is learning to determine the relative value of the things we have come to accept as in some sense obligatory. That means learning to distinguish between morality and social custom. But, although man-made, social customs have their value too; not all are dispensable like used razor blades or fashions in clothes. They are in large part expressions of natural wisdom, providing a psychologically necessary framework for ordered living or a bulwark against moral anarchy. Unfortunately, too many psychologists regard the psychic "top floor" in a largely unfavourable light. Psychological maturity or health consists in silencing or rejecting its voices.

its father and went to bed with its mother, for instance). So it represses its more disorderly energies and desires and directs them into socially acceptable channels through fear of disapproval. But although now under control, the fundamental nature of these energies remains unchanged. Man is essentially a sexual animal.

From all this, 20th century man has, not surprisingly, concluded that happiness must lie in giving these energies maximum release, and misery or damage to health result from controlling or restraining them. To control is to frustrate. If the post-Freudian world recognises a sin, it is surely "frustration." Even translators of the Bible have not been immune to the idea. Where the older English versions of *Colossians* 3:21 had "Fathers, provoke not your children lest they be discouraged" or "become discouraged" (Douai-Rheims, Authorised, and R.S.V.), the more fashion-conscious translators of the Jerusalem Bible give us "Parents, never drive your children to resentment or you will make them feel frustrated." In an analysis of modern atheism (14th Apr., 1999), John Paul II took issue with the idea that God is a projection of the "repressed image of the earthly father" from whom adults must free themselves if they are to develop properly.

It hardly matters that Freud did not regard sexual licence as a remedy for neurosis, and in his personal life appears to have been a faithful family man. Without Freud's idea that man is a fundamentally sexual being, it is impossible to imagine the degradation of the greatest of natural mysteries into a "fun activity" and a universally discussible subject down to the baldest details, anywhere and everywhere, which is now the distinguishing mark of Western societies. A small language change tells a large part of the story: the use of the expressions "having sex" and a "sex life," for "making love" and a "love life."

The "sexual revolution" that has followed, with its assault on marriage and the family and its policy of explicit sex education embracing every conceivable sexual deviation for younger and younger children, would, without Freud, be just as hard to account for.[132] Once the sexual instinct was presented as the

_____

132. However, it is interesting to note that Freud himself, even though in his earlier years he was in favour of contraception, later came to define sexual perversion as the removal of the procreative aspect from sexual activity: "It is a characteristic common to all the perversions that in them reproduction as an aim is put aside. This is actually the criterion by which we judge whether a sexual activity is perverse – if it departs from reproduction in its aims and pursues the attainment of gratification independently. You will understand therefore that the gulf and turning-point in the development of the sexual life lies at the point of its subordination to the purposes of reproduction.

bedrock of human personality, all this could no doubt have been foreseen.

What could hardly have been foreseen was the speed with which large numbers of Catholics adopted quasi-Freudian ideas about sex after the Council. For some of the clergy, no doubt the way had been prepared by the Kinsey Report of the early 1950s. A proportion, at least, seem to have used that now discredited document[133] to throw what they thought was light on degrees of moral responsibility in the case of sexual sins. But that hardly explains the irresponsible way the faithful were suddenly deluged with ill-considered psychological notions of a kind they had hitherto been taught to eschew, and the wisdom of the ages about handling the "facts of life" was abruptly flung aside like an old plastic bag.

Apparently without thought, young men in seminaries were exposed to courses in which they "explored their sexuality" to find out "who they were," many deciding along the way that celibacy was contrary to nature, probably psychologically damaging, and, except for neurotics, impossible. Guilt came increasingly to be seen as a psychological hang-up. Celibate priests and nuns were put in charge of sex education programmes that would have made Charles II of England and his courtiers blush.[134] Many in authority seem to have forgotten that, in addition to sin, there are "occasions of sin." The Church is now paying the price, not only in lost vocations and lost faith, which is what really matters, but − to compensate for clerical misdemeanours − in cash to the tune of millions. It is unnecessary to dwell on the way all this has contributed to loss of faith among the laity, especially the young.

We also find Freudian ideas being used to keep orthodox young men out of certain seminaries. In a case known to the author, the applicant was asked, by the priest and nun interviewing him to see if he was psychologically suitable, whether "he had ever had a girlfriend." When he said No, he was told to remedy the situation and apply again. Piety and orthodoxy can

---

133. See Judith A. Reisman and E. W. Eichel, *Kinsey, Sex and Fraud, The Indoctrination of a People*, edited by John H. Court and J. Gordon Muir, Huntingdon House, 1990.
134. In the 1980s, the author was asked to take a batch of particularly lurid sex-educational material to the Holy See. The Cardinal who received it sighed and said wearily: "The Holy Father already has a whole pornographic library of stuff like this." Everything that occurs before this conversion takes place, and everything which refuses to conform to it and serves the pursuit of gratification alone, is called by the unhonoured title of 'perversion' and as such is despised." *A General Introduction to Psychoanalysis*, tr. Joan Riviere (New York, Garden City, 1935), p. 277; cited in Janet E. Smith ed., *Why Humanae Vitae Was Right*, (San Francisco, Ignatius, 1993).

also be obstacles to acceptance. They are treated as signs of psychological immaturity. The theory of the Oedipus complex requires a psychologically healthy young man to be to a certain degree rebellious.

With the laity, the logic of Freudian anthropology seems to have fuelled the demand for annulments and opposition to *Humanae Vitae*. If the sexual instinct is the bedrock of human personality, marriage ought to include maximum sexual satisfaction with minimum restriction.

I will not multiply examples and instances. The Church in the West is awash with them. I have given enough, I think, to indicate Freudianism's role in the collapse of Catholic faith and morals.

Chapter Fifteen

MAINLY ABOUT JUNG

Carl Jung (1874–1961) has affected Western thinking differently.

His grandfather was alleged to have been an illegitimate son of the German poet Goethe, and the grandson's capacious untidy mind, roving imagination, voracious curiosity, and love of the mysterious makes him more akin to his alleged forebear than to men of science like Pavlov and Freud. He was also a natural spell-binder. There are numerous reports of the fascination he exercised as a conversationalist and personality. But none of this by itself explains his reputation.

To understand his influence, we have to distinguish between Jung the psychiatrist and Jung the spiritual guru and founder of a quasi-religious cult. It is in the latter capacity that I am concerned with him here. No other famous modern psychologist has mixed up psychology and religion to the same extent.

As a psycho-therapist, Jung began to explore the unconscious around the same time as Freud, and together they founded the psycho-analytical association of which Jung was for a time president. But in 1912, believing that Freud was over-emphasising the role of infant sexuality, Jung broke away and founded his own school of analysis.

For Jung the therapist, the human psyche was a realm of complementary and sometimes conflicting opposites, and the goal of his therapy was to reconcile or integrate them in a way that allowed each of them adequate room for expression. He called the process "individuation." To him we owe the terms "complex" (for a cluster of subconscious or semi-conscious hang-ups); "introvert" and "extrovert" (for the two most common psychological types); "animus" and "anima" (for the masculine and feminine personality traits supposedly present in each individual); "collective unconscious" (for the genetically transmitted memories of racial experiences which he believed each of us carry with us along with drives having their origin in personal experiences), and "archetypes" (for the images through which those collectively acquired drives or ideas express themselves).

Using these principles and ideas, the great majority of Jungian therapists are said to have about the same rates of success and failure as analysts of other schools and to know little about their master's more bizarre religious ideas.

If they are aware of them, they mostly presume them to be symbolic ways of describing psychic phenomena. This is partly because of the volume and obscurity of much of Jung's writings, partly because he only confided the full range of his religious theories to an inner group of initiates, and it is only recently that those ideas have been coming fully to light.[135] They strike a very different note.

As the father of a religious cult, Jung was a typical representative of the *fin-de-siècle* decadence which I described in Chapter 20 of *Turmoil and Truth* as one of the factors influencing early modernism. From adolescence on he was fascinated by oriental religions, gnosticism, magic, Hermeticism, alchemy, spiritualism and the occult. He was also influenced by Wagner, Nietzsche and the Germanic movements and cults reviving Teutonic paganism in the thirty years before the First World War.

Eventually, combining the fruits of his wide reading on these subjects with his experiences as a psychiatrist, he put together what a distinguished ex-Jungian has described as "a mystical pagan polytheism in which the 'multiple images of the instincts' (Jung's most concise definition of the 'archetypes') are worshipped as 'gods.' "[136] Just as many of the mystery religions of the ancient world re-enacted the descent of a hero into the underworld, from which he emerged purified after a series of tests and battles with subterranean powers, so the adepts of Jung's path to salvation reach their goal after battling with spiritual powers in the depths of the unconscious. Of these "the terrible Mother," representing the principles of matter and the earth, is the most fearsome.

Did Jung himself see these powers as purely psychic phenomena? Or did he attribute an objective reality to them? The answer seems to be the latter. Throughout his life Jung dabbled in spiritualism and believed in a spirit guide he called Philemon.

In Jungian religion and spirituality, the instincts and drives of the unconscious appear as reflections within the individual psyche of the

---

135. See Richard Noll, *The Jung Cult*, Princeton University Press, 1994, and *The Aryan Christ*, London, Macmillan, 1997. Dr Noll is a clinical psychologist and post-doctoral fellow in the history of science at Harvard. Ever anxious to protect his reputation as a scientist, Jung tended to give more or less place to his religious ideas depending on the audience he was addressing.

136. Dr Jeffrey Satinover, a former Jungian analyst, graduate of the C. G. Jung Institute in Zurich, and one-time president of the C. G. Jung Foundation of New York. The citation is from his long letter-article in *The Wanderer* for 27 July, 1995, quoting liberally from Jung's followers and admirers.

activities of transcendental beings, who, like the gods and goddesses of Greek mythology are always fighting and quarrelling with each other. The role of the Jungian neophyte is to conquer and tame them so that from their union can emerge the higher being whom Jung calls the Self (with a capital "S"). As in Hermetic philosophy, the One God is born from the union of the many. The Self is the "God within" or "the God-image in Man" that Jungians are always urging us to make contact with. But, as will be seen, it is not the God of Judaeo-Christian revelation; it seems to be closer to the "Universal Self" or "World Soul" of Hinduism, through which the enlightened man discovers that in his ultimate self he is God too.

Two other things are to be noted. Jung's psychiatry aims at reconciling complementary facets of the personality which are good in themselves – things, for instance, like masculine vigour and feminine tenderness, or the need to balance work with play. His religion aims at reconciling good and evil. In forcing the warring instincts to lie down together like the lion and the lamb of Scripture, the Jungian neophyte, like the Nietzschean superman, passes beyond good and evil into a realm where these categories no longer apply. For Jung the spiritual guru there are no evil instincts or passions. What we call "evil," Jung would call the dark side of life, and darkness is just as necessary a part of existence as light. All instincts and drives are in theory good. I say "in theory," because Jung would certainly not have recommended robbery or murder as socially acceptable forms of behaviour. What he chiefly seems to have been preoccupied with was the free enjoyment of sensual pleasures without feelings of guilt which, like other cultivated Europeans of his period reacting against strict Protestant upbringings, he erroneously appears to have regarded as the hallmark of pagan antiquity.

It is therefore not surprising to find his religion containing a decidedly erotic element. This he justified in terms of alchemical theory and practice. In the reconciliation of complementary opposites, or good with evil, he saw an analogy with the alchemist's blending of base metals to produce gold, a work which, in alchemical literature, was often carried on with the help of a "mystical sister" (*soror mystica*) and culminated in a mystic marriage from which was born a bi-sexual being or "androgyne."[137]

---

137. It is ironic that Freud, who is associated above all with sex, should have been more chaste than the reputedly "spiritual" Jung. For my account of Jung's "religion," I am indebted chiefly to Dr Noll and Dr Satinover. The latter's masterly article enables one to see the jungle of Jung's religious ideas in perspective.

In a Jungian context, the analyst would be the alchemist, his patient (if a woman) *the soror mystica*, the climax of the analytical process the mystical "marriage," and the fully individuated person resulting therefrom, the bi-sexual offspring – bisexual because giving equal expression to the masculine and feminine sides of the psyche. That, in practice, the mystical marriage could have a physical side seems to be well established. "Jung himself, and a small number of his closest disciples," Dr Satinover tells us, "had found a way to live out not only symbolically but explicitly the core practices of occultism." Jung's principal *soror mystica* was his mistress for 40 years.

All this explains why Dr Satinover can say that most Jungian analysts have no idea what they "have been fellow travellers to" and that "the occult ideas embedded in Jungian theory and practice, even taken symbolically, tend to undermine moral standards." The psychology, as it were, floats on top of the "spirituality," absorbing some of the "brine," as the hull of a wooden boat would absorb sea water.

Jung and Christianity

Jung was also, beneath a lot of seemingly fair words, deeply anti-Christian. As an expression of psychological and spiritual realities, he considered Christianity greatly inferior to the gnostic, Hermetic, occult ideas on which his own theories were based. Descending from the shamans of the remotest times, known to the mystery religions of the ancient world, repressed by Christianity for two thousand years, those ideas had survived in the teachings of heterodox sects but could now be directly tapped by psycho-analysis and the interpretation of dreams. Here, rather than in Christianity, lay the deepest wisdom of the human race.

Christianity was a grossly patriarchal, "misery" religion. There might be value in some of its symbols and doctrines, but to be of any use today they would have to be radically re-interpreted. "The Christ-symbol lacks wholeness in the modern psychological sense," Jung tells us, "since it does not include the dark side of things but specifically excludes it in the form of a *Luciferian* (sic) opponent."[138] To rectify the situation Jung, at one point, suggested including the Blessed Virgin in the Trinity. To be psychologically correct, the Trinity must have a shadow side. It must be a Quaternity rather than a Trinity. And this, without knowing it, was what the Church had made it with the dogma of the Assumption. Mary had been taken into the

---

138. See Satinover, *op. cit.*

Trinity to become the necessary fourth person. The Church's only mistake was making her a symbol of purity and light. Jungians should see her as the principle of maternal darkness.[139] Other reinterpretations have a typically Manichean ring. In his *Essay on Job*, Jung represents the Lord God as a senseless tyrant indifferent to human misery. Eventually, under the influence of his second wife Sophia or Wisdom (Jung gives the Lord two wives: Israel is wife No.1) God repents and becomes a man to atone for his sins.

"What Jung foresaw as a possible future for Christianity," writes the eminent Jungian analyst Murray Stein, "would in many ways be continuous with Christian tradition, but also very different from it...The New Testament would become for the transformed version what the Old Testament became for Christianity, a prefiguration and forerunner of the new revelation."[140]

It would be truer to say that Jung not only foresaw the transformation of Christianity, he intended it and worked for it. He did not mean his psychologised neo-paganism to remain the preserve of his intimates for ever. With or without a Christian veneer, he intended it for the spiritual regeneration of the whole world.[141]

By a different road to the early modernists, Jung arrived at much the same goal. Since religious knowledge wells up from the subconscious and speaks to the conscious mind in myths and symbols, there is no need for a public revelation, a Church, or sacraments – except in so far as they are themselves useful as symbols.

How much should all this be, or have been, a matter of concern for the Church?

Thirty years ago one would probably have said "very little." Jung was never

---

139. Jung's reinterpretations of Christianity are taken from an unpublished paper by Dr Pravin Thevathasan MB BS MRCPsych MSc, of Shrewsbury, England. See also, David Wulff, *Psychology and Religion*, John Wiley and Sons.

140. Satinover, *op. cit.* In 1912, Jung, according to Noll, called for "an intrapsychic overthrow of custom, a revolution in the internalised European traditions that enslave the individual personality." (Likoudis, *The Wanderer*, 29 December 1994.)

141. Noll, *The Jung Cult*, p. 254. For Jung's belief that he had received a special call for this work, see Philip Rieff, *The Triumph of the Therapeutic*, (Harper Torchbook), pp. 112–113. The author describes how, at the age of 12, Jung had a series of dreams, culminating with God dropping an enormous piece of dung on Basel cathedral and crushing it. Jung later described the incident, which gave him a prophetic sense of mission, as, in Rieff's words, his first and formative "experience of grace," and interpreted it as a call to "help those like his father, who suffered from the failure of the Christian miracle of grace, to a new grace." The father had committed suicide.

a household name the way Freud became. His appeal was initially limited to spiritually uprooted middle-class Europeans and North Americans looking for a meaning to life, with a smattering of Christians like the English Dominican Fr Victor White, an early enthusiast for Jungian psychiatry. Jung's early Christian admirers do not seem to have appreciated the extent to which his psychiatry was a wrapping for a rival religion. However, in the 1960s the situation changed dramatically. As the number of spiritually uprooted Westerners soared, so did Jung's following, both inside and outside the New Age Movement. Ten years or so later, religiously disoriented Catholics started moving in the same direction.

Since the late 1970s, writes Dr Satinover, "Jungian and Jungian-related spirituality, with its emphasis on gnostic 'wisdom,' sexual freedom, eastern mysticism, pantheism, goddess worship and accommodation with evil has infiltrated deeply into the churches (especially in the Anglican and Roman communions)," and a stream of newspaper reports over the last decade and a half are there to confirm his words. According to the US journalist, Paul Likoudis, "Catholic spirituality as it is taught in the majority of US dioceses is almost entirely Jungian"; advertisements for retreats show that a high proportion are Jungian inspired; the best selling books on spirituality in many Catholic bookstores are by popularisers of the Jung cult.[142]

A spirituality that is truly Jungian is, of course, no longer Catholic. Catholic spirituality aims at helping the individual draw closer to God, with the help of grace, through self-forgetfulness, the practice of virtue and mortification, and submission to God's will. The goals of Jungian spirituality are self-enhancement, self-fulfilment and inducing feelings of psychological well-being. The former lifts the soul into the supernatural order, the latter, in so far as it has any contact with reality, leaves it firmly planted in the natural or exposed to the praeternatural.

Catholic education is also suffering from injections of Jungianism. In *A New View of Religious Education* [Twenty-Third Publications] we find an American author, Dr Kevin Treston, advising teachers to "compose a prayer service with the theme 'the Earth our Mother,' telling them that "Christians are being challenged to listen to and celebrate the divine revelation in the various religious stories and traditions of the world" and asking, "Have you noticed that our myths and symbols are disintegrating?" This is pure

---

142. Likoudis, *The Wanderer*, Dec–Jan 1994–5. "The Kordes Enrichment Center, run by Benedictine sisters in the diocese of Evansville, U.S.A., has programmes with titles like, 'Discover how to heal yourself through dream analysis,' 'Nurturing spirituality and sexuality,' and 'Dreams and spiritual growth.' "

Jung. As an English reviewer shrewdly comments, "to these people, symbols means sacraments and myths doctrines."

English Catholic teachers are receiving similar doses of Jung mixed with New-Ageism. In a talk given under diocesan auspices, by a priestly "social scientist," Fr Diarmuid O'Murchu, a member of the Sacred Heart Missionaries and author of a book titled *Reclaiming Spirituality*, a group of teachers were told that "official religion" is "not merely inadequate; it may in fact be a great delusion, based on the inflated patriarchal instinct of a power-crazy species. We need to shed the whole thing with its trappings of dogmas, ritual, laws and regulations." In contrast, "Witchcraft, totemism, shamanism, divination merit a fresh evaluation ... to dismiss worship of sun, moon or elements of nature as primitive pagan practices highlights the appalling spiritual ignorance of 'civilised' humanity."

After reading stuff like this, one does not find Richard Noll's verdict, that Jung represents the greatest threat to the Catholic Church since Julian the Apostate, as startling as one might otherwise. Gently correcting Noll, Satinover calls Jung "the greatest threat ... since the father of gnosticism, Simon Magus, with whom and his disciples Basilides and Valentinus, Jung openly and explicitly identified both himself and his work." One can at any rate say that, faced with a choice, Jung's "spirituality" looks more dangerous than Freud's crude atheism.

It is perhaps indicative of the disoriented state of the Western intellectual and spiritual life that Alfred Adler (1870–1937), Freud's other early disciple/associate, who, like Jung, eventually broke away and founded a school of his own, should be the least known and least influential of the three pioneers.

Adler did not construct a grand system like Freud and Jung. If less imaginative, his grasp of basic realities was firmer, and although for most of his life he had little time for religion, he was not hostile and his ideas are more adaptable to Christian use. Life, he maintained, presents us with three tasks: family, work and social living. Neurosis is the result of running away from them, and successful therapy is getting the patient to face up to them. The ego, not the libido, is the really important part of the psyche, and the will to power, not sex, is the dominant subconscious drive. Reinforcing the ego, the rational self, was the heart of his therapy.[143]

---

143. According to Fr. Louis Bouyer, before Adler died, he "arrived at a religious and Christian conversion through practising an individual psychology that was speculatively modest, but wholly honest in practice." *The Invisible Father*, Edinburgh, T.& T. Clark, 1999, ch. II, pp. 35–36.

Some Later Figures

After its initial launching by the original triumvirate, modern psychology produced numerous different schools and talented freelances, of which, for present purposes, I only need mention two: the developmental psychology of the Swiss, Jean Piaget (d. 1980), and his Canadian disciple, Laurence Kohlberg, and the humanistic or non-directional psychology of Carl Rogers (d. 1987).

Piaget was an experimental psychologist mainly concerned with the mental development of children and their real or supposed capacity to take in or not take in different kinds of ideas and information at different ages. At each age or stage, the mind is said to produce its own special "cognitive structure," and trying to feed it with matter appropriate to a cognitive structure not yet in place is like trying to push software into the wrong kind of computer. From this the conclusion has been drawn by many Catholic educators that children are incapable of absorbing ideas of right and wrong or moral obligation until relatively far on in childhood, and should therefore not be taught about them till the necessary psychological equipment is supposedly in place. According to Piagetian principles, it can also be argued that small children do not have the cognitive structures for learning about the Trinity.

Kohlberg's chief contribution was maintaining that morality develops spontaneously and if it is to develop properly must above all *not* be taught. The teaching of specific moral principles he dismissed as "indoctrination" or the transmission of "a bag of virtues." Instead of instructing, teachers must help to stimulate children's moral understanding through reflecting on their own experience. Kohlberg was not a Catholic, but he was discovered by the generation of Catholic educators hit by the first tidal waves of post-conciliar misinterpretation.

Among the most influential writers of catechetical texts to apply these ideas to the teaching of faith and morals was Kohlberg's Canadian follower, Christianne Brusselmans, whose catechetical texts have been widely used on both sides of the Atlantic. In Brusselmans' books, the children are to reach their own ideas about morality through learning about peace, justice, sharing, caring and love, etc. Her text on preparing children for first Holy Communion, *The Gold Book*, teaches them that the Eucharist is about celebrating, making peace, listening, caring, sharing a meal, in which they receive a very special bread.

Piaget's and Kohlberg's theories also underlie the refusal of certain priests to teach children how to make their first confession before they make their first Communion. Often the children have lapsed before the appropriate "cognitive structures" are judged to be in existence, and so they never learn how to go to confession.

The American Carl Rogers, on the other hand, is famous for the large numbers of religious vocations he helped to destroy in the late 1960s and the '70s.

Starting as a disciplined therapist of strict Lutheran upbringing, he established his reputation in the Chicago area in the 1940s and '50s among mildly troubled or neurotic mid-Westerners, who, like Rogers himself, still had some religious principles. With people like this, his method and message worked well enough. By listening to whatever his patients said, without expressing approval or disapproval, Rogers made it easier for them to open up and, in doing so, to get back on the right track more or less by themselves. He had no arcane theories like the Oedipus complex or collective unconscious to confuse them with. Later, he headed a research team in Wisconsin. Meanwhile he had been pouring out books. By 1960 he was the best-known psychologist in America. Then in 1963 he moved to California, and California transformed him. From being principled and responsible, he became in the words of one critic a "70-year-old teenager"; in those of another, "one of the most important social revolutionaries of our time." The roles are not incompatible.

By this time his interests had switched to what he called "Therapy for Normals" (TFN), that is to say ordinary people without psychological problems. They might be normals, but Rogers believed that his non-directional therapy, by releasing the full "human potential" inside them, could turn them into "supernormals." In other words, he was moving out of psychology into spiritual direction or character formation.

To implement the idea, he invented the "encounter group" or "sensitivity session." In an encounter group, people explore their feelings together to discover "their real selves." The irony is that this is just what normal people, as long as they remain normal, don't usually want to do. They sense there is something unhealthy about it, and the results proved them right. Rogers' encounter groups were a recipe for turning large numbers of hitherto normal people into sentimental nincompoops or sexual libertines. Rogers was initially disturbed by the results, but pushed on nevertheless. The trouble was that he did not believe in the obvious fact that everybody's "real self" contains a great deal that is not very nice. He did not, in other words, believe in evil. Also his basic message had changed. "Be your real self" no longer meant "Do what you know is right," but "Do what your real self wants to do," and "anything you have been trained or told to do by someone else is not part of your real self." It is surprisingly like Jung's message without the sophisticated underpinnings. Fame and folly had turned Rogers into one of the founders of the permissive society, and fathers of the "ME generation." As a psychologist, he is no longer esteemed as he was. But the consequences of the revolution he helped to work remain.

This was the situation when, between 1965 and 1967, the heads of Catholic religious orders and organisations in America started calling on Rogers and his assistants to help them carry out the reforms called for by Vatican II, which had just ended. They had been told to renew their institutions in the light of the charisms of their founders. That for this purpose they too turned to psychologists rather than theologians or spiritual directors is revealing. "Dozens of Catholic religious organisations" received the Rogers encounter-group treatment.[144] They included Jesuits, Franciscans, and a raft of women's orders. The results were catastrophic. Priests and nuns, first by the score then in hundreds, discovered that their response to God's call had not come from their real selves. Some had affairs with each other or their therapists. Others left their orders without more ado. Demands to be laicised multiplied. Within about a year and a half, a well-known and respected women's teaching order was reduced to rubble: numbers dropped from 615 members to a bare two dozen; of their sixty schools, only one remains. Among Jesuits "the third way" was seriously discussed. The third way was proposed as a legitimate alternative to marriage and celibacy; it meant priests having girlfriends.[145]

Rogers' ideas have been influential in the field of catechetics as well. In his *Freedom to Learn* (1969), regarded as the Bible of "humanistic"

---

144. For this account of Rogers' ideas and career, see William Coulson: (1) "The Californication of Carl Rogers," in *Fidelity*, November 1987, and (2) "We Overcame their Traditions," in *The Latin Mass*, January–February 1994. Dr Coulson was for eight years Rogers' closest assistant.

145. In humanistic psychology, "the proof of authenticity ... is to go against what you were trained to be, to call all that phoniness, and to say what is deepest within you... What's deepest within you, however, are certain unrequited longings, including sexual longings. We provoked an epidemic of sexual misconduct among clergy and therapists." (Coulson, *op. cit.* 2). The encounter group has been one of modernism's most effective weapons in its campaign against Catholic faith and morals. As a method of changing people's attitudes and ideas it has proved quite as effective as machine guns and bombs in modern warfare.

education, he delivered himself of the following opinion: "To my mind the best education would produce a person very similar to one produced by the best psychotherapy," by which he says he means "an exploration of increasingly strange, unknown and dangerous feelings in oneself, this exploration proving possible only because the individual gradually realises that he is accepted unconditionally."

Bad psychology has also afflicted the Church outside the English-speaking world. In the late 1980s, a renewed exodus from the priesthood began in Germany provoked by the priest-psychotherapist Eugen Drewermann and his book *The Clergy: Psychogramme of an Ideal* (1989). This and Drewermann's 35 other books, said to have sold over a million copies, appear to be a blend of Jung and modernist biblical scholarship. The doctrines of the Church "have a symbolic character." They "are not expositions of facts external to man but contain a reproduction of his inward experience." They put us in touch with "an absolute person," through "images that are inherent in our spirit." However they are much better expressed by other religions. We would be more "truly Christian" with a good dash of ancient Egyptian religion. As for the Catholic Church, it is an institution "of constraint, repression, de-personalisation and the destruction of feeling." [146]

The Drewermann case is interesting not because Drewermann has anything at all new to say – it is mostly threadbare stuff – but because of the support he has had from middle-class German Catholics and the weak response of the majority of the German hierarchy. Archbishop Dyba of Fulda, who spoke of Drewermann's "profound apostasy," seems to have been one of a minority. For Bishop Lehmann of Mainz (now Cardinal), the head of the German Episcopal conference and a leading theologian, Drewermann was "right in his attempt to rescue the treasures hidden in biblical faith" and he subsequently rebuked German theologians for "having failed" to follow Drewermann's lead.

The Church's Voice

As I explained at the beginning of the last chapter, the chief purpose of this brief survey of psychological theory and its impact on Catholics is not to write off psychology completely, but to show where it is lumbered with erroneous philosophical, ethical and religious ideas which it badly needs to shed if it is to reach its full potential as a science.

---

146. Guido Horst, *30 Days*, No. 4, 1992.

The first Pope to recognise this fact officially was Pius XII. The boom in psycho-analysis following the end of World War II had just begun. During the 1950s, he tackled the subject in four addresses (14th September 1952, 13th April 1953, 2nd October 1958, and 10th April 1958). He was mainly concerned to defend free will and moral responsibility.

While the Church "looks with satisfaction on the new psychiatry," he said, psychiatrists must "not lose sight of ... the obligatory precepts of ethics." Our psychic dynamisms "are not irresistible ... nature has entrusted their direction to the centre-post, the spiritual soul ... which is normally capable of governing these energies." Nor, "without further consideration" should psychotherapists treat inhibitions of the ego "as a kind of fatality." "Every man must be considered normal until the contrary is proven ... Abnormal psychological conditions are not always of compelling force."

In dealing with the limits of research and treatment, he cautioned against unrestricted exploration of the patient's sexual life. A "man is not free to arouse in himself, for therapeutic purposes, each and every appetite of a sexual order." Nor may he suppress at will the religious spirit, self-esteem, modesty and decency. The therapist, on his side, when faced with "material sin" (what is objectively sinful whether or not the patient realises it is such) cannot remain neutral. A therapist cannot counsel a patient to commit serious sin on the grounds that it would be without subjective guilt. Moreover, in regard to guilt, morbid guilt must be distinguished from real guilt. "No purely psychological treatment can cure a genuine sense of guilt." In the case of real moral fault, the means of eliminating it do "not belong to the purely psychological order."

The Pope also addressed the wider question of the origins of religion. Referring to the possibility of a psychic dynamism directing man towards God, he said that, should its existence be demonstrated, it would merely confirm St Augustine's words: "You have made us for yourself, Lord, and our hearts are restless until they rest in Thee." However, he rejected the idea that such a dynamism was the basis of religious belief. "We know," he said, "that ... the natural and supernatural knowledge of God and the worship of Him, do not proceed from the unconscious or subconscious, nor from an impulse of the affections, but from the clear and certain knowledge of God by means of His natural and supernatural revelation."

However, any results that the Pope's admonitions may have had at the time when they were made, were quickly undone by those who took the lead in interpreting modern psychology to the faithful after 1965.

The beginnings of a restoration of sanity, at least in regard to sex and its significance, started in the early 1980s with John Paul II's allocutions at his Wednesday general audiences, in which he developed his "theology of the body." Removing sex from centre stage, the Pope returned it to its rightful place as the physical expression of a fundamentally spiritual, because personal, union, and in doing so restores its dignity. The message still has to permeate to parish level. But when it does, it will, I believe, have a tremendous attractive power for men and women in flight from the world-wide "Playboy"/"Playgirl" culture and mentality.

Chapter Sixteen

MAN IN THE PLURAL

The influence of sociology and anthropology on Catholic thinking and the development of neo-modernism has not been proportionate to that of psychology, but it has been significant nevertheless. The clergy have probably felt it most. For instance, in July 1999, John Paul II told a group of visiting Irish bishops that "a sociological rather than a theological concept of the Church" was responsible for calls in Ireland for an end to priestly celibacy. Basically, this means losing sight of the Church's supernatural dimension.

Sociology and anthropology, unlike psychology, are relatively new sciences whose rise in the later 19th century can be partly attributed to loss of the idea, after the end of the age of reason, that it is natural for men to live together in society, or indeed that there is such a thing as "nature." If God made men and women for each other, along with the power to generate new human beings with a need for food, shelter, companionship and the exercise of their faculties, then social living and everything that flows from it – the tribe, the nation, government, agriculture, architecture, crafts, etc. – become self-explanatory. But if there is no God, no nature and no ultimate reason for things, if nature is a football field of interacting faceless physical forces, a whole host of questions arise which hitherto hardly seemed worth asking. Why do men live in society? Why do societies vary? What keeps them from falling apart? Is one form as good as another? Are fundamental forms like the family necessary, or can we organise ourselves in any way we please? What are the main causes of social change? Are there discernible laws of social change?[147]

The destruction of traditional social forms which started with the French Revolution, or their transformation by the Industrial Revolution, also contributed to the rise of sociology. What was to replace the institutions that were, one after the other, being swept away or found no longer socially useful?

Some of these questions had already been addressed by thinkers not usually classified as sociologists: men like Montesquieu, Rousseau, Saint-

---

147. As the sociologist Peter Berger has put it, with secularisation, social life has become "problematic" (Berger, *Sociology: a Biographical Approach*.)

Simon ("the science of man is the new religion"), his one-time assistant Auguste Comte (who coined the name "sociology" for his science of man which, in his "positivist" religion, was to take the place of theology), Herbert Spencer, and, of course, Marx and Engels. The Catholic thinkers de Maistre, de Bonald and de Tocqueville are also included among the forerunners. But all these men were more social and political philosophers than sociologists in the modern sense.

Sociology as a science in its own right begins with the attempt to study social life and institutions with all their variations and changes as though it could be an exact science like physics or chemistry, beginning with the amassing of sociological facts, then seeking to explain them as far as possible in terms of non-rational causes and general laws.[148] Also included were the study of collective thinking and collective behaviour. If chemicals could be put under the microscope, and physical bodies rolled about on inclined planes to discover the laws determining their movements, why could not men in the aggregate be treated in a similar way? I am talking about an attitude of mind, rather than an explicit agenda. The term "social physics" had already been suggested as a name for the new science.

The amassing of facts can be seen in works like Frédéric Le Play's study *Les ouvriers européens* (1877–99) and Booth's *Life and Labour of the People of London*, (1892–7). However, the Germans Ferdinand Tönnies (1855–1936), Max Weber (1864–1920), and Georg Simmel (1858–1918), the Frenchman Émile Durkheim (1858–1917), and the Italian Vilfredo Pareto (1848–1923), an economist as well as a sociologist who relied heavily on mathematics, are generally regarded as the true founders of sociology.[149]

In his *Gemeinschaft und Gesellschaft* (1887) Tönnies distinguished between societies and communities. All major social problems were due to the shift from the communal, status-based, concentric societies of the past to the individualistic, impersonal large-scale societies of the industrial period. Communities, whatever their faults, have a human quality. They are "natural." Societies, which are artificial, tend to be inhuman. The lament finds echoes in Weber, Simmel and Durkheim. Not that any of them thought a return to the past possible. But somehow the impersonal modern industrial society must be made more human and communitarian. Simmel

---

148. In so far as human beings are rational and free, their behaviour is not, of course, subject to laws. There are only tendencies varying in strength.
149. Le Play was an exception. He did not believe in universal progress or evolution, which is not the same as saying he was indifferent to particular social evils.

stressed the relative helplessness of the individual in modern society. Weber, who opposed German foreign policy during World War I and helped draft the Weimar constitution, had earlier favoured imperial expansion in the hope that it would make the German middle classes more responsible. For Durkheim the ultimate aim of sociology should be directing people's behaviour towards "greater solidarity."

And here, right at the start, we come on the dilemma at the heart of sociology. If it was to be a pure science, it had to confine itself to providing facts and explanations of facts, leaving it to other authorised or more or less competent bodies – governments, industrialists, manufacturers, social reformers, even, if need be, churches – to decide in what way the facts and explanations should be applied in order to remedy evils or promote the good, which is how many sociologists have always seen their task. The extent to which legislation to improve working and living conditions has been made possible by accurate social studies hardly needs stressing.

In a different field, the late 1960s and early 1970s saw Catholic sociologists beginning to raise questions about the wisdom of some of the liturgical reforms from a sociological standpoint.[150] Down-playing the Catholic character of Catholic institutions (universities, schools, hospitals) by certain Diocesan bureaucracies has been criticised from a sociological standpoint too. According to sociologists, in order to survive and flourish over a long period, every community needs a "plausibility structure" – the technical term for a network of organisations and practices embodying the community's particular beliefs or convictions, which together make up the community's cultural and spiritual "home." This is above all true of religious communities. They cannot live permanently in a cultural vacuum, or, without radically adapting it, in a culture of someone else's making. In other words, the assault on the "Catholic ghetto" (the dissenting theologians' term for the Catholic "plausibility structure") violated a fundamental sociological principle. Pope John, it will be remembered, had merely asked for the windows of the "home" to be opened a bit wider.

However, a much larger number of sociologists, including the fathers of the discipline as we have just seen, have believed that it was up to them not only to provide explanations but to have the final say in how their findings

150. See Victor Turner, *The Ritual Process, Structure and Anti-structure*, Ithaca, 1969; Mary Douglas, *Natural Symbols, Explorations in Cosmology*, London, 1970; David Martin, *Two Critiques of Spontaneity*, London, 1973. By the 1990s they had been joined by Anglican theologians of the "Radical Orthodoxy" movement.

should be used. More than that, as believers in progress and evolution, many of them had strong views not only about particular social problems but about the way society as a whole should be organised, or its direction pointed. Human behaviour and institutions may be largely determined by extra-human factors, but they are very definitely not to be left as they are. From its first appearance, sociology has been the most "prescriptive" of the sciences. In other words, what in the name of "value-free" science had supposedly just been pushed out of the front door (metaphysics and ethics) almost immediately came in again through the patio windows at the back in a different form.

Thus, with the advent of sociology, there came into being an awesome new force for good and ill not unlike atomic energy – its rise and existence being itself a sociological fact as much in need of analysis and discussion as social class or class conflict, and not a little of its attraction lying in the sense of power it gives. When it comes to applying their "values," sociologists have always had the advantage over the ordinary citizen of being armed with information and techniques that make it far easier for them to win the ear of the authorities or people of influence. To such an extent is this the case that political conservatives have often seen sociology as an instrument of revolution. Sometimes it has been. Revolution apart, "social engineering" is now a recognised activity indulged in by governments and by pressure groups like NGOs, mostly with only an appearance of public consultation. As far as the changes themselves are concerned, each has to be judged on its own merits.

It is not possible or necessary here to describe the different schools and approaches (at least a dozen) which immediately appeared once sociology had established itself as a recognised science, but they tended to fall into one of two classes: those which focused on societies as stable self-regulating systems, like the human body, adjusting themselves gradually to irregularities and new conditions (organismic or structural functional sociology); and the social action schools preoccupied with change and conflict. Both types have run side by side throughout sociology's now roughly one hundred and fifty years of history, fluctuating in fortune according to events in the outside world.

The majority of sociologists in the United States, which dominated the field from the early 1920s to the early 1960s, in spite of sociology having initially been a European product, favoured the functionalist approach. The Chicago school, and later that of Talcott Parsons at Harvard, promoted a deterministic, positivistic (only observable facts exist), supposedly "value-free" sociology, which chimed with the pragmatic side of the American temperament and the relative stability of American institutions. Neither school was of course really value-free, but the members at least paid deference to the idea of scientific objectivity.

In Europe, the political upheavals of the inter-war decades (1918–1939) restricted interest in the new discipline, but it revived with the return of peace in 1945 under socialist and Marxist influences, which invaded American sociology in the 1960s. This and other social-action currents like feminist sociology, a product mainly native to America, were unashamed in declaring that, for them, objectivity was subordinate to ideology. Sociology was to be a tool for advancing causes higher than that of any science. Largely because it suited them, their approach was also less deterministic than that of hitherto mainstream American sociology. This was true even of the Marxists, whose Marxism derived more from Frankfurt than Moscow. They made more room for human free will and individual initiative as causes of social change and handmaids of revolution.

The main thing that both sociological approaches had in common was an almost exclusive preoccupation with advanced Western societies.

Meanwhile, anthropologists had been studying traditional, tribal or primitive social groups. This more or less fortuitous division of labour persisted until after World War II. Anthropology was also, originally, more truly "value-free." Societies were studied for what they were. One might be more interesting than another. But all social forms – except perhaps eating enemies, burning widows, and things of that sort – were regarded as equally legitimate, and worthy of conservation. Anthropologists might believe in evolution, but they were against social change for primitive societies or cultures. It was like preserving coelacanths and other threatened species.

The anthropologists' approach, in other words, was descriptive and explanatory, rather than "prescriptive." The studies of South Sea islanders by the American anthropologist Margaret Mead (1901–1978) are typical examples. But these raise the question of whether even the descriptive approach can always be value-free. Her account of some of the islanders' easy-going sexual habits was long taken as proof that marriage is just a man-made construct, and promiscuity a harmless social alternative. On some issues, to be ethically "neutral" can itself be the announcement of a "value."[151]

---

151. Some of Mead's successors in the field have claimed she was dishonest in her presentation of the facts, subordinating facts to theory.

However, after World War II the boundaries between sociology and anthropology began to dissolve, their fields of study became more alike, and psychology (under the name "social psychology") was called in to throw light on the obscurer social motivations.

The study of social groups, whether primitive or advanced, also of course includes the study of their cultures; not just the way the members organise themselves so as to live together in harmony, but everything they think, make and do. On this topic, sociology and anthropology today give conflicting messages.

On the one hand, there is a tendency to present each civilisation or culture as a fortress, whose members can barely communicate with the inhabitants of other fortresses. We can call it "cultural compartmentalisation." Each culture, Hindu, Arabic, Confucian, Native American, has its own private way of thinking and expressing itself. The best its inmates can do is shout basic messages across the intervening space between fortress and fortress. Anything but basic messages will be unintelligible. Cultural compartmentalisation is the result of defining man in terms of what is *accidental* to him (his tribal habits), instead of what is *essential* to him, and is the same everywhere. We have already met it at the time of early modernism in the supposed opposition between the Greek and Hebrew minds – an idea that still finds advocates in spite of the evident accord between both types of mind in the later biblical Wisdom literature.

Contrasting with cultural compartmentalisation is "multi-culturalism" or cultural pluralism – the notion that, even over the long haul, a single state can embrace a variety of different cultures without serious strains and stresses and without an overarching master culture. Cultural pluralism is proposed as the sociological ideal for Western societies with large immigrant populations. It is promoted partly in the interests of social harmony, and that is where its appeal lies. But it would be naive to think that was the only motive. For dedicated Western secularists, cultural pluralism is seen as a way of clearing away the surviving remains of Christian thinking, practice and legislation throughout the once-Christian West.

But can a society survive if the component cultural groups retain enough spiritual vitality to maintain what must often be conflicting viewpoints? Deliberately to foster cultural differences would seem to be a recipe for creating social problems. The notions of pluralism and community do not sit easily together, in spite of so often being promoted by the same people. The essence of a community is that the members think and feel alike to a large degree on what matters most to them. A nation made up of communities thinking and feeling differently will therefore not itself be communal.

An example from England will illustrate the point. Arranged marriages have long been a part of Pakistani culture (and, of course, of many others) and quite a number of English Pakistani parents still decide who their children shall marry. This can include sending a son or daughter back to Pakistan to a pre-chosen spouse there. Meanwhile, English feminist groups are agitating against the practice. Whether they are right or wrong is not here the point. What the feminists are saying, and it is what Western liberalism as a whole is saying, is that we approve of your culture provided it does not conflict with Western liberal principles; or, in other words, as long as its expression is confined to trifles and externals – like headgear or special foods. The doctrines of the Enlightenment are to be the informing principles of the overarching culture in Western societies.

In fact, neither cultural compartmentalisation nor cultural pluralism in their extreme forms stands up to examination. All the evidence suggests that cultures can only remain fixed and stable where there is a degree of isolation, a truth recognised by Chinese governments over a period of 3000 years: members of alien cultures were "foreign devils." Indeed without some kind of isolation it is difficult to see how distinct cultures could come into existence in the first place. But this does not mean that the "structure" of the human mind is not the same everywhere, or that, given time and good will, mutual comprehension remains impossible. Indeed, once cultures come in contact, cultural borrowings are the rule rather than the exception. They may be superficial (like the adoption of tea-drinking by the English in the 17th century) or profound (like, say, the influence of transcendental meditation in the 20th). If profound, they will eventually give birth to a new culture, in the way Byzantine culture emerged from the Graeco-Roman.

In these cultural transformations, cultural "pluralism" seems to be a transitional state owing to foreign invasion or mass immigration. Here, unless one of the cultural components is strong enough to predominate, giving some kind of shape to the whole, the body politic is likely in the end to split apart, or the dominant culture, in absorbing large elements of the lesser culture, will once again be transformed into a new culture.[152]

---

152. The two principal blind spots of Western liberals are their reluctance to face these obvious cultural facts and their refusal to recognise that they themselves represent a powerful all-engulfing culture demanding general assent to its fundamental premises, whether expressed in good activities like famine relief, evil ones like abortion, or absurdities like prosecuting people for not being kind enough to bats.

How has sociology influenced Catholics? Its main effect since Vatican II, one regrets to say, has been to "secularise" Catholic thinking to a degree even greater than did deism in the 18th century. By "secularise" I here mean creating a frame of mind which looks at the Church and the faith from a primarily natural standpoint, tips it overwhelmingly towards a concern with natural things, and relies mainly on natural means to achieve spiritual ends.[153] Sociology has this effect more than psychology, if only because the human psyche is of its nature more mysterious than human society. It is much easier to think of the latter as a piece of machinery to be operated by levers.

That some such result was likely unless sociology was humanised and Christianised, had already been seen by the far-sighted group of American Catholic sociologists who in 1938 founded the American Catholic Sociological Society, a body sufficiently effective to influence figures as eminent as Pitirim Sorokin at Harvard. Since the 1920s, "thousands of sociology courses," mainly secularist and deterministic in outlook, had been taught to "millions of American students" throughout the States, with an impact on its culture at large which was bound in the end to affect American Catholics unless countermeasures were taken.[154] These pioneers had recognised what had in fact been apparent from the beginning, that

---

153. The word *secular* (belonging to the present world or age in contrast to the world to come) and its derivatives *secularise, secularism, secularity*, can have a neutral, an a-religious, or an anti-religious connotation. Secular humanists reject God and the supernatural. A secular or secularist state refuses to give public recognition to a particular religion or the existence of God. *Secularise* can mean seizing the property of religious orders and turning out their members. But it can also have the meaning I have just given, and the terms "*secularity*" or "*secular* realities" are today used in an orthodox Catholic context to mean things and activities belonging to the natural order, or not having a directly religious significance. The natural or secular world or order obviously cannot exist apart from the supernatural order. But a distinction between them is dictated, among other things, by common sense, and recent attempts to do away with it have ended in pantheism.

154. See "Secular Sociology's War Against *Familiaris Consortio*," Joseph A. Varacalli, in *Proceedings of the Fellowship of Catholic Scholars' Convention*, 1992. Dr Varacalli is a founder member of the recently inaugurated Society of Catholic Social Scientists which has taken up again the work of the earlier Society, and publishes *The Catholic Social Sciences Review*. Ironically, according to Varacalli, the situation for Catholic sociologists has improved since the arrival of the more ideologically oriented schools, whether Marxist, feminist or "post-modernist." Realising that the idea of a "value-free" science of man has to be self-contradictory, they are more willing to recognise the possibility of a specifically Catholic sociology than their older mainstream counterparts are.

a sociology not embodying a philosophical or anthropological standpoint is an impossibility. Unfortunately, their efforts to get this fact across were aborted in the wake of Vatican II. To the new Catholic "knowledge class" opposed to the magisterium – ranging from certain Church bureaucrats and social activists to various teachers of theology and philosophy – the idea of a specifically Catholic sociology, that is one based on a Catholic view of what human beings are, had become taboo. They embraced mainstream American secular sociology as though it were a pure science. In the process, the Catholic Sociological Society died for lack of support.

Today, we are told, "the sociology departments of both the major and minor Catholic colleges and universities in the USA do nothing more than reflect and propagate an anti-Catholic world-view on the family and all other aspects of social existence."[155] Even in a school or college where the catechetical instruction or theology is orthodox, the work is often partly undone by a secularised sociology course.

Outside the educational world, the secularising influence of sociology is best seen, I think, in the reliance of Church bureaucrats on sociological surveys and the relish with which they apply them.

One example out of a multitude is the Australian bishops' costly 500-page survey, *Woman and Man: One in Christ Jesus*, published in 1999, purportedly the results of an attempt to discover what the faithful think about the role of women in the Church. Leaving aside its aspect as a piece of attempted social engineering – it aims at creating the impression that the majority of Australian Catholic women feel "pain and alienation ... anger ... marginalisation ... powerlessness, irrelevance, and lack of acknowledgement in the Church" – all it actually revealed after three years of labour was what had been manifest for thirty years without any resort to statistics. The vast majority of church-going Australian Catholic women do not feel the way the church bureaucrats want them to.[156]

Underlying the whole project, moreover, is a theology or mindset completely at variance with that of Vatican II, namely that, unless you have a

---

155. Varacalli, *ibid.*, p. 164.

156. *Catholic World Report*, October, 1999. The U.S. bishops had earlier embarked on a similar project. In 1992, after 13 years, and the consultation of 75,000 Catholic women, they wisely abandoned the project. The fact that objections are often raised to spending money on enhancing the beauty and dignity of divine worship (silver instead of pottery chalices, for instance – the money should be given to the Third World) but not to expenses of this kind, is further evidence, I suggest, of a general de-supernaturalisation of outlook.

Church-funded job of some kind, you are not "participating" in the Church. To which one could add that any Catholic woman, or man for that matter, who feels aggrieved at being "powerless" has missed the whole point of Christianity. To be powerless is to be blessed. What such people need is not church jobs, but spiritual guidance and religious instruction.

The deference paid in certain American Episcopal circles to the opinions of the American Catholic sociologist, Fr Andrew Greeley, is another example of the de-supernaturalising effect of a secularised sociological outlook. In 1987, Father Greeley in collaboration with Bishop William McManus published a volume called *Catholic Contributions: Sociology and Policy*. The purpose of this statistical survey was to discover why Catholics were giving less money to the Church. The best answer the authors could come up with was dislike of *Humanae Vitae*. For a sociologist like Fr Greeley, opposition to *Humanae Vitae*, it appears, constitutes an irremovable sociological datum which can only be circumvented by submitting to its opponents' demands. One would have at least expected the bishop to see that the reasons for declining financial contributions were supernatural not sociological in origin. The Catholics opposing *Humanae Vitae* had begun to lose their faith. The Catholics who had kept their faith were not going to give money to a priest or bishop they considered heterodox.[157]

In so far as the parish clergy have been affected by the secularised sociological mindset, it will have been through mandatory courses on updating the Church, radicalised Justice and Peace commissions, or the teaching of pastoral theology in liberal seminaries.[158]

Owing to Pope John's statement that Vatican II was to be a mainly pastoral Council, pastoral theology has received much greater emphasis than in the past, with, in liberal seminaries, a heavy psychological and sociological input not excluding a knowledge of some of their manipulative techniques. The secularised sociological mindset may not have been the principal cause of the vanishing "sense of the sacred" leading to the vandalisation of churches and indifference towards holy things, but it has unquestionably contributed to it. Where it prevails it is as though a steel shutter had come down, not just hiding the supernatural world from view, but rendering it

---

157. Varacalli, "Sociology, Catholicism, and Andrew Greeley," in *Lay Witness*, June 1992.
158. Pastoral theology is not theology in the normally understood sense. It could be called "applied theology" or how to get the Church's message across in practice. It includes learning how to administer the sacraments, prepare people for marriage, visit the sick, comfort the dying, and so on.

largely unreal.

The conflicting messages of sociology and anthropology about culture have chiefly affected missionaries. There have been two tendencies. Those influenced by the "compartmentalist" approach have tended to attribute a kind of metaphysical substantiality to each culture which must remain untouched as far as possible.

This has given rise to the idea that each area of the world must have its own special theology or version of the Catholic faith, its own completely distinct liturgy, and the preservation of any pre-Christian practices deemed essential to its culture. At more than one Synod in Rome there has been pressure for the Church to allow polygamy on the grounds that polygamy is a fundamental expression of the African soul.

This is the reverse of "inculturation" as the Church has hitherto understood and practised it, and can lead to the faith and liturgy being submerged in the local culture and transformed out of recognition in the process. It is, of course, right that missionaries should love the people they have come to evangelise and appreciate what is good in their culture, but not that they should conduct a love affair with it. Successful inculturation is not something likely to be achieved either rapidly or by Church bureaucrats according to a plan.

Addicts of cultural pluralism, on the other hand, tend to be cultural egalitarians. There are no higher or lower cultures, or if there are, it is rude to mention the fact. This can lead to denigrating or undervaluing the cultural achievements of the Church's past, above all the fact that ancient Jewish culture and Graeco-Roman culture must always have a pre-eminent place in any authentic presentation of Christianity because they were the vehicles chosen by God for divine revelation and its earliest explication in the teaching of the Fathers.[159]

Seeing that, until the present century, religion has been the heart of every known culture, the pluralist and egalitarian cultural mindsets have also contributed to the spread of religious syncretism (i.e. the notion that all religions are valid vehicles of salvation).

Fr Karl Rahner laid the foundations for this particular deviation, whose implications have since been more fully developed and expressed

---

159. The point appears to be better appreciated in Africa than in Europe. In 1990, a Senegalese bishop told the Episcopal Synod in Rome on Priestly Formation that in his seminary the students learned Latin and Greek in order to get as near as possible to the mind of the Fathers to whom, as recent converts, they felt especially close.

by the Sri Lankan theologian Tissa Balasuriya, who objected to the idea of Jesus as "unique universal redeemer," and by the French theologian, Jacques Dupuis SJ.

In his *Towards a Christian Theology of Religious Pluralism*, (Maryknoll, N.Y., Orbis Books, 1997), Fr Dupuis argues that religious pluralism is "part of God's plan," that all religions are valid paths to salvation, that all are directly willed by him and all are converging towards the same end. They exist "*de jure* and not merely *de facto*." To make his point he quotes Fr Schillebeeckx. "The multiplicity of religions is not an evil which needs to be removed, but rather a wealth which is to be welcomed and enjoyed by all." Is Christianity the one absolutely *true* religion? "Talk about absoluteness" should be avoided, Fr Dupuis tells us, because "absoluteness is an attribute of the Ultimate Reality of Infinite Being which must not be predicated of any finite reality, even the human existence of the Son-of-God-made-man. That Jesus Christ is 'universal' Savior does not make him the 'Absolute Savior' – who is God himself" (p. 282). The words "universal" and "unique" can have a relative meaning. There are other "universal" saving figures. "The principle of plurality" rests "primarily on the superabundant richness and diversity of God's self-manifestations to humankind" (p. 387). One is left wondering about Baal worship and the Aztecs.[160]

On 28th January 2000, John Paul II intervened personally. In an address to the Congregation for the Doctrine of the Faith, at the end of a four-day meeting of the plenary assembly, he insisted that the Christian revelation is "definitive and complete" and spoke of the "errors and ambiguities" regarding the uniqueness and universality of Christ's salvation, which, he said, were spreading. "Therefore," he went on, "the theory of the limited character of the revelation of Christ, which would find its complement in other religions, is contrary to the faith of Christ ... it is erroneous to consider the Church as a way of salvation equal to those of other religions, which would be complementary to the Church, although converging with her toward the eschatalogical Kingdom of God" (*Tablet*, 5th February 2000). On 6th August 2000, these strictures were confirmed and reinforced by the important document from the Congregation for the Doctrine of the Faith

---

160. Archbishop D'Souza of Calcutta has expressed his support for Fr. Dupuis, his regret that Rome is investigating his theology, and his belief that "those who still build walls around the faith" will "rob it of the rich insights which it can get from the sharing and interchange with the Spirit's presence outside" (*The Tablet*, 21 November 1999). For Balasuriya, see *The Tablet*, London, 11 May 1999.

on the uniqueness and universality of Christ's salvific office, *Dominus Iesus*.

Coming back to cultural egalitarianism, in contrast to religious egalitarianism, there is no reason, I believe, for anyone to take offence at the idea of there being higher and lower cultures, if they think seriously enough about it. The Germanic and Scandinavian tribes from whom most northern Europeans today are descended had little if anything to boast about in the way of culture before they met Rome and Christianity. This did not prevent Tacitus from recognising that they had virtues which the more cultured Romans lacked, or hinder God from choosing the "least of all peoples" to be the cradle for the salvation of the nations.

Chapter Seventeen

WORDS AND THEIR MEANING

Linguistics, semantics, and the *philosophies of language* – the study of the way we use words to communicate with each other – may seem topics too recondite to have much relevance for the theme of this book. But we have only to recall that divine revelation and the Church's teaching are conveyed through words, to realise that new theories about the significance of words as signs or vehicles of meaning could well affect the faith of Catholic scholars, whose business it is to concern themselves with these matters.

And in fact, as I hope to show shortly, that is exactly what has happened. Following in the footsteps of some of the most prominent exponents of this branch of study we find certain Catholic theologians arriving at the conclusion that it is impossible to reach certainty about anything except strictly scientific propositions.

In so far as the above-mentioned subjects have helped to make us more careful about how we use words or more sensitive to their meaning, they have done and no doubt continue to do a great service. However, taking the work as a whole, they have often ended by making the expression of what we want to say seem more difficult rather than easier.

Starting with *linguistics*, the scientific study of the way languages are formed, hang together, change and are related, we could call it old-fashioned grammar and philology under a new name. However, it is grammar and philology conducted with some rather new premises and with a greatly extended territory. For one thing, it is no longer assumed that God endowed man with speech from the start. Man started as a brute and his first words were grunts. How then did words evolve, and their stringing together grammatically as speech? How, too, are they related to our thoughts?

Certain leading ideas can be found as far back as the French philosophers Condorçet (1743–1794) and Maine de Biran (1766–1824), but the Swiss linguist Ferdinand de Saussure (1857–1913) is generally considered the father of modern linguistics, in which we find two not mutually exclusive tendencies.

One is to see language as a kind of mathematics with laws and a life of its own which dictates our thoughts to us rather than being the medium of their expression. Without words, so the argument goes, it is impossible to formulate our thoughts, and if we can't formulate our thoughts, we can't know what we are thinking. But words come to us from the language group we are born into. Our thoughts are therefore always expressed in a form not of our own making.

This was, for a long time, a ruling idea in "pure linguistics," but was modified by Noam Chomsky (b. 1928), who gave "deep structures" (unformed thoughts) priority over "surface structures" (language). He recognised that thoughts come first. Gilson also defended the primacy of thought over language. In his *Linguistique et philosophie* he points to the simple fact that we often have to cross out and rewrite a sentence several times before it accurately expresses our thinking. The thought is there before we find the right words in which to clothe it.

The second tendency has been to regard language as a system of signs reflecting patterns of behaviour or needs. The human animal plays "language games"; for each set of activities it arranges, it uses the signs in a different pattern (a basic idea in socio-linguistics). Lawyers play one kind of game, computer programmers another. Worship has its special pattern, differing from that of medicine. Each is a reflection of the way groups of individuals "structure" their lives.

Neither tendency, one has to say, does much justice to the primary purposes of language: to mirror reality and convey our ideas about it from one mind to another.

This brings us to the next step in the story. It was out of these studies and theories about language as a system of signs, their use and history, that the philosophies of language or language analysis grew up. The philosophies of language stand in somewhat the same relationship to linguistics as physics to metaphysics. Linguistics provides the matter about the significance of which philosophers then speculate. They study the meaning of what we say, rather than the medium through which we say it.[161]

Originating with the Cambridge thinkers G E Moore, Bertrand Russell and Ludwig Wittgenstein before and during World War I, linguistic philosophy was then taken up and developed by the Vienna Circle of Moritz Schlick (d. 1935) and Rudolf Carnap (1891–1970), the founders of *logical positivism*. In 1935, Carnap emigrated to the United States where he became professor of philosophy at Chicago and then at UCLA. The later Oxford

---

161. *Semantics*, which studies the relationship between words and their meaning in a more technical way, is, in so far as it can be considered a distinct discipline, the stepping stone between linguistics and linguistic philosophy.

school of analytical philosophers (with Ryle, Ayer and J L Austin among the best-known names) spread the ideas of the Vienna Circle in England.[162]

Heavily influenced by logic, analytical philosophy has little to tell us about the human person, the user of language. It "is more characterised by styles of argument and investigation than by doctrinal content. It is thus possible for people of widely different beliefs to be practitioners of this sort of philosophy..."[163]

One of the purposes, if not the main purpose, of the Vienna, Cambridge and Oxford schools was to clarify the meaning and use of words for the benefit of science and mathematics, and this no doubt is where the value of their contributions chiefly lies.

Unfortunately, most of their members were unvarnishedly hostile to metaphysics and religion. Not only, they maintained, do ordinary people not know what they mean most of the time; the same has been the case with the majority of philosophers. When metaphysical statements are properly

---

162. Some people see Gottlöb Frege (1848–1925), as the "father" of linguistic philosophy. A professor of mathematics at Jena, who tried to construct a universal mathematically based "ideal" language incapable of error, he influenced both Russell and Wittgenstein. When it was found that language cannot be made to work with the precision of mathematics, Wittgenstein (c. 1930) turned to ordinary language. Frege, together with Boole, de Morgan, Russell and Whitehead, was also one of the founders of modern logic, a subject too technical to go into here. But opponents of St Thomas sometimes draw arguments from it against his proofs for the existence of God. They are said not to satisfy the requirements of modern logic. If this is so, one is inclined to think either that modern logic is demanding more than is required for this kind of proof (mathematical strictness) or that it has some more work to do.

163. "Twenty Opinions Common Among Modern Anglo-American Philosophers," Elizabeth Anscombe, in *Persona, verità e morale*, Rome, 1986. The paper circulates privately in English translation. Anscombe, a Catholic, was Wittgenstein's pupil and literary executor. The twenty opinions Anscombe finds "implicitly or explicitly among analytic philosophers," are all ones she finds inimical to Christianity. They include the following: "There are no absolute moral prohibitions which are always in force." (No. 8). "Calling something a virtue or vice is only indicating approval or disapproval of the behaviour that exemplifies it ... Evaluations or 'value judgements' are not as such true or false." (No. 10). "It is necessary, if we are moral agents, always to act for the best consequences." (No. 13). "God, if there is any God, is mutable, subject to passions, sometimes disappointed, must be supposed to make the best decisions he can on the basis of the evidence on which he forms his opinions." (No. 19). "The laws of nature, if they can be found out, afford complete explanations of everything that happens." (No. 20). For Wittgenstein, science cannot explain everything, but about what in its nature it is incapable of explaining we must remain silent.

analysed, most of the problems that have vexed philosophers throughout history simply melt away. The words they use, when unverifiable by the senses, are meaningless. Philosophy has in fact nothing positive of its own to say about the world. It can only clear the ground of metaphysical rubbish before the advancing triumphal chariot of empiricist science. Under this aspect linguistic philosophy represents the last ditch stand of the anti-metaphysical tradition, attempting, like Hume, to conjure philosophy out of existence.

In England, the ideas of the Cambridge school reached a wider public through the writers and artists known collectively as the Bloomsbury group, with which Moore and Russell were associated. It included the satirist Lytton Strachey, the novelists Virginia Woolf and E M Forster, and the economist John Maynard Keynes, Franklin Roosevelt's adviser at the time of the New Deal. A typical Bloomsburyite retort to a commonplace remark like "What a pity we are having such bad weather" was likely to be "What exactly do you mean by 'weather' " or "Why do you call it bad?"

When therefore today we hear a theologian telling us that the Church is re-examining some part of its moral teaching to discover exactly what it means, or that the word "person" in reference to the Blessed Trinity has to be reconsidered in the light of modern knowledge, and years of research may be necessary before experts come up with an answer, we are not just hearing the voice of a single disoriented ecclesiastic, but echoes from linguistic analysis.

The late Cardinal Siri of Genoa has given us an interesting summary of the opinions of the German-speaking world's premier theological "problem child" on this subject. "The Church could never formulate sure propositions to define her faith because 'she will have to reckon with the problematicity inherent in all propositions in general' and no truth can ever be conceived and expressed with certitude." According to the new philosophy of language "the propositions of faith are never the direct word of God," they "do not correspond to reality," they "are only relatively translatable," they "are in motion," they can be "ideologically exploited" – even "the proposition 'God exists.' " "It is thus," the Cardinal concludes, "that Hans Küng expounds in five points his creed on the impossibility of ever having a sure creed."

The words in single quotes in the above paragraph are Küng's own.[164]

---

164. *Gethsemane, Reflections on the Contemporary Theological Movement*, Joseph Cardinal Siri, English translation, Chicago, 1981, pp. 270–1. The Cardinal is quoting from the Italian edition of Fr Küng's *Infallibility*, pp. 114–118. Fr Rahner, more cautious than Küng, seems no less anxious to keep the Church from speaking with authority. "In the future," he says "the magisterium will only be able to issue very few doctrinal

Among the thinkers Küng cites in support of his views, in addition to existentialists like Heidegger, Jaspers and Merleau-Ponty, are Wittgenstein, Frege and Chomsky.

We are here at the very heart of the modernist theological enterprise. Pope John, it will be recalled, had said that the Church's teachings were to be expressed in ways suited to modern man but always with the same sense and meaning, while Fr Küng and his friends had wanted from the outset to alter the meaning of much of that teaching. Now in Chomsky's "surface" and "deep structures" he seems to have believed that he had found the right excuse for his stance and tool for his task.

Where does meaning reside? As I pointed out towards the end of Chapter 1 of *Turmoil and Truth*, everyone knows you can usually express the same ideas or concepts in different words. That was precisely what Pope John had in mind. But can you express the same reality with a different idea or concept without finding you are thinking or speaking about a different reality? Can one think of a replacement for the *idea* of justice that still retains the *meaning* of justice?[165] Küng, who wants the meaning of ideas to be as fluid and as open to different interpretations as the meaning of words can be, appears to say Yes. For Küng, it seems, in so far as our thoughts have any connection with reality, it is only at the level of Chomsky's "deep structures" (unformed, or, as Rahner calls them, "unthematic" thoughts). As soon as we try to "conceptualise" or formulate these subterranean communications, they turn into "surface structures" which can never reflect reality with complete accuracy or bear an unchangeable meaning.

This, one assumes, is why Fr Küng finds the propositions of faith forever "problematical." God revealed Himself to the prophets, apostles, and inspired

---

declarations."This, according to Rahner, is because to make a universally and permanently valid statement you have to know everything about everything. But the sum of human knowledge is now so vast that the necessary omniscience is no longer possible. No one mind can comprehend and synthesise it all. Also, the kind of theological agreement necessary for doctrinal definitions has gone for good. Theological pluralism, including it seems theological contradiction, is now an irreversible fact (Siri, *op. cit.*, pp. 134 & 352.) This causes him to wonder whether heresy is any longer possible.

165. There were people in the reform movement who wanted grace redefined as a "relationship" rather than a quality. (US Bishop Austin Vaughan to the author, Rome 1993). But if the new definition is intended to exclude the idea that grace is something new added to and inhering in the person receiving it, then the meaning has been changed. The idea that grace is purely a matter of being in a new relationship with God without any substantial change in the recipient, would be a Lutheran understanding of grace.

writers of the two Testaments at the level of "deep structures." The words and ideas in which the divine communication is embodied, being a surface structure, are entirely of human origin and therefore endlessly changeable. Changing the ideas as well as the words in which the faith is expressed has been called "reconceptualisation." Reconceptualisation moves the attack on the stability of revealed truth and doctrine from the level of language to the level of concepts, or from the form in which they are expressed to the substance of what is expressed.

After all this, it would seem difficult to create a more impenetrable "cloud of unknowing." The attempt has been made nevertheless under the influence of the movements presently known as *post-modernism* and its sub-current *deconstructionism*.

Post-modernism, as I explained a few chapters ago, is a general mood rather than a strictly philosophical position, generated by the nihilistic existentialism of the late 1960s and early '70s and affecting, though in different ways, the higher intelligentsia and the general public alike. It is a symptom of the widespread, though far from universal, loss of confidence in the idea of perpetual progress, and its replacement by a radical individualism which, in the public sphere, justifies itself as the only sensible attitude in a meaningless world in which we have only one life to enjoy.

It was against this background and under the influence of this mood that in the late 1960s the post-modernists conducted a sort of philosophical rape of the Sabine women.

Up to this point linguistics and language philosophy had been regarded as more or less the private property of the arid, unemotional Anglo-Saxon philosophical school. But around the time just mentioned they were suddenly captured and carted off by German and French philosophers, mainly followers of Heidegger of some kind, and put to work for purposes of their own.

The Anglo-Saxon school had been content to use linguistics to help them abolish metaphysics. The goal of the newcomers was more radical – the "deconstruction" of the ordinary notion of truth in order to replace it with their existentialist notion of truth. Believing, as they did, that there is no stable reality to attach a permanent meaning to, they invoked linguistics to discredit the power of words to reveal the true nature and meaning of things and to reinforce the idea that it is impossible to make a statement which will always have the same meaning for everyone everywhere. Man makes words, his own and other people's, mean whatever he wishes. The leading "deconstructionists" have been the German Hans Georg Gadamer

(b. 1900) and the Frenchman, Jacques Derrida (b. 1930). Using a different technique from that of Kant, they have been carrying his undertaking, the divorce between mind and reality, to its last resting place.[166]

The deconstructionists' main field of interest has been "hermeneutics," or the science of interpretation, particularly the interpretation of ancient texts. Can we know what their authors actually intended to say? Their answer is No, or, at the best, Not really.

Human beings are constitutionally incapable of, in the first place, reporting events accurately or objectively, and secondly of understanding what men of an earlier age have written. Every witness of an event interprets it in terms of his own subjective and conditioned vision of things (he sees only what he wants to see or is programmed to see), and every subsequent reading of the text is an equally conditioned interpretation. No statement exists which is not an "interpretation." Indeed, according to Heidegger, language itself is an interpretation; he who speaks is already "interpreting his world."

This being the case, it would seem reasonable to follow the example of the Chinese cultural revolutionaries. What is the use of hoarding documents and texts that can no longer be understood? Why read Plato or the Bible if we can have no idea what the authors were trying to say? The obviously sensible thing would be to burn the lot in order to make more shelf space, or – so as not to sin against political correctness – recycle them. And recycling is in a sense just what Gadamer has proposed. Not of course a recycling of the papyrus, parchment or paper on which the texts are written. They are to be reverently preserved. What is to be recycled is the *meaning* of the texts. Each generation will use them for its own purposes, attach to them its own meaning; will interpret them so as to give expression to its particular way of looking at the world at its particular time.

A text, says Gadamer, "whether law or gospel ... must be understood at every moment, in every particular situation, in a new and different way"... "To interpret means precisely to use one's own preconceptions so that the meaning of the text can really be made to speak for us." Trying to understand what the original author meant to say would "be no more than the recovery of a dead meaning." "An interpretation that was correct 'in

---

166. "The meaning of a word is its use," was a slogan of the Vienna school, implying that words have no objective meaning. There is also an affinity between "deconstructionism" and Zen Buddhism. For Zen, too, language is an arbitrary construct unrelated to things. Consciousness is real but its objects are not.

itself" would be a foolish ideal that failed to take account of the nature of tradition."[167]

It is true that Gadamer speaks of a possible "fusion of horizons" between the original author and the modern reader of a text, but whatever this ambiguous phrase means, it does not seem seriously to limit the interpreter's freedom to make any text mean more or less what he wishes.[168]

Since the "new hermeneutics," as it is called, renders any kind of historical knowledge impossible, it is difficult to see what the deconstructionists have in mind, unless it is to render the meaning of the Bible totally inaccessible. For the deconstructionists, no amount of historical and linguistic research will really open the biblical authors' minds to us.

In spite of this, a well-informed observer speaks of the "breath-taking advance" of post-modernism and deconstructionism "not only in the discourse of high culture, but in academic theology too." "The crisis of interpretation," says the same author, "is deepened by the turmoil into which, with post-modernism, the philosophy of language has entered." [169]

Pope Paul VI seems already to have been aware of all this as early as 1968. "The purpose of interpretation – hermeneutics," he writes in his *Credo of the People of God*, "is to understand and elicit the meaning conveyed by the text, taking into account the words used, not to invent some new sense on the basis of arbitrary conjecture."

Two years later the Pope returned to the subject in an address to the Bible Week organised by the Italian Biblical Association. While at pains to make clear that he recognised the subjective element that enters into

---

167. See, Brian Harrison, *The Teaching of Paul VI on Sacred Scripture* (doctoral thesis, Pontifical Athenaeum of the Holy Cross), Rome 1997, chapter 4, "Modern Hermeneutical Problems." Also A. Nichols, *Christendom Awake*, Edinburgh, T. & T. Clark, 1999, p. 58. It may require an effort to enter the minds of people of different times and places. But that presumably is why we have been given *imaginations*.
168. It is difficult to see much difference between Gadamer's position and that of Lewis Carroll's Humpty Dumpty:
"When I use a word," Humpty Dumpty said, in a rather scornful tone, "it means just what I choose it to mean – neither more nor less."
"The question is," said Alice, "whether you can make words mean so many different things."
"The question is," said Humpty Dumpty, "which is to be master – that's all."
Lewis Carroll, *Alice Through the Looking Glass*, ch. 6, p. 190 (OUP combined edition 1971, reprinted 1992).
169. Nichols, *op. cit.*, p. 55.

all historical writing, reporting and subsequent interpretation, the Pope insisted that the meaning of the original author of a text is both recoverable, immutable and intelligible.

That he had to insist at length on these obvious facts indicates the extent to which "new hermeneutical" thinking had begun to affect Catholic biblical scholars. Indeed, much of it had already reached them via the Protestant biblical scholar Bultmann, as we shall see in the next chapter.

Chapter Eighteen

THE MEETING WITH PROTESTANTISM

Through contacts made during the Second World War, many French and German Catholics discovered for the first time the virtues and love of Christ of their Protestant brothers and came to a better appreciation of the beliefs they had in common with them, which in turn, when the war was over, led to interest in the movement for Christian unity.

However, not a few began, it seems, to look sympathetically at what, from the Catholic standpoint, are Protestant errors. These were of two kinds, reflecting the great divide within contemporary Protestantism between historic Protestantism and modernist Protestantism.

Historic Protestantism offered those perennial temptations: no Pope and so no final arbiter about what must be believed; the Bible privately interpreted as the only source of revelation; the supremacy and infallibility of the individual conscience; and the Eucharist as a simple memorial meal. For Luther, the Gospel had done away with priesthood, sacrifice and ritual. The prophet or teacher of the Word had replaced the priest as leader of the community. Between Gospel and law, (law meaning for Luther ecclesiastical authority, institutions, and pious practices), there was a radical opposition. Christian freedom meant liberation from this "law."[170]

Protestant modernism offered temptations of a different kind. In *Turmoil and Truth*, we looked at the state of Protestant modernism around 1900. What Catholic scholars now encountered were the developments worked out during the 1920s and '30s in Germany and Switzerland by neo–Protestant theologians like Barth, Brunner, Bultmann, Tillich, and Gogarten.

As men of the same generation, they had a number of things in common. All were in reaction against the optimistic liberal Protestantism of Schleiermacher, Ritschl and Harnack. What use was Harnack's simple religion of the heavenly Father's love, universal benevolence, progress, and the belief that men would be naturally good if they were only given the right ideas, to people who had just come through the horrors of the First

---

170. For the influence of these ideas on Catholic exegetes and theologians, see Ratzinger, *Called to Communion*, Ignatius, 1991, Chapter 4, a slightly edited version of the Cardinal's opening address to the 1990 Synod on priestly education.

World War and the collapse of the old European order?

At the same time they were confronted with the theories of the social historian and philosopher Ernst Troeltsch. Troeltsch and his disciples of the "history of religions" school were teaching that Christianity originated in a hotchpotch of Jewish, Greek and Oriental ideas resulting from the fusion of nationalities within the Greek and Roman empires. Christianity is important for Europeans because it formed their culture. It is God's instrument for talking to Europeans. But it won't do for other cultures, whose religions are God's instrument for speaking to them. Western missionary endeavour ought therefore to cease.

The situation of a hundred years earlier appeared to be repeating itself. Schleiermacher's attempt to base Christianity on religious feeling or experience having failed, Christianity, as a religion of universal significance, seemed once again to be at its last gasp.

This time it was Barth who led the rescue operation. The son of a Calvinist or evangelical minister and himself a pastor in the small Swiss town of Safenwill, Karl Barth had been shocked, not only by the failure of his theology teachers to concern themselves with social questions, but even more by the fact that they had all signed a manifesto supporting the German imperial government's war aims. In 1916 he began a close study of St Paul and in 1919 published his *The Epistle to the Romans*. The second edition (1922), which seemingly marked his final break with liberal Protestantism, was a theological *succès de scandale*. In the ensuing controversies, Bultmann, Brunner and Gogarten rallied to Barth's defence and for about ten years they worked together to develop an alternative to the reigning liberal ideas, propagating their views through the influential little magazine *Zwischen den Zeiten* (*Between the Times*), which ran from 1922 to 1933.

Their alternative came to be called "dialectical" or "crisis" theology. Crisis theology, a blend of Kierkegaard and certain early Lutheran themes which had fallen somewhat into the background, was designed to shake their fellow Protestants out of what they saw as their self-satisfaction, lack of fervour and spirit of routine.[171]

To combat these evils, they emphasised the dark sides of life, showing that the struggle against sin is as fundamental a component of human existence

---

171. Dostoevsky was another important influence. Dostoevsky's chief missile against the Catholic Church – the legend of the Grand Inquisitor in his novel *The Brothers Karamazov* – was to have a deeply unsettling effect on the Catholic intelligentsia of the 1940s and '50s, contributing to the general loss of nerve about the exercise of authority in the Church.

as breathing and thinking; that men are incapable of raising themselves out of the state of sin by their own efforts; that, once God's grace does strike, the essence of Christian faith and life is dramatic decision-making and commitment more than conforming to established laws and practices. They also made much of the astonishing, paradoxical nature of Christian beliefs, the affront they offer to received views of life.

On the other hand, they were equally convinced that the conclusions of critics like Schweitzer, Weiss and Loisy were more or less irrefutable. Searching for the "historical Jesus" in the New Testament was fruitless. He was buried too deeply under the layers of mythical rubble ever to be brought to the surface again.

But if the Bible was unreliable as a foundation for belief, and Schleiermacher's attempt to substitute feeling and experience had failed, on what was their alternative to be based? It was over this question that, around 1930, the crisis theologians began to go their separate ways.

Although Barth was the leader of the group, I will take Bultmann and Gogarten first, since they offered the most uncompromisingly modernist answers.

Bultmann's "Demythologised" Christianity

Rudolf Bultmann (1884–1977), who was more Scripture scholar than theologian, spent most of his long life teaching at Marburg. There was one interlude, but it was an important one. Between 1912 and 1921 he lectured at Breslau, and it was at Breslau that he wrote his influential *History of the Synoptic Gospels*. However, it was only after his retirement in 1951 that he and his now famous "demythologizing" of the Bible made an international name for him.

His alternative to liberal theology was a blending of existentialism and "form criticism," or blind faith coupled with a rethinking of Christian origins in the light of the latest theory about the origins of the New Testament. Form criticism had been invented by two Old Testament scholars and then applied to the New by Dibelius and Gunkel.

For form critics, the creator of Christianity was not Christ but the early Christian community or communities, whose members, to help themselves cope with the psychological shock of seeing their leader put to death like a common criminal, persuaded themselves, contrary to the facts, that Christ had risen bodily from the tomb and was still alive somewhere. Easter, the Ascension, and Pentecost do not describe separate events forty and fifty days apart. They are attempts to express in symbolic language the whole overwhelming psychological upheaval or "faith experience" of the first Christians. Thus were the "Easter Faith" and "Easter People," a group of well-intentioned self-deceivers, launched into history.

Rapidly the early Christians added other myths. Christ was a pre-existing Divine being. He had come to atone for men's sins. He would return at the end of the world to judge the living and the dead. The Gospels therefore do not tell us about Christ. They tell us about the spiritual and psychological needs and religious beliefs and practices of the early communities. But these are not presented systematically. For the form critic, the New Testament is a patchwork of oral traditions in different literary forms reflecting the circumstances or "life situations" which gave rise to them. The form of some of the stories or sayings is dictated by the requirements of preaching, of others by those of catechesis, others again by those of worship. The task of the form critic is to sort out and classify the different forms in order to evaluate their true meaning and unveil the *kerygma* or central Christian message at their heart. It is impossible to separate the facts of Jesus's life from the way they were received by those who witnessed them. In other words, since every historical fact is in some degree affected by the subjective impressions of the witnesses, objective reporting is impossible. Applied generally, the principle as effectively undermines historical scholarship, as Hume's empiricism undermines science.[172]

The rest of Christian doctrine expresses the spiritual and psychological needs of later Christian generations fused with the beliefs of their predecessors.

What is that message? For 4000 years, God has been confusedly trying to tell men, first through the Old Testament myths, then through the New Testament myths, what in the 20th century Heidegger and the existentialists have at last been able to formulate clearly: that the purpose of human existence is to turn from inauthentic (or selfish) to authentic (or unselfish) living. By imitating the "kerygmatic Christ," the largely fictional figure of the early community's proclamation, people will learn to be "men for others," becoming themselves more fully human as they move from one responsible decision to the next. This kerygma is "God's final and definitive Word" to mankind. More or less everything else in Christianity belongs to an outdated world-view no longer intelligible to modern men.

---

172. Bultmann and his school are here, as we saw in the last chapter, following the lead of Hans-Georg Gadamer, who applied the principle in the fields of literary criticism and philosophy.

Bultmann called this conversion of the Bible into a foreshadowing of existentialist philosophy "demythologisation." Since it actually involved turning facts into myths, not myths into facts, "mythologisation" would have been a more accurate name for it. "And what a primitive mythology it is" was his final patronising judgement on the sacred text.

For Bultmann, therefore, the sole purpose of Christian life, teaching, worship and practice is to stir people up to make existentialist "decisions of faith." This is achieved chiefly through the Sunday scripture readings and sermon. They are God's way of inspiring His people to perform various kinds of good works: feeding the poor, caring for the sick, even, one assumes, where necessary, overturning unjust governments. Such inspirations are known as "revelatory acts."

When revelatory acts are followed by "decisions of faith," the two together are said to constitute "an eschatological event." For Bultmann, "eschatology" does not mean – as it has hitherto – the Second Coming, the resurrection of the dead, the last judgement, the final establishment of God's kingdom. These are merely metaphors for describing the way men respond in the here and now to God's "revelatory acts." Heaven is acting authentically, hell acting inauthentically, and the decision to follow one or other path carries with it its own judgement. Bodily resurrection, whether Christ's or that of mankind in general, is a metaphor for the spiritual turnabout of the individual from selfish to unselfish living. That is why we sometimes hear it said from the pulpit today, "It doesn't matter what happened 2000 years ago; what matters is whether Christ rises in the hearts of the Christian people." Christ "has risen" whenever someone decides to become "a man for others."

The sacraments are likewise instruments for stirring up decisions of faith – not special means of grace instituted by Christ. They are "signposts" or "landmarks" set up by the pilgrim community to celebrate its self-understanding as it marches towards the last horizon.

As for leadership in the community, it arose out of popular need sanctioned by popular consent. To begin with, presiding over the Eucharist was only one of a dozen or more different kinds of "ministry" open to everybody. Prophets, apostles, lectors, wonder-workers, guardians of the widows and orphans, jostled each other for place in what Cardinal Ratzinger aptly characterised in his opening address to the 1990 Synod, as "pneumatic (or Spirit-inspired) anarchy." Only in the second century, as the community felt the need for stronger, more centralised leadership, did permanent presidents of the Eucharist or priests (as they mistakenly came to be called) appear.

Why, it may be asked, did it take the "Easter people" nearly 2000 years to discover that its beliefs were not meant to be taken literally? Because of their relative poverty and backwardness. Given the hardness of life in the past, it was natural for them to put all their hopes on a better life after death. Progress and intellectual maturity, however, have brought this century's Western Christians (the "faith community's" advance guard) to the realisation that references to "salvation" and "the kingdom" in God's book of holy fairy tales refer mainly to this world.

But if the New Testament does not give a truthful account of Christ's words and miracles, how does Bultmann know that God is somehow speaking through its pages? There are no demonstrable reasons. When the Word of God "confronts" a man, he either knows it to be that intuitively or he does not. But he cannot explain why. Christianity cannot be proved. There are not even motives of credibility. However, neither can it be disproved. No one can state categorically that such and such a man or such and such a community have not had such an interior illumination.

The only vaguely Christian elements to survive in Bultmann's demythologised Christianity are that men are constantly in need of conversion; that they are incapable of achieving perfection without God's help; and that Christianity is in some way unique. Bultmann may not have believed in original sin, but he believed that men are in some Heideggerian sense "fallen." Living authentically is not something they do easily or naturally, even if it is not their fault.

Paul Tillich (1886–1965), whose name is often linked with Bultmann's, only needs a brief mention, since his existentialised "Christianity" differs from Bultmann's mainly in inessentials. He began his teaching career at Berlin immediately after World War I, was subsequently a professor of theology at three other German universities, and was at different times a colleague of Bultmann and Heidegger. He is said to have developed his theology in opposition to Karl Barth's "neo-orthodoxy."

His chief importance, however, lies in his having carried his existentialised "Christianity" to the United States where he moved after being deprived of his teaching post by the Nazis. He taught mainly at Union Theological Seminary and Columbia University in New York, and between 1951 and 1964 he published his three-volume *Systematic Theology*. On his retirement in 1955, he was given a position as University Professor at Harvard. His free-ranging speculations about God and the meaning of human life are closer to natural philosophy than Christian theology.

His starting point is the human condition, and this far at least no Christian need quarrel with him. Man, he finds, comes into the world in a permanent state of "estrangement" from his true self (the existentialist equivalent for the effects of original sin), a state which cannot be resolved by any secularist panacea or purely human means, and which only begins to improve when he makes religion his "ultimate concern."[173] Salvation, or "healing" as Tillich prefers to call it, has to come from outside nature. And this is Jesus's function. Jesus appears in the middle of history as the exemplary authentic "unestranged" existentialist man, on whom men from now on can model themselves, thereby entering a new state of existence. Jesus is the healer of man's state of estrangement not only from God but himself. Substituting healing for salvation has the advantage of making sin sound less nasty. It suggests we are mostly victims of illness rather than wrongdoing.

Is it only through Christ that men can learn how to live authentically? No: time and space are filled with similar "revelatory events" encouraging men to turn from inauthentic to authentic living. But like Schleiermacher, Tillich would probably say that of the various religious medicines for man's ills on offer, Christianity is probably the best. He resembled Schleiermacher in being anxious to make religion acceptable to its "cultured despisers."

Does he believe that Jesus is God? He would seem to be a Nestorian. The Incarnation is "a community between God and the centre of a personal life which ... resists the attempts within existential estrangement to disrupt it."

After Bultmann and Tillich, it would seem impossible to go further in emptying Christianity of its content. However, to think that would be to underestimate human ingenuity, or the power of logic to carry ideas to their necessary term.

Secular and Religionless Christianity: Gogarten and Bonhoeffer

Secular or religionless Christianity, which swept through Western Europe and North America during the 1960s, the decade of the Second Vatican Council and the Church's first steps to implement it, is one of those grotesque notions, like belief in the noble savage or the best of all possible worlds, that have captivated the fancy of the Western world from time to time over the last 300 years and about

---

173. Existentialists are at least to be commended for opposing an unqualified Rousseauistic optimism about human nature. On the other hand, experience hardly justifies the belief that large numbers of men live in a state of guilt, anxiety and dread. The most noteworthy feature of Westernised societies is surely the number of people who *don't* feel anxious or guilty when they ought to.

which one does not know whether to laugh or cry. Laughter is probably best. As a theological theory, it rapidly burnt itself out, as meteoric follies of this kind tend to, but not without the fumes of its combustion continuing to hang around and affect many people's mental respiratory systems. Paul VI spoke of "the smoke of Satan" entering the Church after the Council. The fumes of religionless Christianity, if not the most harmful, were among the most immediately pungent.

Its starting point was Kant's idea that "modern man has come of age."[174] The process of growing up began with the people and religion of Israel. The great achievement of the religion of Israel was "desacralizing" nature and the state. Desacralisation freed men from the idea that nature was subject to tutelary deities, and that any particular state had the permanent blessing of God.

The full implications of desacralisation, however, remained for long unappreciated. Only with the 17th century did the truth begin to dawn. The result was the "secularisation" and "historicisation" of man's understanding of himself and his destiny. "Secularisation" means realising that man no longer needs God to help him run the world. Improving the world is the only thing that matters and God wants man to do it on his own. "Historicisation" means realising that nature and society are not systems based on unchanging principles, but ever-changing processes. Consequently men can manipulate them at will. The only impossible things are those which men themselves judge harmful.

These ideas were first propagated by Barth and Bultmann's ally in their initial assault on liberal theology, Friedrich Gogarten. However, it is unlikely that Gogarten's secular Christianity would have enjoyed the notoriety it briefly and disastrously did in the 1960s, had it not been taken up and amplified by the much younger Lutheran pastor, Dietrich Bonhoeffer (1906–45), who was put to death for his part in the plot to kill Hitler.

It was Bonhoeffer's *Letters and Papers from Prison* which got secular Christianity off the ground.[175] His courage and selflessness seemed to confirm the truth of his ideas, which unfortunately was not the case.

He constructed his theology in order to explain to himself the fact that so many of his contemporaries whom he respected or admired neither believed, nor seemed capable of believing. This he attributed first to the bad

---

174. About modern man having "come of age," two things can be said. To be mature does not mean to be better. With maturity the possibilities of wickedness become greater. Secondly, the idea that man is capable of controlling his destiny all by himself is surely a sign of adolescence rather than maturity.
175. First published in 1951; American edition, *Prisoner of God*, 1954.

example of Christians (about which we won't quarrel) and secondly to the absurdity of the Church's teachings (with which we will).

It had hitherto been assumed that man was by nature a religious animal. But that, Bonhoeffer maintained, had now been proved false. History had given birth to a religionless man, whose respect could only be won by seeing Christians equally keen to make this world a better place. The Church must therefore confine herself to the silent service of her fellow men. About God, who is largely unknowable, she should say nothing. Worship, sacraments, public prayer should be abandoned. The age of religion is past. And this should not be regretted. "Secularisation" is something good – a sign of man's emergence from an immature dependence on religion. "God is teaching us that we must live as men who can get along very well without Him." God should be thought of more in connection with man's triumphs and prosperity than his sufferings and failures, about which "it seems to me better to hold our peace and leave the problem unsolved."

However on this last point – struggling as he was with the promptings of a generous heart and the absurdities of a theological school in its death throes – he was not consistent. He equally speaks of God as in some way identified exclusively with powerlessness and suffering. We can now only find God, if at all, on the margins of life.

To encapsulate all these ideas, he took up and popularised Nietzsche's notion of the "death of God," which resulted in the rash of 1960s "death of God theologies." But by "death of God," he did not mean what Nietzsche meant – the realisation that God does not exist. He meant that all hitherto existing notions of God had become untenable. A Supreme Being absolute in power and goodness is "a spurious conception."

Secular or religionless Christianity can be seen as the Anglo-Saxon social Gospel at its last gasp. In the 1970s Harvey Cox's *The Secular City* was to carry it far and wide through English-speaking countries.[176]

---

176. For what is said in this chapter and the next, I am greatly indebted to James C Livingstone for his *Modern Christian Thought, from the Enlightenment to Vatican II*, London and New York, Macmillan, 1971. Catholics who want to understand the developments within 19th and 20th century Protestantism that have affected Catholic thinking in the second half of the 20th century, and the role played in those developments by philosophy, mainly German philosophy, could not, I think, find a better guide. *Twentieth-Century Religious Thought* by John Macquarrie, SCM, 1971, though not nearly as detailed, is also good. One would only like to know whether it was a joke or an oversight which led the publishers to print photographs of Schweitzer, Lenin, Bertrand Russell, Tillich and Teilhard de Chardin on the cover of the paperback edition as examples of the 20th century's best religious thinkers?

Chapter Nineteen

BARTH AND NEO-ORTHODOXY

After his split with Bultmann, Brunner and Gogarten, Karl Barth (1886–1968) developed an alternative to liberal theology mid-way, or seemingly mid-way, between historic Protestantism and Protestant modernism.

The Epistle to the Romans had not only made him famous. It turned him from a pastor into a professor of theology, eventually of world renown. Between the appearance of the first and second editions of *The Epistle* he was offered a chair at Göttingen, moving to Münster in 1925 and Bonn in 1930. With the rise of the Nazis, he joined the minority German Protestant opposition, and took the lead in drawing up the Barmen Declaration against the Nazis' pseudo-religious claims (1934). When forced to leave Germany in the following year, he was offered a post at the university of Basle, and at Basle he remained for the rest of his life.

Throughout World War II he used his reputation to stiffen Swiss resistance to the Nazi regime, even joining the Swiss army as a gesture of solidarity with the anti-Nazi opposition. But afterwards, like Buber, without in any sense excusing the Nazi war crimes, he worked to reconcile Germany and its conquerors. During the Cold War, on the other hand, he took what was then the "politically correct" line for the bulk of the Western intelligentsia. He made a point of dissociating himself from anti-communist campaigns.[177] In 1962 he retired from teaching, but continued to write and generally be an oracle on religious, political and social affairs until his death six years later.

Meanwhile, from the late 1920s, he had been working on his formidable *Church Dogmatics*, a survey and reinterpretation of the greater part of pre-Reformation and Reformation theology in the light of his newly found principles and approaches. By the time of his death it was longer than St Thomas's *Summa*. There are 13 volumes in 4 parts, devoted respectively to The Word of God, God, Creation, and Reconciliation.[178] As the volumes

---

177. The phenomenon "no enemy to the left" – communists are always in some way to be excused, Nazis not – can be partly explained, I think, by the fact that the communist idea is naturally more marketable. Communists were claiming they could make the world perfect for everybody. Nazis were only offering to make it more agreeable for Germans.

appeared one by one, so his reputation expanded until it was greater than that of any other Protestant scholar of the time. The rewritten first volume, published in 1932, marked the final break with Bultmann. The fifth and final part on the Redemption remained unwritten.

His reputation can also, I think, be attributed to the fact that he was more than just a theologian. He was a character, a "personality," in the sense that the English Prime Ministers Gladstone and Churchill were personalities. One feels that whatever he had done in life he would have made a mark. He had an exceptionally strong will, and an astounding self-assurance and stubbornness which enabled him to maintain the most obviously wrong-headed positions against opposition from all directions without losing his nerve or prestige. Without being malicious or vindictive – his natural combativeness was tempered by a sense of humour about himself – he also loved a good fight. He was both fascinated and amused by his success.[179]

At first sight, Barth's blend of Kierkegaard, Luther and a reconstructed Calvinism looked like a total rejection of modernism. Hence the name neo-orthodoxy.

God, Barth insisted against every current of fashionable Swiss-German theological thinking, is not an immanent, semi-pantheistic, possibly evolving

---

178. *Dogmatics*: "In Christian theology, the systematic presentation of doctrines so as to form a coherent whole ... most familiar in connection with the Barthian attempt to cover the whole theological field afresh in the light of a new understanding of the Bible" (*Fontana Dictionary of Modern Thought*, London, Collins, 1981). The word "dogmatics" gives theology a relatively substantial sound without making it too solid. Barth was averse to the idea of universally binding truths implicit in the word "dogma." For a summary of *Church Dogmatics* by a Catholic admirer, but not an uncritical one, see *Grace versus Nature*, Hugo Meynell, London, Sheed and Ward, 1965.

179. For example, he is said to have had portraits of famous theologians lining the wall of his staircase ending at the top with a mirror. However, as has been the case with similarly powerful characters, the mixture of qualities and quirks which distinguished him did not always make life easy for his wife and children. There is a certain ruthlessness in unusual men when they are not saints. He undoubtedly saw his secretary Charlotte von Kirschbaum, who seems to have been of a higher level of intelligence than his wife, as indispensable to his work and the development of his ideas, and possibly she was. Nevertheless it was fairly insensitive to insist on her living in the house with the family, and quite often to go off on holiday with her, leaving his wife behind, an arrangement which is admitted to have caused tensions "which shook (the family) to the core" and caused "unspeakably deep suffering" (*Karl Barth, his life from letters and autobiographical texts*, Eberhard Busch, London, SCM Press, 1976, pp. 185–6). Barth, says Busch, "did not hesitate to take ... the blame for the situation which had come about ... but he thought that it could not be changed."

Being, speaking to men mainly through religious feeling or experience. Equally to be deplored were Bultmann's attempts to put Christianity at the service of Heidegger's existentialism. No. All these attempts to cut God down to the level of man's understanding had as little to do with the one true God as Hinduism and Buddhism have. The real God, the God of the Bible, is an all-powerful, incomprehensible, transcendent Being, completely "Other," standing in judgement above and outside His creation, though in complete control of it. Between this God and His creation, the gulf is unbridgeable. Poor miserable man, sunk in sin, is incapable of remedying his situation in any way until God takes the initiative.

Only if man opens himself to God's Word and grace when it "confronts" him in the Church's never-ceasing "proclamation" and responds with faith do things begin to improve.[180] The Word of God, not human experience, is the source of our knowledge and salvation. His full and final Word is the Person of Jesus Christ, God and man, the one and only Lord and Master of creation, who truly rose from the dead, not just in spirit, initiating a kingdom not to be confused with any earthly utopia. Christians must love and do good to their fellow men, but in no way is the building of the kingdom of God to be equated with human progress. There is no way of harmonising the wisdom of this world with the folly of the Cross.

In the theological climate of the 1920s and '30s, all this was astonishing enough. Traditional Protestants began to take heart, and Catholic theologians to prick up their ears. What Barth was saying might not coincide exactly with Catholic teaching. But it sounded a great deal better than most of what had been coming out of German Protestant theological faculties for the last 100 years. Here at last, surely, was a major Protestant figure with enough solid belief to make discussion worthwhile.

Moreover as time went on, Barth began to make his Calvinist God less remote and forbidding; to speak less about "God the Other" standing in judgement over men and nations and more about "the humanity of God" and the "God who is *for* man" and involves Himself in human history. Although God often has to say No to man, He is primarily a God who says Yes to him. This meant having to find a way around Calvin's doctrine of double predestination (from all eternity some are predestined to salvation, others to damnation).

Nothing daunted, Barth set to work and concluded that double

---

180. The word "proclamation" has a special significance in Barthian theology. The faith can only be proclaimed. It is incapable of rational justification or explanation.

predestination only applied to Christ. As representative of guilty humanity, Christ was first rejected on the Cross, then at the Resurrection accepted and raised to glory. Barth's later theology is spoken of as "swamped in grace." As a pastor, which he remained in spirit throughout his life, he repeatedly insists on the need for Christians to put all their trust in Christ and be cheerful and hopeful. "God was in Christ, reconciling the world to Himself." Such is the core of the *kerygma* or the Church's earliest "proclamation." Such is the good news to which it is the Christian community's principal task to bear witness. What more can anyone want? As the bearer and transmitter of God's Word, the Church is as important as the Bible, indeed more important.[181]

Contacts with Catholic theologians had begun as early as the 1920s. In 1928, Barth had been studying St Thomas, whom he found "uncannily instructive" and difficult to answer, so he invited the German Jesuit theologian Fr Erich Przywara (1889–1972) to a debate in his seminar. Przywara had just made a name for himself with his *Philosophy of Religion*. Barth was impressed, and the following spring asked Przywara to give a lecture on the Church. Przywara, Barth recorded, "shone for another two hours in my seminar and finally overwhelmed me for two whole evenings..." [182] By this time Barth was teaching at Bonn, and that he was feeling the attractions of Catholicism seems indisputable. He was in contact with other Catholic theologians besides Przywara and often visited the monks at Maria Laach, sometimes with his students. In the preface to Part I, Volume 3 of *Church Dogmatics*, he speaks of being reproached by Protestant colleagues for studying St Anselm and St Thomas and of having to defend himself against the accusation of "Catholicising." In 1931 he could find only one reason for not becoming a Catholic; all the other Christian denominations were "short-sighted and frivolous." This seemed to include the Orthodox. After a visit from the Orthodox theologian Georges Florovsky, Barth spoke of not having "an overwhelming impression that we really needed this Eastern theology," and referred to the "obscurantist effect of Russian thought-patterns."[183] The one stumbling block to becoming a Catholic, apparently, was the Church's teaching that God can to some extent be known from his works. (The technical term is *analogia entis*, which Barth came to describe as "the invention of Anti-Christ.") Why this was such a stumbling block we shall see shortly.

----

181. On this point, Barth's theology of revelation, as we shall see, turns Lutheranism upside-down. For *sola scriptura*, it substitutes *sola ecclesia*, or rather *sola communitas*.
182. Busch, *op. cit.*, p. 183.
183. *Ibid.*, p. 215.

By the end of the decade, however, there had been a change. Barth was entrenching himself more and more in a position which involved fighting off the objections of traditional Protestants and Christian existentialists like Bultmann and Brunner on the one hand, and justifying himself against the positions and practices of "Rome" on the other, with Rome as the principal target of his polemics and sarcasms.

The younger generation of Catholics who started visiting him in the following decade after the publication of the early volumes of the *Church Dogmatics* therefore had a tougher, more self-confident figure to deal with. Barth was no longer discovering marvels in Catholicism. Instead his Catholic visitors were to some extent looking to him for light. Anxious as they were for a loosening of Catholic theology, they saw him as a possibly useful ally.

In 1940, Fr von Balthasar, a pupil of Przywara, attended Barth's seminar on the Council of Trent, thereby starting a long friendship, and in 1948-49 he gave a series of ten much-discussed lectures, later published as *Karl Barth and Catholicism* (1951). The French Jesuit, Fr Henri Bouillard, followed with a 1200-page thesis on Barth, with Barth attending Bouillard's *viva voce* at the Sorbonne. Later, Fr Hans Küng did a doctorate on Barth's theory of justification and became for a time a regular correspondent, as did Fr Karl Rahner. Barth himself spoke of a "whole chorus of German and especially French friends," who "in different ways and with different emphases all seem to want to look in a new way towards the centre," and "who alone can make possible theology itself or any attempt at ecumenical understanding."[184] The Belgian Dominican Fr Jérome Hamer also did doctoral work under Barth, but subsequently distanced himself from him.

Meanwhile more and more volumes of the *Church Dogmatics* had been appearing, and by the mid-1950s, even Rome was recognising Barth as a figure of consequence. He was invited to be a lay observer at the Council but refused on grounds of poor health; in 1966 he took part in an international congress of Catholic theologians in Rome "where he was greeted by those present with a long ovation"; Paul VI received him in audience, and from time to time he and Barth exchanged letters; and John Paul II has spoken of him as one of the theologians contributing to the renewal inaugurated by Vatican II.

The aspects of his theology which seem most to have attracted the members of the reform party were: his "Christo-centrism" – he relates

---

184. As Barth saw it, his visitors "envisaged a kind of reformation of the Catholic Church and of Catholic theology from within. And now I was to be introduced like a new Trojan horse to bring it about (against St Thomas and also against Augustine)." *Ibid.*, p. 362.

everything to the Person and Work of Christ, who alone makes it possible for men to understand who they are[185]; his "universalism" – God wills and makes salvation possible and readily available to all men; the omnipresence of grace; his emphasis on the importance of Christian witness; his making the Church rather than the Bible the primary vehicle of revelation; his insistence that the Church is a community more than an institution; and the fact that it exists for the benefit of all humanity, not just of its own members.

However, there was more that is "neo" and less that is "orthodox" in Barth's theology than at first appeared. The novelties took time to manifest themselves, partly because, as his *magnum opus* progressed, he kept shifting his position on certain points, partly because, although using the same terminology as Catholics, it was often with a different meaning. The *Church Dogmatics* are Protestant in tone but not all Protestant in substance, and it is possible to read long passages without noticing anything strikingly novel or heterodox. I will confine myself to the more salient "irregularities."[186]

Reason and Revelation. Barth's great problem was that he wished to preserve the idea of an historical divine revelation, while at the same time, as we have said, having as little belief as Bultmann in the historicity of those parts of the Bible whose authors manifestly intended them as history.[187]

---

185. We can perhaps see an anticipation here of the Council's teaching that "Jesus Christ reveals man to himself."

186. A devout Catholic friend, a great lover of the old liturgy, distressed by most of the post-conciliar changes, told me she once read all thirteen volumes of the *Church Dogmatics* without realising there was anything amiss. A Presbyterian reader, on the other hand, began to suspect that Barth "wasn't as orthodox as he sounded" when he noticed how "many former Barthians became 'Death of God' theologians." (J C O'Neill, Professor of New Testament Language, Literature and Theology, University of Edinburgh; private letter to the author.)

187. "Opponents of Barth like Bultmann were infuriated by (his) seeming to say that he believed that the Resurrection happened (in the normal sense by which the grave became empty and the transformed body of Jesus left this universe) when he did not believe anything of the sort – but Barth never really concealed his actual position from those who took the trouble to read carefully what he wrote... (He) is perfectly explicit that the history of the forty days is not part of the facts of history to which the life of Jesus from his birth to his death belong" (*The Bible's Authority*, J C O'Neill, Edinburgh, T. & T. Clark, 1991, p. 273). To justify his position, O'Neill says, Barth distinguishes between "Mirakels" and "Wunders." A "Mirakel" is what all Christians up to the 19th century have always taken miracles to be – acts of God which, no matter how extraordinary, enter into the continuum of historical events. A "Wunder" is seemingly a sign from God that enters people's minds independently of the continuum of historical events. The Resurrection and the Virgin Birth are both "Wunders" not "Mirakels."

How were these two positions to be reconciled? Somehow revelation had to be given a form, or lifted into a realm, where it was impervious to the inquiries and criticisms of philosophers, scientists and biblical scholars. This he did first by digging an unbridgeable chasm between natural and revealed knowledge.

Whatever validity natural knowledge, including radical biblical scholarship, has in its own sphere, we cannot have any genuine knowledge of God and His intentions until He tells us about them Himself. Up to then we are completely in the dark. Attempts to reach a natural knowledge of God by reason and analogy are worse than no knowledge. Indeed the distance between God and man is so enormous, they are so utterly unalike, that the use of analogy is close to blasphemy. The God of natural theology is a caricature, an idol, a non-Being. Efforts by philosophers, particularly existentialists and Roman Catholics, to link this non-Being to the God of the Bible must therefore be resolutely resisted. This is why Barth begins his *Church Dogmatics* with the Word of God, and only in Part II does he come to God Himself.

The mystics' efforts to know God by direct contact are likewise futile. So too, for salvation, are all that men busy themselves about in this world. Although Barth had a lot to say about the duties of Christians in this world, the logic of his scheme of things leaves as little room for a Christian humanism as for natural theology.

The Word of God. Barth's next step was to detach the Word of God from the Bible. Most people on first coming across Barth probably assume that when he speaks of the "Word of God" he means the Bible. But, while claiming to base his theology exclusively on the Bible, he maintains that it only "witnesses" to the Word of God. It is not itself the Word of God. It is true that to distance himself from Bultmann's "demythologising," he makes a distinction between myth and saga. Myths are symbolic ways of expressing timeless truths; a saga has some kind of basis in historical events. But about how much of the Bible is myth and how much saga we are left in the dark. That is for biblical scholars to decide. The theologian has more important concerns, as we shall see shortly.

In so far as God does speak to men, it is through events and actions rather than words – through the "mighty deeds" recorded in the Old Testament, culminating in His Final Word, the "Christ event" – the Incarnation, life, death and resurrection of the Word made Flesh – witnessed to by the New Testament.[188]

---

188. The neologism "Christ event" seems to owe its origin to the "process" metaphysics and theology of the English philosopher Alfred North Whitehead (d. 1947). For Whitehead, the world is a compound of events and processes rather than things.

The advantage of making revelation primarily the manifestation of a Person rather than a body of knowledge or the imparting of a message is that is does not then matter so much whether what the Person is reported to have said is literally true. A person's character can be conveyed through imaginary events and conversations as in an historical novel.[189]

As to the way we are to understand the meaning of the deeds and events recorded in the Bible, God has left it up to men to interpret them as best they can. There has never been any guarantee they would get them right. Both the prophets and inspired writers of the Old Testament and the apostles and evangelists in the New Testament "were guilty of error in their spoken and written word." "The more clearly the biblical witnesses of Jesus Christ speak, the more what they say gets lost in what we today call the realm of pure legend." [190] Nor is the Church any more reliable as an interpreter. The Church, says Barth, "passes on its way through history... in understanding and misunderstanding of what is said to it."[191]

The Word of God, in other words, is not located in any particular text or teaching. It floats in a void behind the stream of historical events which the biblical "witnesses" were struggling to interpret. Neither inspired nor inerrant, the Bible is merely an instrument which, as in Bultmann's system, God uses to convey to the community what He wants them to understand about Himself and His plans in the here and now. People are supposed to

---

189. Since Vatican II, Catholic scholars affected by radical biblical scholarship have shown a similar preference for regarding revelation as the manifestation of a Person rather than the communication of a message. For example, Fr William Nicholson SJ, formerly of Fordham University, New York, tells us that "the Church's magisterial task is to preserve in itself and communicate the revealing Word of God, not *something* (e.g. 'an interpretation of reality'), but *Someone.*" Quoted in the American *Fellowship of Catholic Scholars Newsletter*, Sept 1994. For the Church, revelation culminates in a Person, it is true, but a Person who spoke, and whose words very definitely involved "an interpretation of reality." Christ, says Vatican II, "completed and perfected revelation... by the total fact of his presence and self-manifestation – by words and works, signs and miracles" (*Dei Verbum*, 4). And He "commanded the apostles to preach the Gospel ... which he fulfilled in his own person and promulgated with his own lips" (*ibid.*, 7).
190. See "The Christian Understanding of Revelation" in *Against The Stream: Shorter Post-War Writings, 1946–51*, SCM Press 1954, p. 222. In his strange, sometimes almost perverse way, Barth tries to make a virtue of this supposed unreliability of Holy Scripture, even to glory in it. "For is it not of the very nature of revelation that the form in which it confronts us is relative and problematical." *Ibid.*, 223. The more incomprehensible revelation is, the more reason is humbled.
191. *Dogmatics in Outline*, London, SCM Press, 1960, p. 10.

hear the Word of God through listening to the Bible regardless of whether the human words they hear are true or false. Revelation, which is going on continually, is a purely interior thing. It takes place whenever a man or woman "responds in faith" to the Church's proclamation, which can be either the Scripture readings or the Sunday sermon. (Logically, it is difficult to see why God could not as effectively use the plays of Shakespeare or the *Iliad* and *Odyssey*.) God also speaks through everyday events, which is why the Barthian theologian goes about with his Bible in one hand, and the daily newspaper in the other.

But how can the faithful know whether they have understood all these messages correctly? Barth's official reply is the same as Bultmann's; that a man who has understood rightly knows it intuitively. That he can't explain why is beside the point. In practice, however, it is theologians who hold the key that unlocks the door to right understanding of the Word.

Theology and Theologians

In the original evangelical or Calvinist churches, the preacher or minister of the Word determined how the Bible or the Church's "proclamation" was to be understood. However, it was assumed that the Bible had a stable, ascertainable meaning, and for the most part it would be the meaning laid down by Calvin. However, as scholars holding views like Barth's and Bultmann's about Holy Scripture have supplanted the minister of the Word, the Church's proclamation has come to be regarded as being continually open to revision. Theology, Barth says, is "not a matter of stating old or even new propositions that one can take home in black and white... If there is a critical science at all, which is constantly having to begin again at the beginning, dogmatics is that science." Theologians must constantly question the biblical texts "as to whether and to what extent authentic witness of God's Word may be actually heard in them." This continual re-assessing of the "proclamation" applies not only to the Bible but to the whole corpus of Christian doctrine and theology. The "thought and speech of the community have behind them a long history which is in many ways confused and confusing." The chief task of the theologian, therefore, Barth tells us, is to check that current Church proclamation is in keeping with the Word of God.[192]

---

192. *Ibid.*, p. 12., and *Evangelical Theology: an Introduction*, Edinburgh, T. & T. Clark, 1963, pp. 44 & 45.

Here, however, he starts to go round in circles. "Dogmatics," he says, "measures the Church's proclamation by the standard of Holy Scripture," and elsewhere "by Scripture and the Word." But Scripture, we have been informed, cannot be relied on to transmit the Word faithfully. So who is left to tell the flock what God has been trying to say through His holy book: the Church's past proclamation, or this week's newspapers? Who, but the theologian. And what standard has he to go by apart from an inner intuition?

"Like the pendulum which regulates the clock, so theology is responsible for the reasonable service of the community." [193]

Although, Barth tells us, theology is a humble science, he has in fact elevated it to a position indistinguishable from divine revelation, and theologians to a status equivalent to that of the prophets and apostles. It is true he speaks of primary and secondary witnesses to the Word. The prophets and apostles belonged to the first category, theologians like St Irenaeus, St Augustine, St Bonaventure, St Thomas, or Barth and Bultmann to the second. [194] The former were direct witnesses of God's deeds down to the Christ event. But since God continues to speak through public events, is there really any substantial difference between the two categories? Jeremiah witnessed the fall of Jerusalem, Barth the fall of the Hitler régime. Moreover, as we saw a moment ago, all have been equally liable to misread the meaning of God's actions as they have unfolded through history. There is, in other words, no boundary between revelation and theology. All there has been, from the earliest Old Testament writer, down to the most recent book by a contemporary critical scholar, is a stream of "theologising," constantly changing ground. In this shifting tide of speculation the only fixed points seem to be the affirmations that "Jesus Christ is Lord and Saviour" and "God was in Christ reconciling the world to Himself."

In spite of its seemingly solid structure and coherence, Barth's *Church Dogmatics* is in reality like a vast fairy castle floating on air. This is somewhat as Barth himself saw it. He compared his theology to a bird in flight. All

---

193. *Ibid.*, p. 42. Prof. O'Neill comments: "As he (Barth) is the only true guardian of 'revelation,' this all means that we have to humble ourselves in his presence" (letter to the author).

194. "The witnesses to the Old and New Testaments ... were *theologians*" (E.T., p. 30, Barth's emphasis). For other characteristic statements on this topic, see E.T. pp. 44, 46, 47. Theology must "risk" taking Holy Scripture "as a working hypothesis." "No dogma or article of the creed can be taken over untested by theology from ecclesiastical antiquity." What theology "supposes to know and think *today* (sic), will only seldom agree completely with what the fathers of yesterday thought and said."

theology, besides floating on air, is moving through the air, changing shape as it goes. Barth loved and was fascinated by theology, the whole sweep of opinions and controversies about the Christian mysteries down the centuries, but in the way that a collector loves his acquisitions. It would not, I think, be unfair to compare his ideal theologian to a juggler tossing coloured glass balls in the air just to make them spin and flash in the sunlight. What the juggler must never do is let any of the "balls" come to rest long enough in one of his hands to become a doctrinal definition or dogma.[195]

The Trinity

According to a well-known Dominican theologian, Luther's subjective attitude to truth, his preoccupation with what God has done "for me" or us and relative indifference to what God is like *in Himself*, is one of two classic Lutheran themes to have recently found their way into Catholic theology via Karl Barth.[196] Luther himself characteristically summarised his attitude: "Christ has two natures: how does that concern me? Be He by nature man and God, that is his affair. But that he has ... poured out his love to become my salvation ... it is in this that I find my consolation and my good." With Barth, this approach would seem to have affected his view of the Trinity. He refused to consider the Trinity in itself apart from the acts of creation and redemption, with the apparent implication that, had God not chosen to create the universe and redeem men, He would not have been the same God. The creation and human history thus come to look like part of the being of God. "The idea of a self-contained ontological Trinity" (that is, of a Trinity for which creation was not in some sense a necessity) was the object of "consistent attack" by Barth and Brunner.[197] The idea appears in a

---

195. "I think the clue to the audacity of the *Church Dogmatics* is that Barth believed all great works of art were self-sustaining, suspended in a void ... all human thought creates in a void" (O'Neill, letter to the author). This attitude, O'Neill maintains, was characteristic of many of Barth's contemporaries in Germany (*op. cit.*, pp. 277–8). We must act, they held, *as if* certain things were true even if they are not, or can no longer be proved to be: *as if* God existed, *as if* there were a natural law, *as if* men have free will – *as if*, we could add, there has been a divine revelation. O'Neill gives a list of names and works expressing this viewpoint from Spengler's *Decline of the West* to Freud's *The Ego and the Id*, to which he says Barth's *Epistle to the Romans* belongs. Perhaps it explains Barth's dislike of Bach and love of Mozart. Bach, he complained, "preached." Mozart, presumably, just played about with beautiful sounds.
196. Aidan Nichols OP, *The Shape of Catholic Theology*, Edinburgh, 1991, p. 315.
197. Cornelius van Til, *The New Modernism*, London 1946, p. ix.

more marked form in the later Karl Rahner.

Christocentrism

Although Barth's "Christocentrism" has been much praised, there is a marked difference between the way he understands the word and the way the Church understands it. The Church's teaching is and always has been "Christ-centred" in the sense that it proposes Christ as the model of human perfection, as the one mediator between men and God, and as mankind's Head and King. A representation of the crucified Christ hangs in every church. The risen Christ is present in every tabernacle. But as a system of beliefs, Christianity is first of all Trinitarian. The doctrine of the Trinity is what distinguishes it from all other religions, and its earliest statements of belief, the creeds, are Trinitarian in form. Barth's Christocentrism, on the other hand, means that the "Christ event" is the sole source of knowledge about God and the meaning of human life. The "Christ event" is like a small aperture in the otherwise impenetrable wall separating the natural from the supernatural world.[198] Barth's theology has, rightly I think, been called "Christomonist" rather than "Christocentric."[199]

---

198. It is impossible here not to see the influence of Kant. The Christ event gives us our one peep through the veil of phenomena into the world of "things in themselves."

199. Barth even goes so far as to maintain that "for Christians the existence of the God revealed in Jesus Christ is the ultimate certainty; and that Jesus Christ came into the world as a man is the proof of the existence of the world and man"– an example of Cartesian doubt surely carried to an extreme. (Meynell, *op. cit.*, p. 89, summarising a passage from *Dogmatics*, Part 3, Vol. 1). In 1951, von Balthasar had referred to Barth's "Christological narrowness," an observation leading to a temporary cooling in their relationship. But the word "Christomonism" was first used by Barth's Protestant opponents, as Barth himself tells us (*Church Dogmatics*, Part 3, Vol. 3, p. xi). More recently it appeared in an article by Cardinal (then Father) Avery Dulles SJ on the theology of John Paul II, (*Communio*, Winter 1997, p. 720). The Pope's Christology, Cardinal Dulles says, is Christocentric but "avoids *Christomonism*." (Italic added). Cardinal Dulles does not mention Barth, but he seems to be distancing the Pope's teaching from Barth's. He concludes the paragraph with the words, "The theology of J. P. II, while remaining Christocentric, is pneumatological and Trinitarian." Barth's Christomonism was not entirely original. "We find God in nothing but Christ," was a dictum of his teacher Wilhelm Herrmann. Did Barth, in spite of all this, truly believe that Christ was God? Von Balthasar has spoken of a "downplaying" of the Incarnation in modern theology "because it is impossible for the *holy* God to be incarnate (as in consistent Protestantism), for example, Karl Barth..." ("The Fathers, the Scholastics and Ourselves," *Communio*, Summer 1997).

Reconciliation

The reconciliation of God and the human race resulting from "the Christ event" is without doubt the central theme in Barth's theology. This, for Barth, is what the Church fundamentally exists to proclaim.[200] But he gives it an all-embracing significance that Catholic teaching does not allow. Catholic teaching distinguishes between reconciliation and justification. God and humanity have been reconciled in Christ. As representative of the human race, Christ has paid the price of all men's sins. But not all men have taken advantage of the fact. Only those who have made an act of faith and received the baptism of water or desire are, through the infusion of sanctifying grace, "justified," and only if they persevere in that state will they reach salvation.

Barth, on the other hand, tends to identify reconciliation and justification. God and humanity have not only been reconciled "in Christ." "According to Barth's teaching in the *Dogmatics*, a man is justified in Christ whatever he may do ... and whether he is a member of the Church or not. A man does not enter the Church to be justified, but to be a witness to the world outside the Church of the accomplished fact of justification." [201] The only difference between Christians and the rest of mankind, for Barth, is that Christians know they have been justified, the latter so far don't. Does this mean that everyone is saved too? Although we cannot affirm it, Barth says, we cannot deny it.[202]

Grace, Nature, Creation, Evil, the Moral Law

Following some of the early Greek Fathers, Barth tends to make little or no distinction between grace as the gift of divine life to men and the creative act by which God brings the universe into existence or the sustaining power by which He keeps it there. Everything God does is "grace." This widening of the word's meaning not only obscures the importance of grace in the usually understood sense as something vital for perseverance in virtue and

200. The greater emphasis in the Catholic Church on the concept of "reconciliation," as for example in the use of the word to describe the sacrament of penance, could also reflect Barth's influence; likewise the conciliar teaching that, through the Incarnation, "Christ has in a certain sense united himself with every man" (*Gaudium et Spes*, 22).

201. Meynell, *op. cit.*, p. 257.

202. "According to Barth all men are saved by God in Christ, and the Christian differs from others only in his knowledge of this fact" (Meynell, *op. cit.*, p. 161). For Barth's universalism, see *Dogmatics* 2.2.

ultimately salvation, it makes the activity of creatures as secondary causes superfluous or non-existent. It creates the impression that, as men need grace to reach salvation, bees need a special divine assistance, beyond what is given with their nature, in order to make honey. He has not endowed created things with any existence or consistency independent of a succession of direct interventions on His part.

To some extent all this flows from Barth's bizarre ideas about God's initial act of creation. In creating the universe, we are told, God turned his back on nothingness or chaos, and it is only his minute-to-minute watchfulness that keeps the world from returning to that state. This continuing tendency of things to relapse into nothingness or chaos is the origin of suffering and evil. There are no evil spirits. Angels have a sort of existence, but only when they are acting as God's messengers, not, it seems, the rest of the time. Are they merely symbolic manifestations of God's power? It seems so. The human soul is not naturally immortal. It survives death by a special act of God. This makes hell problematical. Does God have to intervene to make it possible for people to go to hell, when left to themselves they would simply cease to exist? In morals, Barth has lent his authority to the development of situation ethics; there can be no rules applicable to all situations.

The Church.

For Barth, the Church or Christian community is all Christian denominations together regardless of disagreements. Some have understood God's Word better than others, Barthian evangelicals presumably having understood it best of all. But no denomination since World War II has made such a poor job of interpreting God's Word that it can be considered as no longer belonging to the Church. Heresy, possible in theory, is hardly so in practice. In practice, too, it would be better if we could avoid the word "Church." "Christian community" better describes what we mean. The way Christians have organised themselves at different times and places is a matter of personal choice or cultural accident.

In spite of this, the Church or Community stands at the very centre of Barth's theology, since it is only through the Church's existence and evolving proclamation that we can know anything. This is why he asserts so emphatically that, in the last resort, "the subject of dogmatics is" – not God or the Incarnation – but "the Christian Church."[203]

---

203. *Dogmatics in Outline*, SCM Press, 1960, p. 9.

Faith and religion.

"Religion" is something distinct from faith, and on the whole harmful to it. Faith, true biblical faith, comes from God. Religion is of man's making. So is any seeking after God before God has personally summoned him. Only the man who has biblical "faith" finds the true God. Religion is all the practices and pieties that collect around the worship of God, and which not only can be, but most often are, the grave of faith. Until the latter part of his life, Barth would seem to have regarded the Catholic Church as the form of Christianity in which faith was buried deepest under "religion."

Summing up, we could say that Barth unquestionably believed, indeed deeply believed, in God, and His sovereign power, justice and mercy; in Christ as, in some sense, God's spokesman and agent in bringing peace between earth and heaven; in the existence of a special people summoned to bring the Good News to the rest of the world: in the Sermon on the Mount as the rule of Christian life; and in the importance of prayer, fasting and almsgiving. But almost everything else in his theology seems to be problematical.

Soon after Barth's death, his influence in the Protestant world began to wane, something which can happen for a time even to writers whose works are of enduring value. But in Barth's case there was, I think, an additional reason. He was attempting the impossible. There is no way of maintaining a solid body of Christian doctrine or belief once you accept the conclusions of radical biblical scholarship, and I would say this has been demonstrated by the course of Protestantism since his death. "Advanced" Protestant "ecclesial communities" and theologians, taking their stand on the infallibility of the critical method, have continued to move further and further into doctrinal and moral relativism, while "conservative" Protestants anxious to uphold traditional teachings (from highly educated evangelical scholars to the members of fundamentalist sects) have entrenched themselves with more or less effectiveness in the defence of the Bible's authenticity. For Protestantism, there is no middle way as Barth thought there could be. Everything indeed suggests that in the long run only the Catholic Church will be able to handle critical scholarship without being blown up by it – even if in the meantime many of her scholars have received serious cuts and burns or even been mortally wounded.

That the influence of Barthian neo-orthodoxy on Catholics has not, as was hoped, been all benign will, from what has been said in this chapter, be easily seen by Catholic readers, so I will confine myself to a few of the more obviously adverse effects for the sake of non-Catholic readers.

We cannot in fairness lay all the blame for the Catholic theological revolt on Barth. He did not have Catholic faith. But his views on the nature of theology and the role of theologians have provided dissenting Catholic theologians with precisely the arguments they needed in their attempts to raise themselves to a position of authority on a level with that of bishops.[204]

He was not the only theologian to promote the notion of "on-going revelation." But he was probably the most authoritative.

His separation of faith from reason helps to explain why Paul VI had several times to lament the spread of "fideism" among Catholics – making belief a totally irrational act – and the widespread abandonment of apologetics. Apologetics, the art of explaining the rational grounds for believing, was anathema to Barth. Its abandonment after the Council, when apologetics became all but a dirty word, is, I believe, one of the main reasons so many Western Catholics are now incapable of seeing why one version of Christianity is to be preferred to another, or even one religion to another.

Among scholars, his irrationalism has led to a revival of what is known as "Averroism" – the theory that revelation and the findings of reason can contradict each other yet both in some unexplained sense be "true."[205] This was not only Barth's position; it is now common among Catholic scholars. An example is the American biblicist Fr Raymond Brown in regard to the Resurrection and Virgin Birth. As a critical historian, Brown knew they were pious legends; "by faith," he believed they were real events.

Finally we should mention Barth's continuing polemic against most things Catholic. Except for the period when he was feeling the spell of Fr Przywara, and towards the end of his life when he mellowed under the influence of ecumenism, he never ceased making the Church the butt of his sallies and denunciations. It is difficult to think that this barrage of unfavourable comment from a man of his scholarly standing, with whom it was the Church's policy to remain on good terms, was not at least partly

---

204. For instance, "no ecclesiastical authority should be allowed by theology to hinder it from honestly pursuing its critical task, and the same applies to any frightened voices from the midst of the congregation" (E.T., p. 43).
205. Averroes wanted to advance philosophical propositions contradicting the Koran. His theory was therefore partly designed to appease Muslim theologians. Repudiated by the Church in the 13th century, it had a brief revival among Catholics in the early 16th century under the title "Latin Averroism."

responsible for so many influential people in the Church at the time of the Council, from the late Cardinal Suenens to countless conciliar *periti*, having come to believe and start propagating the idea that everything had been going wrong in the Church since the reign of Constantine.

Barth's influence on the Catholic faithful at large was more indirect. Like Bultmann and Bonhoeffer, his influence only made itself felt in a significant way when the clergy began to read books applauding them, when students for the priesthood started attending courses in Protestant seminaries, and when the results made themselves felt in Sunday sermons.

PART III

IMPACT WITHIN THE CHURCH: A THEOLOGIAN AND THE LITURGY

Chapter Twenty

BIG BROTHER

This last part of the book is intended to high-light the influence of the tendencies we have been following on Catholic thinking at every level by studying their effects first of all on a major theologian, and then on the attempts to make the liturgy more telling as an instrument of spiritual transformation. Three chapters will be devoted to the theologian and two to liturgical change.

The theologian I have chosen is Father Karl Rahner, chiefly because during the 20 or so years following the Second Vatican Council he became for many people its most authoritative interpreter.

As I said in Chapter One, "theologians (or major theologians) are the principal channel through which doctrinal developments, or deviations, enter the main stream of Catholic thinking. They also create the intellectual style through which, at any particular epoch, divine revelation is transmitted via the clergy to the Catholic people. In both these respects, Fr Rahner, above all other theologians of the period, deserves studying." Furthermore, he illustrates better than any other figure of the conciliar period what I said in *Turmoil and Truth* about Catholic scholars who fall in love with their special subject and start subordinating the faith to it.

For Rahner, "my subject" was, of course, German idealist philosophy. However, before looking at the ways in which it affected his theology and faith, I will say something about his life and career in so far as they throw light on the development of his ideas.

A Bavarian, he came from what he called a "normal middle-class Christian family." It was normal for those days. His father, a professor at a teacher-training college at Freiburg in Breisgau, had seven children. To supplement his salary he tutored on the side and his wife went out baby-sitting. The couple never had a house they owned themselves.

At 18, Karl, the third child, entered the Jesuit novitiate at Feldkirche in Austria. His brother Hugo, who became a well-known religious writer himself, had joined the order three years earlier. There followed the usual course of Jesuit training: three years of philosophy, mainly at Pullach near Munich (1924–7); two years teaching Latin to novices back at Feldkirche (which gave him a command of Latin later invaluable for communicating with non-German speakers at the Council); for his theological formation

(1929–33) he was sent to Valkenburg in Holland. He was ordained in Munich in 1932 by Cardinal Faulhaber. His studies over, it was decided that he should teach the history of philosophy, and he returned to his home town Freiburg to get the necessary doctorate.

Because Heidegger was teaching there, Freiburg university was at this time considered one of the most stimulating centres of philosophy in Germany. However, owing to Heidegger's support for the Nazis, Rahner's superiors considered Heidegger unsuited as a supervisor. Instead, Martin Honecker, the holder of the chair of Catholic philosophy, was chosen as guide for his studies. He and Rahner were not well suited. Honecker was unsympathetic to the new trends in philosophy and theology. Rahner, on the other hand, was already a devotee of German idealism. During his time at Pullach he had made a careful study of Kant, Maréchal and Rousselot, and his life-long antipathy to scholasticism, for which the way that theology was taught at Valkenburg may have been partly responsible, was already well developed. The relationship with his supervisor was an anticipation in miniature of the clashes that would take place at the Council.

For his doctoral thesis, Rahner chose a text from St Thomas. The thesis was intended to be an historical study of St Thomas' theory of knowledge. But Rahner, who was never in awe of authority – at any rate not ecclesiastical authority – and whose "innovative and systematic spirit" [McCool, *A Rahner Reader*, p. xix] was already making itself felt, used it to demonstrate what he believed to be an affinity between St Thomas's epistemology and that of Kant and Heidegger. Honecker rejected the thesis and forced Rahner to leave the university without a degree. However, sympathetic superiors intervened. Rahner was precipitately transferred to Innsbruck, given a degree in theology, and made a professor at the Jesuit theological faculty. Rahner was to teach theology for the rest of his life.

In 1939, an amplified version of his rejected doctoral thesis was published under the title *Geist im Welt* (*Spirit in the World*) and two years later a series of lectures on the philosophy of religion, delivered in the summer of 1937, appeared as *Hörer des Wörtes* (*Hearers of the Word*). These two books, which established his reputation, "were the seminal and foundational works from which Rahner was to develop his philosophical theology." [206]

---

206. William V. Dych, *Karl Rahner*, Geoffrey Chapman, Outstanding Christian Thinkers Series, p. 8. Fr. Dych, a pupil of Rahner, acted as interpreter on his American lecture tours and has translated *Spirit in the World* and, at Rahner's own request, *Foundations of Christian Faith*.

Although Rahner would always insist that he was a theologian not a philosopher, his subsequent career suggests that philosophy always mattered more to him. In an address on the occasion of Heidegger's 80th birthday, Rahner referred to him as "his one master ... without whom Catholic theology would no longer be thinkable."[207]

On the invasion of Austria, the Nazis closed the Jesuit college and ordered Rahner to leave the city. But they do not appear to have taken further measures against him. Most of the war years he spent in Vienna as a theological consultant to the archdiocese and a member of the diocesan pastoral institute. He also gave lectures on theology there and in other Third Reich cities. Meanwhile he had gained the confidence of the Archbishop of Vienna, Cardinal Innizer.

In January 1943, the Archbishop of Freiburg, Rahner's home town, wrote a letter to all the bishops of Germany and Austria warning them against dangerous innovations in doctrine and liturgy, and Innizer, who disagreed with him, used Rahner to draft his reply. The reply showed an "acute sense of the need for ... reform in Church teaching and liturgy" (Dych, p. 9). Gradually Rahner was becoming a name to the whole German-speaking episcopate.

In 1948 the theological faculty at Innsbruck reopened and Rahner's long career as a teacher and professor of theology began in earnest.

A former pupil has called him "a stimulating teacher." "I think the main reason for his attractiveness to students was that his classes were alive – he did not just repeat what was in the textbook. In fact he rarely referred to the textbook" though "he told us to learn what was in it. He would take thesis by thesis and ask what it really meant and how it relates to the situation of the Christian today... He was also quite witty in his own way. He often amazed us by giving brief summaries of the theologies of various theologians ... or philosophers." The writer also speaks of the regularity of his life. "He was ... up very early, Mass and Breviary before 7 a.m." After breakfast, "he went to his desk for the rest of the day. He had that old German *Sitzfleisch*."[208]

Without this old-time self-discipline, one feels, his enormous output

---

207. *30 Days*, no. 10, 1992, p. 53. By way of contrast, in 1931, Heidegger told Edith Stein, whom he mistakenly thought was applying for a job as his assistant, that if she "intended to take a Catholic line, then it would be impracticable to work under him" (*Edith Stein*, by Sister Teresia de Spiritu Sancto, O.D.C., Sheed and Ward, 1952, p. 92).
208. Letter to the author from Fr. Kenneth Baker SJ, editor of *The Homiletic and Pastoral Review*. *Sitzfleisch*: an old German expression for perseverance.

would hardly have been possible. For Rahner, the 1950s were a formidably prolific period of writing and publishing. Most of his work was in the form of articles that began as lectures and later appeared in journals, lexicons and encyclopaedias. He was an active member of several learned German theological societies concerned with ecumenism and the relations between faith and science. He was co-editor of a half dozen ambitious publishing ventures, which included the more than one-hundred-volume series *Quaestiones Disputatae* (Disputed Questions), to which he contributed eight books of his own and 8 in collaboration with others. Meanwhile he was editing the 28th–31st editions of Denzinger, the definitive collection of the doctrinal decrees and statements of Councils and popes. The encyclopaedic knowledge of Catholic doctrine he thereby acquired would stand him in good stead the deeper be entered into difficult theological waters – an entry that had indeed already begun.

In 1950, Pius XII's *Humani Generis* had singled out existentialism as liable to undermine "the validity of metaphysical reasoning," even when it didn't undermine the very belief in God's existence, and as Rahner was known to be an ardent Heideggerian it was widely assumed that the authorities in Rome had Rahner in mind. The idea, the encyclical said, that existentialism could be harmonised with Catholic doctrine merely by adding "a few corrections" and filling in "a few gaps" was "a palpable illusion."

Being a controversial figure does not of course of itself mean that a theologian is unsound. That depends on whether his ideas accord with Catholic teaching – something not always instantly apparent – and on the Church's final judgement. However, the next brush with authority did reveal an increasingly typical Rahnerian character trait.

In 1951 the Jesuit authorities forbade him from publishing a lengthy paper entitled "Problems in Contemporary Mariology." It was Rahner's way of voicing his opinion on Pius XII's proclamation of the Dogma of the Assumption the year before. Purportedly a learned defence of the doctrine, it began with the statement on p. 1:"Let's make one thing clear from the outset. Every word in this definition seems to us at first hearing to be off-putting" (*Tablet*, 14 July, 1984). This lordliness of tone would grow over the years until eventually it acquired an imperial ring suggesting that the entire body of the Church's teaching was his private property to dispose of as he wished.

Three years later, someone drew Rome's attention to an article Rahner had published in 1949, "The Many Masses and the One Sacrifice." In addition to advocating concelebration, which the Church has since restored (a positive contribution), the article raised questions about "the fruits of the Mass" and the value of multiplying the number of masses. Without mentioning Rahner by name, Pius XII contradicted part of it in a talk in 1954.

There was yet another skirmish a few months before the opening of the Council. In 1960, Rahner had published an article on Our Lady's perpetual virginity in which he drew a distinction between "the real content and substance of a doctrine and what can be considered part of the historically conditioned form in which it is expressed" (Dych, p. 12). What did he mean? Surely, either Our Lady was or was not perpetually a Virgin? How could historical conditioning affect this central fact?

To begin with, the article seems to have passed unnoticed. Then suddenly in October 1962, Rahner was informed that in future everything he wrote had to be passed by Rome before publication. Rahner replied that in that case he would give up writing altogether. However no such drastic step was called for. The three German-speaking cardinals, Frings of Cologne, Döpfner of Munich and König of Vienna, the leaders of the German-speaking wing of the reform party at the Council, intervened and persuaded Pope John to suspend the censorship. A learned society of professors in the sciences and humanities, the Paulus Gesellschaft, was also mobilised in Rahner's support. Two-hundred-and-fifty signatures were gathered for a petition to Rome asking for the censorship to be dropped.

Because of these *contretemps*, Rahner played little part in the work of the conciliar preparatory commissions. The restoration of the permanent diaconate seems to have been the only subject on which he was officially consulted. Nor was he initially made an official *peritus* or theological adviser of the Council. He came to the Council as Cardinal König's personal adviser, a role he also filled for Cardinal Döpfner, and was only an official conciliar *peritus* after the Council began. From then on, with the backing of his patrons, he rapidly became a dominant figure.

Fr Congar speaks of his influence as "enormous." "The climate," Congar says, "had become: *Rahner dixit. Ergo verum est.* Let me give you an example – there were two microphones on the table, but Rahner had monopolised one … It often happened that the Cardinal Archbishop of Vienna, Franz König, whose expert Rahner was, would turn to Rahner and say, as if prompting him to intervene: *Rahner quid?* Then, of course, Fr Rahner would intervene." [209]

"Traces of his theology," writes Fr Dych, "can be found in the Council's teaching on the Church, on papal primacy and the episcopate, on revelation and the relationship between Scripture and Tradition, on the inspiration of

209. Congar, interview in *30 Days*, no. 3, 1993.

the Bible, on the sacraments and the diaconate, on the relationship of the Church to the modern world, on the possibility of the salvation outside the Church (the visible Church) even for non-believers and in many other areas." However this does not mean that the Council adopted Rahner's views wholesale on all these subjects. We do not have to deny that he made positive contributions to the texts. But there is also evidence of his having exerted a negative influence, in the sense of traditional positions having been less strongly upheld than they could have been.[210]

However, the main thing at this point is his having emerged from the Council as, unofficially, the most authoritative interpreter of what it had all been about. "Who today does not take his point of reference from Karl Rahner?" wrote von Balthasar about this time.[211]

Meanwhile, with his impressive capacity for work, he had continued teaching theology at Innsbruck, until he moved to the University of Munich in 1964, and finally, in 1967, to Münster, where he was professor of dogmatic theology until his retirement in 1981.

After the Council, his position vis-à-vis Rome could be compared to that of a 19th century Austrian Archduke backing independence movements in the subject territories of the Empire without personally taking to the field or breaking off relations with his father in Vienna. Direct confrontations with authority were left to Fr Schillebeeckx, Fr Küng and lesser subordinates. Ever watchful of his reputation as a "great theologian," Rahner took much more care than the revolution's "shock troops" to make his ideas look like legitimate theological developments rather than the innovations they increasingly were. This was the period of tours abroad lecturing to ecstatic audiences of priests, religious and laity.

Rome on its side did its best, for strategic reasons, to disguise the degree of his responsibility for the rebellion and the precise nature of what he

---

210. Some of his less happy endeavours can be found in Ralph Wiltgen's account of Vatican II, *The Rhine Flows Into the Tiber*, Hawthorn Books, U.S.A., 1967. The great merit of this book is that while "full of precise details" (Yves Congar), the author, a Divine Word missionary, knew how to keep on top of them. He ran an international news service during the Council, and met and interviewed numberless Council Fathers and *periti*.
211. Quoted in *30 Days*, no. 10, 1992. "I thought I ought to discover what the new theology is all about" said a future archbishop to the author in 1967, brandishing a book by Rahner. For the first two-and-a-half decades after the Council the new theology meant Rahner, Schillebeeckx and Küng for the majority of Catholics, as could be seen from a glance at most presbytery bookshelves of that period. At least in England, it was unusual to find much if anything by De Lubac or Congar.

seemed to be saying. He was, for instance, one of the first members of Pope Paul's International Theological Commission. Later it was agreed that he and the Commission should "go their separate ways" owing to "incompatibilities" of theological outlook.[212]

In November 1963, over a decade earlier, he had written to his friend Vorgrimler from Rome that a *festschrift* in honour of his 60th birthday would stand him in good stead because it was by no means certain that "my 'most dangerous' things have yet been written" (*30 Days*, no. 4, 1993, p. 61). But now the "dangerous things" were being written, and as they multiplied, so did the prominence of his critics.

Cardinal Frings and Fr Ratzinger had begun to have reservations about aspects of his theology before the Council ended.[213] The critics would eventually include not only "traditionally-minded" figures like Cardinal Siri of Genoa but one-time sympathisers or colleagues such as Frs von Balthasar and de Lubac. Von Balthasar had rapidly revised his opinion of Rahner as "a point of reference."[214]

In spite of this, at no time was any of Rahner's teaching officially called into question, nor, as happened to lesser men, was he invited to Rome to explain it. He can be seen as revolution's heavy artillery, firing from behind the lines to soften up a doctrine before his followers went in to the attack.

He spent his years of retirement writing and lecturing at home and abroad. For his 80th birthday in 1984 there were celebrations in Freiburg, Innsbruck, London, and Budapest. He died three weeks later, by which time entire generations had absorbed his way of thinking. One of his last acts was a letter to the bishops of Peru supporting the liberation theology of Gustavo Gutierrez.

---

212. Cardinal Seper, to the author, October 1980. The cardinal was at that time head of the Congregation for the Doctrine of the Faith. In 1993, in a rather cautious letter to the international monthly *30 Days* (no. 3, p. 7), Cardinal König, while admitting that "there might be the desire to disagree with some aspects of Rahner's theology," defended Rahner from the charge of heterodoxy on the grounds that, had any of his writings deserved censure, the Congregation for the Doctrine of the Faith would have been bound to take action. The Cardinal must surely have known that with his former protégé constantly accusing Rome and the CDF of trying to sabotage the Council, any such action had become next to impossible.

213. Wiltgen, *op. cit.*, p. 285.

214. *Cordula oder der Ernstfall*, 1966 (*The Moment of Christian Witness*, Ignatius Press 1994) pp. 100–130. For Cardinal Ratzinger's criticisms see *Principles of Catholic Theology*, Ignatius Press, 1987 (German original, 1982), pp. 162–171.

Chapter Twenty-One

THE EMPEROR'S CLOTHES

That a man who reflected on the teachings of the Church for a good fifty years and poured out books and articles about them will almost certainly say a lot of things that are useful and true can be taken for granted. We can also assume that up to a certain point in his life, Rahner believed all the Church's teachings as the Church has always understood them. Men fall into errors by degrees. This explains the great, though by now perhaps diminishing number of Rahner's Catholic admirers. There is always something refreshing about hearing the same truths expressed in new words or from a new angle. It is like reading the Gospels in a different language.

But as we have just seen, by the mid-1960s, one-time admirers were beginning to realise that something was going seriously wrong. It was not a question of the odd error here or there but of a transformation of the underlying substance of his thought from Catholic to something less than Catholic, and it is the more or less final state of that substance that I shall try to outline as it had come to be when he published his *Grundkurs des Glaubens* in 1976 (*Foundations of Christian Faith* (FCF), New York, Crossroad, 1982, translator William V. Dych). Von Balthasar and Ratzinger both note symptoms of the transformation on the devotional level: the first mentions Rahner's waning interest in the Sacred Heart, the second his cooling feelings for Our Lady.

Before the publication of *Foundations*, most of his strictly theological writings had appeared in the form of articles on particular subjects in periodicals. These were gradually collected and published in the multi-volume series, translated into English under the title *Theological Investigations*. Others could be found in dictionaries and encyclopaedias. All this made it difficult to see what he was saying, as it were, "in the round." His famously contorted style was another obstacle to comprehension. All this however changed with the appearance of *Foundations*, which Ratzinger calls a "comprehensive Summa." But it is a summa in one volume of under five-hundred pages. It is not exactly a pleasure to read. Nevertheless anyone with a reasonably good education, a measure of determination and a rudimentary knowledge of Kantian epistemology should be able to get the gist of it.

Since then comprehension has been made easier still by Fr Dych's book. This illuminating survey of his teacher's career and theology had

Rahner's personal approval, and the author's candour and clarity of style give it additional value. With these two books, it becomes possible for non-experts to understand the basics of Rahner's later theology.[215]

One should also be aware at the outset that Rahner was essentially a theologian with a mission, which is not quite the same as a vocation. Every theologian has a vocation – to meditate on and expound the Catholic faith, and we can be certain that that is what Fr Rahner too saw himself called on to do. But early on he formed two specific further aims.

The first was "the need to dispel the notion that Catholic theology was a monolith in which everything of importance was settled" (Dych p. 10). This was a viewpoint shared by the majority of the conciliar reformers. Indeed, the Council itself opened up a number of theological questions for debate without settling them. The difference in Rahner's case was that he came to regard almost everything as "unsettled," which, as we shall see, included the doctrine of the Trinity.[216]

His second objective seems to have taken shape while he was involved in pastoral work in Vienna. Closer acquaintance with pastoral problems had led him to the conclusion we are already familiar with. Faith and practice were in decline because the way the faith was presented was too remote from people's experience. Catholic belief in its entirety must therefore be reformulated in terms corresponding with that experience. Even if this were true, the odd thing was thinking that using the terminology and concepts of modern German philosophy – the most remote of all philosophies from a common-sense view of the world – could remedy the situation.[217]

The undertaking has been compared to St Thomas Aquinas' use of Aristotle. But there is a notable difference. The primary sources for St Thomas' theology were Holy Scripture and the Fathers, whom the saint quotes in abundance, and after that Aristotle, Plato and pseudo-Dionysius whom he uses to bring out the concord between reason and revelation.

---

215. Rahner's articles "Incarnation" and "Jesus Christ" in the theological encyclopaedia *Sacramentum Mundi* also throw light on it, and the introductory passages in Fr McCool's *Rahner Reader* (1975) are a first-rate guide to his theology as a whole. Unfortunately, the latter predates the German original of *Foundations* (1976) by a year.

216. An experienced Divine Word missionary speaks of his "genius for making perfectly clear concepts as hazy as possible" and his gift for "creating problems without solving them." H. van Straelen S.V.D., *The Catholic Encounter with World Religions*, 1966, p. 102. The author was professor of modern philosophy and comparative religion at the University of Nagoya, Japan.

217. See Appendix II.

Philosophy, for St Thomas, was truly the handmaid of theology. Rahner, in contrast, makes theology the handmaid of philosophy. A distinguished German scholar has spoken of Rahner's "diffidence" towards Holy Scripture, and this is easily confirmed by looking at his books. They contain startlingly few references to Holy Scripture, the Fathers or any other ecclesiastical sources either in the text or footnotes.

Kant, then, will provide the "new St Thomas" with his theory of knowledge, Heidegger with his philosophy of man, Hegel with his cosmology or general world-view. Together they will, as it were, permeate his theology from below until they have transformed it into a religious philosophy largely independent of divine revelation.

The extent of the transformation can be judged by his statement that "a 'demystificatory theology,' rightly understood, will need to be aware that propositions like 'There are three persons in God,' 'God sent his Son into the world,' 'We are saved by the blood of Jesus Christ' are purely and simply incomprehensible for a modern man if they remain, in the old fashion of theology and of statement, the point of departure and arrival of the Christian message. They generate the same impression as pure mythology in a religion of the past" ("Fundamental Theological Directions" in *Summary of Twentieth Century Theology*, Herder, 1970, III, p. 539, quoted in "Rahner the Untouchable," *30 Days*, no. 4, 1993). "Modern man feels that thousands of statements in theology are just forms of mythology." He can no more take seriously the words "Jesus is God made man" than the fact that "the Dalai Lama regards himself as the reincarnation of Buddha."

Lesser but still significant influences were Teilhard and radical biblical scholarship. Who in the world of high theology of his generation and outlook could escape them?

Although Fr Teilhard had no time for existentialism – it was too gloomy – from Teilhard, Rahner learned to look at the universe as a process in which each level of being gives rise to the one above through a process of "self-transcendence." It is as though the universe were pulling itself up by its bootstraps. All beings are endowed with this fundamental urge. "If becoming is really to be taken seriously, it must be understood as real *self-transcendence* (his emphasis), as surpassing oneself, as emptiness actively achieving its own fullness..." "It is of the intrinsic nature of matter to develop towards spirit" (*Foundations of Christian Faith*, p. 184).

As for biblical scholarship, while not having much personal interest in it, he seems to have taken its more radical conclusions for granted. "The accounts from which we can acquire knowledge about Jesus of Nazareth, if we can acquire it at all, are ... one and all faith assertions" (FCF, p. 244). From "an historical point of view a great deal has to be left open in an inquiry about the pre-resurrection Jesus" (FCF, p. 248). Our "historical knowledge of Jesus, of his self-interpretation and of the justification he gives for it is burdened with many problems, uncertainties and ambiguities" (FCF, p. 235). "Jesus saw himself not merely as one among many prophets ... but ... as the absolute and definitive saviour, although ... what a definitive saviour means and does not mean requires further reflection" (FCF, p. 246).

However, German philosophy remained the dominant influence, and to understand how it changed Rahner's understanding of central Catholic doctrines we must start with a look at his theory of knowledge. With idealists, this is always where the troubles begin.

For a follower of Kant, it will be remembered, there are three kinds of knowledge: categorical knowledge, transcendental knowledge, and the dictates of "practical reason" which give us our ideas of right and wrong. Here we are only concerned with the first two – categorical knowledge which comes to us via the senses from outside, and transcendental which is somehow or other generated within. For acquiring knowledge of God, Rahner sees categorical knowledge as decidedly inferior to transcendental knowledge. Categorical knowledge – which includes divine revelation and the doctrines of the Church – because it comes from outside, can never tell us how things really are "in themselves." Categorical statements therefore can only be approximations to the truth, ever open to revision. Interiorly, on the other hand, we are the direct objects of God's "self-communication." We have a contact with Him or "pre-grasp" (*Vorgriff*) that, no matter how vague (or unthematic), is much more genuine. "When," says Rahner, "we assume for the miracles and mighty deeds of Jesus and for his resurrection the function of grounding the faith, this is not to maintain that such knowledge induces and justifies faith from outside as it were" (FCF, p. 239). Faith corresponds with "our supernatural ... experience of God's absolute self-communication." This is why doctrinal formulations always have to be brought into line with inner experience. It also explains Rahner's growing agnosticism (not about God's existence but about the possibility of knowing almost anything about Him) and, I think, what Fr McCool of the *Rahner Reader* has in mind, when he speaks of "the dialectic between the mind's categorical knowledge of sensible reality and its conscious, though unobjective grasp of God as the term of its dynamism" being "crucial for Rahner's dogmatic theology" (*Rahner Reader*, pp. xxv–xxvi). This could be translated as "the dialectic between what the Church has said its doctrines mean and what Rahner's 'unobjective grasp' of God has told him they mean. This is what is crucial for Rahner's dogmatic theology." [218]

We are now ready to look at the way the dialogue between transcendental knowledge and categorical knowledge in Rahner's theology, along with the philosophies of Hegel and Heidegger, altered Rahner's understanding of the Incarnation and the Trinity.

Who and what is Christ? The Church has always said "God and Man," and when asked how He could be both, has replied, through the Council of Chalcedon: by taking a human nature without losing His divine nature. He is a single divine person with two natures, a divine one and a human one. But this idea Rahner simply will not have.

Already at the beginning of the Council he was writing from Rome to his friend Fr Vorgrimler: "When I sit around a table with Daniélou, Ratzinger, Schillebeeckx and so on, I realise that I have not yet grown old. In my view they are still not aware of how little water Christology approached from the top down will hold today. It begins by declaring simply that God was made man" (Note, *30 Days*, October 1992, p. 50).

Subsequently he carries on a persistent polemic against the idea that Christ was a "pre-existent divine being." Chalcedon's "descendency Christology" – Christ descending to earth and assuming a human nature without ceasing to be God – smacks, he repeatedly tells us, of mythology. It leaves the impression that Christ's human nature was just a disguise the Divinity put on during a visit to earth like a Greek god. It suggests that God did not become a real man. Such an idea is incomprehensible to modern man, or if he can understand it, he won't buy it. Chalcedon's out-dated descendency Christology must therefore be replaced by a properly worked out "ascendency Christology" that modern people can understand.

How then does "ascendency theology" differ from "descendency theology"? It could, of course, mean that Christ was a good man who gradually became more and more "god-like," or that at some point God came to dwell in him, or adopted him as a son (the old adoptionist heresy). But it wasn't in Rahner's character to peddle such a tired idea, even if he had not had other reasons for thinking differently. [219]

---

218. Obviously we can never know God as He is in Himself, just as we can never know other people as God knows them. But we can still say things about God and other people that are lastingly true.
219. A charitable member of the Congregation for the Doctrine of the Faith once tried to persuade me that "ascendency Christology" simply meant that we should start by concentrating on Christ's manhood because that was the order in which the apostles

To understand Rahner's "ascendency Christology" we have first to look at his doctrine of the Trinity, which, if left to ourselves, we might find hard to understand, but to which we have happily been given a key. The key was provided by Msgr Theobald Beer, a German scholar, in a series of articles and interviews about Rahner, appearing in the international monthly *30 Days* in late 1992 and early 1993. Von Balthasar has called Beer "the greatest living Luther expert." The interview was conducted at the Gustav Siewerth Akademie in Germany, and the founder and director, Prof. Alma von Stockhausen, a Hegel authority, also took part in it.

Basically, the Monsignor claimed, Rahner does not believe in the Trinity as the Church understands it. He has replaced the God of Christianity with a God resembling Hegel's Absolute Mind of which the universe and humanity are thought-projections.

The article produced a chorus of infuriated protests from Rahner enthusiasts throughout Germany. A professor Neufeld of the Rahner archive in Innsbruck claimed that Rahner never revealed "any kind of debt" to Hegel. In reply the author of the interview, Guido Horst, quoted Hans Küng – on a matter like this surely an authority. "The great mind," writes Küng, "behind this closely considered deepening of classical Christology is, while allowing for the influence of Heidegger, none other than Hegel" (*The Incarnation of God*, Edinburgh, T & T Clark, 1987, p. 539). Frs Dych and McCool, both dedicated Rahnerians, likewise take Rahner's debt to Hegel for granted. But perhaps the most convincing evidence for the truth of Msgr Beer's contention is not this or that authority but the flood of light it throws on the whole drift of Rahner's later thought.

If Msgr Beer is right, for Rahner, the Son and the Holy Spirit are not persons in the Church's sense. They did not exist with the Father from all eternity. They are functions of God, or "modes of subsistence" which only come into operation as He begins to create or "objectify" Himself. Rahner, says Msgr Beer, "does not accept as having a biblical foundation the personhood, distinct from the Father, of the Son and the Holy Spirit ..." He "seeks a God for whom the history of the created world is only one moment in the history of God himself" (*30 Days*, no. 10, 1992).

Rahner confirms this. "One ... must take every care" he writes, "to keep everything that might suggest 'three subjectivities' away from the concept of person. Hence, even within the Trinity there is no reciprocal

---

got to know Him. Rahner does in fact make this point. But such a simple idea on its own would hardly have required him to devote so many pages to the subject.

'Thou.' The Son is the self-expression of the Father, which, yet again cannot be conceived of as 'speaking'; the Spirit is the gift which yet again does not 'endow.' " (*Mysterium Salutis* II, p. 462, quoted Horst, *30 Days*, no. 4, 1993.) Thus, to quote Beer again, in Rahner's theology there is "no inter-Trinitarian love, no true Thou for the Father to give his heart to." Indeed, Rahner contemptuously dismisses attempts to understand the inner life of the Trinity. Of "the imposing speculations in which, since the time of Augustine, Christian theology has tried to conceive the inner life of God ... perhaps we can say that ultimately they are not all that helpful" (FCF, p. 135). Like Luther, Rahner is only interested in God in so far as he does things "for us." Besides, prior to the creation, there was in effect no Trinity to have an inner life to speculate about.

However Rahner's God is not as loveless as Hegel's. Hegel's Absolute Mind "objectifies" or becomes "other" than itself in order to understand itself. In its objectification it discovers what it is. Rahner's God wants to communicate Himself to "the other" in order to awaken a response of love. This is where ascendency Christology or Rahner's way of understanding the Incarnation comes into the picture. Christ is the climax of God's efforts to produce a creature capable of responding adequately to his self-communication when he sets the evolutionary process going. "When God wants to be what is not God, man comes to be." [220] One is tempted to add: and lots of other things too. Dinosaurs, coelacanths, giraffes. And why omit angels?

But evolution is a slow business. Even when man at last appeared, his response to the divine self-communication remained minimal for hundreds of thousands of years. Eventually, however, the long process of cosmic self-transcendence reached a climax. The initial breakthrough, presumably, had been the first fully hominised anthropoid. Man represents "the basic tendency of matter to discover itself in spirit through self-transcendence." The end of the process will be man's "full self-transcendence into God by means of God's self communication," and it is this final stage of the upward journey that begins with the birth of Christ. In Christ, evolution produces the first man whose "Yes" to God was total, and in reply God said "Yes" to mankind as a whole.

The "absolute guarantee that this ultimate self-transcendence ... will succeed and has already begun is what we call the 'hypostatic union.' The God man is the initial beginning and the definitive triumph of the

---

220. F.C.F., p. 225. Alternative translation: "If God wants to be non-God, man is born, that and nothing else." Von Balthasar, *Cordula*, Ignatius, p. 106.

movement of the world's self-transcendence into absolute closeness to the mystery of God. In the first instance this hypostatic union may not be seen so much as something which distinguishes Jesus from us but as something which must occur once and only once when the world begins to enter on its final phase" (FCF, p. 181).

It is only in this sense that Rahner (we are talking of course about Rahner in his latter years) is willing to accept Christ as saviour and redeemer. He is as averse to the idea that the passion and death of Christ were a sacrifice for sin as he is to the idea that He was a "pre-existing divine being." There is no place in his system for a theology of the Cross. He tells us we should not take as much notice of Christ's "bitter sufferings" as of his death. He carries on a "constant polemic against a legalistic doctrine of satisfaction." He makes no attempt to explain the New Testament statement that Christ bore our sins on the Cross. He attributes our redemption to God's saving will rather than to anything Christ did for us.[221]

"For Rahner," Msgr Beer says flatly, "Christ was just a man" (*30 Days*, Oct. 1992, p. 53). And taking the words in their normal sense, Msgr Beer is of course right. But you can seldom make such a forthright statement about Rahner without eventually finding you have to qualify it in some way.

For instance, in the pages of *Foundations* (212–228) where he deals with the Incarnation, he repeatedly asks his readers to consider what the Creed means when it says that Christ *became* man, with special emphasis on the word *became*. We must not, he tells us, "understand this fundamental dogma of Christianity in a mythological way" (FCF, p. 180). What does he mean? After enough repetitions, the penny drops. He is using the notion of *kenosis*, God's self-emptying, to imply that God, or the part of Him that turned into non-God, was literally transformed into a man. He or It ceased to be divine. (The Latin creed, of course, says that Christ "became incarnate" or "took flesh," which is rather different.) However, since what is non-God has all emanated from God and will eventually be absorbed back again into God, everything from Christ down to pebbles on the beach can in this sense be considered divine.

Here is how Rahner puts it. After rejecting the idea that God could assume a human nature without its affecting his nature as God, he writes: "On the contrary, the basic element according to our faith, is the *self-emptying* (sic), the coming to be, the *kenosis* and the *genesis* of God himself,

---

221. Von Balthasar, *op. cit.*, pp. 108–9.

who can come to be by *becoming* another thing ... without having to change his own proper reality which is unoriginated origin. By the fact that he remains in his infinite fullness while he empties himself ... the ensuing other is his own proper reality." (*Theological Investigations*, vol. IV., pp. 114–115, quoted by Beer, *30 Days*, no. 4, 1993.) If one tried to bring consistency into these speculations, one would have to say that the Incarnation really began with the Big Bang or when God said "Let there be light," and that the millions of years preceding the historical appearance of Jesus were the time of his gestation in the womb. All this is highly ingenious. But it is hardly Christianity.

Chapter Twenty-Two

NAKED BUT NOT ASHAMED

The other main novelty in Rahner's theology is his teaching about the relationship between the natural and the supernatural worlds, and between nature and grace. Most of the leading 20th century reformers were in some degree critical of the way the Church presented her teaching on this subject. Nearly all had proposals for improved or alternative explanations. Nor were their proposals just one item among others on their agenda. Recasting the way the relationship between natural and supernatural, nature and grace was conceived was the heart or nerve centre of the "new theology."

Their criticisms and proposals can be grouped as those of the moderate school led by de Lubac and those of the extreme school led by Rahner, and in order to show how Rahner's theology deviates from the traditional teaching and from the Council's new orientations, I will start with a look at what the Church has to say, and then at de Lubac's ideas and proposals.

One cannot understand Catholic Christianity without understanding its teaching about grace, to which one could add that if you don't understand its teaching about grace, you will find it harder to tell what is and is not Catholic Christianity. However, although what the Church has defined is clear enough, we are of course dealing with a mystery, and there are still unsettled questions and unresolved problems connected with her teaching.

The two sets of terms "natural and supernatural" and "nature and grace" are often used interchangeably as if they applied equally well to two different if related topics – the relationship of God to the created universe, and the action of God in the human soul – and this, for non-theologians, can often be the cause of not a little confusion. I will therefore use "natural and supernatural" for the former, and "nature and grace" for the latter.

The teaching about the relationship of the supernatural world (God, heaven, eternity) to the natural world raises relatively few problems. God brought the natural world into existence, holds it in being from moment to moment, and is "immanent" in it, or present by his power, everywhere. At the same time He transcends it in the sense that it is not part of Him. It is not an extension of His being or substance. This is the traditional teaching about the relationship of the natural and supernatural orders.

As for the word grace, down to about the fifth century it was loosely used for every kind of gift from God, natural and supernatural, material and spiritual, both for the benefits and wonders of the universe and equally for holy inspirations and endowments. However, in the Latin West, after the fifth century the word came to be reserved exclusively for God's supernatural spiritual gifts. Moreover, as she reflected on the Scriptures, the Fathers, and her own sacramental practice over the centuries, the Church gradually came to distinguish between these different supernatural gifts with ever-increasing clarity. (Meanwhile the looser use of the word by the Greek Fathers continued in the East and was reintroduced in the West by the movement for *ressourcement* associated with the new theology.)

In Western doctrine and theology, grace meant in the first place the life of God Himself (uncreated grace) and then (the main subject of theological discussion) the "share" in that life which God imparts through His Holy Spirit to angels and men so that they can reach their final end, the beatific vision. Within the realm of created grace, a further distinction was made between *actual* grace and *sanctifying* grace. The term "actual grace" is used for separate acts of supernatural assistance which God gives to all men at different times as need arises or in answer to prayers. "Sanctifying grace" is the term for the enduring state of friendship or justification which men enter when they assent to God's offer of the gift of faith, receive baptism, and keep His commandments. It is customarily referred to as the "state of grace." The "state of grace" is what makes the soul worthy to be a "temple of the Holy Spirit." One must be in a state of grace when one dies if one is to achieve salvation.[222]

This teaching about grace was given its earliest formal articulation by St Augustine, was further developed and clarified by St Thomas and the scholastics, and when challenged by the 16th century reformers led to disputes among the Catholic theologians who tried to answer their objections. The objections were mainly about the relationship of grace and free will. When the disputes began to threaten the peace of the Church, the pope of the time forbade further discussion, and for three centuries tranquillity reigned. But in the late 19th century, Blondel brought the relationship of natural to supernatural to the fore again in a philosophical form, whence, lifted to the theological plane, it became the heart of the conflict between de Lubac and the new theologians, and the neo-scholastics headed by Fr Garrigou-Lagrange.

The core of the teaching around which the 20th century controversies have gravitated, is the fact that grace and the promise of eternal life, which

222. See CCC, articles 1987–2029.

grace prepares for and helps to realise, are free gifts. They are "gratuitous." They do not belong to human nature as such. As creatures of the natural order, men have no right to them. Nor can they gain access to them by their own efforts. They can or cannot co-operate with grace once offered. They can pray for it. But they cannot even begin to want to pray without a grace to get them going.

This teaching about the "gratuity" of grace and eternal life was too well established for anyone to wish to challenge. But on one point all the new theologians were agreed. Whether dealing with God and the cosmos, or God's action on the individual soul, the reigning theology, by making too sharp the distinction between the two realms or orders – natural and supernatural – left the impression that God had not initially intended man for a supernatural destiny but had only added it as an afterthought. The reigning teaching was described, often mockingly, as the "two-floor" or "two-tier" theory. However there were differences of opinion about how the two tiers could be brought into closer proximity without colliding with defined doctrines or dogmas.

De Lubac's criticisms focused in the first place on the neo-scholastics' teaching about man's final end.

Man has, in fact, only one final end – the beatific vision in a transfigured universe when the natural order will be assumed into the supernatural. The scholastics on the other hand, St Thomas included, had talked about man's two ends: one natural, the other supernatural. Their purpose was twofold: firstly, to bring out the difference between what men can do in this world by their natural powers alone, and the things for which they are dependent on grace; secondly, to show that God was in no sense bound to reward us with eternal life in heaven. The question could be put this way: God made us with a need for food, we can therefore count on Him to provide it. You could almost say goodness constrains him to provide it. But there is nothing in our nature as such that absolutely "requires" Him to give us either grace or a heavenly reward in the way his goodness "constrains" Him to give us food. An eternity of natural happiness would be a fair and sufficient reward for us (what traditional theology called the "limbo" of the just). Grace and heaven are unmerited gifts, apart from and on top of natural existence.

The importance of this teaching is best seen in the spiritual climate its omission generates. Where it is not explained, Christians easily come to think not only that it is jolly good of them to give God some of their time and attention, but that they have a right to heaven. Anything less would be scandalously unjust. They cease to understand their own insignificance or the immensity of God's generosity.

The scholastics did not of course mean that men's service of God in this world with their natural faculties and capacities (their natural end) was on the same level as their supernatural end, or that the latter could be won without the help of grace. They saw the pursuit of these two ends as interwoven and running concurrently.

However, to clarify the issue still further, their 16th century successors introduced into the debate the concept of "pure nature." The state of pure nature was an hypothesis about what an ideal natural man would have been like if God had made him for life in this world alone and without the need for grace. The purpose was to protect the "gratuity" of the supernatural."[223]

The "state of pure nature" was de Lubac's second target. Since, he maintained, God did not in fact create us for a purely natural existence or purely natural happiness, but (provided that we co-operated) destined us for the beatific vision from the beginning, discussion about "pure nature" could only be misleading.

The neo-scholastic justification for the hypothesis was a principle borrowed from Aristotle: every created being must have within it the power to achieve the purpose for which it was created. If, therefore, men are incapable of reaching their supernatural end by their own powers, they must have an identifiable natural end which is within their natural capacities.[224]

Nonsense, replied de Lubac. Man is not like the rest of nature. As a spirit, with reason and free will, he is an exception in nature. It was a good point, which would have been even stronger if he had added that each spirit, being made directly by God, comes from outside nature.

However, he kept the bulk of his fire for what he saw as the consequences of the neo-scholastic treatment of the two orders. By over-stressing their difference, he insists again and again, the 16th century scholastics had prepared

---

223. Without an adequate distinction between man's natural and supernatural ends, Vatican II's teaching about the "autonomy of the secular" becomes unintelligible. If the natural order could not be studied by reason independently of revelation, or were dependent on grace for its day-to-day functioning – in the sense the word "grace" has had for 1500 years – scientists would have to call on theologians to help them understand what is going on in the laboratory. The fact that the "autonomy of the secular" does not sit easily with the complementary idea of bringing the natural and supernatural orders closer together, gives an idea, I think, of the complexity of the crosscurrents affecting the composition of some of the conciliar texts.
224. I have put the neo-scholastic position more or less as de Lubac presents it in *Mystery of the Supernatural*. The way he saw it was what he was arguing against.

the way for 18th century deism and modern atheism. They had provided atheists with a largely self-explanatory natural order from which God could easily be removed without doing it any observable damage. An over-emphasis on God's transcendence had had similar consequences. For this over-emphasis, de Lubac invented the term "extrinsicism." By "extrinsicism" he meant thinking of God as largely external to His creation, and he suggested that, from time to time – no doubt he was being deliberately provocative – that "extrinsicism" could be a heresy as dangerous as modernism. The remedy was to give more place in theology to God's immanence and all-pervading activity within the cosmos.

De Lubac's other main criticisms had to do with the way the scholastics handled the relationship between nature and grace in the individual soul. Any effective teaching about man must somehow show that "the natural presupposes the supernatural." This, as we have seen, was the starting point of Blondel's philosophical apologetic, which de Lubac was to some extent simply developing. This, he believed, was the only way to answer scientistic atheism.

Up to a point, de Lubac already had St Paul on his side: "The whole creation groans, waiting for the adoption of the sons of God." And St Augustine: "Our hearts are restless until they rest in Thee." And, though he may not have known it, Chesterton in *The Everlasting Man*: "Nature is … looking for something; Nature is always looking for the supernatural." But this only suggests that Nature senses a lack, an absence, and, in the case of men, all that the current teaching allowed was that they have an *obedientia potentialis*, a capacity to receive grace when it is offered. However, de Lubac wanted something more and believed he had found it in the passages where St Thomas speaks of men having a "natural desire" to see God. "Every intellect naturally desires the vision of the divine substance," St Thomas says in the *Summa contra Gentiles*, Bk 3, ch. 57.[225]

Unfortunately, there seems to be no general agreement about what St Thomas meant by this "natural desire." He returns to the idea more than once, and the passages where he speaks of it are not easy to harmonise. The difficulty is that if you interpret the "desire," as De Lubac initially seemed to do, as some kind of natural movement towards God embedded in the human soul from the outset, you come into conflict with the teaching that "without God's grace (man) cannot of his own free will move himself towards justice in God's sight." (CCC 1993, citing Council of Trent.) It also

---

225. Similar texts can be found on pp. 21, 22, and 75 of *Mystery of the Supernatural* (Eng. trans., 1967).

makes heaven something seemingly "owing" to human nature, something God is "bound" to give us, like food.

"The nature of the problem," writes the Anglican Thomist, Eric Mascall, "is impressively shown by the difficulty, which has exercised generations of Thomist scholars, of reconciling St Thomas's repeated assertions that the end of man – the purpose for which he is made – is the supernatural vision of God, with his no less emphatic insistence that man has neither the right to grace and the supernatural nor any powers of his own to attain them" (*The Openness of Being*, p. 152).[226]

It was De Lubac's efforts to solve the problem in his two books, *Surnaturel* (1946) and *Le mystère du surnaturel* (1965), that got him into trouble with Rome in the 1940s and '50s.[227] The second was intended to clarify his position in the light of the objections to the first. Later he wrote a more popular book on the subject, *A Brief Catechesis on Nature and Grace* (Ignatius, 1984; French original, 1980), in which, faced with the devastation wrought by Rahner's speculations, he re-emphasised the distinction between natural and supernatural.

That de Lubac had a case against the way the scholastics presented their teaching about man's two ends and the "state of pure nature," that there could be dangers in over-stressing the distinction between natural and supernatural, we have already seen in Maritain's handling of the question in *Integral Humanism*.[228] On the other hand, the new theology's attempts to reduce the gap by emphasising God's immanence would, with Teilhard and Rahner, as we have seen, lead in the direction of pantheism. So the debate between the neo-scholastics and the new theology was not academic hair-splitting. It would

---

226. De Lubac himself admits that the existence of this "natural desire" cannot be demonstrated from experience, while Professor Alice von Hildebrand in an address at Oxford in the 1990s, spoke of men only too often manifesting "a natural aversion to the supernatural."

227. His friendship with and defence of Teilhard would have been another factor. It was de Lubac's Achilles' heel. There is an interesting parallel with Theodoret of Cyrrhus and Nestorius in the 5th century. Although Theodoret was approved by the Council of Chalcedon, he would, out of loyalty to his one-time friend and fellow student Nestorius, never say a critical word against him in public. Tixeront, vol. II.

228. *Integral Humanism* in effect removed social and political life from any direct influence by the Church. This may not have been a matter of concern to de Lubac. But it explains why we find Cardinal Siri criticising Maritain, the leading luminary of neo-scholasticism, along with de Lubac and Rahner, who stood on the opposite side of the great philosophical divide. For the historical background to the debate between the neo-scholastics and the new theologians, see Appendix III.

affect the faithful's whole way of perceiving the most fundamental realities.[229]

How the Church will eventually resolve this question we do not know. The only point that needs making here is that, both with regard to God and the cosmos and God and the individual soul, de Lubac was endeavouring to correct what he saw as, and what seems to have been, a genuine theological imbalance, and to resolve a genuine theological problem.

Rahner, on the other hand, whatever his original intentions, in effect abolished the problem by substituting an altogether different teaching. We have looked at his theories about the relationship of God to the cosmos; the natural and supernatural worlds are two aspects of a single Hegelian divine *becoming*. With his theology of nature and grace in the individual, we move from the world of Hegel into the world of Heidegger.

First of all, Rahner widens the meaning of grace to include any kind of divine gift. The distinctions between created and uncreated grace and between actual and sanctifying grace to all intents and purposes disappear, or if mentioned become irrelevant. For the most part, Rahner uses the

---

229. Ratzinger sees another and more recondite motivation underlying Rahner's doctrine of grace. Since the 18th century, the world of German academic theology (Protestant to start with, but more recently Catholic as well) has been agitated by an objection to Christianity first raised by the playwright and critic Lessing. No particular historical event, Lessing asserted, can ever have universal significance. By a particular historical event he meant, of course, the life and death of Christ. The simple answer seems to be, Why not? If the earth collided with another planet, the explosion would have "universal" significance at least for the human race. In spite of this, Lessing's objection has continued to be regarded by certain German Christian academics as a stumbling block that must at all costs be removed. The problem is described in Ratzinger's *Principles of Catholic Theology*, (pp. 153–190) along with Rahner's solution and its implications. Ratzinger, while up to a point admiring Rahner's "ingenuity," compares his undertaking with trying to "square the circle." If I have understood Ratzinger's account rightly, the solution, in spite of its ingenuity, ends in dissolving the particular in the universal to the point where the particular all but disappears. Christianity is reduced to a set of commonplaces about man as an historical self-transcendent being which any modern pagan could assent to. As Ratzinger puts it, for Rahner, Christianity is just "a particularly successful apprehension of what is always more or less consciously acknowledged," or in Rahner's own words "The Christian and the Church do not say something that can be opposed. Rather they say that the Unutterable ... that reveals itself ... is Nearness." To this Ratzinger replies that "Christians say much that is particular. Otherwise how could they be a 'sign that is rejected.' " (*op. cit.*, pp. 164, 165, 166.) The only specifically Christian feature Ratzinger can find in the theology of Rahner's *Foundations* is the "person of Jesus," and the only thing that makes Jesus special is the fact that He is "the most successful form of human self-transcendence" – the first member of the evolving human species to achieve complete "openness to God." This is surely a high price to pay to satisfy Lessing.

word "grace" for God's gift or communication of Himself (uncreated grace) without further distinctions. Since God is everywhere, this allows Rahner to say that grace is everywhere. "Now God and the grace of Christ are present as the secret essence of every reality we can choose" (F.C.F., p. 228). Or to sum up Rahner's view critically: "God and the grace of Christ are in everything as the secret essence of all changeable reality" (von Balthasar, *Moment of Christian Witness*, p. 102, citing *Schriften*, 4, p. 153). Grace permeates the whole of nature like water in a sponge.

Paradoxically, the idea that grace is everywhere led to grace becoming a word scarcely heard in Catholic teaching after the Council until it was brought to the fore again by the CCC in the 1990s. The gift was identified with the Giver and many of the faithful started talking as if their actions were all done under the direct inspiration of the Holy Spirit.

What about the recipient of the gift? When and how is grace received? At this point the problem of the non-Christian's salvation begins to impinge on Rahner's thinking. He is anxious – one does not blame him for that – to open the net of salvation as widely as possible, and in the philosophy of Heidegger and his own new loosely defined conception of grace, he believes he has found the means.

In Heidegger, as we already know, men no longer have a human nature. There is only human existence or experience, or "human reality" as Rahner likes to call it. Every individual experiences life differently. However, there are a few basic experiences common to us all which Heidegger calls "existentials," and to these Rahner adds a "supernatural" one. What does it mean? "The self-communication of God," Rahner explains, "is present in man as an existential" (F.C.F., p. 146). Elsewhere he calls it part of "the transcendental constitution of man." To which his pupil, Fr Dych, has added "God's self communication is an existential which pervades all history" (Dych, p. 72). It is not, in Rahner's words, "a-cosmic, directed only to an isolated and individualised subjectivity" (F.C.F., p. 193). [230]

---

230. Holy Scripture takes a different view. Although God wills the salvation of all men, the New Testament tells us that in past times He left the nations in a state of "ignorance," and "allowed them to walk in their own ways." Nor was this ignorance altogether blameless. They could have at least known of His existence and something about His nature from the signs of them stamped on His creation. Thus far they were "without excuse" (Acts 14:16 & 17:30). These strictures of St Paul do not contradict what St Justin said about the "seeds of the Word" to be found in other religions, which have recently been emphasised by the magisterium. But they describe a state of affairs hardly compatible with Rahner's continuous, all-pervasive, undifferentiated "divine Self-communication."

But how can the idea that the self-communication of God is part of men's "constitution" be reconciled with the Church's constant teaching that grace is not part of nature? A common interpretation has been that, just as, according to Rahner, every man has a semiconscious if unarticulated knowledge of God, each of us also enjoys the kind of in-dwelling presence of God which the Church has always taught is possessed only by those who have received baptism by water, blood or desire.[231]

One of the conclusions drawn from this teaching is the now widely held idea that the sacraments do not communicate grace but merely "celebrate" the presence of what is already there.

Even better known is the conclusion drawn by Rahner himself, namely that the world is full of "anonymous Christianity" and "anonymous Christians." "Anyone," he says, "who ... accepts his existence in patient silence (or better still in faith, hope and love) ... is saying Yes to Christ even if he does not know it," just as "anyone who accepts ... the humanity of others, has accepted the Son of Man because in Him God has accepted man" (FCF, p. 228). "The Christian is not so much an exception among men as simply man as he is" (quoted by Ratzinger in *Principles of Catholic Theology*, p. 166).

On the contrary, replies Ratzinger. "Is it not the faith ... of both Testaments that man is what he ought to be only by conversion, that is, when he ceases to be what he is? ... Spiritually," Ratzinger concludes, "this intermingling of being a Christian and being 'man as he is,' amounts to man's self-affirmation" (*ibid.*).

That God is always and everywhere giving actual graces to Christians

---

231. According to a report in *The Wanderer* (29 May, 1999), Fr Richard McBrien claims that the Sri Lankan theologian, Fr Tissa Balasuriya, like "Karl Rahner and a growing number of other Catholic theologians, is contending that we are all born in a state of grace." As far as Rahner is concerned, Fr McBrien could be mistaken. Rahner may have meant no more than that God is continually offering everyone grace; this continuing offer is one of the basic conditions of human existence. Unfortunately, for existentialists like Rahner, the conditions of our existence constitute our existence. We are their product. From there it is easy to infer that grace itself, not just the offer of grace, is part of our existence. It is also worth noting that while, in 1953, Rahner was upholding the doctrines of original sin and the Immaculate Conception, by 1968 he was maintaining that the Immaculate Conception "does not mean ... that the birth of a being is accompanied by something contaminating, by a stain and that in order to avoid it Mary must have had a privilege." (quoted in Siri, *op. cit.*, pp. 87–88). It simply means that "from the beginning of her existence" she was "enveloped" in grace like the rest of us. His theology of omnipresent grace has apparently led him to upgrade us while simultaneously down-grading Our Lady.

and non-Christians alike is not in doubt. But after that we know little if anything about how He distributes spiritual gifts outside the Church. As far as I know, there is nothing in Scripture or Tradition to indicate precisely when, if they persevere in good living and good works, non-Christians receive baptism of desire, which is the only thing that can make them Christians. From *The Acts of the Apostles* we know that anyone who fears God and does what is right, like the centurion Cornelius, is pleasing to Him. But, mysterious though it is, the New Testament also teaches us that even the holiest people of the Old Testament enjoyed a "status" or "condition" in some way inferior to the least of the children of the New Covenant. St John the Baptist was the greatest of the sons of women; he was sanctified in his mother's womb. But the least member of the kingdom of heaven, the Redeemer tells us, is in some indecipherable fashion "greater" than he was during his earthly existence. St Peter certainly did not baptise Cornelius just to celebrate an indwelling of God or an adopted sonship already present in him. He baptised him in order to bring it about (see von Balthasar, *Cordula*, p. 120, and CCC 1987–2029).

As von Balthasar writes:"Anyone who speaks of'anonymous Christians' cannot avoid the conclusion that there is ultimately no difference between Christians who are such by name and Christians who are not. Hence – despite all subsequent protests – it cannot matter whether one professes the Christian name or not" (M.C.W., p. 120).

He also takes issue with Rahner's handling of the two "greatest commandments." Since Rahner's God is an "Absolute Mystery" about whom next to nothing really definite can be said, love of God can only be truly expressed in love of neighbour. This means that strictly religious acts are inferior to good works. Of this von Balthasar says: "anyone who presents ... the love of one's neighbour as the primary meaning of the love of God must not be surprised ... if it becomes a matter of indifference whether he professes to believe in God or not. The main thing is that he has love." And he concludes with the comment:"a theology that develops from catchword principles is always a theology that ... finally liquidates and sells out. Whether it wants to or not, it asymptotically approaches atheism."[232]

It is true that Rahner allows room for men to say "No" to God's universal and continuous self-communication. But saying "Yes" involves so little positive belief or conscious knowledge that it is difficult to envisage what

---

232. *Asymptote*: a curve approaching a straight line and running as close as possible to it for a time without ever quite touching it.

saying "No" would consist in. Here we have the roots of the theory of the fundamental option in moral theology. Provided you have said this obscure "Yes" to God in the depths of your psyche, even without knowing it, and do not act unkindly to your neighbour, nothing you do can seriously offend Him.

As for revelation, the evangelist or missionary who preaches the Gospel message "has not really produced the understanding ... (he) has only brought it to the level of objective conceptualisation ... which is offered to the listener as the interpretation of his already presupposed understanding of faith." "An understanding which is offered to the freedom of faith is already present at the centre of the listener's being" (F.C.F., p. 233).

Other religions are less successful interpretations of this "understanding" said to be at "the centre" of everyone's being. They are vehicles of revelation and salvation nonetheless. "The history of salvation and revelation is co-existent with the whole history of the human race" (F.C.F., p. 142). Christianity is "only a species, a segment of the universal categorical history of revelation" (F.C.F., p. 155). Or as Dych puts it, "revelation is the presence of the very reality of the Trinity itself, not the communication of an idea about it" (*op. cit.*, p. 157). "As a whole, the morality of a people and an age is the legitimate and concrete form of the divine law." Because of this, "in preaching Christianity to non-Christians, the future missionary will not so much start with the idea that he is aiming at turning them into what they are not." [233]

As for the reasons why Christians believe, Rahner starts by saying that they believe on the basis of evidence (the miracles, the Resurrection, etc.), but then claims that they only accept the evidence because they already believe. "The relationship between historical events which ground faith and faith itself comes into existence within faith" (F.C.F., p. 241). One could hardly think of a more typical example of what Cardinal Siri calls Rahner's "interminable linguistic acrobatics." The acrobatics were unavoidable as his theology increasingly became an attempt to reconcile the irreconcilable. He indulges in them here, partly because he does not accept the objective reality of the Gospel accounts, partly because he does not want to be accused of promoting an extreme Protestant conception of faith (faith as a leap in the dark), and partly because he refuses to recognise any distinctions between

---

233. Van Straelen, *op. cit.*, pp. 105 & 29. The second quotation is from an address to German students. Fr. van Straelen speaks of the "crippling effect" of statements like these on missionary efforts, and Rahner's ignorance both of Asian religions and the actual state of affairs in the East.

the different ways in which God "communicates" himself to us. Yes, we cannot come to the fullness of belief without the help of grace. But grace takes different forms. As all converts know, what they initially receive as they inquire into the grounds for believing are "actual" graces, not the "gift" or "supernatural virtue of faith" possessed by the full believer. Actual graces set them going and keep them going. But until convinced, with God's help, of the truth of the evidence, they are still unbelievers. The "gift of faith" only comes at the end of the process, when they say Yes to what is proposed.

Rahner, quite as much as Barth, has been responsible for the spread of "fideism" among Catholics, a fact lamented by Paul VI.

With his growing agnosticism about the possibility of saying anything definite about the nature and attributes of God, it is also not surprising to find Rahner's later theology acquiring a marked socio-political dimension. He finds it necessary "to elaborate the principles of 'a political theology' ... only thus will the individualist reduction of revelation to the salvation of every man be surpassed" (Siri, *op. cit.*, p. 173). This could have been expected. If there is very little we can say with certainty about God, and the Church is not, in any recognisable way, ultimately necessary to men's salvation, it is difficult to see what purpose other than improving society the Church can have. But in this area Rahner was tagging along behind his disciples Frs Schillebeeckx and Johann Baptist Metz. Although he had prepared the ground, he was here a follower rather than a leader.[234]

Rahner also seems to have been touched by the "religionless Christianity," of Bonhoeffer and the death-of-God theologians. "With the advance of the history of grace, the world becomes ever more independent, mature, profane..." This "growing 'mundanity' of the world – in spite of blameworthy ambiguities and deformations ... is not a misfortune which obstinately opposes grace and the Church, but on the contrary is the way that grace is realised little by little in the creation..." (quoted by Siri, *op. cit.*, p. 172).

These, presumably, were the "dangerous things" Rahner said he was planning to write in his letter to his friend Vorgrimler in 1963. But why would a Catholic theologian want to write "dangerous things"? One can imagine Abélard or Luther saying it. But St Irenaeus, St Augustine, St Thomas, St Bonaventure, St Francis de Sales, St Alphonsus Liguori?

---

234. In his *Principles*, pp. 167–8, Ratzinger sees a direct connection between the banality of Rahner's later "Christianity" and the Marxist-inspired theologies of the next generation of theologians.

Chapter Twenty-Three

LITURGICAL CHANGE:
THE HISTORICAL BACKGROUND

From our study of a major theologian we now pass to an examination of the factors influencing liturgical change, and their consequences in the fields of belief and practice.

Nowhere more than in the revision of the liturgy have the strands of reform and rebellion been so closely intertwined. I will try to separate them so that each can be seen for what it is. But it is not easy. To no other part of the conciliar enterprise does the image of the six men pushing a car with three of them meaning to push it over a cliff, so well apply (see *Turmoil and Truth*, p. 34).

Extensive changes in this area were bound to have been disturbing regardless of circumstances, seeing that, for most of the faithful, Sunday Mass and the rites of baptism, marriage, extreme unction and Christian burial are their chief external points of contact with the Church. But it is unlikely they would have been as disturbing as they have been if the changes had been less sudden and numerous and if heterodox reformers had not taken advantage of their implementation in order to try and alter belief.[235] This is why I have postponed any discussion of the liturgy until after I have analysed the ideas and ideologies that have disoriented it. However, I will come to abuses later. To understand the reforms one must have some idea as to how and why the demand for them arose, and of the history of the movement that led up to them.

The Church's Public Worship

In classical times, the word "liturgy," of Greek origin, meant public service to the state, and it was then adopted by the Church for its official worship. In this century, in his encyclical *Mediator Dei* (1947), Pius XII gave two definitions: the liturgy is "the public worship which our Redeemer, the Head

---

235. The revision of the Russian Orthodox liturgical books by the Patriarch Nikon in the 17th century provoked opposition even though there was no attempt to change doctrine. The schism of the "Old Believers," who rejected the changes, persists to this day.

of the Church, offers to the heavenly Father and which the community of Christ's faithful pays to its Founder and through him to the Eternal Father" (art. 20); and more succinctly, "the common prayer of the Mystical Body of Christ, which is the Church" (art. 4).

There are three main components: the prayers and ceremonies surrounding the Mass; the prayers and ceremonies used in the administration of the sacraments and sacramentals; and the "divine office," the daily recitation of psalms and other prayers and readings by individual priests or by monks, nuns and other religious groups in common, for all of whom it is obligatory. Lay people who say the divine office are not obliged to do so. The divine office ensures that the praise of God goes on continuously, day and night. Whatever else changes, this core of the liturgy does not.

But to leave the matter there would give a very inadequate idea of the liturgy's overall significance. Nearly all religions have public worship with prayers and ceremonies of some kind. But the liturgy of the Catholic Church is far more than that. It is the instrument which activates the mystery that the Church herself is. One could say that the final goal of the liturgy is the worship and adoration of the Father, and the antecedent goal is the sanctification of men so that the Father may have true worshippers in "spirit and truth." [236]

The Church's first concern, therefore, is that the Mass should be said and the sacraments administered validly. That does not mean that the liturgy or the environment surrounding and activating the mystery is unimportant. But provided the prayers and ceremonies are reverent and appropriate, that is to say provided they convey a sense of the sacredness of what is taking place, and do not contain statements contrary to the Church's belief about the mystery which would prevent it from being realised, they should be seen as subordinate to the mystery itself. [237]

---

236. See Louis Bouyer, *The Liturgy Revived*, p. 44, Darton, Longman and Todd, 1965. This is the best short account known to the author of what the orthodox reformers wished to achieve.

237. I have drawn this distinction between the liturgy and what it enshrines, because of the way Catholics who have developed an allergy to the liturgy of Paul VI usually speak about it as "the new Mass." There can be no such thing as a "new Mass." When a priest stands before the altar, either the mystery is enacted or it is not, depending on whether he is validly ordained, says the right words, uses the right matter, and does not deliberately form an intention contrary to that of the Church. If these conditions are fulfilled, then what takes place beyond the range of human sight and touch is incomparably more wonderful than the most beautiful liturgy.

Why was it thought necessary to change the liturgy? Over the centuries there had been additions and developments and occasional prunings. But the Latin liturgy had existed in the form that it had down to 1970 with little substantial change for over a thousand years. The bulk of the Church's most devout Catholics would seem to have loved it, and as the fountainhead of great music and art and even as a work of art in itself, it was valued even by cultivated non-believers.[238]

Taken together, all the arguments for change and adaptation have had as their starting point Fr Rosmini's complaint of 100 years earlier. In his *The Five Wounds of the Church*, it will be remembered, the first wound was the excessive separation of clergy and faithful at Mass, leaving the impression, and helping to create it in the minds of the faithful themselves, that they were, if not just spectators, then more or less passive recipients of the benefits of what was occurring. The 20th century reform of the liturgy is closely connected with the return to the more populist and "organic" view of the Church initiated by thinkers like Möhler and Newman.

The need for reform, with at least some element of the vernacular (the local language) in the liturgy, might not have become so urgent had Catholic countries remained Catholic. Where the faith is a constituent part of the surrounding culture and unchallenged from outside, it could be assumed that the Catholic people had a sufficient if implicit knowledge of their role as part of the Christian people. Many liturgists, I believe, have exaggerated their supposedly servile and uncomprehending condition in the past. There is plenty of evidence to the contrary. But, once this was no longer so, once Catholics found themselves a minority and their beliefs the subject of questioning if not attack, it became necessary for understanding to be explicit rather than implicit.

However, before coming to the movement for liturgical change which led up to the Council's reforms, I would like to look at three considerations of a general kind which can affect people's judgements in matters liturgical.

The first is a simple matter of taste. In art, architecture and music, some people are attracted by simplicity, others by ornament and complexity. These are personal inclinations. They have nothing to do with right or wrong, good or bad. But they are usually the subject of strong feelings, especially when it is a question of what is thought fitting for the worship of God. A striking example of the degree to which these differences of

---

238. The London *Times* for 6 July 1971 carried a letter signed by a mixed group of writers, artists and critics appealing to the Holy See to preserve the old liturgy.

taste can cause conflict is the famous dispute between St Bernard and Peter the Venerable, abbot of Cluny in the 12th century. The relative austerity of Cistercian architecture and liturgical style is explained partly by St Bernard's opposition to the elaborate ceremonial of the nearby Benedictine abbey.

My second point is not about how elaborate or ceremonious the liturgy should be, but, granted a particular liturgy is held to need trimming to some degree, about how much trimming there should be. Here what I will call "the interior-decorator syndrome" can come into play. An interior decorator has a natural itch to change things around, whether it is necessary or not. It is a very human weakness. Anyone with expertise or skill of some special kind wants to show it off, whether it is called for or not, and liturgists too, I believe, are not immune from the temptation. With liturgists it takes the form of wanting to revive ancient prayers and practices just because they are ancient and they happen to know about them. Pius XII censured this in his encyclical *Mediator Dei*. He called it "archaeologism." Ancient prayers and practices, he said, should only be revived if they could be shown to be of benefit to the faithful of today. All respectable liturgists accept the principle in theory. But it is difficult to think that all those responsible for the recent reforms have always kept to it in practice.

Finally there is what could be called "the Protestant temptations." They could be summed up as "What is earlier must be better than what is later because it is nearer the 'source,' " and "Everything apart from the essence is superfluous."

While it is reasonable to suppose that the earliest Christian liturgy was fairly simple, to conclude from this that the simplest form of worship, the one with least ceremony, is the one most pleasing to God, has no warrant in Scripture or anywhere else. The idea that Christian worship is best when simple and unadorned springs from a state of mind that wants to keep the mustard seed of the parable perpetually a mustard seed.

It is also a fact that, as soon as the Church was free to "go public," and hence there exists more concrete evidence about her liturgy, it was already elaborate and ceremonious, and so all Christian worship remained in East and West until the 16th century. Ceremonious worship is also in keeping with the glimpses we get in the Old and New Testaments of the heavenly liturgy, of which the liturgy on earth should fittingly be a reflection.

Remote Beginnings

Coming now to the movement for liturgical reform, its remote origins lie in the great tide of research into the documents of the past which began in the

Renaissance, and of which the study of the history of the liturgy soon became a part. However, serious research only began in the 17th century with figures like Cardinals Bona and Tommasi in Italy, and in France with the Benedictines Dom Mabillon and Dom Martène, and the Oratorian père Lebrun.[239]

Although all this scholarship did not initially include a demand for change – it was only a short time since St Pius V, in conformity with the wishes of the Fathers of the Council of Trent, had legislated a uniform liturgy for the entire Latin Church – it was perhaps inevitable that such a demand eventually would be made. The notion of reform was in the air and, by making more people aware that the Latin liturgy, like other liturgies, had not been always the same but had developed over the centuries and to some degree varied from place to place, it was almost bound to suggest, at least to some minds, that adapting the liturgy could be another means of raising the level of the faithful's spiritual life and practice.[240]

Among Catholics, the demand for changes first made itself heard in France about the middle of the 17th century, spreading in the following century to Catholic Germany, Austria and Italy. Unfortunately, most of those making the demands were to some degree heterodox and therefore understandably suspect. The demands came in the main from Catholics under Jansenist or Gallican influence.

For the Jansenists, a perfect liturgy would be a reconstruction of what they believed the liturgy to have been like in St Augustine's day. But this was also a way of expressing their hostility to Rome. If the Roman liturgy could be exposed as a mass of liturgical "impurities" or "corruptions," it would suggest that the same could be true of her doctrines. The Gallicans, on the other hand, were for reviving ancient French liturgical practices and prayers, effectively removed by St Pius V's reform, in order to emphasise Gallic distinctness or independence. Some of these "neo-Gallican liturgies" survived until the late 19th century.

---

239. It is now more or less agreed that Luther, Melanchthon, Calvin and Cranmer knew little about the history of the liturgy. If they had, it would have been much more difficult for them to justify the changes they introduced.

240. Pius V's reform was not a reform in the 20th century sense; it was more a tidying up. Before Trent, the Latin liturgy had been basically the same everywhere, but there were many minor variations. These, unless they were over 200 years old, were suppressed, mainly to avoid doctrinal deviations. The Reformation was at its height. It is even possible that "reform" is the wrong word for the 20th century changes, since "reform" suggests there is a moment when a liturgy reaches a point of perfection to which it is always necessary to return. "Revision" would perhaps be more accurate.

We get some idea of the way minds were moving from the innovations of the famous abbé Jubé of Asnière, a village near Paris, in the late 17th century. The abbé insisted first of all, Fr Louis Bouyer tells us, "on the public and collective character of the Mass." He never, for instance, "used the high altar in his church, except on Sundays and feast days when the congregation gathered together. He also restored the old Roman usage (which had endured longer in France than in Rome itself) of placing the linen cloth on the altar only just before Mass and of having no other cross or lights on the altar than the processional cross and tapers which were set in place at the beginning of Mass." He said the psalm *Judica* and the *Confiteor* along with the people; sang the *Kyrie*, *Gloria* and *Credo* with them; listened to the Epistle and Gospel sung by assistant ministers; restored the offertory procession "which had never entirely disappeared from French churches" and "had offerings of all kinds ... in this procession which he later blessed ... at the end of the Canon according to the original practice." He never began the Canon until the *Sanctus* had been sung in full, and "said the Canon loudly enough to be heard by the whole congregation."[241]

Clearly the abbé was not only something of a "liturgical specialist." He was ahead of his time in approving of "doing your own thing."

Meanwhile, as the 18th century proceeded, increasing numbers of the higher clergy, scholarly and hierarchical, were being influenced by Enlightenment rationalism. Here we have to distinguish between moderates and extremists: those who wanted to trim what they considered superfluous "extravagances" in order to give "fundamentals" greater prominence, without losing their belief in the essentially mysterious and supernatural character of the faith; and those, like the Emperor Joseph of Austria, and his brother Leopold Grand Duke of Tuscany, who made the "demands of reason," the standard by which they judged what should be kept or discarded. For them, the primary purpose of public worship was moral instruction in order to produce "good citizens."

To begin with, these three bodies of opinion, Jansenist, Gallican and "enlightened," were often at daggers drawn. As long as Louis XIV was alive, most Gallicans were anti-Jansenist, because the king was; while for

---

241. Bouyer, *Life and Liturgy*, London, Sheed and Ward, 1956, p. 53. Fr Aidan Nichols OP in his *Looking at the Liturgy*, (Ignatius, 1996) refers to Jubé as a Jansenist. Fr Bouyer, who admires Jubé as a courageous forerunner of the 20th-century reforms, says that "he can only be reproached for having signed the appeal against the papal bull *Unigenitus*, which condemned the main Jansenist propositions."

"enlightened" people, Jansenist piety was often an object of ridicule. But during the second half of the century, united by their hostility to Rome, these hitherto warring groups were more and more coming to think alike about religious and liturgical reform.

In their combined demands we already see emerging the principles, many of which the Fathers of Vatican II would adopt as the basis for reform in their decree on the liturgy, *Sacrosanctum Concilium*, two hundred years later. The people should play a more active part in worship; the rites should therefore be simplified; they should be as "intelligible" as possible; they should be a vehicle of instruction as well as an act of worship; some parts at least should be in the vernacular; the liturgy should be the foundation and centre of the people's prayer life, and there should be a greater use of Scripture, not only for its own sake, but to facilitate reunion with the Protestants; simplification of the rites would also serve that purpose.

If the Church so long resisted these demands, it was largely because of the circles in which they arose. While the demands were not unreasonable in themselves, the motivation behind them was, as we have seen, often heterodox. A possible "right" or at least tolerable thing was being requested for the wrong reason, a situation which confronts the Church in trying to implement her reforms today.

More specific demands were for concelebration (several priests saying mass together), the temporal cycle to be given priority over the sanctoral cycle (the celebration of feasts of the saints should not obscure the general pattern of the liturgical year), Mass facing the people, more frequent communion, reform of the breviary with the removal of historical errors, the right of local episcopates to alter the liturgy, and permission for parish priests to modify it in so far as doing so would clarify the truths and duties of religion.

We also find among the 18th century protagonists of liturgical reform a prejudice against "popular devotions" (rosary, benediction, eucharistic adoration, devotion to the Sacred Heart, "excessive" veneration of saints) similar to that of many of the 20th century's liturgical reformers. Popular devotions were seen as rivals to the liturgy rather than as complementing it. "Private" masses were disapproved of on the grounds that Mass should never be said without a congregation. There should therefore be only one altar per church. At the same time, the Austrian government was promoting the idea that priests should not be required to say mass daily. Pilgrimages and sodalities or pious associations were other objects of attack, as were statues and images or what was considered an excess of them. For the Emperor Joseph and his like, a religious order devoted to the care of the sick and wounded like the Brothers of St John of God seemed acceptable, while an order devoted to prayer and contemplation was useless.

The more extreme demands reached their apogee at the Synod of Pistoia, 1786, brainchild of the Jansenist Bishop of Prato in Tuscany and his sovereign the Grand Duke Leopold. Pius VI condemned 86 of the synod's propositions in the Bull *Auctorem Fidei* (1794). They included a call for a totally vernacular liturgy with only one altar in each church, and the merging of all religious orders into a single giant order with a common habit.

However, at the time we are considering, outside Austria and Italy, these demands and experiments hardly touched the life of the Church as a whole. They remained the concern of a minority of specialists, and in the 19th century they were reduced to a whisper.[242] The revolution had made the majority of ecclesiastics more sensitive to the dangers of abruptly altering long-established practices, and the romantic movement brought with it a new appreciation of the importance of beauty in worship and of the liturgical achievements of the Middle Ages.

Immediately following the Napoleonic era, the Bavarian theologian Johann Michael Sailer (1751–1832) pressed for "a modest revision of the missal and breviary, with some reduction of the cultus of the saints in both, and a greater coherence in the choice of biblical readings." But at the same time he could write: "I know it is incomparably better to breathe the letter and spirit of the existing liturgy ... than to give the prize to the arbitrary, mutually contradictory improvement of the liturgy by individuals, which lead finally only to a complete liturgical anarchy and, rather than ameliorate the letter of accidental aspects, destroy the essence and spirit of the whole thing."[243]

With Sailer, in fact, we see an alternative approach to the liturgical renewal beginning to take shape. Everyone interested in the subject was agreed that the faithful should have a better understanding of what was taking place. But the new school of thought believed that this could best be achieved by teaching the faithful to appreciate the existing liturgy, rather than by drastically altering it, simplifying it or introducing the vernacular.

---

242. It is true that Rosmini's already-mentioned call for ending the separation of clergy and people at mass can hardly be described as a whisper. It was an anguished *cri de coeur* and briefly caused a sensation, but in obedience to the Holy See he withdrew the first edition of the book and the revised edition was not published until after his death. The modest first edition "for a few friends," which was widely pirated, contained what sounded like a call for the vernacular. The revised edition retained the passages seeming to favour a vernacular liturgy, but included additional passages arguing the case for the retention of Latin.

243. Quoted in Nichols, *op. cit.*, p. 39.

The first and most successful advocate and practitioner of this new approach was Dom Prosper Guéranger (1805–1875), founder of the restored Benedictine community of Solesmes in north central France.[244]

Dom Guéranger, who is perhaps best known for the restoration of Gregorian chant, was not opposed to all change. His initial aim was to remove what he regarded as 17th and 18th century disfigurements – mostly artistic – from the rites and ceremonies. He would therefore have seen his work as one of purification rather than alteration or adaptation. His ideal was the Roman liturgy of Pius V executed in the style and with the artistic forms of the high Middle Ages – the peak, in his eyes, of liturgical development. Once the ideal form had been re-established, all that remained was to make it better understood and loved.[245]

This he set about doing through two series of publications, his *Institutions liturgiques* and his *Année liturgique*, which carried his ideas to a wide Catholic reading public and contributed to the new wave of liturgical scholarship which had begun at about the same time. The foundation of a daughter abbey at Beuron in the Rhineland helped to spread his ideas in Germany.

The next step came from the Church's supreme authority. Between 1903 and 1913, St Pius X issued a series of instructions, three of which, modest as they may now seem, directly affected the laity at large. The first aimed at purifying church music and encouraged the use of Gregorian chant at parish level.[246] The faithful, hitherto all but completely silent at Mass, were to learn to sing the Kyrie, Gloria, Credo, Sanctus and Agnus Dei with or without a choir. The second instruction encouraged frequent communion. The third lowered the age at which children could receive communion to seven or thereabouts.

Two further instructions concerned the missal and breviary. The number

---

244. To appreciate Dom Guéranger's achievement, it is worth recalling what Montalembert tells us in the 2nd chapter of his *Les Moines de l'Occident*. So effectively had the revolution wiped out the religious orders in France that the author grew up without the slightest idea what a monk was and without ever having seen one.

245. After World War II it became customary in liturgical circles to talk condescendingly about Dom Guéranger. He was represented as a romantic aesthete with little appeal beyond the pious and cultivated readers of his *Années liturgiques*. Recent studies have shown this to be untrue. His concerns were as much social and pastoral as those of any 20th century reformer. (See Nichols, *op. cit.*, p. 41.)

246. Much prevailing church music was quite inappropriate. The Italians sang hymns to tunes from Puccini and Verdi operas – not that we are now in any position to look down on them.

of feasts, with their own special readings and prayers, which could supplant the regular Sunday readings and prayers, was reduced. In the 18th century, Benedict XIV had considered such a reform but, according to one account, had been put off by the radicalism of the priest he consulted.

The Contemporary Reform Movement: 1909–1947

However, in spite of the work of Dom Guéranger and St Pius X, the beginning of the movement which culminated in the revised liturgy of Paul VI (1970) is attributed to a paper read by Dom Lambert Beauduin, a monk of the Benedictine abbey of Mont César (Louvain, Belgium) at the Malines Congress on the liturgy in 1909. Given the role of the divine office in their life, the Benedictines, not surprisingly, have continued at the forefront of the movement ever since. The subject of the paper was "the participation of the faithful in Christian worship."

To begin with, the movement's main thrust was to do at parish level what Dom Guéranger had done for the cultivated readers of his *Années liturgiques*: stimulate interest in and appreciation of the existing liturgy. To achieve this, Dom Beauduin and his associates organised liturgical weeks, encouraged the publication of books and periodicals on the liturgy of a popular kind, had missals printed with vernacular translations opposite the Latin and, following St Pius X's instruction, promoted the singing of Gregorian chant. Dom Beauduin's *La piété de l'église* (1914) has been called "the manifesto of the liturgical movement."

Later, the centre of activity moved to Germany. This was partly because Dom Beauduin's interests became divided between liturgical renewal and ecumenism. In 1925, at the request of Pope Pius XI, he founded a monastery at Amay in Belgium (later moved to Chevetogne), dedicated to promoting understanding between Catholics and Orthodox. Then, in 1928, he fell into disfavour and had to leave Amay because of his "bold views" on the liturgy and ecclesiology. However, he continued active in both fields if no longer in the forefront of the liturgical movement, and a retreat he preached in Paris in 1942 led to the foundation of the influential Centre de Pastorale Liturgique in the French capital.

Germany and Austria in the 1920s and 1930s produced a host of fine writers and teachers dedicated to educating the faithful about the liturgy, of whom the most widely read and effective was probably the Austrian Augustinian canon, Fr Pius Parsch of Klosterneuburg outside Vienna. He called his work a "popular liturgical apostolate." Although a considerable liturgical scholar, his first interests were always pastoral, and his many popular explanations of the liturgy led to his monastery being described as the "liturgical centre of German-speaking lands." He attached equal weight to deepening the faithful's appreciation and understanding of the Bible. Appreciation of the liturgy and appreciation of the Bible, he believed, had to go hand in hand.

Meanwhile, the Benedictine abbey of Maria Laach in the Rhineland was providing the movement with some elevated theological input. Under the leadership of Abbot Ildefons Herwegen (1874–1946), Maria Laach had already become an important centre of liturgical research. But what attracted attention and eventually controversy was the "mystery theology" of Dom Odo Casel (1886–1948). One could say that where Pius Parsch's work was directed to bringing the liturgy as much as possible within the orbit of the ordinary faithful's comprehension, Dom Odo's aim was to raise their comprehension to a higher level.

Dom Odo's theory is not easy to summarise. But I will try to give the gist of it because of its subsequent influence, both negative and positive.

The entire liturgy, according to Dom Odo, including the divine office, is the making present in sacramental form of the Paschal Mystery, which he defines as Christ's passage or *transitus* through death to eternal life and which includes all his actions from his incarnation to his ascension. By taking part in the liturgy, the faithful are swept up into this single movement from death to life, being transformed in the process. It is as though the liturgy as a whole does for the Paschal Mystery what the words of consecration at Mass do in regard to Christ's Body and Blood. As Christ's Body, Blood and Sacrifice are made present by the words of the officiating priest at Mass, so is the Paschal Mystery made present in its entirety through the liturgy.

To begin with, Dom Odo presented his theory of the Paschal Mystery as the fulfilment of what the "mystery religions" of the ancient world were seeking to achieve, an idea that did not make the theory more acceptable in many quarters, and he eventually played down this aspect of his case.[247] However, he did not modify the theory itself, which Fr Louis Bouyer, an ardent admirer of Dom Odo, claims was canonised by the Council's document

---

247. The earliest mystery religions of the ancient world were vegetation rites. By re-enacting the death and return to life of a god, the revival of nature in spring was assured. In the mystery religions flourishing at the time of Christ, this element had largely disappeared. Those joining in the rite hoped thereby to ensure their survival after death. It was this latter kind that Dom Odo saw as a providential foreshadowing of Christianity. Confusion about which he had in mind may have caused the misunderstanding.

on the liturgy, *Sacrosanctum Concilium*.[248] This, I think, is an exaggeration. While one can certainly detect traces of Dom Odo's influence there, the theory as such is not explicitly expounded or taught. This seems to be the view of Fr Aidan Nichols OP, who points out nevertheless that a dash of Dom Odo's mystical conception of the liturgy would be a good antidote to today's liturgical functionalism.

But whatever Dom Odo may have meant, did his lofty theological ideas matter all that much? How could they have any practical consequences? The fact is that, as interpreted by some of his admirers, they did. For instance, we find them reproaching the faithful when at Mass for concentrating too much on Our Lord's Passion and being too pre-occupied with the Real Presence. Yet, in the context of Dom Casel's mystery theology, that is quite logical. If the whole of Our Lord's life from conception to ascension was a single undifferentiated process, then no single episode has any more redemptive value than another.[249]

With this interpretation of Dom Odo's theory, Pius XII took issue in his encyclical *Mediator Dei*, on Christian Worship (1947):

"Since His (Christ's) bitter sufferings constitute the principal mystery of our redemption, it is only fitting that the Catholic faith should give it the greatest prominence. This mystery is the very centre of divine worship" (art. 164). And in the preceding article but one he had warned those "who, deceived by the illusion of a higher mysticism, dare to assert that attention should not be paid to the historic Christ, but to a 'pneumatic' or glorified Christ. They do not hesitate to assert that a change has taken place in the piety of the faithful" who "by dethroning the glorified Christ ... have substituted in His place that Christ who lived on earth" (M.D., pt. III). For this reason, the Pope observes, there have been voices asking for the removal of crucifixes from Churches.

Meanwhile, the idea, never completely extinct, that explaining the existing liturgy to the people and teaching them to appreciate it was

---

248. Bouyer, *The Liturgy Revived*, p. 31.
249. This seems to be the view of Fr. Ambrosius Verheul, in his *Einführung in die Liturgie*, (Herder, 1964; Eng. trans., *Introduction to the Liturgy*, Anthony Clarke, 1972, p. 166), where the faithful, and the Church of recent times, are reproached for "dividing" the Paschal Mystery by treating the Passion and Resurrection as separate events of different significance. We are not to think of the Cross except as Christ's kingly throne and a sign of victory. For Jungmann's critique of Casel, *op. cit.* p. 161. "You cannot for instance say at Christmas, when *Hodie Christus natus est* is sung: the birth of Christ is made present ... Similarly at Easter, the resurrection of Christ is not in any true sense realised anew."

not enough, that if it was to have a really transforming effect on their spiritual lives the liturgy itself must be changed, was growing in strength and finding more and more supporters. The period between the two wars in Germany was a time of widespread liturgical experimentation, the majority of it unofficial. Fr Parsch, for instance, had already tried Mass facing the people – for the benefit of students on cross-country hikes – and in German-speaking countries there was much unauthorised use of the vernacular.

Perhaps the most interesting thing about these experiments and the accompanying demands for change, was how closely many of them resembled the demands of the 17th and 18th century liturgical reformers we looked at earlier, even if the motivation behind them was not always the same: where the approach of the Enlightenment reformers was utilitarian – the liturgy is primarily for instruction and the moral improvement of the faithful – the reformers of the 1920s and '30s still saw the liturgy as primarily the enactment of a mystery directed to the worship of God.[250] However, this situation was not to last. The re-emergence of the Enlightenment's utilitarian approach in the period after World War II and its triumph in the wake of the Council, will, as we shall see, be responsible for most of the misinterpretations of the new liturgy.[251]

The controversies roused by the liturgical experiments of the 1930s and '40s were largely responsible for Pius XII's encyclical.

Mediator Dei was not intended to crush the developing liturgical movement. Rather it was intended to lay down the boundaries within

---

250. The similarity of the goals of the Enlightenment reformers and the 20th-century reformers only came fully to light with the republication in 1979 of a book by a Fr Waldemar Trapp, first published in Regensburg in 1940. Until its republication it seems to have been little known even in its country of origin. A liturgical scholar and reformer, Fr Trapp appears to have been not a little disconcerted by his discoveries. The details are in Fr Nichols' book, to which I am deeply indebted. Its 126 pages throw more light on why the reforms have been partly derailed than any other book I have come across.

251. No one understood the dangers to the liturgy of the utilitarian approach better than Fr Romano Guardini, a supporter of liturgical reform and leader of the Catholic renewal in Germany in the 1920s and '30s. In his famous little book *The Spirit of the Liturgy*, he explains that while the liturgy has meaning (the glorification of God) the attempt to give it a directly pragmatic purpose destroys it. "Only those who are not scandalised by this understand what the liturgy means. From the very first, every type of rationalism has turned against it." Sheed & Ward, 1930, pp. 105.

which it could operate. However, it has to be said, that while the liturgical movement is praised for its efforts, there are as many if not more passages devoted to warnings against heterodox ideas and abuses. The elements which will disorient the reform are already present in the movement. Prominent on the Pope's list was the idea that there is no difference between the ordained priesthood and the priesthood of the baptised; the priest is merely a delegate of the community. Treating the Mass as just a fraternal meal is also censured.

In spite of this, shortly after the encyclical's appearance, the Pope set up a commission to consider the possibilities of reform, and this in turn led to the already mentioned liturgical changes of the 1950s (restoration of the Easter Vigil and reform of Holy Week services, evening mass, shorter preliminary fast, etc.)

The Reform Movement: 1947–1970

The figure enjoying the greatest reputation in the post-war period was the Westphalian liturgical scholar Josef Jungmann SJ, who taught pastoral theology, catechetics and liturgy at Innsbruck from 1925 to 1963, and who became world-famous with the publication of his *Mass of the Roman Rite*, in 1948. He was a *peritus* at Vatican II, working on the preparatory and conciliar commissions for the liturgy, and afterwards acting as a consultor to the commission which implemented the conciliar decree.

The post-war period also saw two important developments. The first was a new and vigorous French input into the liturgical movement, inspired, says Fr Bouyer, by "some Dominicans and a few seculars," and also, as we have seen, by Dom Beauduin. Its headquarters were the Centre de Pastorale Liturgique in Paris, with *Maison Dieu* as its house journal.

From this French offshoot would come many of the more radical demands and experiments in the years ahead. Its leaders do not seem to have had much interest in the liturgy itself, its history or its beauty as a vehicle of worship and expression of the Church's faith over two millennia. They seem to have seen it largely as an instrument to be adapted and changed at will for purely missionary ends, the neophytes in view being workers, students, and modern pagans generally. They were little interested in "helping faithful Christians ... rediscover their own treasures." [252] Many were ready to abandon the parish as the normal centre of Christian worship.

---

252. Bouyer, *Life and Liturgy*, p. 67.

The second development affected the mainstream of the movement, still a largely German and Austrian affair. "The decisive epoch of the liturgical movement," Fr Nichols writes "was ... what we may call its 'political phase,' when it set out to be a force on the stage of the world Church from 1945 onwards." By this, the author does not mean that liturgical scholars mounted the pulpits or took to the streets, in order to stir up the masses. The term refers rather to the gradual formation within the movement of a party, in the sense of an organised group of like-minded men with a programme of practical goals. They were not without allies in Rome. Chief among them was the secretary of Pius XII's liturgical reform commission, Msgr Annibale Bugnini. But the Congregation of Rites, the department of papal government responsible for the liturgy, was not sympathetic to their aims. They therefore advanced their cause by preparing private measures of reform and "gaining the ear of well-disposed national Episcopal hierarchies." Much of the preparatory work was done at a series of international conferences of liturgists beginning in 1951, "the brainchildren of the Centre de Pastorale Liturgique and the Liturgical Institute of Trier."

"The extraordinary thing about these meetings," writes Fr Nichols, "was that with few exceptions they were held behind closed doors, by invitation only, and ... even in the case of the exceptions, the sessions to which a wider public had entry were always preceded by what (Dom Bernard) Botte calls a *réunion de techniciens*." Dom Bernard, himself one of these *techniciens*, for whom "practical revision of the external form of the liturgy was exceedingly important," will become one of "the principal authors of the revised liturgy." "Considerable continuity," Fr Nichols goes on, "links these reunions of the 1950s to the composition of the consultative body set up to draft the (Council's) schema on the Liturgy, and, after that ... to the post-conciliar *Consilium*" (the commission which implemented it).

We have here, I think, the first of the weak spots in the reform process. The old liturgy was in a true sense a "community project," the result of multiple small contributions from different times and places over a period of 2000 years. Its 20th century reform was almost exclusively the product of experts, with some of the consequences foreseen over a hundred years earlier by Sailer. "With all its advantages," writes Cardinal Ratzinger, "the new Missal was published as if it were a book put together by professors, not a phase in a continual growth process. Such a thing has never happened before. It is absolutely contrary to the laws of liturgical growth."[253] In a

---

253. Ratzinger, *Feast of Faith*, Ignatius, 1986, p. 86.

similar vein, Fr Nichols describes it as a "revolution by technicians that acquired a general stamp of approval from papacy and episcopate."

However necessary reform may have been and praiseworthy the aims of the reformers, it is difficult to see how this method of proceeding can be reconciled with the Council's injunction that "any new forms should in some way grow organically from forms already existing."[254]

---

254. The *Catechism of the Catholic Church* published nearly 30 years later adds: "Even the supreme authority in the Church may not change the liturgy arbitrarily, but only in the obedience of faith and with religious respect for the mystery of the liturgy" (art. 1125). In contrast, here is a *technicien*'s view: "The Church has always been conscious of the power she holds from Christ for the regulation of the cultural celebration of the mystery of Christ, a power that according to contemporary theologians goes much further than had previously been supposed" (Verheul, *op. cit.*, p. 135). However, Fr Verheul is on the side of the angels in other respects. "Liturgy is in the last resort honouring, praising and worshipping God" (*op. cit.* 32).

Chapter Twenty-Four

THE NEW LITURGY

We can sum up what happened once Rome decided to give more or less free rein to the *techniciens*, under three headings: What the Council asked for; What the Consilium or commission to implement it did; How all this was understood and applied at national and diocesan level.

What the Council asked for

"The reform of the liturgy in the spirit of the liturgical movement was not," Ratzinger tells us, "a priority for the majority of the Fathers," and he includes Pope Paul among them. For many, he goes on, it was "not even a consideration...The liturgy and its reform had, since the end of World War I become a pressing question only in France and Germany." Neither was the fact that the liturgy "became the first subject for the Council's discussions," due to the Council Fathers' being particularly interested in it. It was a tactical move by the reform party to keep other topics from being discussed until the draft documents of those other topics had been rewritten. None of the Fathers, Ratzinger continues, would have seen the text they eventually approved as "a 'revolution' signifying the 'end of the Middle Ages' as some theologians felt they should interpret it subsequently." [255]

Because of this, *Sacrosanctum Concilium*, the decree on the liturgy, was a relatively moderate document. As we have seen, it only laid down general principles, and to the majority of the Council Fathers who voted for those principles, nothing, surely, could have sounded more reasonable than increased lay participation, simplifying the rites a bit so as to make their meaning plainer, and allowing a degree of the vernacular. They must have assumed that all this could be relatively easily realised with some tidying up of the existing texts and the introduction of things like "bidding prayers,"

---

255. Ratzinger, *Milestones*, Ignatius, 1998, pp. 122–3. All the observations about the liturgy and liturgical reform in this book will be found on pp. 122–4 and pp. 146–9. His other easily accessible views on the subject are to be found in *Feast of Faith*, a short book entirely devoted to the liturgy (original 1981; Engl. trans., Ignatius, 1986), and in his two interview-books *The Ratzinger Report*, ch. 8 (Ignatius, 1985), and *Salt of the Earth*, pp. 50 & 174–6 (Ignatius, 1997).

offertory processions, lay readers for the non-Gospel scripture texts, and occasional acclamations from the congregation. However, these general principles were all of them susceptible to degrees of interpretation.

The first weakness for example lies in the meaning of the words "noble simplicity." What is simple to one liturgist may still be too complicated for another, and "nobility" is a quality to which not a few people are blind or deaf. "Noble simplicity" then easily becomes just "simplicity." What too do we mean by "intelligible"? How does one make supernatural mysteries "intelligible"?[256] By cutting down on ceremony, beauty, ornament, ritual? By diminishing expressions of reverence and awe? By encouraging an atmosphere of cheerful *bonhomie*? By exposing everything to view so that the people can see "exactly what's going on"? Or do you in this way make the mystery less intelligible, even if you do not actually mislead people about it? It is the same with "active participation." How much of it? And what sort of activity? Are contemplation or adoration activities? Or does "activity" have to be continually bodily or vocal?

As for the vernacular, given that the Church is a universal Church, and Latin has been the official language of a large part of it for something like 1700 years, the case for keeping a degree of Latin in the Roman Rite is very strong. Latin has been the bond of unity linking ages and nations together throughout the West since the late third century. One only has to attend an all-vernacular liturgy in a foreign country to appreciate how its almost total abandonment has weakened that bond.

The "open-endedness" of the principles laid down in *Sacrosanctum Concilium* and the wide powers the document gives to local bishops' conferences to adapt or reinterpret its more specific instructions, can, I believe, be seen as the second weak spot. Not only did it give the technicians scope to carry out a more widespread revision of the texts than would seem to have been necessary, it unlocked the sluice gates for the heterodox currents hitherto held in check by *Mediator Dei* to flood into the Church more or less unchecked. Attempts to push the liturgical "car" closer and closer to the cliff of heterodoxy have not been the only factor disorienting

---

256. A German missionary bishop from the Philippines called for a Mass liturgy in which everyone present "even if they happen to be attending Mass for the first time can readily understand without involved explanations." This, of course, was the aim of the 16th century reformers, and the result was a change of understanding. You cannot understand the Mass without first knowing the doctrine of the Mass, which the ceremonies and rites reinforce (Wiltgen, *op. cit.*, p. 38).

the use of the new liturgy; but throughout the rest of this chapter it should be kept in mind as a significant factor.

What the Consilium did

The third weak spot was the speed with which the new liturgy was put together. In 1964, soon after the Council's decree on the liturgy had been passed and while the Council was still in session, Pope Paul deputed Cardinal Lercaro, the Archbishop of Bologna, to set up the commission (the Consilium) to implement it. "The projects had to be completed as quickly as possible, consonant with scholarly and pastoral professionalism, lest the momentum created by the Council be lost." The Consilium was composed of prelates, with the *techniciens* as their advisers, and Msgr Annibale Bugnini as secretary. It was at this point that the *techniciens* came into their own. Msgr Bugnini orchestrated and directed their work. "More than any other single person," it has been said, Msgr Bugnini "may be called the chief architect of the liturgical reform ... he occupied the critical position on the successive bodies of the official liturgical revision." [257] In 1969, when Pope Paul suppressed the old Congregation of Rites and merged the Consilium in the new Congregation for Divine Worship, Msgr Bugnini remained on as secretary, eventually being made an Archbishop. Before Pope Paul abruptly dismissed him in 1975,[258] he only suffered one setback: he was not appointed secretary of the conciliar commission on the liturgy; he was only a *peritus*. But the setback only lasted a year.

How did this relatively minor official come to wield such extraordinary power in a field that would deeply affect the life of Catholics everywhere for generations? The fact that he was the principal intermediary between Pope Paul and the Consilium during the work of revision is a partial explanation. For the rest, the situation is not all that unprecedented. The Monsignor, whatever one thinks of his views, clearly had those qualities which throughout history have commended subordinates to men in high stations: industry, dedication, single-mindedness, the capacity to organise,

---

257. Both the quotations in this paragraph are from *New Catholic Encyclopedia*, vol. 18, art. "Bugnini," F R McManus.
258. In 1975, Pope Paul abruptly removed the Archbishop and sent him into diplomatic exile in Iran, where he remained until his death in 1982, and where, in answer to his many opponents, he wrote his own account of the liturgical reforms, *La riforma liturgica (1948–1975)*, a work of nearly 1000 pages. It was published posthumously.

handle people, get them working together, all of which in the end make them seem indispensable. One thinks of Thomas Cromwell, Richelieu's Père Joseph, or Roosevelt and Harry Hopkins.

Together with Msgr Bugnini, the *techniciens'* chief failing seems to have been their unwillingness to leave anything to time and God, and their determination to push the reforms through, not only as quickly as possible, but with as little consultation as possible. There was no systematic sounding out of episcopal conferences, as collegiality surely required; and when an experimental model Mass was enacted for the benefit of the bishops attending the first Episcopal Synod in 1967, although it had a mostly unfavourable reception, it was implemented regardless. The changes were also much more far-reaching than had been generally expected.

"It was reasonable and right of the Council," Cardinal Ratzinger writes, "to order a revision of the missal such as had often taken place before and which this time had to be more thorough than before ... but more than this now happened: the old building was demolished and another was built" even if largely "using materials from the previous one and even using the old building plans." This "did enormous harm."[259]

Finally, when after a period of introductory modifications the new liturgy of the Mass became the official worship of the Latin Church in 1970, the old liturgy was in effect suppressed.

This too Cardinal Ratzinger regards as a serious error of judgement. He describes the dismay he felt at the "almost total prohibition" of the old liturgy "after a transitional phase of only half a year ... nothing of the sort had ever happened in the entire history of the liturgy." Not only were the faithful deprived of a rite to which the majority were deeply attached and which had hitherto been obligatory; they were now expected to shun and abhor what they had hitherto been taught to venerate. Never before had anyone thought of "setting one missal against another."

---

259. Ratzinger, *op. cit.*, p. 148. The criticisms by the late Cardinal Antonelli are more detailed and stringent. A liturgical reformer and member of the Consilium himself, he speaks of its negative, unjust and destructive spirit; its critical and intolerant attitude to the Holy See; the lack of "true theologians" – it was "as though they had all been excluded;" the absence of "any sense of the sacred" and "concern for real piety;" the rambling disorganised way the discussions were conducted; and the failure to provide a proper voting system. "Normally we proceed by a show of hands, but nobody declares how many participants approve or disapprove. A real disgrace!" *Inside the Vatican*, August-September, 1999, reviewing a doctoral thesis by Fr Nicola Giampietro, published in Rome in June 1998.

Fr Congar seems to have been of the same opinion as the Cardinal. "I can't understand," he says in his *30 Days* interview with Stefano Paci [*30 Days*, no. 3, 1993], "why no authorisation was forthcoming to safeguard the Mass (the old liturgy) ... I personally intervened with the Archbishop of Paris and in the Vatican ... I lodged repeated requests that the two rites be allowed to stand but without success."

Not without reason does Fr Aidan Nichols speak of Pope Paul having been poorly advised.

Traditionalists,too, have a strong case in regard to not a few of the changes, and still more to the way they were introduced. But they do not, normally, pay enough attention to the history of the reform movement and the mixed nature of its membership. The aims and intentions of the men like Romano Guardini, Parsch, Jungmann and Bouyer seem mostly to be unknown or ignored.

It is impossible here to go in detail into the merits and weaknesses of the Consilium's work. Among other things it was the product of men who, while agreed on fundamentals, had different focuses of interest. "Many compromises were needed to satisfy the diverse elements."[260] I shall also speak mainly about the liturgy of the Mass since that is what has affected people most.

The first and most noticeable feature is, of course, the number of opportunities provided for the laity to be audibly and visibly part of the celebration. In this way, one of the two main goals of the reform movement was achieved. The excessive separation of priest and people at Mass is overcome. Fr Rosmini would have rejoiced.

The increased number of Scripture readings can be seen as the second greatest gain. The use of the vernacular, I believe, would have been an unmixed blessing if it had not been so total.

A third striking feature is the quantity of additional or alternative prayers and Scripture readings: three new eucharistic prayers or canons, several

---

260. *New Catholic Encyclopedia*, art. "Liturgical Reform." There are devout people who see criticism of the new liturgy as criticism of the Holy Spirit. This is clearly not the view of the present Pope. As early as 1975, he was writing: "For the present, we cannot go into the question of how far specific steps taken by the liturgical reform were real improvements or actual trivialisations ... how far they were wise or foolish from a pastoral point of view..." (Ratzinger, *Feast of Faith*, cited in *Ratzinger Report*, pp. 119–120). Before the Council, Jungmann had opposed the view that the old liturgy was to be attributed in its entirety to the Holy Spirit. Unless he had taken this position there could have been no liturgical reform movement.

variant Kyries, numbers of new prefaces with many culled from earlier liturgies. Rubrics (liturgical rules and regulations) are fewer and looser. The intention underlying the large range of choices seems to have been to forestall routine and make the liturgy more adaptable to local conditions.

Less obviously beneficial are the many small changes apparently introduced to suit the supposed psychology of "modern man." Liturgists with "modern man" in mind appear to have had an aversion to repetition. Triple invocations are cut down to two, as in the English translation of the Gloria, and doxologies and prayer-endings which invoke the Trinity are frequently omitted. Where prayers from the old liturgy have been preserved, they are often needlessly truncated: for example, the beautiful offertory prayer beginning *Deus, qui humanae substantiae* which Etienne Gilson loved to recite. Also removed are ways of addressing God that might seem too "obsequious." To give another example, in the prayer before communion "May the receiving of your Body" (*Perceptio Corporis tui*), the words "which I though unworthy presume to receive" have been left out. The adjectives "sacred" and "holy" are as much as possible eschewed. This tendency is particularly noticeable in the English translations, where God is often instructed or commanded, rather than entreated to grant favours. Modern man, it is assumed, is practical and down-to-earth. Having come of age, he talks to God as one grown-up to another, he can only take a minimum of ceremony, and his attention span for anything except concrete facts is limited. He is in a hurry as well. He wants to get to the golf-course or the beach on Sunday. Brevity has been added to simplicity and intelligibility as a guiding principle of reform.[261]

Ecumenical considerations played an even larger part in the work of reconstruction. "The Rite of Paul VI contains more features of Oriental provenance than the Roman rite has ever known historically ... and notably in the new anaphoras" – another name for the central Eucharistic Prayer or Canon [Nichols, *op. cit.* p. 121]. But there are many more changes with Protestants in view. The short Second Eucharistic Prayer or Anaphora, for instance, is capable of a Protestant or a Catholic interpretation, and has been lauded for it by a prominent evangelical. These were the changes that attracted most criticism.[262]

---

261. See McManus, *op. cit.*, where he explicitly includes brevity as a criterion of reform.
262. Eucharistic Prayer II, sometimes referred to as "the Canon of Hippolytus," a third-century Church Father, is in fact quite different to the original.

The principal charge was that the new liturgy, particularly that of the Mass, did not protect Catholic eucharistic and sacramental doctrine adequately. And the *General Instruction on the Roman Missal,* the document introducing it, met with even stronger objections. *The General Instruction* is a statement of theological principles about the Mass as well as of rules for celebrating it, and most of its descriptions and explanations of what the Mass is so carefully avoided traditional Catholic terminology that it gave the impression of trying to promote a Protestant theology of the Eucharist. Article 7, for instance, stated that "the Lord's Supper or Mass is the sacred assembly or congregation of the people of God gathering together with a priest presiding to celebrate the memorial of the Lord."

Because of this, the new Missal's publication had to be postponed for six months. In September 1969, Cardinals Ottaviani and Bacci, both prominent figures at the Council, sent a letter to Pope Paul with a document strongly criticising both the new *Order of the Mass* and the accompanying *General Instruction.* As a result the Pope had the *General Instruction* revised and added an eight-page foreword defending its orthodoxy. There were sixteen pages of emendations, but critics continued to maintain that the corrections were more verbal than substantial. The corrections, they claimed, did not alter the document's underlying ethos.[263]

In fact, there had been anxieties about the way the liturgical reform was going from the time of the Council if not earlier. The anxieties had been generated partly by rumours of what was being planned, partly by an explosion of liturgical experiments by individual priests, who had been disoriented by the propaganda in favour of change. The explosions ranged from well-meant if mostly misguided attempts to carry out what it was thought the Church wanted, to straight heresy and vandalism. The Blessed Sacrament having been banished to a cupboard in a side wall or a remote "prayer room," sanctuaries were stripped, altar rails removed, statues and stations of the cross chucked out, silver or silver gilt vessels replaced with pottery cups and plates. Confession was abandoned, along with Benediction, the rosary, and Corpus Christi and May processions. Priests started referring to themselves as "presidents" or "animators" of the assembly, and in the worst cases even said Mass dressed as clowns, as Father Christmas or even as the Easter Bunny (either because St Paul

---

263. Unfortunately the initial *General Instruction of the Roman Missal* left the way open for the very errors which Pope Paul's encyclical *Mysterium Fidei* of five years before was designed to check or refute.

had referred to the "foolishness of the cross" or to keep the kids happy). Liturgical dancing was also tried.

The immediate consequence was the appearance of various "traditionalist" movements, dedicated to preserving the old liturgy, not only for its own sake but as a bulwark against heresy. The best known of these movements is Archbishop Lefebvre's Society of St Pius X, whose leaders were automatically excommunicated when, in 1988, the Archbishop, against the instructions of Pope John Paul II, consecrated four bishops to perpetuate his work and organisation after his death.

However, John Paul II has been more sympathetic than Paul VI to traditionalist aspirations. In 1988 the Priestly Fraternity of St Peter was established, under a commission in Rome, the *Ecclesia Dei* Commission, to train and provide priests to minister to Catholics who found the new rite too unsettling, and to provide a refuge for Lefebvrist priests who, though still attached to the old liturgy, want to be reunited to the Holy See. The Fraternity of St Peter, which has its own seminaries, is in communion with the Holy See and runs extra-territorial old liturgy parishes where the local bishop allows it. The Holy Father has asked bishops to be generous in allowing for the celebration of the old liturgy where there is a demand for it. Some bishops have been generous.

The main points to keep in mind about the new liturgy, it seems to me, are: that it is now the main authorised liturgy of the Latin Church (even if the use of Latin has temporarily all but vanished); that it is clearly valid in the sense that Mass and the sacraments can be effectively celebrated with it (the majority of traditionalists now accept this); that the Church is not going to abolish it and return entirely to a silent all-Latin liturgy for the whole Latin Church or to the 1962 Roman rite for everybody – it would scarcely be possible even if a Pope wanted to make such an about-face; that it has many virtues as well as defects; that the latter can be eliminated; and that, properly executed, it is capable of achieving the legitimate goals of the reform movement.

The key phrase is "properly executed." In a sense one could apply to the Pauline liturgy Chesterton's quip about Christianity as a whole: it has not been tried and found wanting; it has never been tried. That's not quite true: there are cathedrals, parishes and religious houses where the new liturgy is celebrated fully and with dignity. But there is a good dash of truth in this generalisation. Enough at any rate so that, not long after the Council, Fr Bouyer could write: "There is practically no liturgy worthy of the name today in the Catholic Church ... perhaps in no other area is there a greater distance and even formal opposition between what the Council worked out and what we actually have ... I now have the impression, and I am not alone, that those who took it upon themselves to apply the Council's directives ... have turned their backs deliberately on what Beauduin, Casel and Pius Parsch had set out to do."[264]

Since then, Benedict XVI, when he was a cardinal, has spoken of the "disintegration of the liturgy."[265] "One shudders," he says, "at the lacklustre face of the post-conciliar liturgy as it has become." He has also said that there is less difference between the old and new liturgies than there is between the new liturgy properly celebrated and the way it is normally celebrated.

How the New Liturgy Has Been Applied

What then has gone wrong? Why are so many celebrations of the new liturgy "lacklustre," or as others have put it, "banal," "secularised," or lacking a "sense of the sacred," to such an extent indeed that criticisms are no longer coming from traditionalists but from Catholics of distinction who accept the new liturgy and see in it potentialities for good?

We can attribute some of the trouble to the influence of the surrounding culture. Western society as a whole has less and less time for, and understanding of, ceremony, symbolism and the idea of sacredness. There is nothing to symbolise. There is only what you can touch and see, objects and physical forces – and how many of us can say we are wholly unaffected by this ethos? But this is only the tip of an explanation. The Church has often had to resist cultural influences of this kind.

To get to the root of the trouble, we have to start with the way the liturgical establishment began to change during the Council and how it has developed since. It no longer consists of a relatively small number of European scholars. It is now an international affair. Each national bishops' conference and each diocese has a liturgical commission, whose leaders have become the official teachers and judges of "politically correct" liturgical thinking and acting.

The original basis of this thinking, as we have seen, had been the liturgical purism of the older generation. The Roman liturgy of the 4th and 5th centuries was the ideal; only liturgical prayer has real value; popular devotions should be discouraged if not abolished; popular participation

---

264. Bouyer, *The Decomposition of Catholicism*, London, Sands & Co, p. 99.
265. Ratzinger, *op. cit.*, p. 148.

should be the first consideration in any liturgical theory or practice. Men of this type saw the liturgy of Paul VI as the apex of liturgical perfection; the liturgy of Paul VI should be treated as sacrosanct.

The liturgy of the 4th and 5th centuries has been the ideal of liturgical reformers of this type since the 18th century, because after the 5th century visible participation by the people diminished, and with the invasion of the barbarians, Latin ceased to be a language understood by the majority of the faithful. At the same time we should remember that in some respects the later liturgy, especially the Mass, developed in a way that showed an understanding of what is happening in the Mass which was less well expressed in the earlier Latin liturgy. A "return to the sources" that excluded development would be against the mind of the Church.[266]

However the Pauline liturgy was hardly in place before it was being regarded as merely a door to further developments.

Latin was already being abandoned before the Council was over, and Mass facing the people became all but universal shortly after. Then a succession of further changes were introduced at national level, sometimes with, sometimes without, encouragement from the local bishop, against the wishes of Rome; for example, Communion received standing and Communion in the hand. When these practices became sufficiently widespread, Rome would be petitioned to authorise the innovations on the grounds that they had become an established tradition or local custom. The motives behind these and other measures, which we shall come across shortly, varied. But their general tendency has been to weaken understanding of and reverence for the Real Presence, and the Mass as a Sacrifice.

The trend continues. In *A Rereading of the Renewed Liturgy*, published in 1994, the late Dom Adrien Nocent, one of the co-founders of the Pontifical Liturgical Institute in Rome, proposed further abbreviations of the Missal including the elimination of the pentitential rite at the beginning, the washing of the priest's hands at the offertory and the elevation of the sacred species at the consecration, all so that there would be more time for Scripture readings and the sermon. He also wanted each language group to write its own collects on the grounds that Latin concision cannot be replicated in other languages. Even if the author's proposals are never taken

---

266. It is also well to remember that our knowledge of the earliest Latin liturgy is "a hypothetical reconstruction," and, for that of the 4th and 5th centuries, is dependent mainly on sources "for the most part from the 6th and 7th centuries" (Jungmann, *op. cit.*, p. 288).

up, they represent a well entrenched outlook.[267]

Meanwhile, liturgical thinking was being increasingly transformed not only by Protestant theories about the Church and the Eucharist, but by the other ideas and ideologies we have been examining in this book: the doctrines of the Enlightenment, philosophical subjectivism, Teilhardian evolutionism, Buber's communitarianism.[268]

So as not to get lost in too much detail, I will single out the four dominant ideas in current liturgical thinking which, it seems to me, have been chiefly responsible for debasing the celebration of the Pauline liturgy.

In the first, exemplified by Dom Nocent's proposals, we see the influence of Enlightenment rationalism. According to this mind-set the primary purpose of the liturgy is *to instruct*. No one explicitly says that the worship of God is not the liturgy's primary object; but where this mind-set prevails, worship tends to become a junior partner. Of course, the liturgy has a place for "instruction" – the Scripture readings and the sermon. But the sermon is the only part of the Mass for which the word "instruction" is really appropriate. We do not learn from the Scripture readings and the rest of the liturgy in the way that we learn in catechism class or by studying books about the faith, where things are set out in a logical order. In the liturgy, divine truth is conveyed into our souls differently. When the liturgy is used primarily as a teaching tool, it can cease to teach.

The second dominant idea is that the liturgy should be used to generate social cohesion. The people at Mass should feel themselves to be, and be noticeably seen to be, a strongly united community. The influence of Buber in this area has been overwhelming. Of course, Christians should be recognisable by their love for one another; but that should be apparent from their lives as a whole. There should be no need to show it off in church. The spirit of worship suffers from the focus of attention being directed away from God to the congregation.

Here I cannot do better than quote Fr Nichols again. "A community sense that does not arise from the ritual celebration of worship but is aimed

267. Nichols, *Looking at the Liturgy*, Ignatius, 1996, p. 116. The opposite argument has been advanced by the initial English translators of the liturgy. They cannot follow the Latin faithfully, they claimed, because Latin is so florid and modern English so concise.
268. Even Marxism left its traces! In 1983 the French *Missel des Dimanches* mentioned the centenary of the death of Karl Marx. And I recall a statement by a member of the US bishops' commission for the laity two or three years later: "The action of the Mass leads to the action of the street."

at, in and for itself, soon appears evanescent or superficial or both." The best it can do is produce a "transiently benevolent atmosphere" which is ultimately "frustrating." And he adds, still more pertinently, "like happiness, community is not produced by aiming at it directly; rather it is a vital, indirect consequence of immersion in other things."[269]

Much the same point had been made long before this by Guardini. In *The Spirit of the Liturgy* he explains why the liturgy has to be detached, objective and well regulated, why it does not and should not provide room for the expression of personal feeling. The universal Church, he points out, embraces men and women of every kind of temperament. For them to be united in worship, the liturgy must be above the level of their emotional differences. Expressions of personal feeling and enthusiasm in public worship, he points out, are a characteristic of religious sects.

These first two dominant ideas in current liturgical thinking, that the primary purposes of the liturgy are (a) to instruct and (b) to generate community feeling, established themselves early on in international liturgical thinking as sacred precepts. The third and fourth took longer to make headway but are now widespread too.

In the third we see the influence of philosophical subjectivism combined with democratic political ideas. The liturgy is not something we receive from God working through the Church; the liturgy should be an expression of popular experience and human creativity. Each parish or community should therefore make up its own liturgy. Cardinal Ratzinger had already foreseen this as one of the consequences of a reform conducted mainly by experts. By introducing "a breach into the history of the liturgy," the impression was created that the liturgy is not "something given in advance," but "something 'made' and consequently lying within our own powers of decision." From this it follows that "in the end each and every 'community' must provide itself with its own liturgy."[270]

The fourth idea expresses the prevailing evolutionism. The liturgy must be constantly changing because the people's situation is constantly changing.

It is difficult to think of a kind of worship better calculated to drive normal men and women with a longing for God away from church than

---

269. Nichols, *op. cit.*, pp. 33 & 42.
270. Ratzinger, *op. cit.*, pp. 146–8.

a liturgy celebrated according to these principles. A liturgy that is too "instructive" is like a conversation with a king constantly interrupted by courtiers and secretaries. A liturgy designed to generate community feeling instead of lifting us momentarily out of the everyday and commonplace leaves us firmly planted in it. A liturgy "created" by the local community means a liturgy concocted by the dominant figures in the parish group. And a constantly changing liturgy violates the fundamental sociological and anthropological principle that what people want and need in worship above all is permanence and stability.

If these views were to persist for any length of time it would be the end not only of the Latin rite but of any rites at all. I do not believe they will persist, because wherever they prevail Mass attendance and vocations to the priesthood continue to plummet. They will die eventually, even if they have a protracted old age.

In the meantime we cannot assume that even orthodox parishes remain immune to them. The faithful absorb them unconsciously, from books, from the Catholic media, from the odd remark overheard after Mass, at diocesan get-togethers, or in a sermon in a strange parish, along with a host of other ideas which have the effect of undermining the dignity and nobility of Catholic worship. They read or hear, for example, that "the Church is not the house of God but the house of the People of God," meaning that God wants you to "socialise" in church as you would at a parish get-together. Or they pick up a little book on the Eucharist by Fr Bernard Haering where they discover that Teilhard de Chardin "liked to cry out joyously 'Everything is sacred!' " But if everything is sacred, the sanctuary is no more sacred than the body of the church, and the church no more sacred than the street outside. So one can behave in the same casual way in both. The consecration of churches also becomes meaningless. Why would the bishop do it? Presumably it's just a symbolic hang-over from the past.

The second reason, I believe, why so many celebrations of the new liturgy are "lacklustre" or "banal" lies in the difficulties inherent in the fundamental conciliar enterprise. In the chaotic situation after the Council how was the average parish priest and congregation to understand and carry out the required shifts of emphasis without pushing them too far and thereby endangering both doctrine and the dignity of the celebration?

Let us take the four main aspects of Catholic worship which the Church has been trying to re-appropriate or bring back into prominence.

The social dimension.

The Church did unquestionably want the faithful to be more explicitly aware of being a priestly people, or, to use Dom Guéranger's beautiful phrase, "the society of divine praise," but not that the liturgy should be turned into a social event. The principal message the liturgy of the Eucharist should convey is that what is taking place at the altar is something wonderful, awe-inspiring, glorious and different, even remote, from everyday life and things. The wrong means have produced the wrong result.

The unity of priest and people at Mass.

Following Rosmini and others, the Church just as certainly wanted the roles of priest and people at Mass to be more fully integrated and the people's role more fully expressed. Priest and people should be seen to be, and be aware of being, engaged in the same work, even if the priest is identified with Christ and more necessary for the celebration in a way the people are not. There are changes in the new Missal which traditionalists, I believe mistakenly, assume to have had a heterodox intention, that in fact had the above purpose in mind. The rearrangement of the prayers before Communion is an example. But many innovations introduced since the new Missal was promulgated stress lay participation to such an extent that they too tend to introduce a note of the commonplace, as well as obscuring the distinction of roles, even where no heterodox intention is at work. The chief example is the introduction of lay ministers of the Eucharist.

At the Synod in Rome on the Laity in 1987, concern was expressed about "the laicisation of the clergy and the clericalisation of the laity" (the clergy concerning themselves overmuch with political and social affairs, and the laity being used unnecessarily for what had hitherto been regarded as specifically clerical tasks). In spite of this, the Holy See soon afterwards authorised what had already been going on since the mid-1970s, if not earlier: lay people conducting communion services in countries where few people have cars and there are no resident priests for long distances. According to the new regulations, they were to be called "extraordinary ministers" of the Eucharist and only used where the circumstances genuinely called for them. However, at national and diocesan level they were rapidly introduced everywhere whether needed or not, re-named "eucharistic ministers" and employed on a regular basis, so that the faithful have become accustomed to seeing numbers of lay people in ordinary clothes moving about the sanctuary in an unceremonious matter-of-fact way, doing things like opening the tabernacle – which only the priest formerly did – and handling the hosts without first having to purify their fingers as the priest still has to.

Thanksgiving and joy.

There were, no doubt, many Catholics before the Council who needed to be reminded that *eucharistia* means, in the first place, "thanksgiving." Fr Jungmann was particularly insistent on this point. But what we are chiefly giving thanks for at Mass is our redemption, for which the price was Christ's passion and death. Our thanksgiving therefore has to be different in style from the kind of gratitude we feel on receiving a large sum of money or an extra-generous Christmas present.

It is the same with Christian joy. Christian joy is not the same as natural or worldly joy. We rejoice in the prospect of eternal happiness. But we know at the same time that it is only reached through the narrow gate. Nothing has debased the celebration of the Pauline liturgy as much as confusion about the meaning of the word "celebration": the idea that a party atmosphere should be the key note of Christian worship – even for funerals and Lent. The loss of the "sense of the sacred" seems to be closely related to the loss of the "sense of sin," which the assembled fathers at the 1983 Synod on penance deplored.

Recovering the "meal" aspect of the Mass.

In Catholic belief the sacrifice or self-offering to the Father which Christ made once on Calvary for our sins, and which He continues to offer eternally in heaven, is made present again in time, though bloodlessly, by the words of the consecrating priest. This has always been the focal point of the Mass. For a short while, eternity and time intersect. To this self-offering of Christ, with which the people spiritually unite themselves, the "sacred banquet" at the end of Mass is the complement or fulfilment, without being something additional or accidental. In the past this relationship between the two components was understood well enough. But it was perhaps inevitable that once the Church started to encourage frequent Communion, the Communion rite would attract greater attention.

However, not only is the use of the word "meal" in this context ambiguous, throughout most of the West it has been so over-stressed that many of the faithful now think the people's Communion is the single high point of the celebration. Even when they continue to believe in the Real

Presence – and polls in the United States and elsewhere have shown that something like 75% of Catholics no longer do – many appear to see the consecration as simply a way of making our Lord present so that they can receive him in Holy Communion.[271]

In the average parish, diminished awareness of what is fundamentally taking place at Mass, due to faulty catechetics and the misplaced emphases we have been looking at, seems to be the main reason why there are so many uninspiring celebrations. Far from the potentialities of the new liturgy being exploited, they are mostly ignored or scanted. The dominant guiding principle is only too often "brevity." Of the four eucharistic prayers available, the two shortest are the most commonly used. Ceremonies like the blessing of ashes, or the Palm Sunday and Easter Vigil liturgies are usually carried out in their briefest form. Incense, a powerfully symbolic way of honouring God and sacred things and representing the faithful's prayers, is in many places all but unknown. The reformers' hope that Morning and Evening prayer from the breviary (Lauds and Vespers) would become part of the laity's prayer life has not been realised. Only a handful of parishes have Morning Prayer as a preparation for Mass or Vespers on Sunday evenings. And so that modern man's attention span will not be over-stretched, even the new Sunday Scripture readings seem to be in danger. In France and Germany, the first of the three is often omitted, showing once again that where an alternative is permitted, the least time-consuming is the most likely to be chosen.[272]

A Glance Ahead

The situation just described would presumably be one of the reasons why, in October 1998, John Paul II, after speaking of liturgical "abuses" and "grave scandals," told a group of US bishops that, while active participation of the laity should be encouraged, their fundamental disposition "must be,

---

271. The 1920s and '30s, Ratzinger tells us, saw a learned debate in Germany about the basic "structure" of the Mass, in contrast to its dogmatically defined "content." Was the basic structure a "meal"? Ratzinger, following Jungmann, shows decisively that it is not. According to Jungmann, there is only one reference in the New Testament to the Eucharist as a "supper" (1 Cor 11:20). After that the word is unheard of until the Reformation. Ratzinger, *Feast of Faith*, original 1981, English trans., Ignatius, 1985.

272. See the *General Instruction of the Roman Missal*, art. 318. For the appropriate way to celebrate the Pauline liturgy see *Ceremonies of the Modern Roman Rite, The Eucharist and the Liturgy of Hours*, by Mgr Peter Elliott, Ignatius, 1995, and his more popular *Liturgical Question Box* from the same publishers. If every parish conformed to the requirements and suggestions of these two admirable manuals, liturgical chaos would cease.

reverence and adoration." It would also explain why Joseph Ratzinger asked for "a new Liturgical Movement which will call to life the real heritage of the Second Vatican Council."[273] Indeed, inspired by this, there is already a movement for the "reform of the reform." This does not mean a restoration of the traditional rite, which will continue as an alternative (following John Paul II's *motu proprio, Ecclesia Dei adflicta*). The aim is to adjust texts, tighten some of the rubrics, and above all recover the lost or dimninished "sense of the sacred." It will doubtless take time. But that is the traditional way in which the liturgy has changed.

The chief problem areas ahead would seem to be communion services conducted by lay people, and radical feminists pushing for inclusive language and women priests.

Lay-conducted communion services with hosts that have been consecrated by a priest, as we have seen, were originally intended for mission countries. In the West, where they are now common too, many of the faithful are beginning to see them as a handy substitute for Mass, if indeed they are still aware there is any difference.

Radical feminism represents a much bigger challenge since it is aiming for something unallowable in itself. The problems here began with the decision to permit lay eucharistic ministers. Restricting the privilege to men would have looked like treating women as inferior. But women giving communion makes it much more difficult for the faithful to see why they cannot say Mass as well. Certainly the radical feminists see women eucharistic ministers as a step towards their goal, and during the 1980s and '90s there were signs that numbers of priests and even bishops were beginning to side with them. Few if any ask for the ordination of women outright. The plea is made for the question to be left open for further discussion. But if the question is susceptible to discussion, it is not settled – women priests become a possibility. This is why in 1996, John Paul II finally put his foot down. In his Apostolic Letter *Ordinatio Sacerdotalis*, he solemnly re-affirmed what had always been believed: the Church's inability to ordain women. In Catholic belief, 500 bishops could lay their hands on a woman while invoking the Holy Spirit and she would still not be a priest.

The main reason for this is that, in fundamental things, the Church holds that what she has always done or not done was either instituted by Christ or inspired by the Holy Spirit.

---

273. Ratzinger, *op. cit.*, 149.

How do the advocates of women priests surmount such a major obstacle? In the main they put forward two arguments: either that, in not ordaining women, Christ was limited by the mentality and customs of his time; or that he was making a temporary concession to them. However, only a little reflection shows the inadequacy of both positions.

If the former were true, if Christ's understanding and will were limited in the way suggested, then he could no longer be the universal Saviour. It would imply that his divinity was submerged in his humanity to the point of being inoperative, while at the same time making the Gospel no longer a universal message, the same for all times and places.

On the other hand, the argument that Our Lord was making a concession to the prejudices or spirit of his times until men's minds were better prepared to receive what he really wanted to teach is contradicted by the most obvious historical facts. The pagans were quite accustomed to the idea of women priests; women priests would have been no obstacle to their conversion. As for Our Lord's own people, the Jews, he was prepared to challenge their ideas about divorce, the necessity of circumcision, and their rules about the Sabbath. His attitude to women, as we see from the Gospels, was also in conflict with Jewish custom. If he *had* wanted women to be ordained, then, why did he stop short of doing so himself?

The demand for women priests shows how deeply the doctrines of the Enlightenment are embedded in Western Catholic thinking. It has the same origin as the demand by homosexual men to be surgically altered so that they can have babies. Equality demands that what one sex can do, the other must be able to.

However, a Christian who wants to know the mind of God on some subject does not take a secular thinker like Jean-Jacques Rousseau as his starting point or guide. If he cannot accept the authority of the Catholic Church, he will at least begin with Holy Scripture, and it is there above all that we can discover the reasons why Our Lord instituted an all-male priesthood. Those reasons will not of course be understood by people who fail to recognise that God's ways are not always our ways, that we are dealing with a supernatural mystery, or appreciate the importance, in conveying it, of religious symbolism.

Basically, these reasons boil down to the teaching of Holy Scripture on God's relationship to the human race. Throughout both Testaments it is cast in the mould of human marriage. God is the husband, the human race the wife. Christ is the bridegroom, his people are the Bride. Having women as priests would make the message unintelligible. We may not understand or like this way that God has chosen of explaining our relationship to Him. But that He attaches importance to it is indisputable.[274]

Shortly after *Ordinatio Sacerdotalis*, John Paul II finally gave permission for women to be altar servers, a decision that would seem to have been intended to make it easier for disappointed lay women and nuns to accept the fact that they could not be ordained. Up to this point he had resolutely resisted the pressure for female altar servers since the beginning of his pontificate.[275]

The pressure for inclusive language (the substitution of the word "person" or "people" for "man" or "he" when used collectively for both sexes) is another item on the feminist agenda, already causing headaches. After a tussle with the US bishops' conference bureaucracy, Rome managed to get inclusive language excluded from the English translation of the new Catechism, but it is common in convents and is encouraged in some parishes, the ultimate feminist objective being to get the pronoun "He" for God banned, or to substitute "Creator," "Redeemer" and "Sanctifier" for "Father," "Son" and "Holy Spirit."

---

274. It is difficult not to see a close connection between the movement for women priests and the depreciation of motherhood. But the latter should be impossible once we look at motherhood from a truly Christian standpoint. What is a child for a Christian? A potential brother or sister of Christ and a future citizen of heaven. That normally the mother plays by far the greater role both in bringing the child into existence and in preparing him for this destiny is obvious. Why then should women be discontented at not being able to be priests as well? Is there not a kind of spiritual gluttony in all this?

275. There are several good reasons against female altar servers. They have nothing to do with women being thought inferior. The first is a common-sense reason. Normal men, which most priests are, are going to find a beautiful girl or woman serving at the altar distracting. They would hardly be normal if they did not. Secondly, service on the altar has long been recognised as a seed bed for priestly vocations. But equally well recognised is the fact that at a certain stage in their development, boys dislike doing what could be seen as girlish things. This is all the more likely to happen where an activity involves both sexes wearing robes that could look like dresses. Having girls as altar servers is therefore likely to lead to a decrease in the number of genuine vocations among boys and an increase of imaginary "calls to the priesthood" among girls and young women. A third and final reason against female altar servers has to do with the theological symbolism mentioned above. The Mass under one aspect is the nuptial banquet of Christ with the Church. Since the priest represents Christ the Bridegroom, it is fitting that he should be surrounded by male attendants. This is how bridegrooms have always come to their weddings, not with bridesmaids. Women altar servers, like women priests, send the wrong theological message.

However, the lay-run Communion service is proving radical feminism's most effective tactical weapon. A woman eucharistic minister, dressed in some kind of ecclesiastical robe, who recites the entire Mass liturgy before giving Communion, already seems to be a practice in some North American parishes. She then only has to include the words of consecration and elevate the host and chalice and the main feminist goal will appear to have been achieved. When this has become "a local custom," all that will then apparently be needed is the local bishop's blessing and the laying on of hands.

The Church will come through in the end. But it looks as if the battle with those who seek to deny the innate differences between the sexes is going to be as tough as the battle with the early great heresies.

PLEASE LEAVE BY THE BACK DOOR

It is probably unnecessary to have to ask you to read this final chapter because we tend not to have the same repugnance for postscripts, conclusions and epilogues as we have for prefaces and introductions. Indeed, our expectations about postscripts, conclusions and epilogues tend, if anything, to be too high. We subconsciously look forward to them as the point when everything will end happily or be tied up neatly. But that, of course, is impossible when we are reading about historical events rather than fiction. A book of this sort is designed to help you on your way as Christians and Catholics through the years ahead, not to predict what the surrounding conditions are likely to be. So you may be disappointed – although I hope you won't be.

As I said in Chapter I, although this book is like the previous one, *Turmoil and Truth*, in that both are concerned with the crisis provoked by the disintegration of Christendom and the take-over of Christendom by a powerful intellectual and spiritual rival, the accent in the earlier volume was on debates and conflicts inside the Church, while here it is mainly on debates and disagreements with groups and bodies of opinion outside the Church, and the moral and spiritual crisis through which the entire Western world is passing.

So in order to make a final assessment of that crisis and its impact on the Church, let us begin by recalling the path we have been following, moving back from the point we have now reached to our starting point in chapter one.

In the last five chapters we have explored the influence of modern Western thought and culture on two of the most sensitive areas of the Church's life: theology and the liturgy. The resulting problems only the Church can sort out. This is in the first place a matter for the magisterium, and the matter at stake is the protection and propagation of divine revelation.

With the greater part of the book, however, it is different. Leaving aside the chapters on Karl Barth and liberal Protestant theology, the seventeen chapters between pages 13 and 202 are concerned with recognised fields of scholarship, or philosophical and scientific inquiry, where the predominant factor is reason rather than revelation. The debate here is between the Church's scholars and thinkers and their non-Christian counterparts – who, in theory at least, are all solely interested in and committed to discovering the truth about those things which are within the compass of the human mind operating on its own. In this debate, impartiality is the virtue to which everyone taking part should and would like to be able to lay claim, and the chief issue is whether a particular proposition or hypothesis can be shown to be true. If it undoubtedly can be, then the question of how it affects our understanding of this or that revealed truth comes second, and is of concern mainly to the Church.

Finally, our backwards journey brings us to the first seven chapters, which are different again. Here in the doctrines of the Enlightenment we found ourselves confronting an ideological construction based on a mixture of natural truths, inherited Christian attitudes of mind and aspirations, a great deal of wishful thinking, and a missionary zeal that could well put a lot of Christians to shame. It is the universality of the Enlightenment message and its missionary zeal, as we said, which, following the example of Pope Paul VI, justify our describing it not only as a religion and a Christian heresy but as the soul of modern thought and as the Church's main religious rival today.

How far have the Church's efforts to reach an accord or *modus vivendi* with this new rival succeeded since they were initiated between forty and forty-five years ago at the Second Vatican Council? On the surface, not far. On both sides of the Atlantic, but particularly on the European side, the "committed cadres" of secularism as we could call them have been conducting an increasingly aggressive campaign against Christianity as a whole and the Catholic Church in particular, with the ultimate purpose, apparently, of reducing Christian influence on public law and social life to vanishing point.

No gestures on the part of the Church, as far as one can see, have softened the hearts of secularist hard-liners or persuaded them that the Church could make a beneficial contribution to their quest for an ideal society. Not even Pope John Paul II's unprecedented apology in the millennium year for the crimes, misdeeds and mistakes of Catholics during the 2000 years of the Church's history awoke a sympathetic response. The gesture was ignored, as was the Pope's invitation to other groups, nations, religions, and bodies of opinion to make similar apologies for enormities and crimes committed in their names over a much shorter span of time.[276]

---

276. It is difficult to see how an accommodation with truly committed secularists is possible, any more than it would have been possible with Calvin or John Knox, as long as they persist in seeing the Catholic Church as a secularist equivalent to the Anti-Christ. However, one can never be sure. In the 19th century, the Marquis of Ripon, who had been Grand Master of the English freemasons, became a Catholic, and used to go straight from meetings of Gladstone's cabinet to meetings of the Society of St Vincent de Paul.

What could highlight secularism's total lack of response more clearly than the recently drafted European constitution, whose preamble attributes the formation of European civilisation exclusively to the cultures of ancient Greece and Rome, and then – jumping over 1500 years – to the Enlightenment, omitting any reference to Christianity whatsoever.

Even more tell-tale is the growing number of court cases in which religious believers are prosecuted for offending secularist sensibilities, or violating secularist substitutes for the Ten Commandments. They range from police investigations for saying what has been recognised as true in the majority of societies since the beginning of history, namely that homosexual practice is unnatural, wrong, and socially harmful, to court cases for the removal of Christian and other religious symbols from public view. I think that it is not unreasonable to foresee, at least as a possibility, the ultimate absurdity of an anti-Christian persecution conducted by people who once called themselves liberals or freethinkers.

All this of course is conducted under the rubric of the separation of Church and State. However, there is a marked difference between the way a non-confessional liberal state of the Anglo-Saxon type understands this rubric and the way a secularist state of the French anti-clerical type interprets it.

A non-confessional state is one in which no religious belief is given precedence over any other. The government refrains from favouring or imposing one particular world-view, and, without being dogmatic about it, tries, in so far as is possible, to treat the different religious communities even-handedly. This, presumably, was what the American founding fathers had in mind. One could call it a pragmatic solution to a particular historical situation.

Whether a non-confessional state can or should treat different codes of behaviour impartially is a separate question. This is a matter I touched on in the chapter *Human Rights and Human Wrongs*. You can hardly have a state or nation with a plurality of codes of behaviour, at least not about fundamentals, since if that is the case, where are the basic precepts for such a code of behaviour to come from? This is a problem the founding fathers do not seem to have considered. Since the majority were deists, it probably never occurred to them that any considerable body of citizens would one day question the existence of a Creator or the truth of the natural law as formulated in the Ten Commandments.

A secularist state on the other hand is one in which religion as such

– the notion or even the mention of God – is as far as possible excluded from public life, public affairs, public documents and public places, with the purpose of eventually making godlessness, coupled with a humanistic adulation of man and his achievements, the reigning belief of the majority of citizens.

Were the American founding fathers being inconsistent when, in establishing equal treatment – at least in theory – for all bodies of opinion, religious and irreligious, they allowed references to God and the natural law in their declarations of independence and constitution? No, because belief in a Creator, the natural law and a moral conscience are not matters of faith. They are logical inferences based on the evidence of the senses or internal experience, and as such are acts of reason within all men's reach. It is much more reasonable to believe that the universe is the work of a Mighty Intelligence –regardless of the mystery of suffering and evil – than that it generated itself by accident and sustains itself without a cause. Atheism, by comparison, is an act of unreason.

Obviously I am not arguing that atheists may not be men of the highest intelligence. There are many reasons why people become atheists. The Second Vatican Council gives as one of them the bad example of believers. This is a melancholy truth. However it no more constitutes an argument against belief than the existence of bad lawyers is an argument against having laws or people to administer them. So when, in a genuinely non-confessional state, devout secularists and their offspring claim that they feel "intimidated" or "provoked" by references to God in public places, religious believers should enjoy an equal right to feel intimidated and provoked by His exclusion.[277] Toleration, to which our secularist brethren still at least give lip service, means putting up with what you regard as your neighbour's peculiarities and foibles, provided they are not grossly immoral or socially disruptive, no matter how much they offend your sensibilities.

However, in western Europe, if not so far in the U.S., it begins to look as if the days of the truly non-confessional state are numbered. In practice, if not yet in law, as I pointed out in Chapter Three, what is being attempted is the establishment of atheism as a state religion – just as it was, and still is,

---

277. According to a recent French government document, the wearing of religious symbols by children in state schools (in this case Muslim girls wearing headscarves), constitutes an act of "intimidation" and "provocation" for unbelieving children and their parents. *Daily Telegraph*, London, 20th September 2004.

under Marxism.[278]

Were the Fathers of the Second Vatican Council mistaken, then, in trying to come to terms with the Enlightenment and its more dedicated adherents? While not a few Catholics would say Yes, on this point I have to disagree. The work had to be done for the reasons I gave at the end of *Turmoil and Truth*. It was necessary for the sake of the faithful, who in many respects are children of the Enlightenment without knowing it. It was necessary for the sake of the waves of immigrants pouring into the Western countries as the native populations of the West decline. They too need to know how much in the culture of the countries of their adoption is due to Christianity and how much is not.

And there is another consideration. Although secularists are increasingly influential throughout the West and are able to sway public policy and public opinion in a way that should not be under-rated, they are still a minority, even a small minority.[279] Of the millions of Western or Westernised men and women subscribing more or less consciously to Enlightenment principles and aims, by far the greater number are liberals of the un-dogmatic Anglo-Saxon kind, whether they live in England, North America, France, Spain, or anywhere else. Liberals of this kind have always been strong on works of philanthropy. They are *par excellence* the "men of good will" referred to so often in recent documents of the magisterium. Their main weakness has always been a defective or inadequate philosophy of nature and of man, which leads them repeatedly to underestimate the obstacles to be overcome in the attainment of their goals. One could say that a good liberal of this kind wakes every morning in a state of frustration and disappointment on finding that the world is still a very long way from perfection. But they do really value one's being able to say what one honestly thinks, and with them discussion has always been possible, leaving aside the fact that they have

---

278. In Europe today "there is an aggressive secular ideology that is worrisome ... In politics, it is considered indecent to talk about God – as if it would be an attack on the freedom of unbelievers." Cardinal Ratzinger, interview in *La Repubblica*, 19th September 2004. "Secularism means that there is no religion but the state – it is nothing short of state atheism." Cardinal Jean-Louis Tauran, Vatican archivist. For both, see *Catholic World Report*, December 2004.

279. Cardinal Ratzinger, citing the historian/philosopher Arnold Toynbee, observed in an interview on Vatican Radio that Toynbee "was right when he said that the fate of society always depends on creative minorities." (Reported in *The Wanderer*, 16th December 2004.) The Cardinal was actually foreseeing a possible role of Christians in an increasingly hostile environment. But Toynbee's insight applies equally to secularists.

always included large numbers of Christians.

How then are liberals of this kind going to react as the rule of their one-time secularist allies becomes more and more oppressive under a polished surface of "best intentions" and "caring concern," and increasingly incapable of coping with the social problems which their policies are already producing?

About a decade ago, for example, I attended a conference in Stuttgart on the family, where for the best part of a week we listened to politicians and officials from Bonn explaining how they were coping with the breakdown of the family. After listening to them for two days, the thought came into my mind: "This is liberalism trying to cope with the consequences of its own philosophical follies." Since then the situation, in Europe at any rate, has deteriorated still further. It is no longer a question of governments coping with unforeseen consequences, but of governments actively promoting policies regardless of the consequences. It is not the family alone which is under attack. The moral and spiritual life of whole populations is being debauched, and I am not thinking at this point of the "sexual revolution." I have in mind the preaching of politicians and cultural elites who have nothing better to offer than an "ever higher quality of life" (for many of us, it could be argued, the quality of life would be higher if it were "lower"), and a lop-sided doctrine of human rights (which turns rights into wrongs and wrongs into rights). The two together, coupled with the unprecedented rain of riches and conveniences, seem to be making large swathes of the populations of the West as demanding as 18th century aristocrats, and increasingly ungovernable.[280]

I am not envisaging the imminent collapse of Western society. As long as it keeps economically afloat, that seems highly unlikely. But I do see it set on a course that future historians could well label "the decline and death of liberalism."

How in fact do you govern a nation where the majority of the citizens are at least practical atheists? How indeed are people of any kind governed?

This is a problem which liberal and secularist governments have never until recently had to face, and appear not yet to have even recognised as a problem. Although there have been liberal governments of one sort or another for 200 years, they have been living off other people's capital. They

---

280. It is only a small point, but for some years now, English state-owned hospitals have been displaying notices warning that anyone insulting or assaulting doctors and nurses will be handed over to the police.

have been ruling over societies where the majority of the citizens were still Christian or deeply influenced by Christianity.

The Marxists of course had no problem. If only as a last resort, they had the secret police, the prison camps and the torture chamber. This is why neo-Marxists, jockeying for a position in Western-style political systems where such things are not acceptable, discuss what they call "the problem of social control." With their sombre view of human nature inherited from their founder, they at least recognise that there is a problem; that people en masse will not automatically behave in a reasonable, orderly, co-operative way unless they have been trained from childhood to listen to reason and conscience and provided with adequate motives for continuing on the same course.

It could also be called "the problem of the interior and exterior policeman." As you weaken the interior police force, you have to enlarge the exterior one.

So there is hope that as secularists become, like their forebears during the French revolution, more and more dictatorial, entangled, and at cross purposes in their efforts to make godless populations absolutely free, indistinguishably equal and enforcedly fraternal, genuine liberals will at last begin to see the light and start opposing them. For their sake too, therefore, it has been necessary for the Church to come to terms with the Enlightenment.

To conclude – if conclusion there must be – the irony and complexity of the relationship between the Church and the Enlightenment can perhaps best be expressed by adapting – if that is allowable – the parable of the Prodigal Son.

There was once, as in the original story, a man who had two sons, and the younger said to his father, "Give me my share of the inheritance." Then, having received it, he went off to a far country taking all his newly acquired wealth with him. However, instead of wasting it on riotous living, he used it to start a lot of highly profitable businesses. Within a short time he had become a billionaire and, returning to his country of origin, began buying up large tracts of his father's property, which the elder brother was managing while the father was away on a world tour.

To begin with, the elder brother tried to fight off the younger brother's incursions. But he lacked his brother's financial astuteness. Each time he was outwitted. What was he to do? He had to admit that his brother's businesses were well run. They benefited the employees as well as the customers and shareholders. He also had instructions from the father to stay on good terms with his younger brother in so far as that was possible. At first, he thought of suggesting that he and his brother go into partnership and run the two inheritances as one. However, on reflection he saw that, short of a radical change of heart on the younger brother's part, this would be impossible because not all of the younger brother's businesses were of the kind, or run in a way, that the father would have approved. Recently, for instance, he had been financing an international chain of high-class brothels. He had also been telling people that there was no need to worry about what the father thought, since the father was dead. His agents had even been spreading rumours among the younger customers and employees that the father never actually existed. He was an invention of the older brother. In the past people didn't have fathers. The earth generated people spontaneously.

Will the older brother be able to bring the younger brother to a better frame of mind? When the father returns will he find his two sons running the estate together in fraternal harmony according to the principles he, the father, had laid down? Or will he discover that his elder son has had to take refuge in a far country while the younger son lords it on his own, and according to his own lights, over the ancestral patrimony?

Except for the rare man or woman endowed with the gift of prophecy, these are things which it is not given to us to know.

APPENDIX I
(see chapter 14, note 127)

In the period before 1920, it will be remembered, the history of dogma had been a major topic of interest – dogmas, as we already know, did not spring into being fully formed at the start, like Athena from the head of Zeus – and during that time the Church had had to combat two inter-related ideas or tendencies, jointly called "historicism." The first presented the history of dogmatic formulations as an evolution rather than a development; the second tended to see the formulations as entirely determined by the culture or way of thinking of the time in which they took their definitive shape. Dogmatic formulations, it was therefore argued, only have a passing value. In time they become meaningless or unintelligible. The underlying "truth" then has to be rethought and reformulated (though there is no evidence that the Church had ever before found this necessary or attempted it).

After 1920, these concerns and the attendant problems spread to theology as a whole. The demand arose for scholars to be allowed greater freedom to examine the way historical factors had to some extent affected the manner in which theological problems had been posed and answered over the course of time and for the results of their researches to be included in theological courses for students. Theology and doctrine should not be presented exclusively as a timeless whole. The historical approach would enable scholars to enter more deeply into the minds of the theologians of the past they were studying, making it easier to distinguish what was enduring from what was ephemeral in their ideas, and to bring out the connection between the deposit of faith or the "sources" and current teaching.

In itself, the demand was reasonable enough. All the more so, seeing that scholars outside the Church were examining Christian theology from an historical standpoint. It was necessary to know what they were saying, if only to correct what, from the Catholic standpoint, would be erroneous conclusions. But could the demand be satisfied without introducing the problems which had been haunting the study of the history of dogma? Would students leave their courses in historical or *positive* theology, as it has since come to be called, believing that one theological opinion was as good as another, and none could permanently stand the test of time? The question is particularly pertinent because the introduction of the historical approach in all branches of religious studies would be a central feature of the new theologians' reform programme. Some would even speak as though a sense of history had been discovered for the first time.

The answer to the question will, of course, depend, on the wisdom and sense of proportion of the individual scholar or teacher. As a Dominican versed in the subject has neatly put it, "instead of saying that there is an important place for historical study within theology," will it be a case of "history becomes everything"? (Aidan Nichols OP, *The Shape of Catholic Theology*, p. 332)

The transition from the first frame of mind to the second is well exemplified by the course of events at the French Dominican house of studies, Le Saulchoir, between its establishment in 1904 and its closure after the Council, when the order started sending its students to ordinary universities; or between the attitudes of its first rector and, in a certain sense, founder, Fr Ambrose Gardeil, and what eventually became the attitudes of its second most prominent son, Fr Marie-Dominique Chenu.

Chenu, Historical Theology and Historicism

Fr Gardeil initially set out his position in a series of lectures, later published as *Le Donné révélé et la Théologie*, at the Institut Catholique in Paris in 1908. It was a brave move. The first modernist crisis was at its height. Subsequently in collaboration with the medievalist Fr Mandonnet and with the support of the biblicist, Fr Lagrange, he introduced the historical approach at Le Saulchoir. Teaching and research focused on medieval theology with particular attention to the theology of St Thomas.

Authority, more sensitive at this period to dangers than possible advantages, eventually accepted Fr Gardeil's approach, but for a long time reluctantly. One could say perhaps that historical theology was something which *had* to be taken on board, like critical biblical scholarship, be there risks or no risks. Rejecting it would have been like refusing to use cars because there are sometimes accidents. And to begin with, all went well. But, by the late 1930s, historicist tendencies began to manifest themselves. Rome first became aware of the situation through a little book by Fr Chenu, based on a lecture celebrating the feast of St Thomas in March 1936, and printed the following year for private circulation within the Dominican order under the title *Une école de théologie: Le Saulchoir*. Fr Chenu was, by this time, rector of studies, and the book described the methods of research and teaching currently pursued at Le Saulchoir. In 1942 the book was condemned and Fr Chenu was forbidden to teach. Later he was reinstated and, as we have seen, became an active member of the reform party at the Council.

But was Rome, or were the officials in Rome who were responsible at the time for the measure, entirely mistaken about him? There was no public edition of his book until 1985, when it was published by Les Editions du Cerf, Paris, with lengthy commentaries by a group of prominent theological dissenters. In what follows, the letter "S." will refer to quotations from this book, and the letters "T.L." to quotations from *Un Théologien en Liberté*, an interview with the journalist Jacques Duquesne (Le Centurion, Paris, 1975). In both cases the translations are mine.

That Fr Chenu had much that was attractive about him and much to his credit is the impression left by this interview and also by the obituary in *30 Days*, by his fellow Dominican, Fr Spiazzi, in spite of Fr Spiazzi's representing a quite different theological position. Fr Chenu was not an original thinker, but he was clearly an excellent historian and a first-rate teacher, with an almost boyish enthusiasm for his task and love of his subject. Had he not been, Gilson would hardly have engineered his appointment by the French government to found the new Institute of Medieval Studies in Montreal where, from 1930 on, he lectured for two months a year up to the war. Of his *Toward Understanding Saint Thomas*, Fr Spiazzi says "Thousands of us were formed by that book." He was also refreshingly honest (he did not try to disguise his views like Teilhard), appears to have been quite without personal ambition, and had a genuine love of the poor and desire to better their conditions. His support for the worker priests can be attributed to this love and this desire, as can, no doubt, the activities of the majority of worker priests themselves, even if they were mistaken in many of their ideas and methods.

The weakness which eventually led him astray, I would say, was another boyish trait. He was a natural partisan. Once a cause or an idea had captured his imagination he went overboard for it. Everything thereafter was black or white, or perceived in terms of "us" and "them." He would have hotly denied it, but the interview with Duquesne bears repeated witness to it.

We see it first at the very outset of his career. Having refused Fr Garrigou-Lagrange's offer of a post as his assistant in Rome (Garrigou had a high opinion of his talents) and having repudiated neo-scholasticism in favour of historical theology and the school of Le Saulchoir, the historical approach became to all intents and purposes the only worthwhile approach. No theological proposition could be properly understood without a knowledge of its historical context. "Archaeology, ethnology, linguistics, philology, which could seem a peripheral part of sacred studies, are in reality the indispensable keys ... to an intelligent faith" (S., p. 170). This lack of a sense of proportion opened the way to a more and more radical historicism leading eventually to a full-blown modernism, where the deposit of faith takes the form of an unverbalised instinct in the faithful's collective subconscious from which it is continually bursting forth as it endeavours to express itself, though never with complete success, in ever new forms.

"The understanding of the mystery can only be had through the history in which it unrolls – a sacred history. Clearly this goes against the conception of a timeless theology, unchanging across space and time. Theology is thus relativised. That is to say it is drawn into the complex interplay of relations which continually modify, not of course the radical content of the faith, but its expressions" (S., pp. 7–8; T.L., p. 119). "The word 'deposit' is open to criticism because it creates the impression of a truth exterior to me, spread out in front of me" (T.L., p. 47). "I discover the Word of God not in a whole series of propositions taught by a magisterium. I find it, even if conditioned by that magisterium, in act, in effervescence, in a people, who, with the eyes of faith, I see as the locus of the Holy Spirit" (T.L., p. 69). Theology "is not a knowledge fallen from the sky to fix itself in propositions guarded by the magisterium," but "is immersed in the life of the people of God linked to the world" (T.L., p. 68). "The fundamental concern of the theologian ... is ... the whole life of the Christian people, including its economic activities, which are the ground of its culture" (T.L., p. 119). "The Church–community in act is the immediate object of the theologian's study" (T.L., p. 119). "The collective experience of the People of God as an hierarchically organised community must be the basis of the revision of formulas" (T.L., p. 199). "The bearer of the Word of God ... is humanity in process of construction by science and human work" (S., p. 176).

This last passage suggests that Fr Chenu had steeped himself in Fr Teilhard as well as in Maritain's *Integral Humanism* which, he tells us, he had read many times.

In view of all this, how does Fr Chenu see the relationship of theologians to bishops? There are, we learn, two fundamental forces at work in the Church: *pouvoir* (power), exercised by the bishops, and *savoir* (knowledge), the province of theologians, and between them a great gulf is fixed. Bishops, it is implied, will for the most part always be theological ignoramuses, and theologians objective and disinterested. The need for some degree of *pouvoir* is not denied, but since *savoir* is infinitely superior, its superiority should be publicly admitted and the authority of the possessors of *pouvoir* radically restricted in the interests of *savoir*. This means more *pouvoir* for theologians, which, as it turns out, is just what Fr Chenu's theories about the nature of theology have prepared the ground for.

"The theologian ... is better suited to give a pure disinterested witness than the man of power" (T.L., p. 20). "Theologians are not merely experts at the service of power ... they have an autonomous function..." The theologian "is the conscience of the community, the critical consciousness of the world in labour under the influence of faith" (T.L., p. 21). He "watches the word of God at work in the community ... day by day he follows it as it expresses itself in history ...The theologian has to be in a certain sense a prophet, taking the pulse of a world on the march" (T.L., p. 22). "Power," on the other hand, "is tempted to claim that it comes directly from God" (T.L., p. 19). "The Episcopal charism as such does not imply any prophetic element." (T.L., p. 23). "The Pope ... sometimes uses vocabulary adapted to the Italian Christian community ... The theologian's business is to use discernment, to take account of the fact that the people's outlook and situations are not the same in France and Germany. What the Pope says has to be adapted to them" (T.L., p. 19).

Historical theology has its place in Catholic studies. But I think it will be seen that the forebodings of those who had reservations about it were not all illusory.

APPENDIX II
(see chapter 21, note 217)

The other main advocate of "experience" as the primary source of religious knowledge, or the factor which ought to determine the way it is expressed, has, of course, been Fr Edward Schillebeeckx.

Schillebeeckx and Experience

As leader with Fr Küng of the revolt against the magisterium since the Council, and a theologian almost as widely read as Fr Rahner, he too would seem to deserve a chapter or chapters to himself. However, he resembles Fr Rahner in so many ways that this would involve going over much the same ground a second time. Although half a generation younger than Rahner, both men had been subject to the same cultural influences, had mulled over the same questions, acquired a similar aversion to scholastic philosophy and theology, and, in their later years, as they moved further and further from the fullness of Catholic belief, adopted much the same positions about fundamental doctrines.

Fr Schillebeeck differed from Rahner in being less original as a thinker, less systematic and ponderously philosophical as a theologian and in giving an even heavier emphasis to the role of "experience." His later theology is little more than politicised Bultmann with a strong dash of the new hermeneutics. "Christ is no longer present as the Incarnate son of God but as a prophet enjoying the highest relationship with God; the Resurrection is no longer the event in which Christ rose from the tomb...The narratives of the apparitions ... express the experience by which Jesus was recognised as God's salvation for man" (J Galot SJ, reviewing Schillebeeckx's *Expérience humaine et foi en Jésus* in *Esprit et Vie*, 23 July 1981). Onto all this, with the collaboration of Fr Johann Baptist Metz, he grafted his own version of liberation theology. He also took less trouble than Rahner to disguise his departures from Catholic belief and support for dissent. One cannot imagine Fr Rahner, for instance, publicly celebrating Mass with two excommunicated priests and two women ("E. Schillebeeckx and the Catholic Priesthood," van der Ploeg, *Homiletic and Pastoral Review*, March 1982).

What is perhaps most interesting about him, as well as being revealing about the state of many of the faithful immediately after the Council, are the circumstances which brought about the final collapse of his faith.

Up to the Council his writings are generally considered to be capable of bearing a properly Catholic meaning and even to have positive merit. This includes his widely read *Christ the Sacrament of the Encounter with God* (1959). It is true that in 1962 he began collaborating in the production of the new Dutch catechism. But as late as 1964, it is still possible to say that his teaching about Christ "in no way ... betrays any withdrawal from the dogma of the Church" (Leo Scheffczyk, 'Christology and Experience: Schillebeeckx on Christ,' *The Thomist*, July 1984). However, by 1969, "withdrawals" were becoming increasingly pronounced and the rest of Scheffczyk's article follows them step by step. What it does not mention (it was not the article's purpose) is the dramatic nature of the events which precipitated the change.

The year 1966, we are told by Schillebeeckx's admirer and fellow Dominican Philip Kennedy OP (*Schillebeeckx*, London, Chapman, 1993, p. 43), marked a turning-point to be "highlighted at all costs in the consideration of Schillebeeckx's history," and initiated "a time of intellectual ferment" lasting until the mid-1970s. Impelled by what Schillebeeck himself calls an "almost feverish sense of urgency," he began "a frenetic search to reformulate the meaning of faith in God and Christ and the function of faith in secularised societies" (Kennedy, p. 37). From now to the end of the 1960s, his writings would be punctuated by the words "crisis," "newness," "change." Fr Kennedy lists eighteen subjects in all, which, during this period of ravenous reading and rethinking helped to transform his beliefs, with the "new hermeneutics," language philosophy and the "critical" Marxism of the Frankfurt school inflicting the deepest wounds.

What had happened? Why in 1966 did he suddenly decide that Catholic doctrine was no longer intelligible unless it conformed to human experience – which, Scheffczyk astutely remarks, is like saying that the recipient of a letter will only be able to understand and accept it if he has first decided on the contents and written it himself (*op. cit.*, p. 407).

A contributory factor seems to have been his appointment to teach a course in hermeneutics at Nijmegen, which exposed him to radical biblical scholarship in a way he had not experienced before. Another was an article by a Dutch Augustinian, Fr Ansfried Hulsbosch, maintaining that the teaching of the Council of Chalcedon about Christ's human and divine natures was "dualistic" and must therefore be abandoned because in conflict with modern anthropology. But the really crucial event, it seems, was his first visit to the United States in 1966, followed by a second in 1967.

To understand the effect of these visits, we need, I think, to take into account the tightly knit Catholic world in which the majority of practising Dutch and Belgian Catholics before the Council mainly lived – more tightly knit, it seems, than that of their counterparts in France and Germany, and certainly far more so than in the Anglo-Saxon world.

In the U.S., by contrast, he met a society which was not only dazzlingly successful and expansive, but was characterised by a wide diversity of religious and philosophical views, which its members were not embarrassed to discuss and publicly express. It is as though in the U.S. he met, for the first time, the modern world he had spent so much time writing and thinking about, and it knocked him sideways.

He also found the rapturous audiences of priests, religious and laity to whom he lectured not only conversant with topics he had scarcely dipped into but in a more advanced state of religious uncertainty than he had reached himself – he records, for instance, having been frequently asked "Is Christ really God?" This is a point worth noting, I think, when assessing the post-conciliar collapse. By 1966, the sheep were undermining the faith of the shepherds. In certain cases, the faithful had been quicker to see the implications of some of the new theological trends than the men promoting them.

By 1968 the results of his transatlantic visits and "frenzied" reading had begun to show in his writings. In that year, Rome informed him that it was investigating his theology, particularly his views about revelation, since they appeared to imply a continuing revelation through religious experience. There was further investigation in the 1970s, this time into his two widely read volumes, *Jesus: An Experiment in Christology* (1974) and *Christ: The Christian Experience in the Modern World* (1977). In the 1980s he was asked to explain passages in his book on the priesthood, *Ministry: a Case for Change* (1980), which argued that the sacrament of holy orders is not absolutely necessary: in exceptional cases, election by the congregation would be sufficient to make a validly ordained priest. Rome eventually announced that some corrections had been made, but that ambiguities remained (see letters from the CDF, *L'Osservatore Romano*, English-language weekly issues for 13th July 1981 and 28th January 1985). However, there have been no disciplinary measures or formal censures.

For Rome the problem was the same as with Rahner. To stigmatise any of Schillebeeckx's views as heterodox could seem to compromise the Council, and, with the majority of the higher intelligentsia still in a state of at least partial revolt, make the current situation even worse. As a result, since the mid-eighties, Fr Schillebeeckx has been left more or less to his own devices, in spite of his remaining at the centre of organised opposition to Rome internationally and, within Holland, to the Dutch hierarchy.

A few quotations from the little book *I Am a Happy Theologian* (SCM Press, 1994), an interview with the Italian journalist Francesco Strazzari, will perhaps convey the flavour of his later writings.

The Trinity

"I personally am somewhat reticent about the Trinity" (p. 51). The three persons "are forms of existence of God in history" (p. 50). "There is certainly a relationship between God and Jesus Christ ... but is this relation between God and Jesus a third person?" (*ibid.*) "It is not a dogma that we have to accept persons" (*ibid.*).

Christ

"Human beings are the image of God, and Christ is the pure image of God ... but there is a difference. In Jesus Christ the image of God is concentrated; in other words, Christ is the image of God with an exclusive uniqueness" (pp. 54–55). "The creature Jesus is a concentrated condensed creation whose whole participation with God is realised in a unique way, not realised in other human beings" (p. 50). "Human beings are intelligible even without reference to God ... but this is impossible for Christ as such. His humanity as such is related to God" (p. 55).

The Church

"Even if Jesus did not directly institute the Church, because he believed that the end of the world was near and did not believe in a long history in time, in fact after his death the proclamation of the universal and definitive significance of the message and lifestyle of Jesus continued" (p. 73). "Jesus simply handed down a movement, a living community of believers aware of being the new people of God" (p. 73). "It cannot be said that bishops, priests and deacons were instituted by Christ..." (p. 72). "How can the Petrine ministry be exercised? Can it, for example, be a triumvirate? Or a college? Or a Synod? That is a historical question subject to changes" (p. 72).

The Bible

"The Word of God is the word of human beings who speak to God. To say just like that that the Bible is the word of God is simply not true. It is only indirectly the word of God...When the Bible says 'God has said it' or 'Christ has said it,' it is not God or Christ who has said it in the strict sense, but human beings who have told of their experience of God" (p. 42).

Ethics

"There is no revelation in ethical matters; ethics is a human process. It is not God who says 'this is ethically permitted or forbidden.' It is human beings who with reflection and experience must say this and establish it." (p. 70). "For Christians, neither revelation nor faith impose ethical norms, even if there are sometimes inspirations and orientations." "I am against certain ethical positions in the official Church which pass themselves off as Christian ... one thinks in exasperation of the very rigid attitude to sexuality and marriage" (*ibid.*).

Liberation Theology

"Your kingdom come ... this is a policy and action in which both God and human beings can realise themselves and finally achieve happiness – each confirming the other so that both are happy" (p. 104).

About Christ and the Church, the general standpoint seems to differ little from Loisy's a hundred years earlier. In this respect it is amusing to find the authors of the 1992 Catechism younger, and so presumably more "modern" by a decade or two, than Fr Schillebeeckx, and having no difficulty in understanding the teaching of Chalcedon about Christ or proposing it for the belief of the still more modern men and women of the 21st century (CCC, arts. 464–478). Being a happy theologian does not guarantee being an accurate or a faithful one.

APPENDIX III
(see Chapter 22, note 228)

The new theologians' dispute with the neo-scholastics about the most appropriate way of presenting the faith, and their call for a "return to the sources" (*ressourcement*), is best understood if we see it as the latest episode in a debate which has resurfaced from time to time throughout the Church's history.

De Lubac and the Return to the Sources

For Catholics, the "sources" are the Bible and the Church Fathers – those who first explained how Scripture was to be understood and recorded the oral traditions and practices that are not explicitly mentioned in Scripture. The idea of "returning to the sources," therefore, does not mean that the Church has not been employing them. It means basically two things: making greater use of them so that the faithful will have a richer and deeper appreciation of the mysteries of the faith, an appreciation which the formulas and necessarily brief quotations of catechisms and popular theological texts cannot of their nature convey; and reassessing current teaching in the light of them – not to discover whether the Church has been teaching error, but to ensure that all aspects of the faith are getting due attention.

About this there was no debate. All truly Catholic theologians were in agreement. The controversy I am referring to has been about the degree to which in expounding "the sources," the Church should organise her teachings systematically and make use of philosophy and logic to explain, define or defend them. To some extent it has been a disagreement between men of two fundamentally different temperamental types: those with a liking for and those with an aversion to abstract ideas and thought. This in turn has given rise in recent times to disputes of a much deeper kind about the relationship of the sources or the "deposit of faith" to the Church's doctrines and dogmas. Is doctrine to be considered in some way inferior to the sources, and how far is it capable of giving adequate expression to them?

Although, according to present usage, the word "deposit" tends to suggest something small, divine revelation is in fact – as we saw earlier when speaking about the history of dogma (chapter 19 of *Turmoil and Truth*) – an unprecedented outpouring of divinely inspired knowledge, which it was left to the Church to organise and interpret. We can therefore see the

315

"deposit of faith" and its explanation by the Fathers as the flesh and blood of divine revelation with doctrine and dogma as its bone structure. The development and organisation of the bone structure, which, with the help of philosophy, reached a first high point in the scholasticism of the Middle Ages, is like the gradual concretion of a baby's bone structure as it forms inside its body in the womb.

Revelation and doctrine are therefore not rivals, as many in recent years have tried to make them, but part and parcel of the same thing. The only difference is the way in which the one message is expressed. It is a difference of language, style and purpose rather than of content. Scripture, the Fathers, and the Church in her everyday teaching mostly employ the language of metaphor, simile, symbol and image to explain supernatural things. But to protect the meaning of the mysteries from distortion, the Church often has to use more precise and abstract terminology. There is a world of difference in the style and tone of the average bishop's pastoral, or a Sunday sermon, and a conciliar definition or "scientific" theological treatise.

As far as the Church is concerned, it is not a matter of either/or, but of the right blend of styles and methods at the right time and place. In a properly balanced presentation of the faith for general use, the bone structure should be detectable beneath the flesh but not sticking out in an unsightly way.

Or using two different metaphors: we can see doctrine and dogma as a protective fence around the deposit of faith, keeping out alien interpretations; or a map of the paths and other salient features of the terrain. Only those standing within the protective fence or using the map can speculate about the meaning of "the deposit" without danger of misinterpreting it.

Such, more or less, is the background to the periodically recurring debate I mentioned. For most of the time, the two styles or methods, "scientific" theology and the everyday teaching of the faith, have lived side by side or intertwined comfortably enough. A doctrinal or spiritual crisis of some kind, however, can generate strong differences of opinion about which style should preponderate.

The opponents of too much philosophy, reason and logic will maintain that its over-use obscures the essentially mysterious nature of the realities it endeavours to explain, thereby distorting them. Its supporters will argue that the language of metaphor and imagery, being more fluid, more easily lets through ideas and interpretations not intended by the author being interpreted. Religious freelancers have never had any difficulty in making the Bible mean whatever they wish. Without a strong doctrinal component, the faith dissolves into a protoplasmic heap of private opinions.

Maybe, the opposite side then retorts; but a skeleton is not meant for public view, except in schools of anatomy (which is what a theological school is, to a great extent). To the average man and woman, doctrine insufficiently clothed in the flesh of God's word, the teaching of the Fathers, and the works of the Church's great spiritual writers, can seem dry and uninspiring.

These, then, have been the poles of the debate which we first hear about at the time of the Council of Nicaea, when a number of the Fathers objected to the use of the word "substance" to define the divine unity because it was a philosophical term not found in the Bible. But the debate only begins to recur at regular intervals with the rediscovery of ancient philosophy in the cathedral schools and universities of Western Europe in the 11th century. St Bernard in the 12th century protested against Abélard's over-use of logic and dialectic. St Bonaventure, though himself a scholastic, uttered similar cries of distress in the next century. Thomas à Kempis, representing a whole school of religious writers of the 14th and 15th century (the *devotio moderna*) responded in the same way to a scholasticism in temporary decadence. A hundred years later, leading figures at the Council of Trent tended to divide along similar lines over the best way to deal with Protestantism. The *spirituali*, as they were referred to, called for a return *ad fontes* (to the sources), that is for discussions with Protestants based mainly on the Bible, and for postponing clear-cut doctrinal definitions until a more favourable or friendly climate prevailed. Others, who could be called the *teologici*, judged as early as 1541 before the Council opened that confusion about belief was already so widespread and the slide into Protestantism proceeding so rapidly that doctrinal definitions could be delayed no longer.[281]

In Newman's day these two approaches or psychological tendencies reasserted themselves in the debates about papal infallibility prior to the First Vatican Council, in which Newman showed himself a natural *spirituale*. He did not see the need to define doctrines about which Catholics were agreed. Definitions, in his view, were more a painful necessity than a luxury.

And this, I think, fairly neatly summarises the way Fr de Lubac looked at the matter in the 20th century. The new theologians' dispute with the neo-

---

281. See D. Fenlon, *Heresy and Obedience in Tridentine Italy: Cardinal Pole and the Counter-Reformation*, Cambridge, 1972. To the "right" of the *teologici* was what would now be considered as a "hard-line" group called the *zelanti*, typified by Cardinal Caraffa (later Paul IV) whose primary concern was the introduction of practical measures for stamping out heresy as quickly and effectively as possible. But they are not relevant to the point I am making here.

scholastics was in part a revival of the dispute between the *spirituali* and *zelanti* at Trent. Their call for *ressourcement* was partly dictated, as we saw earlier, by what they regarded as the imprint of Cartesian rationalism on Catholic theology. In their view there was not enough flesh and blood on the doctrinal bones of contemporary Catholic theology, and this is what their movement for *ressourcement* was to restore. By the "sources," incidentally, they meant more than the Bible and Church Fathers. It could include the writings of saints and mystics, and even the works of painters and sculptors or any authentic artistic or literary expression of the faith down the ages. These too were seen as able to give greater depth to the understanding of doctrine and dogma.

The first fruit of their labours was the multi-volume edition of early Christian writers, inspired by Frs de Lubac and Daniélou, *Sources chrétiennes*. The second, even though they had no direct hand in it, was the 1992 Catechism. It may not have the clarity and concision of the Catechism of Trent and its offspring (which were written for a partly different audience and purpose). But with its wealth of citations from sources as diverse as the *Epistle to Diognetus*, St Joan of Arc, and St Thérèse of the Child Jesus, it is fuller, richer, even deeper. The Trent catechism was written for a world which took most of the fundamentals of Christianity for granted. The authors of the 1992 Catechism had a world which knows less and less about Christianity in view. For this very different audience it was necessary to show in much greater detail how the doctrines which had been developed over two thousand years were connected with the sources. That is *ressourcement* as it should be.

Modernism, however, looked at it differently. In the sources, as I have said, belief exists in a looser form. Not until the late 4th century, for instance, was the divinity of the Holy Spirit, though continuously taught and believed, formally asserted. A teacher, therefore, who relies only on the sources has far more scope for interpreting particular beliefs in new ways. This explains modernist opposition to the writing of a new catechism after the Council and to the controversy in the 1980s over the French catechetical series *Pierres Vivantes* (*Living Stones*) which was officially abandoned only after the Holy See intervened. The "living stones" were source texts without a doctrinal substructure or framework, which left the pupil or teacher to make what he liked of them.

INDEX